DIVIDED AND CONQUERED

Recent Titles in
Contributions in Military History
SERIES EDITORS: THOMAS E. GRIESS AND JAY LUVAAS

The Image of the Army Officer in America: Background for Current Views
C. Robert Kemble

The Memoirs of Henry Heth
Henry Heth, edited by James L. Morrison Jr.

Against the Specter of a Dragon: The Campaign for American Military Preparedness, 1914-1917
John P. Finnegan

The Way of the Fox: American Strategy in the War for America, 1775-1783
Dave R. Palmer

History of the Art of War: Within the Framework of Political History
Hand Delbrück, translated by Walter J. Renfroe Jr.

The General: Robert L. Bullard and Officership in the United States Army, 1881-1925
Allan R. Millet

The Twenty-First Missouri: From Home Guard to Union Regiment
Leslie Anders

The Politics of the Second Front: American Military Planning and Diplomacy in Coalition Warfare, 1941-1943
Mark A. Stoler

The Anatomy of a Small War: The Soviet-Japanese Struggle for Changkufeng/Khasan, 1938
Alvin D. Coox

Reconsiderations on the Revolutionary War: Selected Essays
Don Higginbotham, editor

The Leavenworth Schools and the Old Army: Education, Professionalism, and the Officer Corps of the United States Army, 1881-1918
Timothy K. Nenninger

In Peace and War: Interpretations of American Naval History, 1775-1978
Kenneth J. Hagan, editor

Pacifying the Plains: General Alfred Terry and the Decline of the Sioux, 1866-1890
John W. Bailey

Jeffery A. Gunsburg

DIVIDED AND CONQUERED

The French High Command and the Defeat of the West, 1940

Contributions in Military History, Number 18

GREENWOOD PRESS
WESTPORT, CONNECTICUT • LONDON, ENGLAND

Library of Congress Cataloging in Publication Data

Gunsburg, Jeffery A
Divided and conquered.

(contributions in military history ; no. 18 ISSN 0084-9251)
Bibliography: p.
1. World War, 1939-1949—France. 2. France—History—1914-1940. I. Title. ii. Series.
D761.G85 940.54'0944 78-22725
ISBN 0-313-21092-6

Library of Congress Catalog Card Number: 78-22725
ISBN: 0-313-21092-6
ISSN: 0084-9251

First published in 1979

Greenwood Press, Inc.
51 Riverside Avenue, Westport, Connecticut 06880

Printed in the United States of America

10 9 8 7 6 5 4 3 2 1

COPYRIGHT ACKNOWLEDGMENTS

The following granted me permission to quote from works under their copyright. My thanks to The Shoe String Press, Inc. for permission to quote from Brian Bond, ed., *Chief of Staff: The Diaries of Lieutenant-General Sir Henry Pownall,* Volume I: *1933-1940* published by Leo Cooper, London, and in the United States as an Archon Book by the Shoe String Press, Inc., Hamden, Connecticut, 1973; to Édition Charles-Lavauzelle for General G[aston] Roton, *Années cruciales: La Course aux armements (1933-1939). La Campagne (1939-1940);* to Constable Publishers for Sir Edmund Ironside (Colonel Roderick Macleod and Denis Kelly, eds.), *Time Unguarded: The Ironside Diaries 1937-1940;* to Desclée de Brouwer, Paris, for General [Raoul] Van Overstraeten, *Albert I-Léopold III: Vingt ans de politique militaire belge 1920-1940,* edited in Bruges; to Librairie Ernest Flammarion for General [Maxime] Weygand, *Mémoires;* and to Librairie Plon for General Maurice Gamelin, *Servir.*

Pour ceux de '40

CONTENTS

MAPS

PHOTOGRAPHS

FOREWORD

The crushing defeat suffered by the French army in May-June 1940 came as an immense surprise to the entire world; was this not the same army that had won the war of 1914-1918, the same army whose pugnacity and experience were feared by the German generals themselves? Certainly, as General de Gaulle had proclaimed at London beginning on the 18th of June 1940, this first lost battle was not an irremediable defeat; at the end of the world conflict, thanks to its great Allies, thanks to Free France and to the clandestine Resistance which remained in the struggle, France found itself in the winning camp, but reduced from then on to the rank of a secondary power; more grave still, the effacement of France turned out to be that of western Europe, which ceased to be the dominating power in the world.

It is not surprising that events so grave and so unexpected aroused diverse, even contradictory explanations. In the midst of the battle Paul Reynaud attributed the first French reverses, which revealed themselves as decisive, to the "treason" of the King of the Belgians. At the "Riom trial," the directors of the Vichy regime attempted to put responsibility for the disaster on the defects of the Third Republic and on the "inefficiency" of some of its leaders, particularly the heads of government of the Popular Front, Léon Blum and Édouard Daladier. The accused counter-attacked by indicting the intellectual "sclerosis" of the French General Staff and the errors, strategic and tactical, committed by the military leaders; they were scarcely gentle with Marshal Pétain.

During the last few years, passions have calmed a bit and, above all, the archives have been opened; a new generation of historians, some born after the conflict, have taken up the study of the catastrophe from a calmer and more objective point of view. Jeffery A. Gunsburg belongs to this new generation.

I willingly preface his book, although we did not consult each other and I had no knowledge of his work. I have arrived at conclusions close to his in my forthcoming book on "the Riom trial," to be published by the Albin Michel press, Paris.

I believe that Gunsburg is right to see the profound cause of the French catastrophe of 1940 in the painful and too costly victory won in 1914-1918; twenty years later France had not recovered from the terrible bloodletting which it had then suffered: 1.5 million dead and 1 million wounded, all young men between the ages of twenty and forty, from a total population of 40 million. Let the readers of this book compare these figures with the some 100,000 dead mourned by the United States in the course of World War I and the 300,000 dead in World War II.

Gunsburg is right to emphasize that intellectually, artistically, and scientifically, France was not a decadent country; it had, nonetheless, become an aged nation, unable to understand why it was necessary once again to face Germany. It was only during the German occupation that all the evils of the Nazi regime were revealed to the French, and that they rediscovered a bit of their warlike ardor and of their combativity in order to contribute to their own liberation.

Above all, and this part of Gunsburg's work is capital, the course of events between the two wars determined that France would have, for an indeterminate time, to face alone a Germany more numerous in population, with a more powerful economy, and with a two-year lead in its rearmament. Certainly in 1939 the British alliance was reestablished, better consolidated than in 1914; but Great Britain had comprehended the error of the policy of "appeasing" Hitler too late, and was far from ready to fight. France had lost, one after the other, all its allies of central and eastern Europe because it did not have the strength to support them. France had not succeeded in reconciling its alliance with Poland with its alliance with the U.S.S.R., and the latter, seeking neutrality in the short term through an unnatural pact with Hitlerian Germany, allowed the Wehrmacht to concentrate all its forces in the west. Further, Belgian neutrality, as justified as it might be from a strictly Belgian point of view, posed insoluble politico-strategic problems for the French General Staff.

Perhaps Gunsburg is a bit indulgent toward that French General Staff, sunk in the lessons of 1914-1918, irresolute partisan of the defensive which was often the same thing as accepting inaction. The General Staff was curiously closed to the spirit of its times—to mechanization and to speed, incapable of measuring the new dimension that the tank-plane team brought to a conflict. But Gunsburg is right to emphasize that the long-term strategy adopted by the French leaders, political and military, with English agreement, was that which, by all evidence, was the correct one. It was necessary to gain time: to complete Franco-British rearmament, to mobilize all the immense resources of the empires of the two Allies, to receive indispensable aid from the United States. That too much importance was attached to the blockade of Germany, and that the period of the "drôle de guerre" was not better utilized, does not change the fact that in May 1940 the Allies could confront their enemy with stronger armies than in September 1939; and that the disequilibrium of forces in their disfavor would reduce itself to their advantage with the passage of time.

But the Wehrmacht still maintained too great a superiority, especially in bomber aircraft, to keep the first battles from threatening to become decisive; above all the Wehrmacht with its armored corps possessed an arm perfectly adapted to its strategy, and it benefited from the advantages of the initiative and surprise. These factors played the greatest role in the extremely perilous attack launched across the Ardennes, demolishing all the plans of the French command, taking the dispositions of its armies from the rear while the French command had neither the originality nor the means to parry the attack—nor to compensate for it in the following weeks.

The logical conclusion of this book is that France was right to accept war with Germany in September 1939, even though it would have to fight alone; the battle was not lost in advance for France. If the struggle was lost at the end of a single battle this was the responsibility, and perhaps the fault, of the Allies of France, as much as of France itself. The conduct of the Allies, whether it is a question of the tragic error of the Germano-Soviet pact, or of the insufficient preparation and cooperation of the British, or of the policy of independence of Belgium, or of the neutrality of the United States, proved shortsighted. The evolution of the war rapidly demonstrated just how wrong they had initially been.

Jeffery Gunsburg makes no pretense to have resolved all the problems, to have answered all the questions; but he has opened a debate, and he asks that others join in it with him. For my part, I earnestly hope that this call will be heard.

Henri Michel
President of the International Committee on
the History of the Second World War
Director of the *Review of the History of the Second World War*

ACKNOWLEDGMENTS

It would have been impossible to trace the policies of two French military institutions for twenty years, then follow a battle involving millions of men from six nations, without relying on the efforts of a great many scholars and writers. In addition to the published works cited in the text, I gained access to much material through the Historical Services of the French Army and Air Force and the *Fondation Nationale des Sciences Politiques.*

The encouragement of Theodore Ropp, William Evans Scott, and Joel Colton, of Duke University, meant a great deal to me. I thank also the readers of my manuscript whose suggestions sparked revisions and cutting of the work.

I owe a debt of gratitude to the *Bibliothèque Nationale*, Paris, and to M. Henri Michel and the staff of his *Comité International d'Histoire de la Deuxième Guerre Mondiale*, who helped guide my research. I owe thanks also to the *Établissement Cinématographique et Photographique des Armées* at the Fort d'Ivry near Paris, which provided illustrations. I owe a further debt to my fellow scholars, particularly to Majors Robert Doughty, Charles Bailey, and John L. Speedy III, of the United States Army, and Jeffrey Johnstone Clarke.

Above all I must recognize those whose efforts enabled me to unearth new material. Colonel Jean Delmas and the staff of the French Army Historical Service, and Generals Hayez and Charles Christienne and the staff of the French Air Force Historical Service, played a crucial role. At the army service I was aided by Mme. Andrée Dupont and Mme. Corvaisier, without whose untiring efforts I would have accomplished little. Colonels Delmas and Dutailly gave me the benefit of their knowledge and their interest. Mlle. Dudon and M. Lechoix of the air force service worked with me over a period of months and took a real interest in my project: may all researchers have such good fortune. Mlle. Geneviève Chevignard of the *Fondation Nationale des Sciences Politiques* guided me through the Édouard Daladier papers which she has so admirably inventoried.

I owe a special debt to those who granted me interviews: Colonel François-André Paoli of the army service (who generously gave me a copy of the proofs of one of his books); General Hayez of the air force service who arranged an interview with General Pierre Bodet and General Bodet who granted it; General Charles Christienne also of the air force service; and the late General André Beaufre. Jean Vanwelkenhuyzen of the *Centre de Recherches et d'Études Historiques de la Seconde Guerre Mondiale,* Brussels, shared with me his unmatched knowledge of the events and his sensitivity toward the people covered in this work, and added much to my views on Belgium. Philippe Masson of the Historical Service of the French Navy, Vincennes, generously granted me permission to cite the paper he presented to the Franco-German colloquium in Bonn, September 1978.

The maps were prepared from information and sources cited in the text, and were drawn by Major Daniel Brittigan of the Virginia Military Institute and Mrs. Alice Williams of Lexington, Virginia. Illustrations from the *Établissement Cinématographique et Photographique des Armées* (the E.C.P. *Armées*) and the French Air Force Historical Service (the S.H.A.A.) are reproduced by permission of those institutions. Mrs. Mary Alice Wise of Lexington, Virginia helped to edit and type the final manuscript, which the staff of Greenwood Press further improved.

Truly, if there is merit to this work, it is due in great part to those named above. I, however, bear full responsibility for errors of fact or interpretation.

INTRODUCTION

Adolf Hitler's victory over France in June 1940 consummated a momentous reversal of world affairs. His conquest of western Europe, pursued with stunning speed and contempt for Allied resistance, ended three centuries of western European dominance in world affairs and made possible the full expansion of Nazism with all its attendant horrors. The campaign was the archetype of modern mechanized warfare. With the armistice of June 22, France abandoned World War II, abandoning its suddenly isolated and unprepared ally, Great Britain, to face the triumphant "New Order" alone. Western civilization seemed to be foundering.

The collapse of the French army, which had won the world's respect during the agonizing years of World War I, and the unexpected danger into which this collapse threw the West, created deep divisions in French and western European political life. These divisions obscured the causes of the collapse in controversy. A great deal has been written about the collapse, and the resulting mass of several thousand works is of mixed quality, much of it partisan and written in partial or complete ignorance of the facts.

France and the French High Command were at the center of the resistance to German resurgence from 1919 to June 1940; most of the explanations for the 1940 disaster center, therefore, on France. Since the defeat was so swift, in contrast to 1914-1918, most authors assumed that political and ideological defects "rotted" France, sapping its will to resist Hitler, making the defeat "inevitable." A small segment of the literature investigated the military aspects of the defeat, concluding for the most part that France "fell" because the French military system failed to adapt to the mechanized warfare—Blitzkrieg—with which Hitler conquered the West. This thesis complements that of "moral decay," which remains the most popular explanation of the collapse.

I contend that these answers are wrong; they draw attention away from the real causes of the catastrophe. The defeat of 1940 was an *Allied* collapse. France was the kingpin of the Western alliance, as it had been in World War I, but by itself France—inferior in population and industry to Germany—was bound to fail. Following World War I France alone worked consistently to restrain Germany. This effort cost France the sympathy and support of most of the Allies of 1918, who—both in revulsion against the horrors of the war and in pursuit of narrow national interests—accepted limited German resurgence. In the midst of the Depression, Adolf Hitler, exploiting these tendencies in France's erstwhile allies and within France too, waged a cold war of rearmament and then territorial annexations. Attempts to "appease" Hitler at the cost of others, such as the Czechs, only whetted his appetite and convinced him that the West had no stomach for a fight. Finally the West rallied: France and Britain in the spring of 1939, Belgium and the Netherlands when they were dragged in by the German invasion in the spring of 1940. The same narrowly nationalistic policies that allowed Hitler's rise played a major part in the conduct of Allied military operations in 1940—and thus in the collapse of the West. True, Great Britain survived that collapse, but it was survival in insular isolation, necessitating Britain's rescue by the Soviet Union and the United States. *Their* victory destroyed Hitler, but it just as surely destroyed the old world order, throwing the powers of western Europe off the center stage of world politics for the first time in three centuries. To concentrate on France alone is to ignore all these facts.

I contend that the French military was *not* technically deficient in 1940, and I draw on the archives of the French army and air force to support this contention. The evolution of Allied strategy through 1940 shows the role the Allied nations played in what was an *Allied* collapse. Certainly there was political division in France between the wars—when was there *not* political division in France? But I conclude that the defeat of 1940 can be explained in terms of the Allied grand strategy—campaign strategy and military operations—with little recourse to ideology and none to "moral decay." The lack of Allied unity that allowed Hitler's rise also enabled him to triumph in 1940—although key mistakes by the French High Command gave him an opening.

This work focuses on the preparation and conduct of Allied military operations by the French High Command from 1919 to 1940. Tracing the French High Command's attitudes toward the means of holding Germany in check, the strategy and the evolving techniques and weapons of total war, I concentrate on elements that played a role in the disaster of 1940.

This focus is not artificial: the French High Command—whether in the persons of Ferdinand Foch and Philippe Pétain or of Maurice Gamelin and Alphonse Georges—never doubted, after the signing of the Versailles Treaty, that it would once again be necessary to wage total war against Germany. For twenty years the best military brains in France worked to meet this challenge. In 1940 those efforts went for naught. I attempt to discover what went wrong.

October 1978

Jeffery A. Gunsburg
Lexington, Virginia

DIVIDED AND CONQUERED

chapter 1

THE EFFORT TO SECURE THE PEACE

The armistice of November 11, 1918, put a victorious end to the hardest and bloodiest war in French history. From those terrible years, from that victory, France as a whole, and its military leaders in particular, hoped to extract guarantees for a secure future. They saw one principal threat—Germany—the enemy just conquered with the aid of an unprecedented coalition of forces. But they saw also that Germany retained its unity, its superiority over France in population and industrial power, its sense of national destiny. The French watched with dismay the disintegration of the coalition that had paid so heavily for victory. From the morrow of the armistice, the French High Command felt itself almost alone facing a potentially threatening Germany. For the next twenty years the gaze of the French High Command remained fixed upon that threat.

THE POSTWAR PERIOD

Following the victory, Marshal Ferdinand Foch, the Allied Commander in Chief, tried to secure a solid guarantee against German revenge: the Rhine River. Foch bombarded Allied leaders with notes on the subject,[1] but they ruled otherwise. The Versailles Treaty limited the German army to 100,000 men serving long-term enlistments, forced Germany to renounce heavy artillery, tanks and airplanes, and forbade German military forces in the Rhineland, which was to be garrisoned by Allied troops for fifteen years. American and British supplementary treaties guaranteeing France against German aggression were never ratified. Instead of adopting Foch's hard line of military checks on Germany, the diplomats at Versailles attempted the reordering of Europe to remove the causes of another war. Central and eastern Europe was divided into a new set of ostensibly national states carved from the empires that had dominated the area in 1914. Diplomacy was to be conducted openly under the auspices of the new association of civilized states—the League of Nations—which would find peaceful

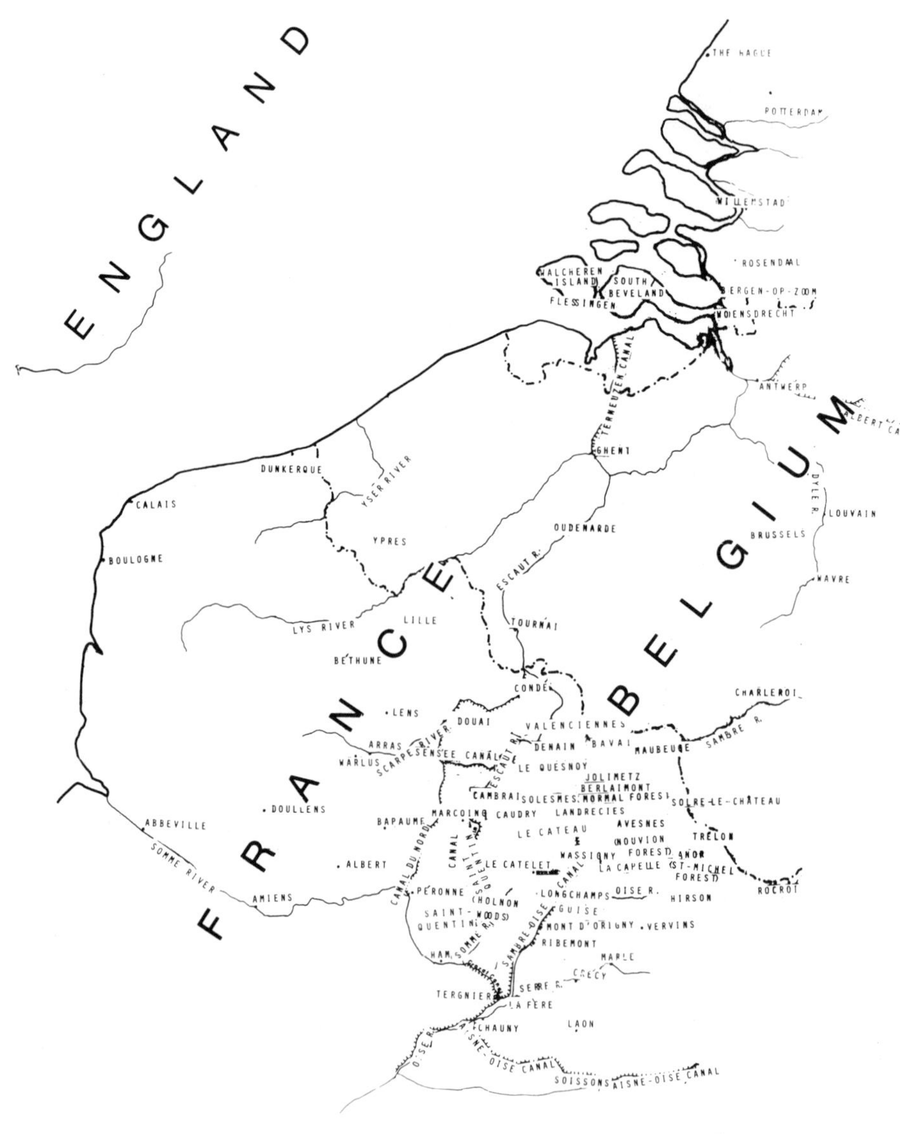

Northwest Europe, 1919-1940

NETHERLANDS
N. Brabant
Limburg
GERMANY
LUXEMBURG
Ardennes
UTRECHT
NIJMEGEN
DORDRECHT
GEERTRUIDENBERG
MOERDIJK
BREDA
TILBURG
GOIRLE
EINDHOVEN
HELMOND
VENLO
THE RUHR
KREFELD
ST. LEONARD
TURNHOUT
BRANCH CANAL
PEEL (MARSH)
MEUSE R.
ROERMOND
RHINE R.
MAASTRICHT
EBEN-EMAEL
TONGRES
GETTE R.
THISNES
HANNUT
MERDORP
LIEGE
GEMBLOUX
HUY
NAMUR
FOSSE
MEUSE R.
OURTHE R.
VESDRE R.
AMBLEVE R.
HOUX
CINEY
DINANT
HAUT-LE-WASTIA
VIELSALM
ST-VITH
SALM R.
CHABREHEZ
MARCHE
PHILIPPEVILLE
ONHAYE
LESSE R.
GIVET
HOUFFALIZE
PRUM
KOBLENZ
CLERVAUX
ST-HUBERT
BASTOGNE
WITTLICH
REVIN
MONTHERME
SURE R.
LIBRAMONT
BERTRIX
SEMOY R.
NEUFCHATEAU
MARTELANGE
ALZETTE R.
BODANGE
MOSELLE R.
NOUZONVILLE
CHARLEVILLE
BOUILLON
MEZIERES
LIART
SERRE R.
TRIER
MONTCORNET
SIGNY-L'ABBAYE
DONCHERY
SEDAN
FLORENVILLE
ARLON
HURTAUT
BOULZICOURT
FLIZE
WADELINCOURT
SEMOY R.
POIX-TERRON
MARFEE
WOODS
CARIGNAN
GARNICH
LA HORGNE
OMICOURT
VENDRESSE
SISSONNE
BOUVELLEMONT
OMONT
BAR R.
VIRTON
INOR
CHATEAU-PORCIEN
RETHEL
STONNE
MONTMEDY
LONGWY
LA CHESNE
AISNE R.
LONGUYON

solutions to disputes between nations or, if necessary, act jointly to provide collective security against any who disrupted the peace. Eventually the world would disarm to the levels imposed on Germany.

But American congressional leaders were offended at the eagerness with which their Allies fought over the spoils of victory. They were further offended by Allied reluctance to repay loans contracted during the war; they were unwilling to accept the Allied desire to link repayment to heavy reparations from Germany. In the end, the American Senate refused to ratify the Versailles Treaty or the treaty by which the United States and Britain would secure France against German aggression. The French felt betrayed. The retreat of America into isolation further weakened the League of Nations, which was already hurt by the absence of another great power, Russia, which was transmuting itself into the Soviet Union. Finally Great Britain, its economy staggered by the costs of the war and its leaders determined that never again would they send the youth of their nation into trenches on the Continent, sought to restore the peacetime business climate and to step as far back as possible from entangling continental alliances. Britain wanted to revert to its traditional role as pivot of the European balance of power.

The upshot of this retrenchment was that the coalition of 1918 was effectively dissolved by 1920. It was replaced only by the League of Nations, minus the United States and Russia. The failure in the following years to give teeth to collective security led to the eventual collapse of the League, despite the hopes of Allied leaders and millions of people eager to have done with war. The result was that Western security, as the French High Command saw it, rested on the ability of France to force the Versailles Treaty on a recalcitrant Germany.

The French army emerged from the World War large and powerful with an abundance of artillery, motorized transport, tanks and aircraft, including France's concentrated bomber strength: the Air Division. But these forces were only part of the coalition; with the rapid evolution of the postwar situation, the French needed a new command structure. Foch retained his interallied command, but within France control of the armed forces was always a sensitive issue under the Third Republic. Learning from the examples of Napoleons I and III, of General Georges Boulanger, and of the Dreyfus affair, the center and left politicians of the Third Republic traditionally regarded *all* French generals as potential military dictators whose powers had to be circumscribed, particularly in peacetime. Catholic and conservative generals could still rise to the High Command (the careers of Foch, Maxime Weygand, and Alphonse Georges proved it), but they were hedged about with obstacles to guarantee their republican loyalty. In peacetime, command resided in the ministers of the armed forces; above them the Superior Council of National Defense grouped ministers charged with defense duties with a permanent secretariat. The ministers dealt occasionally with major, primarily economic, questions. Each minister retained responsibility for his service until 1932.[2]

In early 1920 the War Minister, André Lefevre, established the new military order. Based in part on prewar institutions, the new system rested on the authority of the Superior War Council; presided over by the War Minister or the President of the Republic, it was composed of generals designated for major commands in wartime, plus the Chief of the General Staff of the Army and the Marshals of France. The Superior War Council made final decisions on the organization of the army and its preparation for war. Lefevre named Philippe Pétain, commander of the French armies facing Germany in 1918, Vice-President of the Superior War Council (making him the Commander in Chief designate for wartime) and granted him new powers as Inspector General of the Army. Pétain had the right to inspect and prescribe standards for the whole army; his authority extended over the separate Chief of the General Staff, who served as peacetime director of the army. This last post went to General Edmond Buat, who had served in 1918 as Pétain's chief of staff, directing the wartime General Headquarters (GQG). Under this organization top-level strategy remained with Foch while the demobilization and reconstruction of the army rested with Pétain[3]—but above both of them hovered the Superior War Council which was consulted on everything except strategy. At the summit stood the Minister of War whose civilian authority was supreme in peacetime.

The French army demobilized while maintaining two sets of forces: one standing guard in the Rhineland; the second in France serving as the depot and training center for the Army of the Rhine and France's colonial forces and preparing the mobilization of the nation in arms in case of war. After the signing of the Versailles Treaty, French forces in the Rhineland decreased to six infantry and one cavalry divisions. French air forces, which at the end of the war included almost 1,300 bombers and over 1,000 fighters, decreased by 1923 to only 818 aircraft in France, including 160 day bombers and 240 fighters.[4] But in the Europe of the times this was a powerful force.

Foch was anxious to retain the interallied character of operations to coerce Germany into fulfillment of the Versailles Treaty. Unable to sway Great Britain or the United States toward a hard-line policy, he pressured Belgium into a bilateral Military Accord with France in 1920. Couched in vague terms, it specified that Belgium would maintain a force in the Rhineland and prepare a further force to be sent in case of need. The Accord added a long-term commitment by the two countries to organize a defense system on their eastern frontiers. This system, which would include independent Luxemburg, would serve as a shield once the Rhineland was evacuated. This agreement became one of the key elements in French strategy, for it seemed to bind Belgium into a close alliance. To Belgian leaders, however, its significance was much more limited.[5]

Like the French, Belgian leaders tended to believe that Germany would seek to escape the limits imposed on it and that constant vigilance would be necessary. But Belgium was divided into two linguistic communities: Flemings speaking a dialect of Dutch, and Walloons speaking French. The majority of Belgians were Flemings who, following the war, pressed to make Belgium bilingual. The existence of the Military Accord with France, the terms of which were kept secret, offended many Flemings who saw themselves as an unwilling appendage to an alliance dominated by France. Speeches by French military leaders taking a firm Belgian alliance for granted were particularly offensive to these Flemings; as the years passed, the Accord became an internal political issue quite apart from its role in joint security against Germany. Many Flemings—and successive Belgian governments—would have preferred an alliance with Great Britain, which would have avoided this internal problem while guaranteeing Belgium against Germany. Britain, however, refused to commit itself.

Behind the cover force on the Rhine, the French army demobilized and sought stability. The Recruiting Law of 1923 provided for 100,000 career soldiers (the same number allowed Germany) but supplemented this force with conscription, although it reduced the term of service to eighteen months. The adoption of a conscript force was a political necessity in a country where the words *professional army* aroused fears on the left; it seemed the only solution for a country poorer and less populous than its neighbor.[6] In any case, the conscript army had demonstrated its mettle in the war: the *poilus* of Verdun were already a legend.

The basis of the strategy of the nation in arms was its mobilization plan, whereby its reserves were to be mustered, concentrated, and dispatched to the front. The active cover force stood throughout the 1920s on the Rhine; the French General Staff prepared a series of plans to mobilize the reserves and concentrate for an advance into Germany should that prove necessary.[7] Weapons for the mobilized units would come from World War I stocks; the arms programs of the early 1920s were small, but important in that they started the development of new tanks. The inspector of the tanks, General Jean Estienne, developed prototypes for a light tank to work with the infantry, a medium battle tank, and a heavy "breakthrough" tank. His medium tank eventually became the B tank which formed the backbone of France's heavy armored divisions in 1940.[8]

During the early 1920s the lessons of World War I, which saw more technical development than any previous war, were codified. Now an army's doctrine is the codification of the tactical and technical processes by which it operates. Doctrine appears in official manuals and instructions, and in the textbooks of official courses. The keystone of French doctrine was the 1921 *Instruction provisoire sur l'emploi tactique des grandes unités* (IGU'21). A commission led by Marshal Pétain and General Marie-Eugène Debeney (then director of higher education in the army) drafted this manual. The commission stated its basic assumptions: tremendous progress not only in the power but in the cost and complexity of weapons made war truly total; the end of the war brought only a temporary halt in technical progress, and the doctrine would, therefore, have to be recast when arms underwent important modifications; mass firepower was the key to both offense and defense; aviation, both in its intelligence gathering and combat functions, would play a particularly extensive role; that this manual assumed the enemy would have weapons and motivations similar to those of the French, and a war would be one of coalitions and continuous fronts formed by nations in arms. This last assumption, however, was incorrect in the Europe of 1921.[9] Thus, the manual was a glimpse toward the next total war.

Why did the commission make these assumptions; why the nations in arms, continuous fronts, coalitions? Surely Pétain and Debeney were thinking of Germany; France had no other prospective continental enemies save perhaps the Soviet Union in the distant future. But why implicitly concede to Germany what the Versailles Treaty explicitly forbade? This manual was based on the same assumptions that Foch made when he said that the "eternal Germany" would rise again, that the Treaty of Versailles meant not peace but a twenty-year truce. Pétain and Debeney assumed that France, Belgium, and their former Allies would *not* compel Germany to abide by Versailles. Pétain and Debeney were not the masters of French policy. The Third Republic had hemmed itself in by its commitment to the League of Nations and collective security, abandoning whatever thoughts Foch might have nurtured of a preventive war. And French public opinion earnestly desired a just peace; Frenchmen would not take up arms again until compelled to by a clear threat.

According to the IGU'21, the principal combat mission belonged to the infantry that would conquer, occupy, and hold terrain: the essence of victory. The infantry would be preceded, protected, and accompanied by artillery, and sometimes by tanks and aircraft. Tanks would increase the offensive power of the infantry and should come in two types: a light tank to accompany the infantry and a heavier type, operating more independently, to open the way. But the IGU'21 paid more attention to aircraft than to tanks. Bombers were to attack targets on the battlefield and prolong the action of the artillery; operating en masse, they would produce powerful moral and material effect. The Air Division, engaged directly by the High Command, would intervene massively; a powerful air force and numerous tank units might make it possible to skip the artillery preparation in the assault.[10] Conquering terrain was not enough: enemy forces were to be pursued and dislocated by the advance of frontline troops and cavalry, and by air attacks seeking to "destroy the enemy's capability to maneuver." The manual took no position as to the relative superiority of defense versus offense. It emphasized firepower in all cases, but asserted that the ultimate guarantee of success lay in the spirit of the troops.[11] The commission paid little attention to tanks, an omission already filled by the tank manual of 1920, which defined tanks as offensive instruments destined to work in combination with the infantry. Tanks were to be used in massive, deep formations on wide fronts. Speed was vital against an enemy caught in the open, but precautions against enemy artillery would be needed before taking on an enemy in prepared positions.[12]

The *Aéronautique militaire* codified its own doctrine. The writings of the commander of the Air Division in the early 1920s, General de Vaulgrenant, and the official manuals restated the points made on airpower in the IGU'21. De Vaulgrenant felt, however, that bombers could not work directly over enemy front lines, at least not until airplanes could carry armor. He emphasized the disruptive effect of air attacks on enemy communications during mobilization; the bomber manual stressed the role of the bomber in destroying enemy airpower on the ground.[13]

This doctrine was little more than the experience of World War I codified. But the leaders of the French army were thinking ahead: General Estienne claimed that the appearance of mechanized vehicles (vehicles intended to participate directly in battle) was as great a revolution as the invention of gunpowder; he predicted a 100,000-man mechanized army that could dislocate the mass armies of the recent past.[14] Unfortunately, although Estienne and others provided the vision, the parliaments of the 1920s would not provide the funds. Why spend a fortune on tanks and other "offensive" weapons for which France, secure in the bosom of collective security, had no need?

The climax to the initial postwar period came with the occupation of the Ruhr in 1923. Upset by repeated German obstructions and failures to meet the schedule of reparations payments, Premier Raymond Poincaré ordered the French Army of the Rhine, with Belgian troops, to seize the Ruhr basin. This threw Germany into turmoil: passive resistance and a flood of monetary inflation followed. The violent disruption of postwar life drew the real hostility of Great Britain and the United States upon France. And Poincaré's action, while straining the French economy, failed to break German resistance. In September 1923 a settlement was reached and Allied troops withdrew. But French pursuit of the hard line broke up what was left of the Allied coalition and gained in return only a partial reassertion of French rights under the Versailles settlement. Again the "eternal Germany" demonstrated its unity and its defiance—the policy of armed sanctions had failed. This was the last time that France would try to impose the full measure of the Versailles settlement on Germany by force; the costs in international hostility and economic dislocation outweighed the gains. In 1924 a new parliamentary bloc came to power in France, and with it came Aristide Briand and a policy of conciliation toward Germany.

With the end of the Ruhr occupation, the French army in Europe settled into garrison life. By the Locarno accords of 1925 the powers of western Europe agreed to the permanence of Germany's western frontiers and to the exclusion of German forces from the Rhineland. Germany accepted the accords, thus joining with Britain, Belgium, France, and now Italy to jointly guarantee the status quo in western Europe, including the demilitarization of the Rhineland. The Locarno accords substituted collective security for the wartime alliance. Securing British, German, and Italian agreement was a victory for France. Italy, discontented with its small gains at Versailles and restive under the bombast of Benito Mussolini, had begun to cast threatening glances at French Tunisia and was spending vast sums on its armed forces.

The accords made a repetition of the Ruhr occupation impossible,[15] but failed to settle the situation in eastern Europe. In the 1920s France signed alliances with Poland and Czechoslovakia, while encouraging the formation of the *Petite entente* including Yugoslavia and Rumania. The French intention was to bind these small states into a block on Germany's eastern frontiers to compensate for the loss of the Russian alliance. These powers also formed a protective cordon against the expansion of Bolshevism to the west. Unfortunately, these states did not admire each other—particularly Czechoslovakia and Poland who had wrangled bitterly over the Teschen enclave that the Czechs seized while Poland had its hands full against the Soviet Union in 1920-1921.

Germany was too weak to redraw the map in the 1920s but it continued to refuse to accept the borders of these new states; central and eastern Europe remained a potentially dangerous area that the Locarno accords did nothing to pacify. However, the accords, and the beginning of disarmament negotiations under the auspices of the League of Nations, cast an illusory glow over international relations. As economic prosperity returned, Europe did indeed settle down; Briand's policy of conciliation seemed to work. Meanwhile, the French army kept active with campaigns in North Africa and Syria, while the air forces participated in these campaigns and in the explorations of the heroic era of aviation.

The army perfected its mobilization plans, taking more care to protect its concentration from the threat of a spoiling attack by the small but professional German *Reichswehr.* Key questions of strategy were debated in the Superior War Council in 1926 and 1927; the Council approved Pétain's proposal to mobilize one major force in Belgium opposite the Ruhr and a second in Lorraine. In 1927 and 1928 successive governments in

France passed laws on the general organization of the army and on cadres, personnel, and recruiting. They reduced the active strength of the army from thirty-two to twenty-seven divisions and the term of service for conscripts to one year. This cut, and the need to divert strength to face a growing Italian threat, compelled the army to drop plans for an immediate offensive into Germany in case of war; the French Army of the Rhine would maneuver in retreat to cover the mobilization of the nation in arms, after which offensive operations would begin.[16] In case of war the mobilized nation in arms would have to bear the burden of total war; French strategy thus caught up with the premises of the IGU'21. Despite Foch's contention that security needs must determine the length of service—and not the other way round[17]—France was unwilling to bear extra military service. While Foch was thinking of the German resurgence, which he foresaw just around the corner, public opinion was comfortably ensconced in the present; there was no threat to French security, and if one developed, collective security would meet it.

Colonial campaigns depleted stocks and new mobilization programs required new arms; thus, in the late 1920s the army prepared plans for spending several billion francs. In fact, less than a billion francs were spent through 1931 (barely equaling costs of the colonial campaigns). This money served to buy new automatic rifles and anti-gas equipment for the infantry and to order (from 1929) the first postwar tanks: D1's with tank-killing 47 mm guns. France was actually spending less on the development of its armed forces in Europe than Germany.[18] Unable to secure funds, the innovators in the French military were reduced to "studies." General Maxime Weygand, the director of the Army War College from 1924 to 1930, had Colonel Joseph Doumenc present his views on the use of hypothetical armored divisions; maneuvers offered an opportunity for experimenting with small mechanized units. A trend toward mechanization and motorization appeared in the cavalry, where some of the horse units were traded for armored cars, motorized infantry, and artillery.

The French air forces faced a severe potential threat because of the superior capacity of German industry. The French command felt it had to seize control of the air from the opening of a conflict, lest it face an uncontrollable menace.[19] However, this threat remained a potential one only into the early 1930s. In 1928 France established an Air Ministry, which by 1929 had juridical control of the air forces, although these forces were permanently delegated to the army and navy for operations. An air staff formed in 1929, taking control over the administration of the air forces in May; the Inspector General of the Air Forces was placed directly under the Air Ministry in January 1929. Meanwhile, new aircraft gradually replaced old ones, but expansion was concentrated in the reconnaissance and observation arms necessary for army units under expanded mobilization plans.

France's defense preparations during the 1920s made real progress in one area alone: fortifications. A tightfisted parliament *was* willing to spend to increase that sense of security for which France hungered after being brutalized, like the rest of Europe, into pacifism by the agony of World War I. Facing a more populous and industrially more powerful neighbor and deprived of the Rhine, French military leaders agreed on the need for some form of fortification, although no two agreed on the particulars. By early 1930, as the last French troops withdrew by agreement from the Rhineland, the money and the concrete began to flow and the Maginot Line took shape. Designed essentially to cover French mobilization against surprise attack by the German Reichswehr, the fortification did not extend behind the Belgian border, since it was the intention of the French High Command to advance into Belgium in case of war. This French plan had serious implications.[20] Pétain counted on Belgium as an ally. By pushing into Belgium, the French would hold the Germans away from their industrial northern frontier while simultaneously pushing closer to Germany's vital and vulnerable Ruhr valley. This would be France's response to any German aggression in eastern Europe. The possibility that Belgium might *not* become an ally apparently never crossed Pétain's mind—a disastrous omission. In fact, the Belgian government—frightened at the prospect of being drawn into war with Germany because of some German move against one of France's eastern European Allies—never considered itself automatically committed, in spite of the provisions of the 1920 Military Accord and the obligations of collective security under the League of Nations. When the time for action came in the 1930s, Belgium turned out to be no ally at all, leaving the French High Command in a dangerously uncertain position which was not resolved—and then only partially—until May 10, 1940.

Thus, by the end of the 1920s, the French military had lapsed into a peacetime routine. Lack of funds, lack of an immediate threat from Germany, restrictions on the size of the army, and the shortened term of service for conscripts put the army in the doldrums. However, some promising technical developments were under way in mechanization and in the air forces, while a serious program of fortifications had begun. Then, in January 1930, General Maxime Weygand succeeded Debeney as Chief of Staff of the Army.[21] With Weygand came the ferocious energy and forthright language that had made him the favorite of Foch. It was time for a change.

THE WEYGAND ERA

Maxime Weygand was born of uncertain parentage in Belgium in 1867. Raised in France, he obtained dispensation to enter St.-Cyr, the French military academy, and became a French citizen. Throughout his service

Weygand was tagged as a rather mysterious character with uncertain Catholic and right-wing connections. The rumor that he was the illegitimate son of Léopold II, King of the Belgians, added fuel to the fire. But the largest factor in his reputation was his participation with Foch in the struggle for the Rhine at the Versailles Conference: leftist political circles feared his presence in the High Command. Following his service as chief of staff to Foch after the war, Weygand became director of the Army War College and a member of the Superior War Council in 1924. In 1928 he was chosen to become Chief of Staff beginning in 1930, eventually to succeed Pétain himself. Considering that Weygand had never held a high command in the field, and that a number of prestigious commanders from World War I sat on the Superior War Council, his appointment demonstrated a desire to break new ground. But first, the parliamentary roadblock had to be passed. It was only with the support of the Minister of War, André Maginot, Weygand's written statement of his belief in the Republic, and his acceptance of a "republican" general—Maurice Gamelin—as his deputy, that Weygand could assume his post in 1930.[22]

Weygand immediately became the effective head of the army, and when Pétain retired in January 1931, Weygand climbed to the top rung. Beneath him Gamelin became Chief of Staff; there could be no question of giving both posts to a Weygand. Pétain became the first Inspector General of the Territorial Air Defense. In 1932 the appearance of an ephemeral and weak Ministry of National Defense over all three services led the Premier, André Tardieu, to institute a High Military Committee presided over by the Minister of National Defense and consisting of the Commanders in Chief designate and Chiefs of Staff of the armed services. A Technical Committee, chaired by the Secretary of State for Production, with representatives of various ministries and the military, complemented this new body. Together, these committees represented a first step toward a unified direction of the three services in France. They survived the abolition of the Ministry of National Defense in 1932 and lasted until June 1936.[23]

But leadership of the army belonged to Weygand and Gamelin. Both were progressive in their technical views; both were set on making changes. Unfortunately, they differed profoundly in character. Weygand inherited from his master, Foch, a passionate hostility toward the "eternal Germany" and a forthright determination to wean the politicians from what he saw as the delusions of collective security. The fact that he was a staunch Catholic with a certain fondness for monarchy did not enhance his standing with the center and left politicians of the Third Republic. Gamelin, on the other hand, was a master of tact, particularly skilled in balancing nuances, eager to compromise when possible and content to arrive at his ends (which he usually kept to himself) by indirect means. He swam like a fish through the turbid political waters of the Third Republic.

Maurice Gamelin, descended from an old military family of Lorraine, distinguished himself by his intellectual achievements from his days at St.-Cyr. Joseph Joffre selected him as an aide before the World War and kept him in various posts, including that of his Chief of Staff, until Joffre was retired from command in 1916. Gamelin thus played an important part in the war and was one of the inspirers, perhaps *the* inspirer, of the victory of the Marne in 1914. Later in the war Gamelin commanded a division and then an improvised corps with distinction. Following the war he served overseas, commanded the force that pacified Syria in the mid-1920s, and then returned to command the prized Corps de Nancy in 1927. It was only at the urging of Maginot's military assistant, General Alphonse Georges, and Pétain himself, that Gamelin accepted the post on the General Staff. Gamelin was friend to a number of leaders of the Third Republic; his presence sufficed to push Weygand's appointment through the Parliament, and he was content to work with the politicians whom Weygand found repugnant. Despite the harmony of their technical views, the opposition in spirit and character of the two leaders of the French army meant trouble.[24]

Weygand and Gamelin faced serious problems from the outset: one of Maginot's first decisions as Minister of War was to withdraw the remaining French troops from the Rhineland in 1930, removing the last direct check on Germany. In compensation, he forged ahead on the Maginot Line and on supplementary light fortifications in the early 1930s, spending 4.2 billion francs into 1934.[25] But a solid shield was not enough; a mobile element would have to thrust into Belgium to cover the north, to aid the small but respected Belgian army, and to prepare the engagement of the mass of reserves toward the Ruhr. Belgium was—as the Superior War Council had confirmed—the key front, lying midway between Paris and the industrial northwest of France on the one hand and the Ruhr on the other. Weygand moved to create this mobile element.

Weygand reported to Maginot in the spring of 1930 that the French army was insufficiently trained and motorized; it lacked fast tanks, modern communications equipment, and antitank and antiaircraft weapons. He concluded that a yearly program of 700-800 million francs was essential. In June 1930, the Superior War Council passed his and Gamelin's plan for a major reorganization. Five active infantry divisions were to be converted into motorized infantry divisions, one brigade of each of the five cavalry divisions was to be motorized, and one cavalry division was to become a *division légère mécanique*—the DLM—the world's first standing armored division. Weygand created a Technical Cabinet under Colonel Bloch-Dassault and assembled a Consulting Armaments Council with himself as president. A commission charged with studying the motorization and mechanization of large units operated under Gamelin from 1931. Thus the

French army began, one step ahead of the Germans, to grapple with the technical problems of the future.[26]

Weygand had long urged motorization and mechanization, particularly on the cavalry. Gamelin felt the same way; the saturated fronts which had stifled operations in 1918 would not reappear in the Europe of the 1930s. Maneuver would return to the battlefield; motorization and mechanization, radio communications, and the intervention of air forces in the battle posed new problems for the soldier's imagination. These ideas entered the texts of the Army Staff College in the early 1930s, along with the notion of tactical security necessary to guard the troops—especially inexperienced conscripts—against the surprises such modern weapons threatened. Students of the Army Staff College learned that strategic maneuver by motorized and mechanized forces, particularly on the flanks, would dominate at least the early stages of the next war. Therefore, it was necessary to regain that offensive spirit that had died in the trenches during the War. Strong air reconnaissance, fighters, and bombers capable of disrupting enemy communications and landing commandos in the enemy rear would contribute to the success of motorized and mechanized maneuvers. Nonetheless, decisive success in an assault on an enemy in prepared positions would be unlikely. Given the organization of the French army at the time, however (the one-year service and reduced proportion of active forces), there could be no repetition of the headlong rush of 1914. The students were told ". . . use as much strategic audacity as you wish—but be tactically prudent. . . ."[27] Finally, the French High Command with its tradition of personal control over the battle was unwilling to follow the German doctrine of provoking encounter battles—battles in which both sides happen upon each other in movement—which demanded a maximum of initiative from subordinate commanders in the field.[28] French doctrine in the early 1930s lay halfway between the lessons of World War I and the techniques of 1940, which it glimpsed but did not grasp.

Money began to flow into the arms programs: quantities of the D1 tank and, beginning in 1932, the more reliable D2 appeared along with antiaircraft weapons and new radios. In late 1931 Weygand ordered development of three types of vehicles for the cavalry: two types of scout machines and a combat vehicle.[29] In the spring of 1933, just after Adolf Hitler became Chancellor of Germany, Weygand fixed the composition of the first DLM, and he and Gamelin began development of new infantry accompaniment tanks and more powerful combat vehicles for the cavalry. A June 1934 specification resulted in the superb SOMUA (S35) tank, the best medium tank in the world in 1940.[30] The DLM, as Weygand described it in a note of October 1933, was to be in a balanced, combined-arms, mechanized force capable of offensive and defensive missions, and suited to articulation in two brigade-sized "tactical groupments." Weygand secured orders for armored utility vehicles for the infantry and for half-tracked machines to transport motorized cavalry. Funds, however, were limited; the infantry continued to use 37 mm guns from the war as antitank weapons, and the heavy machine guns intended for the infantry as antiaircraft weapons had to be replaced by ordinary machine guns.[31]

New equipment meant new doctrine; the 1934 manual on the D tank foresaw its use—exceptionally, as the D1 was neither reliable nor well armored—in mechanized formations for independent operations. Such a force was tried in maneuvers in 1932, but General Dufieux, the Inspector General of the Infantry, concluded that the operation would have failed under fire. He advised that such independent formations should be abandoned for the time being, their components reserved and then engaged with full artillery and air support on a narrow front to rupture the enemy position—after which an independent mechanized formation could exploit the breakthrough. This report put a temporary stop to the development of independent armored units in the infantry. But the development of the D and heavier B tanks, and the creation of independent mechanized units in the cavalry, continued.[32]

In the fall of 1933 Gamelin told the Belgian attaché that the French were preparing a quick intervention in Belgium should their governments so order. The force would consist of a packet of motorized infantry divisions preceded by DLM's and would advance to the aid of the Belgian army in a single bound. Gamelin added that he intended to keep information on the transformations within the French army secret.[33] The French command thus continued to count on Belgium as the base for mobile warfare against Germany, while the Maginot Line would secure the rest of French territory. Britain's position in case of a crisis remained highly uncertain, but with the support of Poland and Czechoslovakia in the east, and Belgium as a springboard for a move toward the Ruhr, France could still master Germany—provided the alliances, particularly the Belgian alliance, held—*and* provided that France had the will to act. But France was ill-prepared to mount a fast but limited response to any German threat short of total war; it was this point that Charles de Gaulle first made in print in 1934. The small active force of the French army was designed as the basis for the nation in arms, and was not meant to be an expeditionary force.

Progress in the motorized and fortress formations went unmatched in the cadre force destined to become the nation in arms. During the period 1930-1934 the metropolitan army mustered only 375,000 men (some 260,000 theoretically ready for combat), none too large a force. The Maginot arms programs improved the situation, although these programs never consumed the 650 million called for per year. Elections in 1932 brought in a succession of center-left governments which, facing the terrible dilemmas of the worldwide Depression beginning to hit home in France, cut the military budget. They also refused to extend the length of service to meet the external threat. The Depression hit France later and in milder form than elsewhere, since the French economy had a better balance between industry and agriculture and its exports and imports were less vulnerable. But when the Depression did hit, it brought governments whose preoccupation centered on balancing the budget at home and reinforcing collective security and conciliation toward Germany so that military expenditures could be cut. General Weygand, ever the disciple of Foch, strove constantly to wring funds for military modernization from these governments, and to dissuade Premier Édouard Herriot from granting any further concessions to Germany at the Geneva disarmament talks in 1932. On these issues Weygand clashed directly with the center-left governments. This conflict embittered the remaining years of Weygand's command and opened a breach between him and Gamelin, who tended to defend the government's position.[34]

In the spring of 1932 Weygand wrote the War Minister that the one-year service weakened the army to the point where the cover force could be erected only by calling up reserves—a serious political act. And the units thus formed would be reservist in character, requiring careful handling. Any worsening of the international situation, he wrote, would demand reinforcement of the army. Early in 1933, as Hitler came to power, further reductions forced Weygand to cut back training; he wrote the minister that the French army risked becoming an "illusory facade."[35] Weygand attacked the then-current notion of a defensive army, stressing the necessity for an army capable of maneuvering in the counterattack and of entering Germany should that country attack France's allies in central Europe. For such operations motorized infantry divisions and DLM's would be indispensable.[36]

Weygand's repeated pleas, his protest to the President of the Republic, and his personal embroilment with a new War Minister, Édouard Daladier, raised a crisis and opened a split with Gamelin. In December 1933 Weygand, faced again with proposed budget reductions, found Daladier (backed by Gamelin) opposed to him. Daladier was determined to oust Weygand over the budget issue but the crisis of the 6th of February 1934 blew up, and Weygand's position was saved.

Touched off by a long series of corruption scandals involving high governmental figures, the 6th of February erupted with massive riots of conservatives, Royalist, proto-Fascist leagues, and veterans' groups attempting to march on the Chamber of Deputies. Blood was shed, the cabinet fell—and the Republic almost fell with it. France seemed on the brink of civil war as leftist demonstrators filled the streets of Paris in response to the rightists. France's friends looked on askance, while Adolf Hitler took note of the internal divisions of his adversary. A conservative "national" cabinet under Gaston Doumergue succeeded in restoring order, and Weygand got a reprieve with the appointment of Marshal Pétain to be Minister of War. Pétain, however, out of place in the parliamentary milieu, proved timid, actually cutting the arms budget in spring 1934. He finally opened a five-year program of 3.5 billion francs in October 1934, but refused to request an extension of the term of military service. Pétain's refusal paralyzed Weygand, who could not oppose the prestigious Marshal as he had Daladier. In January 1935, Weygand presented a program to the Superior War Council demanding a guarantee of 800 million per year to equip two DLM's, three cavalry divisions, and seven motorized infantry divisions. On that note Weygand retired.[37] His successor, Maurice Gamelin, inherited Weygand's powers in addition to his own: he had proved his republican reliability.

The early 1930s saw the constitution of another arm of France's defense: an independent air force, the work of partisans of strategic air war. But in France, with its tradition of combined air-ground actions, this idea did not become the obsession it did in the British Royal Air Force. In 1929 an air staff was formed, but air units remained dispersed under the army, the navy, and the Territorial Air Defense, under Pétain from 1931 to early 1934. Confusion reigned as the air staff saw four chiefs come and go from 1930 to 1933; the command structure changed at the same pace. In spring 1931 a Superior Air Council, comparable in makeup and function to the army's Superior War Council, appeared, followed in 1932 by an Air Force Studies Center under General Paul Armengaud. Armengaud believed in the independent air force and received support in this stance from Pétain, who saw a powerful bomber force as a vital deterrent against Germany.[38] At the time, such works as Giulio Douhet's *Command of the Air* and such popularizations as H. G. Wells's *The Shape of Things to Come* foresaw poison gas as a principal weapon of strategic air war. No one knew what effect massive raids with poison gas would have on the populations of large cities, but they posed a deadlier threat than did high explosive and incendiary weapons. Military analysts tended to credit such attacks with an effect comparable to that expected from nuclear weapons in the post-World War II era. To achieve a deterrent effect from this terrifying weapon, France had to preserve a monopoly of such means; Germany had to be kept from using her superior industrial and population base to build up an air force.

In the spring of 1933 a young and active new Air Minister, Pierre Cot, took office. His Decree of April 1, 1933, the charter of the *Armée de l'air* (the French air force), ruled that all air units must be capable of joining in the independent battle for control of the air, as well as cooperating with the other services. The Decree established the post of Chief of the Air Force General Staff, the holder becoming the Commander in Chief of the Air Force in wartime. He would have a Chief of Staff to assist him.

At the end of 1932 the air force consisted of thirty-one day fighter, thirty observation, and sixteen reconnaissance squadrons, all equipped with post-World War I planes. The Territorial Air Defense had four squadrons of night fighters for the defense of cities, plus twenty-seven squadrons of day and night bombers (with machines dating from the early 1920s), and two escort squadrons. The complete French air forces had 1,074 aircraft backed by at least as many more in reserve. This force was large, but weak in offensive (bombing) strength and not up to the technical state of the art except for some of its fighters. But it was far more powerful than anything Germany could then muster.[39]

Both Pétain and the first Chief of the Air Force General Staff, General Victor Denain, felt that the primary role of the bombers would be to attack the infrastructure of the enemy air force, thus contributing to strategic air defense. The 1931 fighter manual, for the first time, asserted that air superiority over the interior of the nation would be a capital factor. Denain was acquainted with the theories of Douhet and General Billy Mitchell, but he saw the limits of such doctrines with regard to France. Denain's primary concern was to modernize his force and adapt it to the needs of strategic air war. In late 1934 he developed a new mobilization system to bring the air force more quickly to readiness, and pushed the development of radio-directed fighters to intercept enemy raids—an innovation at the time. He also backed the unfortunate Bomber-Fighter-Reconnaissance (BCR) concept for multipurpose aircraft which proved all but useless by 1940. On the other hand, he supported the excellent cantilever-wing monoplane Dewoitine 510 fighter armed with an automatic cannon, which was in advance of anything Germany had at the time. But Denain's greatest success was the adoption of Plan I.[40]

Approved by the Superior Air Council in June 1933, this first plan for complete renovation of the air force called for 1,010 new planes: 350 fighters and bombers each plus 310 multipurpose observation and reconnaissance (BCR) planes; Parliament allotted funds to begin work in the summer of 1934. Under Denain's authority, prototype programs developed most of the aircraft with which the French air force fought in 1939-1940. But the French aircraft industry, hit hard by the Depression and still largely at the artisanal level of production, delivered only 607 of the planes of Plan I by June 1936. Although the air force mustered 3,905 warplanes in March 1934, of which 1,581 were in first-line service, these were mostly old and included only 485 fighters and 276 bombers in the first line. A massive effort by the much larger German industry could overwhelm the French lead.[41]

In the early 1930s, France's overall strategy was the prerogative of the army High Command. With the growth of the Maginot Line, Belgium became increasingly important as the likely arena for mobile warfare. Across Belgium lay the only nearby target of value in Germany: the Ruhr.

Mobilization plans then in effect foresaw possible hostilities with Germany or Italy or both. The German threat was foreseen as a surprise attack via Belgium and Luxemburg—by 1935 only one-fifth of the French cover force consisted of active peacetime units. French plans called for an offensive into the Rhineland after completion of mobilization, should Germany attack into central Europe. Within this framework, exchanges between the French and Belgian High Commands continued, particularly after Hitler took power. In the summer of 1933 Weygand, explaining that French mobilization would be slow, complained to the Belgian King that the Belgians had left the "Ardennes gap" undefended without informing him beforehand, compromising the protection of the French mobilization, since no fortifications had been built behind that sector. King Albert I and his military adviser General Raoul Van Overstraeten were much annoyed with Weygand's complaint, since it coincided with complaints from the Walloon Defense Minister, Albert Devèze, who urged an integral defense of Belgium including special mobile units to hold the Ardennes.[42] In fact, the question ran deeper.

Belgium, hit hard by the Depression, was also hit hard by the efforts of Flemings to secure a stronger position. So bitter was the dispute that some Flemings talked of leaving Belgium, possibly to rejoin the Dutch monarchy against which Belgians had fought for independence in the 1830s. Belgian ties to France thus continued to be a political sore point; Belgian leaders at the same time were increasingly concerned about the threat incarnate in Adolf Hitler and about the political weaknesses within France. Under these circumstances, the French generals were very unwise—as events would prove—to take Belgian participation in any action against Germany, particularly German aggression against France's allies in eastern Europe, for granted. In May and June 1932 the Superior War Council debated whether to continue to rely on advancing into Belgium, or to seek funds for fortifications on the Belgian frontier. The Council split evenly on the issue; both Gamelin and Weygand favored fortifications, while Pétain wanted the funds spent on 200 fighters and 200 heavy bombers. The Council finally decided to put the money into tanks and antitank weapons; thus the decision to move into Belgium stood, regardless of the political situation there. It was especially dangerous to Belgium's internal stability for the French to appear to act in concert with Devèze, whose defense proposals clearly favored the Walloon population of the Ardennes at the risk of leaving Belgium's northern frontier (and the Flemings behind it) guarded only by Dutch neutrality. King Albert and his adviser saw the major German threat coming from the open northern frontier opposite the Netherlands. They were determined to leave only a small force in the Ardennes, considering that a German thrust there could not be stopped short of the Meuse River, in any case.[43] Weygand saw it differently.

In September 1933 Gamelin notified the Belgian attaché that the French were preparing a force of motorized infantry preceded by DLM's to be launched through the Ardennes toward the Amblève and Salm rivers, linking up then with the French fortifications facing Luxemburg. Further French forces would aid in the defense of northern Belgium, should the Germans outflank the Belgian fortress of Liège by violating Dutch neutrality. In early 1934 when Weygand was in Belgium for the funeral of King Albert (killed in a mountain-climbing accident in the Ardennes), he invited Devèze to come to Paris for discussions. Devèze came, only to receive contradictory impressions from Pétain (then Minister of War) and Weygand. But in April 1934 Devèze received a note informing him that if Belgium defended the Ardennes, France would send aid, and that from the spring of 1935 the majority of the motorized formations of the French army would assume this mission.[44]

In late 1934 the Chief of Staff of the Belgian Army, General Cumont, visited Paris. Weygand promised to send one cavalry and one infantry division to Arlon, the DLM and two motorized infantry divisions to Bastogne, and a motorized infantry division and a cavalry brigade through Dinant to Vielsam within twenty-four hours after the start of operations. Cumont replied that this was all very well, but what of the danger of a German attack via the Netherlands? Weygand had apparently not seriously considered an attack through the Netherlands; at the next meeting Gamelin took his place. Gamelin proposed to send one infantry and one cavalry division to northern Belgium following the sixth day of mobilization. Cumont found this unsatisfactory; Gamelin agreed: as long as the Belgians held Liège and the French Arlon, the Ardennes front was not dangerous. The key, for both Cumont and Gamelin, was in the north opposite the Netherlands. Neither the Belgian government nor the French expected any help from the Dutch, who were neutral and relatively unarmed (their last continental war ended in 1839 when they recognized Belgium's independence) and thought to be friendly toward Germany. The old Kaiser still resided there, and the Dutchman Anthony Fokker had played a key role in the German air industry during World War I. But for the time being all this was academic.[45]

FIRST CRISIS: THE RHINELAND, 1936

The year following Weygand's retirement was a strange interlude for the French High Command, which faced continuing apathy in Parliament despite new threats: in spring 1935 Hermann Goering openly paraded his *Luftwaffe* and Hitler announced Germany's return to a conscript army of thirty-six divisions—openly flouting Versailles. Worse yet, Britain recognized German rearmament by signing a naval pact with Hitler, acknowledging his right to forces banned at Versailles.

These events were crucial to the destinies of the West. For the first time France, conscious of Germany's overwhelming potential strength, had to choose between openly accepting German rearmament or taking some kind of action. At this time French military strength was weakened by years of budget cuts predicated on collective security and the demands of Depression economics. How real a threat was Hitler? Was German rearmament aimed at conquest, or could Hitler's promises that he sought only equality, not conquest, be taken at face value? Great Britain's frank acceptance of the new situation was a heavy blow. Britain was already pursuing a policy of appeasement toward Germany (although that term was not yet in vogue). To France, Britain's policy seemed another slap in the face, another betrayal by an old ally. At this point there was no hope of restoring the coalition of 1918; France would have to act alone with only the support of Poland and perhaps Czechoslovakia and Belgium, and with the tacit approval, no doubt, of the Soviet Union with whom France had taken the precaution of developing a vague alliance. Any French action at this point would have to come outside the bounds of the League; any such action was bound to attract British hostility. French public opinion was not prepared for France to act alone: economic and political problems at home were too severe, the German threat still too distant, the illusion of collective security still too comfortingly near.

Hitler won the first round in this cold war. In the face of his defiance, France's military leaders were in a difficult position. The Minister of War at the time was General Louis Maurin, one of the leading technicians in the army, and from 1927 the first Inspector General of Motorization. His first task was to convince Parliament to extend the length of service to two years. Maurin asked for retention of the draft class then in service for an extra year; the resulting debates in March 1935 considered the whole range of defense problems and solutions. The left demanded new disarmament negotiations and questioned the extension of service; various members on the right—including Paul Reynaud, who proposed a project sketched out by an officer named Charles de Gaulle—wanted a maneuver corps of professional soldiers armed with mechanized equipment. Caught in the middle, Maurin agreed on the need for equipment but demanded manpower as well. Facing the left, he said the extra men were needed for defense only—there was no thought of an attack on anyone. Maurin got his extra year's service, but he left a false impression of French strategy; the mobilization plan then in effect called explicitly for a military offensive should Germany turn on France's central European allies.[46] The army, meanwhile, saw value in de Gaule's vision of a mechanized maneuver corps, but argued that France must also have a large reserve army to defend French territory and to back up the maneuver corps. The proper solution, Gamelin suggested, was to expand mechanized units already in existence in the army and to add heavy armored divisions, while continuing to use conscripts in these units.

In any case the shortage of personnel was now resolved. Money was also forthcoming, so much so that because of administrative difficulties and the reluctance of industry to accept big government contracts on a long-term basis, 60 percent of the 1.368 billion francs allocated in 1935 was still unspent in 1936. The late spring of 1935 brought further good news: following talks at Stresa, France secured military accords with Italy for joint action should Hitler threaten Austria or act on the Rhine. The Stresa talks and the following Franco-Italian military accord opened bright new prospects for French strategy. Mussolini's annoyance with the meddling of the infant Nazi Reich in Austrian affairs (Austria was then Mussolini's protégé) brought France and Italy together in a joint effort to check German expansion. The Franco-Italian military accord not only relieved France of the need to maintain forces on the Alps and in North Africa as a counter to a possible Italian threat, but added a powerful army and air force to a potential allied coalition. Great Britain, however, steadfastly refused to make any further commitments on the Continent beyond the Locarno accords. Unhappily, the French advantage disappeared in the following months because of the dispute over Italy's Ethiopian adventure. Mussolini's conquest of Ethiopia was popular in Italy, but it aroused strong public reaction in Britain (less so in France). Although the British and French governments were initially inclined to accept the Italian action, the British public reacted so strongly that the foreign ministry there changed hands. Britain adopted a strong stand in the League of Nations on the Ethiopian issue, leading to attempted economic sanctions against Italy. Caught between the contradictory desires to support collective security on the one hand while maintaining Italian friendship against Hitler on the other, the British government—with the French trying desperately not to alienate *either*—succeeded only in destroying the last vestiges of hope in the League while thoroughly antagonizing Mussolini. The French Premier, Pierre Laval, attempted a solution: he promised the British full cooperation against Italy if they in turn would replace Italy as France's Ally against German expansion in central Europe. But Britain, more fearful of the Italian and Japanese threats than of German moves toward Austria, refused. The bright prospects opened by Stresa faded and Italy began its slow descent into the German camp.

In France Jean Fabry, Maurin's successor for a time, continued to build up the army by ordering several hundred more light infantry accompaniment tanks to supplement Maurin's orders for some 500 light and 30 heavy B tanks. Then in January 1936 the government of Albert Sarraut took office to prepare for the parliamentary elections scheduled for April and May; Maurin returned to the war ministry.[47] Sarraut's was a caretaker government, preparing for what promised to be the most contested elections in recent French history: the right versus the new Popular Front coalition embracing all the parties of the center and left up to and including the Communists at whose initiative this "anti-Fascist" movement formed. Belgium too was due for bitter parliamentary elections in May, elections portending victories for the proto-Fascist Rexists and the Flemish nationalists. Hitler saw opportunity knocking.

One step beneath the government, the command of the French army lay in the "soft" hands of Maurice Gamelin.[48] Gamelin had succeeded in acquiring the two top posts in the army—a feat unequaled since his mentor Joffre did it in 1911. Gamelin was appointed despite Weygand's recommendation to Pétain (who as "Dean" of the army approved top promotions) that Alphonse Georges, and not Gamelin, succeed him. Gamelin's new role was demanding; he delegated the operation of the General Staff to its new first deputy, General Louis Colson, and made Georges his executive assistant. But Gamelin dominated the French military down to 1940, and his personality lay at the center of all that was to come.

Gamelin was the son of an officer and *intendant* of the Imperial Guard; family connections stood him in good stead under the Third Republic—his sister married General Picquart, who had played a vital role in the eventual release of Dreyfus. But the key factor in Gamelin's rise was his intellect: graduating at the head of his class at St.-Cyr, he demonstrated diplomacy and tact and military ability under Joffre and in independent commands. All his life Gamelin was marked by a philosophic bent; he could bow before those setbacks that drove Weygand to the brink of insubordination. For Gamelin, the role of the chief was to rise above events, see them in a realistic spirit, choose a proper solution, and then impose it despite all obstacles. He stood by Joffre's side before the Battle of the Marne in 1914: ". . . from a Willpower sure of itself there emanates a real glow, a sort of hypnotism, which galvanizes . . . the subordinates. . . . there are times when one has the impression of a force which actually grapples with and subdues Fortune and . . . 'dominates events.'"[49]

If all this seemed mystical, Gamelin freely admitted it: the faith that gave life to the work was faith in France; that same faith gave the army, in a socially divided France, a vital role as a solid and dynamic element.[50] Despite his faith, despite his advanced technical views and intellectual dominance, Gamelin was handicapped in the conservative officer corps by his "republican" political reputation and above all by his complex and often evasive manner.

Sharing leadership of the army with him was General Alphonse Georges, one of the most widely admired officers in the service. Rising from modest origins, Georges graduated near the head of his class at St.-Cyr in 1897 and fought in the Sahara. Before World War I he graduated from the Staff

College (again near the head of his class) and served on various staffs. He was severely wounded commanding a battalion near Nancy in September 1914 and served out the remainder of the war and afterward in staff positions in the eastern Mediterranean. Following these assignments, he served on the Rhine, in North Africa, and in France. He passed through the War College where his independence and his flair for command made a strong impression. In the early 1930s he worked with André Maginot, commanded the 19th Corps at Algiers, and then took a place on the Superior War Council as Inspector General of the Colonial Troops in 1933. In October 1934 Georges was present at the assassination of King Alexander of Yugoslavia in Marseille; terribly injured, Georges never recovered completely. Nevertheless, Gamelin called him in early 1935 to be *Major-général des armées*; Georges accepted this highly uncertain position only at the urging of Pétain. By the following summer Georges had become Gamelin's deputy, but his position remained consultative, and it was in that role that he worked: preparing statements of doctrine, conducting maneuvers, and so on. This was a difficult task for a man accustomed to independence and to speaking his own mind.[51] Gamelin's appointment of Georges seemed intended to conciliate those elements within the army who supported Weygand (and thus Weygand's protégé Georges) and all that Weygand stood for: forthright pressure on the government (particularly center-left governments) to reinforce the military materially and morally within the French nation. In bringing up Georges, however, Gamelin risked a repetition of the split in the High Command which had opened between himself and Weygand in 1933.

Meanwhile, the construction of the French maneuver force continued. By early 1936 the design of the DLM called for 240 armored vehicles in a balanced all-arms unit. The DLM had fewer armored vehicles than the *Panzerdivisionen* Germany was just beginning to form, but the heavier arms and armor of its combat vehicles made it more powerful. Doctrine evolved to match the formation of new units: the 1935 cavalry manual foresaw the DLM providing tactical security for the maneuver of motorized infantry, while its mobility and the power of its armament would make it, with the air forces, the essential instrument for the exploitation of a battlefield success. Still, given its light armor and the threat of enemy antitank guns and artillery, its armored vehicles could be engaged in an assault only with the support of other arms. The DLM could produce a powerful impact in the assault, but its essential role would be limited to maneuver in free terrain or to exploit a breakthrough; the DLM was just the formation to execute raids into the enemy rear.[52] The use of the DLM was not just paper doctrine, as General Van Overstraeten, the military adviser to the King of the Belgians, saw at French maneuvers in September 1935. He watched a mock battle between a DLM and a motorized infantry division on one hand and another motorized infantry division and a cavalry brigade on the other, complete with tank battles, aircraft, and smoke screens. It was an impressive and professional performance and led Van Overstraeten to wonder why the French ". . . dip their colors to the Reichswehr."[53]

The development of vehicles to fill out the DLM reached its conclusion in 1935; satisfactory scouting vehicles were ordered by then (a total of several hundred machines) but a really powerful combat machine was lacking until the SOMUA appeared in 1935. Gamelin and the Inspector General of the Cavalry planned to increase the assault power of the DLM, while the reconnaissance and observation arms of the air force were oriented toward increasing tactical security against enemy mobile formations.[54]

Gamelin further developed light fortifications on open sections of the French frontier; by 1936 France spent some 5 billion francs on fortifications, although these were of uneven value and generally declined in strength from east to west. In all, France spent some 43 billion francs in arming its services from 1919 to 1936: 42 percent for the navy (particularly in the 1920s), 31 percent to the army, and 27 percent to the air forces. The results were substantial: by June 1936 French industry had turned out (in addition to vehicles for the DLM) some 1,300 antitank weapons, 160 D1 and 17 D2 tanks, 17 powerful B tanks, and 700 armored utility vehicles for the infantry. By the beginning of 1936 as far as French intelligence knew—and it was quite well informed—Germany had 21 infantry divisions and some 550,000 men under arms. By that April French intelligence reported that the Germans were forming three Panzers, but only the first was complete with its 500 tanks and these were all light PzKpfwI's armed with machine guns only.[55] Against these comparatively poorly armed German forces, Gamelin's latest mobilization plan would have fielded a force more than twice the size of the active German army, including a cover force with two DLM's (at least on paper), and seven motorized infantry divisions—plus thirteen further infantry divisions and fortress troops and twenty-four battalions of tanks in reserve.[56]

With these facts in mind Gamelin developed his strategy. The Italian threat was still partially neutralized in spring 1936 by the Stresa agreement. Therefore, Gamelin focused on the two wings of his fortified front facing Germany (Belgium and Switzerland), and on sanctions should Hitler violate the Rhineland. But the sanctions chosen must not compromise French mobilization if war followed. In April 1935 Gamelin addressed a report to Premier Pierre Laval on the strategic situation in the event Hitler attacked Austria or entered the Rhineland. The report stated that the chance to conduct a preventive war against Hitler with certainty of success had already passed. Gamelin hoped that operations would commence with Germany pushing its principal forces into central Europe. France would remain on the defensive behind the fortified frontier until fully mobilized, then take the offensive. It is hard to understand why Gamelin was so cautious at this time, when the German *Wehrmacht* was still in the beginning stages of expansion.

Gamelin's first concern was to set the maneuver into Belgium, the most threatening as well as the most rewarding front likely to open. In April 1935 Gamelin met the Belgian Chief of Staff, General Cumont, and told him that the extra year's service and the lessening of the Italian threat would enable him to further aid Belgium. Gamelin agreed that the real threat to Belgium lay in the north, not the east: he would shift forces away from the Ardennes toward the open Dutch frontier. One infantry division and a half cavalry division would still occupy Arlon in the southern Ardennes, and one infantry division would secure Garnich in Luxemburg; but he would move no further units into the Ardennes initially. He approved Belgian plans to restrict their forces in the area to one infantry division and the mobile *Chasseurs ardennais.* Gamelin planned a much heavier deployment into northern Belgium; he promised that the First Army with one DLM and a motorized infantry division would be in the field by the third day of operations, to be followed by substantial forces on the front from Antwerp to Liège. In the event of a German entry into the Rhineland, the generals agreed that Locarno permitted an immediate French advance into Belgium, provided that precautions were taken so that the Germans could not use that act as a pretext for aggression.[57]

A German occupation of the Rhineland would pose a particularly tricky problem for France: suppose the Germans began to occupy the zone covertly? Alternatively, reoccupation might be the first step toward a massive surprise attack. The international complications would be ferocious with the signatories of the Locarno accords and the League of Nations to deal with. Would a direct violation by Germany bring a strong British response, or would Britain remain wedded to appeasement? The Belgian army seemed to favor joint military action, but the Belgian government was just then working to denounce the Military Accord of 1920: would the vital Belgian alliance operate as planned? Poland and perhaps Czechoslovakia could be counted on, but what action would the Soviet Union (separated from Germany by Poland and Rumania, both hostile to the Soviets) take? Would the demoralized League of Nations react more strongly to German reoccupation of German territory than it had to the conquest of one of its members (Ethiopia) by another (Italy)? And could France hope for any support from Italy? In the end, could France risk acting, without the support of other great powers or the League, to prevent Germany from militarily reoccupying German soil? Would the French public, in the midst of a depression and a heated political campaign, support forceful action? But the stakes were crucial: nothing less than the last guarantee remaining from the Versailles Treaty after all the sacrifices of

World War I. Once in the Rhineland, Hitler could prepare at his leisure for an assault on France, or swallow up France's allies in the east while holding off the French at small cost. With the Rhineland fortified, France could only watch Germany develop the military potential of its 60 million people and its industry; 40 million Frenchmen and an industry two to three times weaker would exhaust themselves in a hopeless effort to keep up. By early 1936 it was clear that Hitler intended to move.[58]

Meanwhile, the French air force underwent major command changes as the army had before it. Denain gave way at the end of 1935 to General Bertrand Pujo, a soldier turned airman in World War I. In the spring of 1936 Pujo's position was enhanced when he received command of the Territorial Air Defense; at last all of France's air forces—save those attached to the navy—were united in one hand. French industry struggled vainly to fulfill Plan I for the modernization of the air force. Although the budget went from 1.8 billion francs in 1934 to 2.8 billion in 1936 (compared with 1.6 billion francs in 1934 to 5 billion in 1936 in Britain) production remained slow; further expansion had to be deferred for financial reasons. Plan I called for the whole fighter force to be reequipped by April 1, 1936, a far cry from the results achieved. Of the 205 bombers in frontline units by March 10, 1936, 158 were new; Armengaud reported that only 95 were ready for action due to the lack of finishing touches and spares. He complained that neither he nor his deputy General Joseph Vuillemin had been consulted on key personnel changes in the units they would command in wartime: a typical complaint in the French military system where wartime commanders had no control over the peacetime administration of their units.[59] The basic problem of aircraft production—excessive division in the air industry—was well known; but recommendations that the state create its own air arsenal as a step toward the concentration and expansion of the industry[60] were not yet politically feasible.

But in early 1936 the *Armée de l'air* was still superior to Goering's fledgling Luftwaffe in quantity and in the quality of its cannon-armed monoplane fighters and its heavy and medium bombers.[61] However, the disquieting potential of the German aircraft industry led Pujo (as it had his predecessors) to plan all-out bombing of German air bases and production centers as the first act of a war. In early 1936 four bomber brigades stood concentrated in France's northeast; Armengaud's deputy Vuillemin specified that the bombers would first attack enemy air forces, second bomb enemy ground forces threatening the army's cover force, and third conduct reprisals on enemy cities and industries should the government so order.[62]

With its armed forces in part evolving toward new roles and in part rearmed to fulfill the new roles, the French command looked toward the coming clash over the Rhineland. No one could doubt the profound popular desire to avoid war; to many the issue of the Rhineland seemed strictly an internal German affair. France's leaders knew the significance of the Rhineland, but what of France's potential allies and the League of Nations? General Maurin wrote to Foreign Minister Pierre Flandin on February 17, 1936, "It might be better for France not to enter the Rhineland in case of German action so as not to appear the aggressor; in any case an operation could not be attempted without British support."[63] Two days later at a conference Gamelin supported Maurin. Still, the demilitarized zone had to be preserved at least until France was stronger. However, there is some reason to think that French leaders were considering conceding the remilitarization of the zone if, in return, they could get a stronger British commitment to Western security. Maurin and Gamelin feared that armed sanctions might disrupt the mobilization plan: the very action that might bring war risked compromising France's preparations to wage it. Thus, if the DLM and motorized infantry units were diverted into the Saar, what would happen if the Germans suddenly attacked through Belgium? Gamelin ordered the preparation of plans for sanctions, but he and Maurin felt that reservists would first have to be called up and Maurin so informed the government.[64]

France's allies proved reluctant. Britain refused to commit itself to any action in advance. Indeed, Foreign Minister Anthony Eden made it clear that Britain did not want France to take any overt action, despite Britain's obligations to keep the Rhineland demilitarized. A question to the Belgian government brought the reply that it would maintain staff talks, but at the same time the Belgians were finishing negotiations intended to free them from the obligations of the 1920 Military Accord—Belgium formally denounced the Accord on March 6, 1936.[65] Although Belgium was still a signatory to the Locarno accords and maintained staff talks with France, it was no longer a firm ally. Coming when it did, the Belgian denunciation of the Military Accord knocked the props out from under French strategy. France had always—unwisely and despite warning signs—counted on the use of Belgium as a springboard for a response to German action. The loss of Belgium was not only a disaster for France in 1936, it disrupted the foundations of French strategy against Germany and ultimately played a major role in the collapse of the West in 1940.

Hitler launched his thunderbolt into the midst of this disarray on March 7, 1936, choosing as a pretext the ratification by the French Chamber of the Franco-Soviet Alliance of 1935. Hitler sent only a few units into the Rhineland, but the gauntlet was down.[66]

As the shock wave reverberated French leaders met. Despite the forewarnings the government had not prepared a detailed response to the coup and was divided between those who urged strong action and those who demanded consultation with France's allies and the League. Gamelin grossly overestimated German capabilities and hesitated to take overt action. He believed French entry into the Rhineland would mean war, and a conflict limited to the Franco-German frontier would see a rapid saturation of the front leading to stabilization. Only the air force could take the offensive in such a situation. But what about Belgium? On March 10 Gamelin discussed with Flandin the possibility of imposing sanctions short of war; he and Georges supported the idea but both agreed that reservists would be needed. That evening the French Premier, Albert Sarraut, met his advisers: Gamelin reaffirmed that this was a favorable moment for action, but first the full cover force must be called up. In case of war he hoped to push rapidly toward Mainz and Köln, but it would be difficult to force the Rhine and thus finish the Germans—France would need allies. On March 11 Gamelin proposed entering the Saar, then moving into the Ardennes. The whole cover force would be needed. This was too much for Sarraut; he could hardly order partial mobilization and risk a war while a pacific France was already in a divisive election campaign and stood without allied support.[67] Actually, the French could count on Polish and perhaps Czech and Rumanian and even Italian assistance against Germany in case of war, but from every other direction they received pleas for inaction, or at best equivocation. European opinion, French and German included, was utterly unprepared for war. Hitler's timing and his claim that he was only restoring sovereignty over German territory left his potential opponents divided, uncertain, and above all desperate to avoid war. Gamelin's supple evasions and equivocations were no aid to Sarraut. Weygand's firmness and forthright language were sorely missed.

Meanwhile, the active French army, including the 1st DLM and a number of tank battalions that had moved to the frontier, began to pull back beginning March 17, although as late as March 28 Gamelin was still preparing plans, including some for a rapid mechanized incursion into the Rhineland. Morale in the activated units of the army and among the frontier populace was almost uniformly high according to a number of officers on the scene; the cadres in particular felt that "grave things" were about to happen. But the peak of the crisis had already passed.[68] In Gamelin's view, as he later put it, everything hinged on the chances for a quick and decisive victory in case of war. What good would it do to throw Hitler out of the Rhineland as long as the "eternal Germany" remained intact? What good had the occupation of the Ruhr in 1923 done? But victory in a war without allies depended on the ability of French forces to decisively defeat Germany before reaching the barrier of the Rhine. French leaders felt that France was simply not ready—not morally, not materially—to wage a total war, and unless quick victory could be guaranteed the prospect of total war had to be faced. In spite of sustained technical and military development, France lacked the allied support and above all the political resolution to risk total war.[69] Hitler, on the other hand, was willing to gamble.

Thus it was that the last benefits culled from the sacrifices of World War I were cast away. The West lost its chance to secure the peace.

At the urging of the Communist party, all the center and left parties of the French political world pooled their strength in an "anti-Fascist" front. Not that they were advocating war; none of them advocated a violent reaction to Hitler's militarization of the Rhineland. But the threat of Hitler combined with Mussolini's adventure in Ethiopia awakened a number of Europeans to the potential danger. In Belgium, meanwhile, elections brought strength to the proto-Fascist Rexists and the Flemish nationalists at the expense of the traditional liberal parties. Western Europe seemed to balance on the edge of internal chaos. Conservative elements were shocked when the French Popular Front triumphed. The success of the Popular Front encouraged French workers to undertake a series of strikes which halted the French economy and panicked French industrialists. France now faced a foreign threat greater than any since World War I, and had to rise from the ruins of the Depression and the social expectations called up by the Popular Front to make a new effort. The alternative was to bow to German hegemony. But only a few Frenchmen had yet thought of that.

NOTES

1. General [Maxime] Weygand, *Mémoires* II (Paris: Flammarion, 1957), pp. 495ff—Weygand was Foch's chief of staff.

2. Weygand, *Mémoires* II, pp. 380ff; Cdt. Jean Vial, "La Défense nationale: Son organisation entre les deux guerres," *Revue d'histoire de la deuxième guerre mondiale* no. 18 (April 1955); Jean-Paul Cointet, "Gouvernement et Haut-commandement en France entre les deux guerres: Contribution à une réflexion sur la défaite de 1940," *Défense nationale* (April 1977).

3. France, Ministère des armées, EMAT, SHA, Col. François-André Paoli, *L'Armée française de 1919 à 1939: La Phase de fermêté* (Vincennes: SHAT, 1971), p. 79; interview with Col. Paoli at the SHA, Vincennes, November 14, 1972.

4. Paoli, *La Phase de fermêté,* pp. 61ff; France, SHAA, Lt.-Col. Hayez, "Organisation du commandement, 1918-1939" (unpublished, 1961), pp. 3ff; Raymond Danel, "Étude succinte sur l'évolution de l'organisation de l'armée de l'air de 1933 à 1940" (unpublished, Blagnac [?], 1966); General [Charles] Christienne and Pierre Buffotot, "L'Aéronautique militaire française entre 1919 et 1939," *Revue historique des armées* 4th year, no. 2 (1977): 9ff. André Van Haute, *Pictorial History of the French Air Force* (London: Ian Allen, 1974 and 1975), 2 vols., has good pictures.

5. *Les Relations militaires franco-belges de mars 1936 au 10 mai 1940: Travaux d'un colloque d'historiens belges et français* (Paris: Centre National de la Recherche Scientifique, 1968), pp. 18ff, 43ff (hereafter cited as *Relations franco-belges*); Jonathan Helmreich, "The Negotiation of the Franco-Belgian Military Accord of 1920," *French Historical Studies* 3, no. 3 (Spring 1967).

6. Paoli, *La Phase de fermêté,* pp. 84ff, 109, 120; General [Marie-Eugène] Debeney, *Sur la sécurité militaire de la France* (Paris: Payot, 1930), p. 51—Debeney succeeded Buat as chief of staff from early 1924 to early 1930.

7. General P[aul]-É[mile] Tournoux, *Haut commandement Gouvernement et Défense des frontières du nord et de l'est 1919-1939* (Paris: Nouvelles éditions latines, 1960), pp. 332ff.

8. Robert Jacomet, *L'Armement de la France 1936-1939* (Paris: Éditions Lajeunesse, 1945), pp. 11ff—Jacomet administered the financing of arms programs from 1936 to 1940; [Engineer General] J. Molinié, "Les Matériels blindés de combat de 1917 à 1967 [Part I]," *Sciences et techniques de l'armement: Mémorial de l'artillerie française* 46, no. 182 (1972): 840ff.

9. France, MG, EMA, *Instruction provisoire sur l'emploi tactique des grandes unités* (Paris: Imprimerie nationale, 1921), pp. 9ff.

10. Ibid., pp. 23ff, 42.

11. Ibid., pp. 10, 62ff.

12. France, MG, EMA, 3e Bureau, *Instruction provisoire sur l'emploi des chars de combat comme engins d'infanterie* (Paris: Fournier, 1920), pp. 5ff.

13. France, Centre d'études tactiques d'artillerie de Metz, Général de Vaulgrenant, *L'Aviation de bombardement* (no publication information given, 1922), pp. 48ff; France, MG, Aéronautique, *Conférences d'aéronautique générale* (Nanterre: Imprimerie de l'aéronautique, 1924 [?]), p. 13; France, MG, Aéronautique, *Règlement provisoire de manoeuvre de l'aéronautique . . . L'Aviation de bombardement* (Paris: Charles-Lavauzelle, 1928), pp. 1ff; Jean-Henri Jauneaud, *De Verdun à Dien-Bien-Phu* (Paris: Éditions du Scorpion, 1960), pp. 18ff.

14. Estienne's remarks in Col. Georges Ferré, *Le Défaut de l'armure: Nos chars pouvaient-ils vaincre en 1940? Enseignements et perspectives nouvelles* (Paris: Charles-Lauvauzelle, 1948), pp. 46ff.

15. Jon Jacobsen, *Locarno Diplomacy: Germany and the West 1925-1929* (Princeton, New Jersey: Princeton University Press, 1972), pp. 3ff, 30ff. See also Maurice Baumont, *La Faillite de la paix (1918-1939)* I, *De Rethondes à Stresa (1918-1935)*, 3rd ed. (Paris: Presses universitaires de France, 1951), pp. 140ff, and the convincing *France's Rhineland Diplomacy, 1914-1924: The Last Bid for a Balance of Power in Europe* by Walter A. McDougall (Princeton, New Jersey: Princeton University Press, 1978).

16. Tournoux, *Défense des frontières*, pp. 79, 334ff; Paoli, *L'Armée française de 1919 à 1939. Livre III: Le Temps des compromis (Juin 1924—Juin 1930)* (Vincennes: SHAT, 1974).

17. [Ferdinand Foch], "L'Armée qu'il nous faut: Les Bases d'une organisation," *Revue des deux mondes* (November 1, 1926): 168ff.

18. Jacomet, *L'Armement de la France*, pp. 91ff; Molinié, "Les Matériels blindés," p. 855; Paoli, *Temps des compromis*; Weygand, *Mémoires* II, p. 313; France, I[e] DA, EM, 3ème Bureau: N°1778/Op., "Manoeuvres de Camp de Mailly 1928: Rapport du service de l'arbitrage" (unpublished, 1928); France, ESG, Cours de tactique générale et d'état-major, *Notes pratiques d'état-major* (Paris: Charles-Lavauzelle, 1939), pp. 39ff.

19. France, *L'Aviation allemande: . . . Tendance du commandent allemand en matière d'aviation* (no place: Imprimerie du bureau cartographique, 1924), p. 30; Hayez, "Organisation du commandement," pp. 6ff; France, SHAA, François Audigier, "Histoire de l'aviation militaire française: Des origines à 1939" (unpublished, [1970?]), Chapter III, p. 3; Danel, "Étude succinte," pp. 8ff.

20. On the Maginot Line see Tournoux, *Défense des frontières.*

21. Weygand, *Mémoires* II, pp. 280ff.

22. Ibid., pp. 280ff, 326; Philip Bankwitz, *Maxime Weygand and Civil-Military Relations in Modern France* (Cambridge, Mass.: Harvard University Press, 1967), pp. 18ff.

23. Weygand, *Mémoires* II, 380ff; discussion of the ephemeral Defense Ministry in Paoli, *L'Armée française: De 1919 à 1939. La Fin des illusions* (no publication information given, [1976?]), pp. 23ff.

24. General R. [Georges-René] Alexandre, *Avec Joffre d'Agadir à Verdun: Souvenirs 1911-1916* (Paris: Berger-Levrault, 1932), pp. 140ff; Bankwitz, *Weygand*, p. 39; Maurice Gamelin, *Servir* II (Paris: Plon, 1946), pp. xxi, 3. See also Pierre Le Goyet, *Le Mystère Gamelin* (Paris: Presses de la Cité, 197[6]).

25. Jean Fabry, *Février 1934-juin 1940: De la Place de la Concorde au cours de l'Intendance* (Paris: Les Éditions de France, 1942), p. 29; Weygand, *Mémoires* II, p. 368; Tournoux, *Défense des frontières*, pp. 135ff, 148, 170ff.

26. Weygand, *Mémoires* II, pp. 349ff, 369ff, 407; testimony of General Dassault in France, Parlement, Assemblée nationale, *Les Événements survenus en France de 1933 à 1945: Témoignages et documents recueillis par la commission d'enquête parlementaire* V (Paris: Presses universitaires de France, [1950?]), pp. 1459ff (hereafter cited as *Événements . . . Témoignages*); [Colonel] André Duvignac, *Histoire de l'armée motorisée* (Paris: Imprimerie nationale, 1947), p. 322.

27. Quote from France, ESG, General L. Loizeau, *La Manoeuvre du corps d'armée dans l'armée* (Courbevoie: P. Chanove, 1932), pp. 7ff, 93, 138ff; Maxime Weygand, "La Cavalerie et la 'Revue de Cavalerie'" *Revue de cavalerie* 4th series, 1 (January-February 1921); Cdt. [Jean] Petibon [notes by Maurice Gamelin], "La 9e Division en 1918," a series of articles in *Revue militaire française* 39 (January-June 1931); France, ESG, Lts.-Col. Voisin, Mouton and Lascroux and Cdt. Caldairou, *Conférences de tactique générale et d'état-major: La Division* I (no publication information given, 1932), p. 70.

28. France, ESG, Lt.-Col. René Altmayer and Cdts. Marion and Trémeau, *Cours de cavalerie* (Paris: Hermieu, 1930), pp. 41, 64.

29. *Automitrailleuses de découverte, reconnaissance,* and *combat:* the first a wheeled vehicle for probing the roads, the second for cross-country scouting, the third for combat with enemy tanks.

30. E. M. von Senger und Etterlin, *Die Kampfpanzer von 1916-1966* (Munich: Lehmanns Verlag, 1966), p. 137.

31. Weygand, *Mémoires* II, pp. 354ff, 408; Molinié, "Les Matériels blindés," 850ff; France, MG, EMA (1er Bureau) et Direction de l'infanterie (Organisation-Mobilisation: N°21 I/II), "Tableaux d'effectifs de guerre de l'infanterie: Formations motorisées et régiment type région fortifiée: Fasicule I" (unpublished, Paris, 1932), pp. 60ff; Paoli, *La Fin des illusions*, pp. 80ff.

32. Weygand, *Mémoires* II, pp. 407ff; France, EMA, Bureau des opérations militaires et instruction générale de l'armée, Première direction, Chars de combat, *Notice provisoire sur l'emploi des chars D en liaison avec l'infanterie: (Annexe à l'Instruction sur l'emploi des chars de combat du 24 janvier 1929)* (no publication information given, 1934), p. 4; Dufieux's report in *Événements . . . Témoignages* IV, pp. 1056ff.

33. Attaché's report in Belgium, Ministère des affaires étrangères, *Documents*

diplomatiques belges 1920-1940: La Politique de sécurité extérieure III (Brussels: C. de Visscher and F. Vanlangehove, 1964-1966), pp. 158ff (hereafter cited as *DDB*).

34. Gamelin, *Servir* II, pp. 12ff; Jacomet, *L'Armement de la France*, pp. 93ff; Weygand, *Mémoires* II, p. 386.

35. Weygand, *Mémoires* II, pp. 384ff, 398.

36. Weygand's report in France, Ministère des affaires étrangères, Commission de publication des documents relatifs aux origines de la guerre 1939-1945, *Documents diplomatiques français 1932-1939* 1st series, II (Paris: Imprimerie nationale, 1966), pp. 457ff (hereafter cited as *DDF*).

37. Weygand, *Mémoires* II, pp. 397ff; Gamelin, *Servir* II, pp. 106ff; General [Émile] Laure et al., *Pétain* (Paris: Berger-Levrault, 1941), pp. 363ff; Jacomet, *L'Armement de la France*, pp. 105ff; Tournoux, *Défense des frontières*, pp. 213ff. See also René Rémond, *La Droite en France de la première restauration à la Ve république* I (Paris: Éditions Montaigne, 1963), pp. 204 passim; Jacques Chastenet, *Histoire de la troisième république* VI (Paris: Hachette, 1962), pp. 77ff; Bankwitz, *Weygand*, pp. 178ff.

38. Audigier, "Histoire de l'aviation militaire française," Chapter III, p. 3; General [Paul] Armengaud, *Batailles politiques et militaires sur l'Europe: Témoignages (1932-1940)* (Paris: Éditions du Myrte, 1948), pp. 11ff; France, Centre des hautes études aériennes, Lt.-Col. Tourre, "La Défense du territoire contre les attaques aériennes" (unpublished, 1937).

39. General [François] d'Astier de la Vigerie, *Le Ciel n'était pas vide: 1940* (Paris: Julliard, 1952), pp. 36ff; Hayez, "Organisation du commandement," pp. 19ff; Tourre," Défense du territoire"; Danel, "Étude succinte," pp. 13ff.

40. Tournoux, *Défense des frontières*, p. 152; Tourre, "Défense du territoire"; France, [MG?], *Règlement provisoire de manoeuvre de l'Aéronautique. L'Aviation de chasse* (Versailles: no publication information given, 1931), p. 5; General Cressaty, ed., *Sous la signe de l'aviation: Le Général d'armée aérienne DENAIN vu par ses amis et collaborateurs* (no place: SERMA, 1969), pp. 9, 75; France, [SHAA], Colonel Bizard, "L'Armée de l'air jusqu'à la déclaration de guerre" (unpublished, no date), p. 12; d'Astier, *Le Ciel n'était pas vide*, p. 36; Audigier, "Histoire de l'aviation militaire française," Chapter III, p. 11.

41. France, MA: N° 15, Letter from General Picard to members of the CSA (unpublished, 1935); France, [MA, EMAA?]. "Historique des plans d'acroissement et rénovation de l'armée de l'air" (unpublished, 1938); France, [EMAA, 4e Bureau, "Programmes 1934 et 1936: Caractéristiques Projets réalisations des différents types d'appareils"] (unpublished, [November, 1938]); Bizard, "L'Armée de l'air," Annex II, p. 3; Pierre Cot, *L'Armée de l'air: 1936-1938* (Paris: Grasset, 1939), pp. 88ff; Danel, "Étude succinte," p. 14. On German airpower see Edward L. Homze, *Arming the Luftwaffe: The Reich Air Ministry and the German Aircraft Industry* (Lincoln and London: University of Nebraska Press, 1976).

42. Belgium is divided into rival linguistic communities: French-speaking Walloons and Flemish-speaking Flemings, the former living in the south including the Ardennes. Hence the dispute over defending the Ardennes and Albert's sensitivity. See David Owen Kieft, *Belgium's Return to Neutrality: An Essay in the Frustrations of Small Power Diplomacy* (Oxford: Clarendon Press, 1972), pp. 34ff, 40ff.

43. General [Raoul] Van Overstraeten, *Albert I-Léopold III: Vingt ans de politique*

militaire belge 1920-1940 ([Bruges]: Desclée de Brouwer, [1946?]), pp. 89ff; Kieft, *Belgium's Return to Neutrality*, pp. 7ff; CSG meetings covered in Paoli, *La Fin des illusions*, pp. 125ff.

44. Belgian attaché's report in *DDB* III, p. 159; Van Overstraeten, *Albert I-Léopold III*, pp. 113ff.

45. Van Overstraeten, *Albert I-Léopold III*, pp. 141ff.

46. Duvignac, *Histoire de l'armée motorisée*, p. 320; [Louis] Maurin, *L'Armée moderne* (Paris: Flammarion, 1938); [France, Parlement], *Annales de la Chambre des députés: Débats parlementaires* (Ordinary session of 1935: I, 2nd session of March 15, 1935) ([Paris: Imprimerie des journaux officiels, 1936]), pp. 121ff, 1045ff. Gamelin's response to the de Gaulle proposal is in the Édouard Daladier papers at the Fondation Nationale des Sciences Politiques, Paris (hereafter cited as E D), 4DA1, Dr4, sdr b, Letter from Gamelin to Daladier and "NOTES: Pour le cabinet militaire du ministre" (unpublished, Paris, July 10, 1936).

47. Jacomet, *L'Armement de la France*, pp. 110ff; Gamelin, *Servir* II, p. 463; Fabry, *Février 1934-juin 1940*, pp. 82ff; William Evans Scott, *Alliance against Hitler: The Origins of the Franco-Soviet Pact* (Durham, North Carolina: Duke University Press, 1962), pp. 240ff. See also Kieft, *Belgium's Return to Neutrality*, pp. 87ff and Daniel R. Brower, *The New Jacobins: The French Communist Party and the Popular Front* (Ithaca, New York: Cornell University Press, 1968). See also *Les Relations franco-britanniques: De 1935 à 1939. Communications présentées aux colloques franco-britanniques tenus à: Londres (Imperial War Museum) du 18 au 21 octobre 1971, Paris (Comité d'Histoire de la 2ème Guerre Mondiale) du 25 au 29 septembre 1972* (Paris: CNRS, 1975), pp. 19ff, 418ff (hereafter cited as *Relations franco-britanniques*); and Donald Cameron Watt, *Too Serious a Business: European Armed Forces and the Approach to the Second World War* (Berkeley and Los Angeles: University of California Press, 1975), pp. 98ff. For further background on the British attitude see Robert Paul Shay, Jr., *British Rearmament in the Thirties: Politics and Profits* (Princeton, New Jersey: Princeton University Press, 1977) and Lawrence R. Pratt, *East of Malta, West of Suez: Britain's Mediterranean Crisis, 1936-1939* (Cambridge: Cambridge University Press, 1975).

48. Gamelin was famous for his "soft" handshake—interview with General André Beaufre, Paris, January 23, 1973.

49. Quote from Gamelin, "Réflexions sur le chef," *Revue d'infanterie* 1 (April 1935); Gamelin, *Servir* II, p. 190; Weygand, *Mémoires* II, p. 427; Louis Garros, *L'Armée de grand-papa: De Gallifet à Gamelin 1871-1939* (Paris: Hachette, 1965), pp. 114, 252.

50. Gamelin, "Réflexions," p. 66 and "Allocutions prononcées par le Général Gamelin au cours de sa visite à l'École polytechnique et de son inspection à l'École spéciale militaire," *Revue militaire française* (April-June 1936): p. 141.

51. General [Édouard de Curières de] Castelnau, "Le Général Georges," *Revue des deux mondes* 53 (October 15, 1939); Georges' testimony in *Événements . . . Témoignages* III, pp. 625, 637.

52. France, MG, Direction de la cavalerie, *Aide-mémoire de l'officier de cavalerie en campagne* (Paris: Imprimerie nationale, February 1936), p. 7; France, MG, EMA, *Notice provisoire sur l'emploi des unités motorisées et mécaniques de la cavalerie* (Paris: Imprimerie nationale, June 1935), pp. 11ff.

53. Van Overstraeten, *Albert I-Léopold III*, pp. 173ff.

54. Duvignac, *Histoire de l'armée motorisée*, pp. 406ff; Gamelin, *Servir* II, pp. 187ff; France, MA, EMG, 3e Section, *Règlement de l'armée de l'air. 1re Partie: Emploi des forces aériennes au combat. Titre III: Emploi des forces aériennes de renseignement au combat* (Paris: Imprimerie nationale, 1935), pp. 3, 7, 44ff.

55. Jacomet, *L'Armement de la France*, pp. 88 passim; France, EMAA, 2e Bureau, "Le Dévelopement de la puissance militaire de l'Allemagne au cours de l'année 1936" (unpublished, February 1937); France, MG, EMA, 2e Bureau: Section des armées étrangères: N° 174/AI, "Note sur l'armement dans l'armée allemande et considérations sur la mobilisation industrielle" (unpublished, April 20, 1936); Georges Castellan, *Le Réarmement clandestin du Reich, 1930-1935, vu par le 2. Bureau de l'état major français* (Paris: Plon, [1954]).

56. Tournoux, *Défense des frontières*, pp. 337ff; France, Parlement, Assemblée nationale, *Les Événements survenus en France de 1933 à 1945: Rapport de M. Charles Serre, Député au nom de la commission d'enquête parlementaire* I (Paris: Presses universitaires de France, no date), pp. 39ff (hereafter cited as *Événements . . . Rapport*).

57. Van Overstraeten, *Albert I-Léopold III*, pp. 162ff; *Relations franco-belges*, p. 50; Le Goyet, *Le Mystère Gamelin*, p. 117.

58. Report of the High Military Committee, January 18, 1936, and letter from Maurin to Foreign Minister Pierre Flandin, January 12, 1936, in *DDF*, 2nd series I, pp. 121ff, 245ff; Armengaud, *Batailles*, p. 27.

59. France, SHAA, Dossier on General Pujo (unpublished, no date); "Dans le haut commandement: Le Général Picard chef d'état-major général: Le Général Pujo devient le grand chef de la Défense aérienne," *Les Ailes* no. 774 (April 16, 1936); Cot, *L'Armée de l'air*, p. 85; France, MA . . ., "Note sur le 'Plan des 1010 avions' de l'armée de l'air" (unpublished, August 28, 1935); Bizard, "L'Armée de l'air," Annex 2 p. 3; France, Inspection de l'aviation de défense métropolitaine et des écoles, EM, 2ème Section, "Rapport du général inspecteur de l'aviation de défense métropolitaine et des écoles sur l'inspection d'hiver des escadres d'aviation lourde de défense, effectuée au cours du ler trimestre 1936" (unpublished, May 1936).

60. France, Comité supérieur institué par le décret du 2 juillet 1935, "Rapports, propositions et avis concernant le ministère de l'air" (unpublished, 1935).

61. France, "Développement de la puissance militaire de l'Allemagne . . . 1936"; Kenneth Munson, *Fighters Between the Wars 1919-1939* (New York: Macmillan, 1970), pp. 127ff, 149ff; Kenneth Munson, *Bombers Between the Wars 1919-1939* (New York: Macmillan, 1970) pp. 137ff, 155ff.

62. France, MA . . . [General Pujo], "Note pour Monsieur le Général Inspecteur de l'aviation de défense" (unpublished, May 13, 1936); France, Inspection de l'aviation de défense métropolitaine et des écoles, EM, 2e Section, "Plan de concentration *actuel* de l'aviation lourde de défense (en vigueur jusqu'au 15 avril)" (unpublished, March 9, 1936); France, Inspection de l'aviation de défense métropolitaine, EM, 2ème Section: N° 19/2.S./I.A.D.M.E., "Instruction générale pour l'emploi initial de l'aviation lourde de défense, dans le cadre du Plan D bis 5" (unpublished, April 23, 1936).

63. Quote from *DDF*, 2nd series I, pp. 290ff, 301ff. For views on French willingness to concede the zone in return for a British commitment, see Anthony Adam-

thwaite, *France and the Coming of the Second World War, 1936-1939* (London: Frank Cass, 1977), pp. 38-40, 150 and James Thomas Emmerson, *The Rhineland Crisis: 7 March 1936 A Study in multilateral diplomacy* [sic] (Ames: Iowa State University Press, 1977), pp. 46-47, 198-200.

64. Documents in *Événements . . . Rapport* I, p. 48; Gamelin, *Servir* II, pp. 197ff.

65. Documents in *Événements . . . Rapport* I, pp. 138ff; Van Overstraeten, *Albert I-Léopold III*, pp. 200 ff; *DDB* III, pp. 494ff; Kieft, *Belgium's Return to Neutrality*, pp. 20ff, 57, 71, 49ff.

66. William Evans Scott, *Alliance against Hitler: The Origins of the Franco-Soviet Pact* (Durham, North Carolina: Duke University Press, 1962), pp. 167ff, 255, 265ff; [Germany, Auswärtiges Amt], *Documents on German Foreign Policy 1918-1945* series C, V (Washington: Government Printing Office, 1966), pp. 11ff, 44ff (hereafter cited as *DGFP*). Details on the Rhineland reoccupation can be found in Col. J[ean] Defrasne, "L'Événement du 7 mars 1936: La Réalité et la portée de l'opération allemande; La Réaction de la France dans le cadre de ses alliances," in *Les Relations franco-allemandes: 1933-1939*, ed. F. G. Dreyfus (Paris: CNRS, 1976); Emmerson, *The Rhineland Crisis*, p. 110.

67. Gamelin, *Servir* II, pp. 201ff; *DDF*, 2nd series I, pp. 444ff; Tournoux, *Défense des frontières*, pp. 251ff; Sarraut's testimony in *Événements . . . Témoignages* III, p. 603. See further Defrasne, "L'Événement du 7 mars 1936" and Eliza Campus, "La Diplomatie roumaine et les relations franco-allemandes pendant les années 1933-1939" and Henryk Batowski, "Le Dernier traité d'alliance franco-polonais: (4 septembre 1939)," in *Les Relations franco-allemandes*, pp. 265ff, 347ff, and 354ff.

68. Germany, *DGFP*, series C, V, pp. 373ff; *DDF*, 2nd series, I, pp. 696ff; *Événements . . . Rapport* I, pp. 56ff; Defrasne, "L'Événement du 7 mars 1936," pp. 259ff, 263ff.

69. Gamelin's testimony in *Événements . . . Témoignages* II, p. 450 and III, p. 586; *Événements . . . Rapport* I, p. 32; Judith M. Hughes, *To the Maginot Line: The Politics of French Military Preparation in the 1920's* (Cambridge, Mass.: Harvard University Press, 1971), pp. 56ff; for differing views see Volker Wieland, *Zur Problematik der französischen Militärpolitik und Militärdoktrin in der Zeit zwischen den Weltkriegen* (Boppard am Rhein: Boldt Verlag, 1973) and two articles by Robert J. Young: "Preparations for Defeat: French War Doctrine in the Inter-War Period," *Journal of European Studies* 2, no. 2 (June 1972) and "The Strategic Dream: French Air Doctrine in the Inter-War Period, 1919-39," *Journal of Contemporary History* 9, no. 4 (October 1974); Ladislas Mysyrowicz, *L'Autopsie d'une défaite: Origines de l'effondrement militaire français de 1940* (Lausanne: Éditions L'Âge d'Homme, 1973). On British attitudes see also Patrick Fridenson and Jean Lecuir, *La France et la Grande-Bretagne face aux problèmes aériens: (1935-mai 1940)* (Vincennes: CEDOCAR, 1976), pp. 25ff.

chapter 2

THE RENEWAL (1936-1938)

The elections of 1936 brought the Popular Front to power. This left-center coalition, led by the Jewish Socialist and pacifist Léon Blum, had to prepare France for total war against Germany. Blum continued to believe that war must be avoided, but by 1936 he also believed that deterrence through strength was the answer. He mastered the social crisis of June, then called in Gamelin to assure him that the national defense had his full support.[1] Blum appointed his Vice-Premier, Édouard Daladier, Minister of National Defense and War, and instituted a Permanent Committee of the Superior Council of National Defense under Daladier. This body had the same composition as the old High Military Committee including Marshal Pétain and the armed services ministers; Daladier had coordinating powers over the service ministers. Prior to this, in March, the wartime organization of the government was fixed by a decree establishing the War Committee presided by the President of the Republic. This would be a select body grouping relevant ministers and charged with the high conduct of a war.[2] Daladier's powers over the navy and air force were limited to dividing the funds available, but this was a step forward.

Obviously the threat of total war demanded a buildup in France's armaments. In the fall of 1936 Daladier went before the Parliament to emphasize that France's demographic inferiority prevented it from matching German numbers. France had to rely on the quality of its forces and material.[3] Daladier demanded an increase in career soldiers and a major arms program. On August 24, 1936, Hitler ordered the two years' service in Germany; on September 7 the French government approved an arms program of some fourteen billion francs. The race was on.[4]

The French program called for production by the end of 1940 of 6,000 25 mm and fifty-one 12-gun batteries of the matchless 47 mm gun to provide a solid antitank base, and fifty new groups of 105 mm guns plus five groups of mechanized artillery for the armored divisions (although prototypes of these last weapons did not appear until 1939 or 1940) to add a modern component to the French artillery. To complete its mechanization, the army ordered 5,000 armored utility vehicles for the infantry and fifty battalions of infantry support tanks. Twelve battalions of B tanks would equip two heavy "breakthrough" armored divisions; 325 excellent SOMUA tanks were ordered for three DLM's: 3,200 tanks altogether. Gamelin asked for vehicles for the seven motorized infantry divisions already planned plus enough for three more divisions. He also requested sums for the preparation of industrial mobilization and antiaircraft weapons.[5] These orders swamped France's metallurgical and much of its remaining heavy industry, particularly the automotive industry. Blum asked the nation to subscribe to massive loans—the French public responded by taking up the first loan by the end of its first day on the market.[6]

The program was designed to respond to Gamelin's concepts; he gave a glimpse of his design in an article for a new periodical intended to open the subject of national defense to discussion. It was the High Command's intention, Gamelin wrote, to transform France's army into more specialized forces in keeping with scientific progress. The army in 1936 had a shield of fortress troops, and an offensive arm composed of major units including mechanized and motorized types. He refused to go into detail—"Well led armies are not in the habit of working in public, and secrecy is a necessity for our new creations." Gamelin claimed credit for accomplishing modernization without reducing the army's combat readiness at a given instant. Then he threw the debate on national defense open: "The leaders of the army are ready to grasp any new ideas which appear to them to hold promise." He added that in case of war, "A clear initial victory is a prerequisite for a short war, especially if it can be exploited. And I include in these considerations the role of the air force whose importance, including participation in the ground battle, constantly increases."[7]

Gamelin also worked to develop conventional strength. The increase in personnel obtained by the Popular Front through expansion of career cadres and formal adoption of the two years' service made it possible to flesh out old units and plan for new ones like heavy armored divisions.[8] Following Hitler's annexation of Austria, Daladier secured another four-year program for twelve billion francs, concentrating on additional artillery and antiaircraft: 6,000 25 mm automatic cannon to hold off low-flying attacks of the Luftwaffe, plus 480 90 mm guns (comparable to the famous German 88) for defense at high altitudes.[9] But none of these weapons could be counted on before 1939. And the French could not match German resources across the board: the commander of the British Small Arms School, visiting installations in France and Germany, was shocked at the crude facilities in France and even more shocked at the lavishness of those in Germany.

France also continued to fortify its frontiers. Following the Belgian declaration of neutrality in the fall of 1936, Daladier got 560 million francs for works behind Belgium, the Jura Mountains facing Switzerland, and the Meuse River-Ardennes region; but Gamelin classed the latter as secondary so the resulting fortifications were light.[10]

France counted increasingly on colonial forces in these years. The Inspector General of the Colonial Troops in 1936, General Gaston Billotte, urged that colonial forces be equipped for modern war; their large numbers of career cadres made them particularly apt for expansion. Billotte felt the colonies could furnish large contingents; the more French policies worked to help native populations prosper, the more willing they would be to serve. The colonial army got a boost in May 1938 when Georges Mandel obtained a decree elevating it to equal status with the other three services, with its own chief of staff, General Bührer. Recruiting of native troops increased from the summer of 1938.[11]

During this period a number of command changes occurred, involving in particular the man whom Bührer replaced, General Gaston Billotte. Billotte was the same age as General Georges, and likewise an outstanding soldier. Gamelin decided to entrust the principal army group to him in case of war, and was eager to compensate him for Georges' precedence. When General Henri-Joseph-Eugène Gouraud retired as Military Governor of Paris, Gamelin appointed Billotte to the post. By this act, however, Gamelin snubbed General Gaston Prételat, Gouraud's chief of staff and the man to whom Gamelin had decided to give a second army group. Gamelin tried to smooth over the ruffled feelings, but he faced further problems when he became Chief of Staff of National Defense[12] in January 1938. Gamelin feared it would be impossible to hold that post as well as command of the armies in France. To reduce his overloaded command, he designated Georges to command the armies facing Germany. Georges would be replaced as wartime chief of the GQG by General Bineau, who had just retired from active duty.[13]

Meanwhile, the army again renovated its doctrine. The new keystone was the IGU'36, written by a commission headed by Georges and including General Pujo of the air force. They took a careful attitude toward new developments, judging that despite new techniques the essential rules established by the 1921 manual still held good. The commission restricted itself to defining the possibilities of modern means of action, fixing rules for the new mechanized and motorized units.[14] Having thus bowed to Pétain, the commission sketched a different vision of warfare from that offered by its predecessors. Noting that victory in the future would be obtained only by maneuver, of which speed and mobility were essential elements, the commission stated that the army had created a whole new system of forces. Although this system of DLM's and motorized infantry divisions could operate independently, it would continue to operate according to the unchanging principles of war. But one of those principles, tactical security, had to be greatly amplified. The commission had no great fear of tanks, which, even in masses, were vulnerable to antitank weapons "which stand before the tank just as the machine gun before the infantry in the last war." Nonetheless the mechanized threat demanded that defenses be developed in depth. The High Command would use bomber aircraft to make its own action felt directly on the battlefield. Nor did the commission ignore the "role of primary importance" played by communications in a modern army; by 1938 the manuals called for the headquarters of each DLM to have a total of forty-three radios, with comparable totals in other formations.[15]

The commission emphasized the need to avoid encounter battles at the opening of a war and to engage young troops under controlled conditions only. Considering modern weapons, particularly tanks, the commission foresaw a commander studying the terrain to choose successive battlefields whose characteristics would determine his maneuver. This concept clearly revealed the methodical bent of French doctrine. But to be methodical did not mean to be defensive. "The offensive is the mode of action *par excellence*," while "The defensive . . . is the attitude momentarily chosen by a commander who does not feel himself able to take the offensive. . . ."[16] The development of motorization and mechanization would accelerate the rhythm of battle requiring more air reconnaissance, antitank and antiaircraft measures, camouflage, dispersion, and defense in depth. Using modern means, strategic surprise attack could be dangerous, but it could be even more dangerous for the aggressor if the defender were prepared. Tanks were to be used in mass, echelonned deeply over wide fronts to produce powerful material and moral effect; once the enemy front had been shaken, enemy forces would be disorganized by independent mechanized detachments and air attacks and ensnared by cavalry units and motorized formations. Should the front be broken by enemy tanks, the friendly troops engaged would cling to cuts in the terrain[17] and would be reinforced by mechanized or motorized reserves, and by as many antitank guns as possible to form a continuous barrage.

The commission examined the use of infantry support tanks against a strong enemy front in two forms: direct support of the infantry, and a more independent mission—the *manoeuvre d'ensemble*—in which tanks would be committed by themselves against the final objective of the assault, with infantry and direct support tanks following in a separate wave. This independent mission would require more powerful and faster machines, but the commission felt that, depending on enemy capabilities, either mission might be accomplished by the tanks then in service. Although the DCR had not yet been created, the commission did consider the DLM. Defining the DLM, which in 1936 had received only a few of the powerful SOMUA tanks, as characterized by mobility, range of action and protection, the commission envisaged the DLM providing tactical security for the motorized infantry. The DLM's armor allowed it to make sudden, brutal assaults. But the armor would require protection against enemy antitank fire. This would come from other troops of the division, artillery and aviation—"The combination of the action of air forces and the DLM is particularly fruitful."[18]

A series of manuals sprang from the IGU'36, the most important being the 1938 infantry manual. The commission writing this manual, led by General Robert Touchon, Inspector General of the Infantry, emphasized firepower and the need for increased tactical security, although it felt that "In the last resort combat is a moral struggle. . . . The vanquished side is not the one which has suffered the heaviest losses in men and material, but the one whose morale has collapsed first."[19] The evolution of equipment preoccupied the commission, which noted that even in the ordinary infantry regiments 25 percent of the horse transport had given way to motor vehicles. Touchon's group emphasized offensive action of the infantry by infiltration and the importance of obtaining surprise, although operations had to have adequate fire support.

Security against tanks and aircraft constituted a permanent obligation for the defense. The commission prescribed a "defense in depth" resting on a series of centers of resistance and strong points[20] on key points of the terrain. Units placed in this fashion were to hold fast even if flanked or bypassed by the enemy. Meanwhile, local reserves would reestablish the continuity of the front while awaiting reinforcements to counterattack; if tanks were available, immediate counterattacks could be envisaged. Touchon and his associates were prescribing an early version of the defense in depth system which became familiar during World War II. These ideas had already taken root to some extent; for example, they were discussed in a manual specifying that the antitank defense was to consist of circular strongpoints, flanking each other and echelonned in depth.[21]

As powerful tanks began to enter the inventory, the High Command divided on their use. Thus the tank manual of 1937 (under Gamelin's signature) stated that it would not discuss mechanized divisions, nor the mechanized detachments intended to exploit a breakthrough.[22] The manual, limited by Gamelin's passion for secrecy, discussed only infantry tanks and the manoeuvre d'ensemble mission. But new developments were on the way. Armored warfare did not daunt France's senior generals: General Debeney portrayed a heavy armored division crashing through an enemy front beneath waves of attack planes, followed by DLM's which would "unleash their armored vehicles on the broken and retreating enemy troops." Debeney added, "There is no element of lyric imagination in this picture—

it is simply the enlargement of actions executed . . . in . . . the battle of France [of 1918] at the scale which our means . . . permitted."[23]

It was one thing to prophesy such actions, quite another to prepare them. The foundation for offensive armored warfare was the order for B tanks to create two heavy armored divisions, although the complex machines came off the assembly line at a snail's pace. But the form of the division proved a serious problem. Gamelin ordered the Inspector General of the Infantry, General Dufieux, to study it in June 1937; his note reveals his uncertainty over the division, particularly in comparison with the DLM. Gamelin proposed a force consisting of two armored brigades, each with two battalions of B tanks, one of mediums and one of mechanized infantry in armored personnel carriers. But the division would have no organic artillery other than a few mechanized guns and antiaircraft. Lacking such essentials, it would be fleshed out with infantry and artillery from the reserves before being engaged. Nor was Gamelin clear on the division's mission: it was well adapted for counterattacks against enemy mechanized units, perhaps for flanking maneuvers and the exploitation of a breakthrough (although less so than the DLM), but Gamelin doubted that the division, as proposed, could break an organized enemy front by itself. It would have to be engaged within the cadre of units already in line; he ordered Dufieux to study this problem.[24]

But equipment came off the lines slowly and the international situation made large-scale training maneuvers with the battle tanks all but impossible. Gamelin felt that the time had come to form the division if only to study the problems involved. He brought the issue to the Superior War Council in December 1937. Dufieux agreed with Gamelin but noted that the necessary six battalions of tanks would not be complete until 1939. These tanks would suffice for one division only, and it was too risky to put all the powerful tanks into one packet. However, Gamelin insisted, proposing that the available B tanks form brigades under the Inspector General of the Tanks, General Julien Martin, who would study the formation and use of the DCR—the heavy armored division. Exercises would be held so that prospective corps commanders could familiarize themselves with the new unit. After further discussion in which the shortage of specialized artillery and infantry units was brought up, and in which General Pierre Héring supported the immediate creation of mechanized tactical groups, the Council approved the proposal, adding that a third DLM should form as soon as material could be produced (then scheduled for March 1939).[25]

Meanwhile, the other branches of the army adapted to the new conditions. The artillery extended the principle of defense in depth by specifying that batteries would organize their own strongpoints with organic automatic weapons, provided for close and antiaircraft defense, and isolated artillery pieces interdicting zones of approach.[26] The increasing danger of German air attacks led the High Command to prescribe the use of ordinary field artillery in an antiaircraft role—a highly unconventional idea! The Inspector General of the Artillery ordered his units to train aircraft observers; it was up to local commanders to decide whether the antiaircraft or the ground battle would get priority. Where antiaircraft was weak or lacking, ordinary 75's could be used for the defense of "sensitive points," although such use could only be momentary. During crises, conventional artillery could throw up barrages which would force enemy aircraft to keep their distance.[27]

The spur to these developments came from the expansion of Hitler's might. Following the German reoccupation of the Rhineland, came Hitler's extension of military service in Germany to two years increasing the peacetime strength of the German army to 800,000 men, allowing the formation of two new Panzerdivisionen. French intelligence credited the German army with forty-four active divisions. In November 1936 French intelligence reported the formation of German parachute units, noting that they might be used as an airborne "fifth column." The 1937 Wehrmacht maneuvers presented a classic display of the use of the Luftwaffe in the ground battle as well as in more independent actions, leading French intelligence to confirm the "primordial role attributed to the air force not only in independent action but also in close liaison with the army. . . ."[28]—thus the diversion of French field artillery to an antiaircraft role.

Finally, Hitler fortified the Rhineland; thus protected from French intervention, Hitler would have a free hand to pursue his designs in the east. The effort began in late 1937; work progressed rapidly.[29] French intelligence noted that the works were of unequal value and had technical faults; nonetheless, in September 1938 the German *Westwall* formed a serious defense. General Fernand Gauché, the chief of intelligence from 1935 to 1940, estimated the field strength of the German army in September 1938 at thirty-five infantry divisions, four motorized divisions, five mountain divisions, five Panzers of which four were ready for action, four light divisions,[30] three fortress divisions, plus nine independent tank regiments in formation. By 1938 the role of General Heinz Guderian and his Blitzkrieg theory was well known.[31] The German army had come a long way since 1936!

During this period the emphasis Hitler gave Goering's Luftwaffe posed an almost insoluble problem for the Armée de l'air which already faced a crisis as the Popular Front's Air Minister, Pierre Cot, sought to impose his views on airpower and to eliminate the more right wing of his generals. Cot was a young member of the centrist Radical party; he believed deeply in the ideals of the Popular Front against Fascism. During a visit to Russia he was impressed by the technical innovations and the mass of the Russian air force; he took his post determined to impose his views. He believed in strategic air war, and in preparing the French air force to fight within a coalition that would include Britain and the Soviet Union, whom he foresaw uniting against Germany and Italy. He began by installing General Philippe Féquant as Chief of the Air Force Staff in place of General Pujo's deputy, General Picard (Pujo remained the Commander in Chief designate until October 1936). Cot faced opposition from the older members of the Superior Air Council, led by General Armengaud. By the late summer of 1936 Cot refused to call the Superior Air Council into session. Armengaud called on his fellow members to resign, but his efforts fell flat; Cot and his adviser Colonel (soon General) Jean-Henri Jauneaud then settled the problem by persuading the Parliament to institute new age limits for senior officers. In October 1936 Féquant replaced Pujo; Cot stocked the Council with people of his own choice, having ousted seven of nine senior generals.[32] Cot restructured the command by the Presidential Decree of September 7, 1936, under which the Chief of the Air Force General Staff was named Inspector General of the Air Force and the Territorial Air Defense by delegation from the minister.[33]

Cot's choice for the top post, Philippe Féquant, was a brother of the famous pre-World War I aviator Albert Féquant. Philippe Féquant won citations and promotions in the war as a fighter pilot, becoming Chief of Staff of the Air Division in August 1918. Despite Féquant's record, he was soon known in the air force as Cot's "strawman"—an uncomfortable position. Féquant's Chief of Staff was General Georges Aubé, a graduate of the *École polytechnique* and an artilleryman who commanded a bomber group in 1918, then joined the technical services of the *Aéronautique*. But behind them was the figure of Jauneaud—held responsible by many officers for Cot's actions. Jauneaud came from a military family and entered World War I in the infantry where he won citations but suffered wounds which forced him into the air service. When Cot first became minister in 1933, Jauneaud began his meteoric rise. Detached to the Army War College in 1935, he returned in 1936 to take his post with Cot, then became Deputy Chief of Staff—becoming France's youngest general at age forty-four.[34]

Whether Jauneaud had the influence attributed to him (*he* felt that he did) is not clear. But there was no doubt of the changes Cot intended to make. Cot's first preoccupation was to secure the interior against air attack. A major reorganization was approved by Pujo and Gamelin: a Commander of the Fighter Forces would have authority over fighters assigned to the army as well as those under the Commander in Chief of the Air Force; initially the whole of the fighter force would defend the interior, save in the case of a surprise ground attack. Once the army's concentration began, the primary mission would be to cover the ground forces. The bombers would initially attack enemy air forces, although they would strike enemy ground forces should ground operations require support.[35]

But this plan was only a stopgap. Cot found that the offensive strength of the air force barely sufficed to support the army; its weakness made French participation in interallied actions impossible. In Cot's mind, the next war would be a coalition war; he foresaw a need for command organs to direct the operations of the coalition forces. Thus Cot obtained the decree of September 3, 1936, which reorganized the French air force into a 1st *Corps aérien* of bombers and a 2nd *Corps* of fighters, each having an enlarged staff—and thus the capacity to command the coalition air force. Only the reconnaissance and observation units, most of which were attached to the army (and composed of reservists), remained outside these new structures. Unfortunately, the basis for Cot's concept—a single interallied air command—was purely his own invention: neither Russia nor Britain accepted such an institution, much less a French command! The Soviets were ready for a military alliance, but even the Popular Front was in no rush to contract a firm alliance with the red régime. Russia lacked a common frontier with Germany over which it could bring military strength to bear. Further, Stalin was just beginning the great purges which decimated the leaders of the Soviet armed forces and the Soviet state: how valuable would an alliance with these Russians be? The concept of a British commitment to France was illusory. Britain accepted limited staff talks with Belgium and France following the reoccupation of the Rhineland, but refused to consider new commitments to France or even to Belgium, who still yearned for a British commitment in place of French ties. Cot was out of touch with political reality. Finally, in October 1936 he ordered the establishment of two groups of parachute infantry (equaling a light infantry battalion) and their transport, one group at Reims and the other in North Africa.[36]

The 1st Corps aérien formed under General Joseph Vuillemin, the legendary bomber pilot and commander from World War I, the 2nd Corps under the young General Gabriel d'Harcourt, who had developed new techniques for the fighters. Amid these transformations the air force suffered a morale crisis. Cadres found themselves the butt of attacks in leftist journals, particularly the Communist *L'Humanité*. More seriously, the reorganization of units and the impending obsolescence of aircraft in service left a profound malaise. Another problem was the unusually rapid advancement of certain officers—Jauneaud, for example. Some saw this as evidence of "political influence." This charge drew a sharp rejoinder from Féquant in August 1937. He reminded senior officers that attacks in the press had no effect on the status of cadres in the service, and he defended the reorganization and methods of promotion. Féquant's response had no effect on the problems,[37] but it compromised his career.

The main area of Cot's concern was the expansion of the Armée de l'air. Even were Plan I completed, the aircraft it provided were insufficient in quantity—and soon in quality—to face the growing Luftwaffe. In June 1936 General Pujo concluded that even with British support the French air force had to expand to at least 1,500 first-line aircraft by the beginning of 1940.[38] From August 1936 Cot worked on Plan II, which called for 2,400 aircraft to be finished by June 1, 1940. The plan called for a major increase in bombers, leaving development of the defensive fighter arm for a later plan should changes in German strength or the diplomatic situation require it. Gamelin opposed the plan in the Permanent Committee of the Superior Council of National Defense, asking pointedly if the fighter force could fulfill the vital needs of the army and the defense of the interior. Nonetheless, the Cabinet approved Plan II in November 1936; the air force at the end of 1939 was to have eight wings with eighteen groups of fighters, twenty-eight wings with fifty-seven groups of bombers, and forty-three squadrons of observation aircraft for the army and nine regional fighter squadrons in the interior. The plan increased personnel to match; Parliament funded the first portion by the law of February 5, 1937.[39]

Unfortunately the Luftwaffe continued to grow at an unexpected rate; Plan II had to be reconsidered. Cot proposed Plan III to expand the antiaircraft artillery and Plan IV for the fighter arm. These plans came before the Permanent Committee on February 15, 1937, but their proposals were beyond French resources, or so it seemed—both were rejected. Plan III called for 770 batteries of antiaircraft guns to add to the 348 on order; the army objected that antiaircraft should take up no more than a "rational" proportion of the total strength—further increase in antiaircraft would come at the cost of the army's own needs. The Permanent Committee also decided to continue to have the air force assign units on an organic basis to the army and navy; the army would retain control of antiaircraft artillery. The Committee decided further to assume a British alliance in case of war.[40]

By allowing Hitler to rearm and then fortify the Rhineland, France surrendered the initiative and could no longer consider action by itself against Germany. Italy was a lost cause after the Ethiopian adventure and Mussolini's participation in the Spanish Civil War, which began in the summer of 1936 between Spanish officers, reactionaries and fascists, and the Spanish version of the Popular Front. The Soviet Union, itself involved in the Spanish imbroglio, remained remote. Britain alone, although refusing to commit itself to France and Belgium and to rearm to back such a commitment, shared French desires to preserve the peace and uphold Western values. France, therefore, shaped its policy more and more to conform to British views, which since 1937 had been dominated by Neville Chamberlain and his policy of appeasement. This policy was not always to the liking of the French government, but France had little choice. The British navy would be a necessity for France which depended heavily on maritime imports, especially in wartime in the face of Germany and Italy; the Royal

General Vuillemin.
Photo Courtesy of E. C. P. Armées

Air Force (which was beginning to rearm) would be a comforting addition as well. Alone, France lacked the capacity to face its foes.

Cot realized France's limitations and sought solutions. The Popular Front nationalized much of the air industry plus some of the armaments industry, expanding production facilities. Cot later claimed that he quadrupled the value of industrial equipment by purchasing some 170 million francs' worth of machinery. He financed the expansion of research in the air industry, and established a state arsenal. Time was required before these investments would bear fruit; meanwhile, production rates remained low and French designs lagged behind German aircraft, principally because their engines were inferior. Nonetheless, by December 15, 1937, Cot had increased the number of squadrons by about 30 percent and the base infrastructure by about 46 percent.[41] But this was no match for the German effort.

By the end of 1937 the inferiority of the Armée de l'air became clear. Pierre Cot had to go. Cot's pro-Soviet attitude and his association with the Popular Front were deadweights in French politics by then. Although the Popular Front Chamber continued to sit, the Popular Front itself foundered on the rocks of continuing economic woes and suspicion of Communist loyalties. During a rearrangement of the Cabinet in mid-January 1938, Guy La Chambre, a member of the Army and Air Force Commissions of the Chamber, became Air Minister. To shore up morale in the air force, he called on Vuillemin to replace Féquant. Vuillemin had entered the air service before World War I; his career during the war was legendary. He first flew and then commanded units of observation and bomber aircraft over the hottest spots of the front. When fighters were unavailable, he personally escorted his crews in the heavy aircraft his units flew—becoming an ace the hard way! He commanded a wing of the Air Division in 1918 and often personally led his squadrons.[42] After the war Vuillemin flew exploratory raids over Africa where he stayed until the early 1930s, impressing his commanders with his skill, his leadership, and his personal prestige, but above all—as his commander in Algeria, General Georges, noted in 1931—his modesty. In 1934 Vuillemin became the Inspector General of the Bombers and deputy to General Armengaud, a position he used in vain to protest against the BCR concept (although by 1935 the air force had come to adopt his views). In 1935 Vuillemin passed through the Army War College; in 1936 he took command of the 1st Corps aérien. He created his new command, calling up an old comrade, Colonel J. Mendigal, as his chief of staff. La Chambre selected Vuillemin to replace Féquant in late February 1938. There is no doubt that Vuillemin's prestige did a great deal to restore morale. This modest—almost timid—hero had to prepare the Armée de l'air to face the Luftwaffe.

La Chambre also restaffed the lower command. Féquant became the Technical Inspector and served until his death after an illness in late 1938. General Aubé, the *polytechnicien*, exchanged posts with the Inspector of the Territorial Air Defense (an essentially technical post) General René Keller, who thereby became Chief of Staff until his retirement in the summer of 1939. General Roger Pennès replaced Vuillemin as the chief of the 1st Corps aérien, while General H. E. Mouchard became the Director of the Air Academy. La Chambre, eager to efface the vestiges of the Cot administration, dissolved the Corps aériens and their staffs in September 1938 and shuffled senior officers into a new system of inspectorates general. The new Superior Air Council included Aubé as Inspector General of Territorial Air Defense; Pennès, Inspector General of the Bombers; d'Harcourt, Inspector General of the Fighters; Mouchard, Inspector General of the Schools; and General Jean-Paul-Marie Houdemon, Inspector General of the

Reconnaissance and Observation Forces and the Land Theaters of Operations.[43]

La Chambre had to expand the Armée de l'air. He increased the budget from 3.866 billion francs (1937) to 6.718 billion (1938). While defense spending rose from about 13 to 17 billion, the air force for the first time received more money than the other two services: 42 percent to the army's 36 percent—evidence of Daladier's work as Minister of National Defense.[44] The Superior Air Council in early 1938 decided to urgently reinforce the fighter arm, giving up thoughts of an offensive air war at the start of hostilities. The new Plan V foresaw massive expansion in first-line strength according to a schedule which would run through April 1, 1941. By the end of Plan V, 2,617 planes were to be in line compared to 1,437 at the start, according to Table 1.[45]

TABLE 1

	1/1/1938	*4/1/1939*	*4/1/1941*
fighter groups	18	24	34
bomber groups (1/6 of which were to be dive-bombers or low-level "assault" bombers)	36	36	60
reconnaissance groups	11	14	14
air observation groups (air scouting groups attached to army units)	47	47	52
regional fighter squadrons	8	8	16

Each fighter group was to have twenty-four planes, each bomber group twelve (the five groups of dive-bombers were to have eighteen each, the six groups of "assault" bombers, twelve), the other formations having from twelve to sixteen. There was to be a reserve of 70 percent of first-line strength. But none of the modern fighters appeared until early 1939.

Hitler did not give the French time: in March 1938 he pressured his native Austria into *Anschluss* (union) with Germany, justifying the action on the Wilsonian principle of national unity. France was in neither condition nor mood to dispute this further violation of the Versailles Treaty. Mussolini, engaged in Spain, granted Hitler a free hand. Thus Hitler added a further portion of manpower and industry to his Reich—and outflanked the fortifications that France's ally, Czechoslovakia, had raised between itself and Germany. Following the Anschluss, La Chambre ordered almost a thousand aircraft (fighters first, later light bombers and dive-bombers for the navy) from the United States, but the first Curtiss Hawk 75 fighters did not enter French service until 1939.[46]

This new crisis did not slow the development of doctrine in the air force which drafted its first general manual, the *Instruction sur l'emploi tactique des grandes unités aériennes* of 1937. Written by a junior officer, Pierre Bodet, this work emphasized the independent role of the air force, the author (like most air force officers) reacting to what he saw as the jealousy of France's senior service. General Féquant, in his preface, pictured a future war in which land fronts would be saturated or closed off by fortifications, leading to a stalemate in which only the air force could maneuver.[47]

Bodet saw the air force as the essential cover force of the nation at the start of a war, engaging its strength in strategic air operations while gathering intelligence on the enemy. Once the army had completed its concentration—the prelude to a general land battle—the air force would throw its strength into combined operations. The army demanded full air support in the ground battle. The manual stressed employment of the totality of forces against the most dangerous enemy threat, whether in the air or on the ground, and the need to apply air action in close combination with land forces. Above all, "The whole art of high command consists in disposing at the desired time and place of air superiority over the enemy."[48]

A number of technical developments influenced doctrine. The air force developed a process known as DEM (*détection éléctromagnétique* or electromagnetic detection) based on the same physical principles as radar, although less effective. Aubé experimented with tactics based on it and on sound location systems. Advances in aircraft construction and the use of light automatic aircraft cannon in the mid-1930s led the command to seek new aircraft types. The lessons of the Spanish Civil War proved useful, nor did innovations in Germany and Italy pass unnoticed. The staff worked on the use of fast light bombers for low-level missions over the battlefield—the "assault" bomber concept—but the 1936 development program ruled that this mission could be carried out by reconnaissance aircraft.[49] In late 1936 Féquant issued a call for ideas on large airborne units and the use of a force capable of assault missions and dive-bombing.

General Vuillemin, then commanding the 1st Corps aérien, worked along these lines. But the bombers then in service were unsuited for these missions. The best Vuillemin could do was request a force of light bombers for assault and dive-bombing missions. Vuillemin wanted at least a third of the 1st Corps to be such aircraft, and suggested that a development of the Potez 63 be used in this role. A small series of these planes was ordered. In its 1937 program the air force issued a particular specification for an assault bomber.[50]

Development of aircraft for the new assault mission was agonizingly slow. Vuillemin wrote an anguished letter to La Chambre shortly after the latter took office, complaining that the Spanish war had revealed the reality of his fears about the vulnerability of French bombers. Vuillemin saw the situation as "extremely grave." In case of war "French aviation will be wiped out in a few days."[51]

Opposed to this picture of slow growth French intelligence painted a terrifying tableau of German developments. It counted 136 German squadrons on January 1, 1937, including twenty-nine of fighters, fifteen of dive-bombers, and forty-eight of medium bombers plus forty-four groups of Flak.[52] This force was larger than the Armée de l'air but was not yet fully organized. By early 1938 the situation had changed disastrously. French intelligence then counted 207 squadrons (thirty-six of fighters, fifteen of dive-, and ninety-three of medium bombers). These units were equipped with Dornier 17 and Heinkel 111 medium bombers and Messerschmidt 109 fighters. The superiority of these new planes plus their overwhelming numbers gave the Luftwaffe a crushing advantage: some 1,450 inferior French aircraft faced some 2,800 superior German planes.[53]

The Armée de l'air made relatively little progress from January to September 1938, although during that period the Luftwaffe expanded to 230 squadrons: fifty-two of fighters, eighteen of dive-, and ninety-six of medium bombers—almost all equipped with new aircraft; the Flak grew to seventy-one groups. To exploit his advantage, Goering invited Vuillemin to visit the Luftwaffe in August 1938 as part of the orchestration for Hitler's move against Czechoslovakia. Vuillemin was impressed, but warned Goering that France would honor its treaty with Czechoslovakia.[54]

Finally, the approach of war and the expansion of technology and production demanded a reordering at the summit of France's national defense to coordinate the action of the armed forces. The appointment of Daladier as Minister of National Defense in 1936 was a first step. Daladier obtained a decree naming Gamelin Chief of Staff of National Defense on January 21, 1938. This appointment touched off a bitter dispute between the heads of the services which Gamelin—despite his reputation for tact—had difficulty controlling. Gamelin passed his principal duties over the army to his deputy, Georges, but by retaining his position as Commander in Chief designate of the army, he was left in an ambiguous position, unable to pose as an impartial arbiter between the three services. Daladier refused to promote Georges, the protégé of Daladier's old nemesis Weygand. By the terms of the laws and decrees in force, the general direction of a war would belong to the War Committee, which would set the general aims of military operations while delegating authority over the commanders of the various theaters of operations to Gamelin. The law of July 11, 1938, canonized these measures. Gamelin declared himself opposed to the establishment of a single staff above the three services, claiming that the cooperation of the three chiefs would suffice.[55] Nonetheless, he proposed in an interservice conference that the air force commander attached to an army theater of operations (the front facing a potential enemy in which strategy was in the hands of a single commander) should have authority over all air forces operating in that theater—whether they belonged to army units or came from the general reserves of the air force. General Mouchard, who by this time had been designated air commander under General Georges on the northeastern front facing Germany, supported this idea. Following Gamelin's suggestion, the three Commanders in Chief would have authority over the military conduct of the war; conduct of operations in each theater would belong to the theater commander. Georges and Mouchard intervened to declare that all operations would be combined air-ground actions. In their opinion, the theater air commander should have control over all air operations in his zone. Gamelin closed the session by underscoring the weakness of the air force; Féquant replied that the Superior Air Council was developing an expansion plan.

Obviously this meeting settled nothing, but Gamelin made no further effort to nail down his attributions under his new title until Vuillemin replaced Féquant. Then he opened a correspondence with Daladier and Vuillemin. His first note to Daladier proposed that he be empowered to issue directives to the Commander in Chief of the air force, just as he could to the commander of a theater of land operations. Vuillemin responded angrily to La Chambre, complaining that Gamelin had gone directly to Daladier and asking La Chambre to use his influence to force Gamelin to settle the issue by agreement between the three Commanders in Chief designate. However, the issue was too important for Gamelin to drop; he wrote again to Daladier, stating that if he did not get this authority, his ability to coordinate air and ground forces would be destroyed—the post of Chief of Staff of National Defense would have no meaning.[56] Gamelin was too much the diplomat to drive the issue to the breaking point. Three days later he sent Daladier a note explaining that he had discussed the question with Féquant, and they had reached agreement along the lines of his first note to Daladier. Gamelin had taken it for granted that Vuillemin was aware of the agreement. The matter was finally settled in a face-to-face meeting. Gamelin received authority to coordinate the action of the air force and the army, but he had to renounce personal command over any theater of operations. His powers were to extend to coordination only, not to command.[57]

This settlement was extremely important in defining Gamelin's role. Gamelin renounced active command over operations on the northeastern front against Germany; this front now fell incontestably to Georges. It was a heavy price for Gamelin to pay, but the coordination of land and air operations was a necessity. From Vuillemin's point of view, the price was also heavy. He was committed to giving the army maximum air support when it engaged in battle, but his air force also faced the separate problem of operations against the air forces and eventually the war-making capacity of the enemy. If Gamelin directed operations on the northeastern front, there was a risk that he would lose sight of the overall conduct of the war and focus on the northeast front alone. By excluding Gamelin from that command, Vuillemin eliminated that problem. But Vuillemin also renounced a portion of his authority to Gamelin, who acquired *some* of the power of a generalissimo.

In the summer of 1938 it became clear that Hitler's next target would be Czechoslovakia, his point of attack being the Sudeten Germans (German-speaking former citizens of the Austro-Hungarian Empire incorporated into Czechoslovakia). Hitler gained the cooperation of Poland and Hungary which were eager to join Hitler's game at Czech expense. But France had an alliance with Czechoslovakia, and Russia had pledged to aid Czechoslovakia if France did. War was no longer unthinkable to European public opinion as it had been in 1936.

As the conflict approached, Gamelin sought to settle the powers of the air and land commanders of a theater of operations: the air commander, titled Commander of an Air Army, would control all air forces and antiaircraft units in his sector; under the land commander of the theater, he would direct operations in support of the ground battle and order interventions over the battlefield itself. The Air Army Commander would receive directives from the Commander in Chief of the air force *and* the land commander.[58] All this meant that Georges, commanding the northeastern front, would have a single air commander, Mouchard, under his authority to command the air forces and antiaircraft facing Germany. Vuillemin would issue directives to Mouchard on the employment of those forces. Gamelin would decide the distribution of land and air forces between theaters of operations.

This measure of coordination came as the specter of war grew ominously. Anxiety extended throughout France: reservists called for training that summer took the business seriously for the first time. Preparations included more air participation in army maneuvers. During the 1937 maneuvers General Héring had emphasized the role of attack aircraft and tanks, criticizing the units involved for paying insufficient attention to precautions against air attack, and warning repeatedly that tactical security against armored attacks must be constant. Tank attacks must be met by a defense in depth. He warned that low-level air attacks—popular with the Luftwaffe—could have considerable effect if the troops were not dispersed and well camouflaged.[59] French paratroops participated in these exercises. Unfortunately the maneuvers confirmed Vuillemin's fears about the vulnerability of his bombers. They "attacked" an infantry division on the march: the infantry was delayed for three quarters of an hour, but the heavy and slow aircraft would have been slaughtered by antiaircraft.[60]

The Munich crisis canceled the 1938 maneuvers, but some preparatory exercises were held. General Laurens, commanding the 3rd Air Division, described the operations of his bombers in June, including reconnaissances of the 1st DLM, simulated air attacks on it, and intervention on the battlefield in support of it.[61] Laurens commented that, given the slow command and communications methods in use, all these missions would have failed in a live action. He recommended that attacking aviation stay in radio contact with the local ground force. He complained that requests for intervention by the ground commander were excessive—and intervention on the battlefield was not a proper mission for his medium bombers. Unfortunately, the general maneuvers, which included the employment of a heavy armored brigade[62] and a squadron preparing tactics for the assault bombers, could not be held.[63]

The weight of the Luftwaffe compelled respect. In April 1938 Gamelin warned of the importance the Germans attached to low-level air attacks on the field of battle.[64] Against this threat he proposed dispersion, vigilance, and barrages using the automatic weapons of the troops. The material and moral danger was greatest for unprepared troops. Therefore, Gamelin instructed the commanders of major units to work with their organic air units to accustom the troops to low-level attacks. The air force ordered participation in these types of exercises.[65] Finally, Gamelin emphasized, the vigorous action of junior cadres would be important in preserving morale.

Thus, as the summer of 1938 drew to a close, the French army and air force worked to prepare for total war. Neither was fully prepared: the army had not yet formed its DCR's nor received all the modern equipment on order. Worse, the air force faced a crisis: the airmen were expanding their forces and adapting doctrine and equipment to modern warfare, but they were in no condition to face the Luftwaffe. This predicament presented obvious problems which Gamelin did his best to circumvent; but the initiative lay in Hitler's hands, and he was ready to cash in on his advantages.

NOTES

1. Maurice Gamelin, *Servir* II (Paris: Plon, 1946), pp. 223-224.

2. [France], Ministère des affaires étrangères, Commission de publication des documents relatifs aux origines de la guerre 1939-1945, *Documents diplomatiques français: 1932-1939*, 2nd series, II (Paris: Imprimerie nationale, 1964), pp. 553 ff; Gamelin, *Servir* II, p. 251; Vial, "La Défense nationale," p. 15.

3. Robert Jacomet, *L'Armement de la France 1936-1939* (Paris: Éditions Lajeunesse, 1945), pp. 279ff; Daladier's report in France, Parlement, Assemblée Nationale,

Les Événements survenus en France de 1933 à 1945: Rapport de M. Charles Serre, Député au nom de la commission d'enquête parlementaire I (Paris: Presses universitaires de France, no date), pp. 177ff.

4. Jacomet, *L'Armement de la France*, pp. 121ff.

5. Ibid., pp. 124ff.

6. [Engineer General] J. Molinié, "Les Matériels blindés de combat de 1917 à 1967 [Part 1]," *Sciences et techniques de l'armement: Mémorial de l'artillerie française* 46, no. 182 (1972): 858; Jacomet, *L'Armement de la France*, pp. 134ff.

7. Quotes from Gamelin, "Hier et demain," *Revue militaire générale* 1 (January 1937): 25ff.

8. Known as *Divisions cuirassées* (D Cu) or *Divisions cuirassées de réserve*—DCR. This last abbreviation became official.

9. Jacomet, *L'Armement de la France*, pp. 128ff; General Sir Francis De Guingand, *Operation Victory* (New York: Charles Scribner's Sons, 1947), pp. 13ff.

10. General P[aul]-É[mile] Tournoux, *Haut commandement Gouvernement et Défense des frontières du nord et de l'est 1919-1939* (Paris: Nouvelles éditions latines, 1960), pp. 265ff.

11. General [Gaston] Billotte, "Les Troupes coloniales et la défense de l'empire colonial français," *Revue militaire générale* 1 (January 1937): 55ff; General X [Bührer], *Aux heures tragiques de l'empire (1938-1941)* (Paris: Office colonial d'édition, 1947), pp. 55ff.

12. Discussed below.

13. Gamelin, *Servir* II, p. 301; Georges' testimony in France, Parlement, Assemblée nationale, *Les Événements survenus en France de 1933 à 1945: Témoignages et documents recueillis par la commission d'enquête parlementaire* III (Paris: Presses universitaires de France, [1950?]), p. 641.

14. France, MG, *Instruction sur l'emploi tactique des grandes unités [IGU'36]* (Paris: Imprimerie nationale, August 12, 1936), p. 15.

15. Quotes from *IGU'36*, pp. 15ff; France, [ESG], *Aide-mémoire pour les travaux d'état-major: 1938* ([Paris?]:[Charles-Lavauzelle?], 1938), p. 188.

16. *IGU'*36, pp. 28, 52, 60ff, 80-84, 109.

17. Rivers, streams, deep ditches, etc.—anything that would stop a tank.

18. Ibid., pp. 81, 147ff.

19. France, MDN and G, EMA, *Règlement de l'infanterie: Deuxième partie: Combat* (Paris: Charles-Lavauzelle, 1940 [originally published 1938]), p. 25.

20. The former including a battalion, the latter a company of infantry.

21. Quote from France, MDN and G, EMA, *Règlement de l'infanterie*, pp. 15, 25, 45, 72, 99ff, 155, 172ff; France, MDN and G, *Instruction provisoire du 12 juillet 1937 sur les bataillons de mitrailleurs* (Paris: Imprimerie nationale, 1938), pp. 17, 19, 26; Major Robert A. Doughty, "French Antitank Doctrine, 1940: The Antidote That Failed," *Military Review* 56, no. 5 (May 1976).

22. France, MDN and G, EMA, Bureau des opérations militaires et de l'instruction générale de l'armée et Direction de l'infanterie, Bureau technique, *Notice provisoire sur l'emploi des chars modernes* (Paris: no publisher given, December 15, 1937), pp. 1, 8.

23. [Marie-Eugène] Debeney, *La Guerre et les hommes: Réflexions d'après-guerre* (Paris: Plon, 1937), p. 78.

24. *Événements . . . Témoignages* IV, pp. 1132ff; deposition of General Julien Martin before the Riom tribunal in ED, 4DA11, Dr 2, sdr c, pp. 12-13.

25. Minutes of the meeting in *Événements . . . Rapport* II, pp. 183ff; deposition of General Martin, Riom tribunal, pp. 12ff.

26. France, MG, *Règlement de manoeuvre de l'artillerie: Première partie: Titre XI: L'Organisation du terrain par l'artillerie* (Paris: Imprimerie nationale, 1938), p. 113.

27. France, Inspection générale de l'artillerie, *Annexe technique à la Note n°5307-3/EMA-M du 5 avril 1938 sur la défense contre les attaques aériennes à basse altitude: Participation de l'artillerie non spécialisée* (Paris: no publisher given, June 15, 1938), pp. 1ff.

28. France, EMAA, 2e Bureau, "Le Développement de la puissance militaire de l'Allemagne au cours de l'année 1936" (unpublished; Paris, February 26, 1937); France, MG, EMA, 2e Bureau: Section des armées étrangères: N° 181/A1, "Note sur les possibilités allemandes suivant l'attitude que prendrait l'Italie en cas de conflit franco-allemand" (unpublished, May 28, 1936); France, EMAA, 2e Bureau, "Note sur la création d'unités de parachutistes en Allemagne" (unpublished, November 3, 1936); quote from France, EMAA, 2e Bureau: N° 232 2-C/S/EMAA, "Les Grandes manoeuvres allemandes en 1937" (unpublished, February 3, 1938).

29. France, EMAA, 2e Bureau: N° 233 2-C/S/EMAA, "Note sur les travaux de fortifications entrepris par l'Allemagne à sa frontière ouest. Décembre 1937" (unpublished, February 3, 1938); France, EMAA, 2e Bureau: N° 2109-2 C/S/EMAA, "Note sur l'état des travaux allemands de fortification sur les frontières français et belge à la date du 5 septembre 1938" (unpublished, September 26, 1938).

30. Units similar to the Panzers but with only a fraction of the tanks.

31. General Gauché, *Le 2e Bureau au travail (1935-1940)* (Paris: Amiot-Dumont, 1953), pp. 135ff.

32. General [Paul] Armengaud, *Batailles politiques et militaires sur l'Europe: Témoignages (1932-1940)* (Paris: Editions du Myrte, 1948), pp. 35ff; Jean-Henri Jauneaud, *De Verdun à Dien-Bien-Phu* (Paris: Éditions du Scorpion, 1960), pp. 37ff; Irwin M. Wall, "Socialists and Bureaucrats: The Blum Government and the French Administration, 1936-37," *International Review of Social History* 19, part 3 (1974): 342.

33. France, MA, EMAA, 1er Bureau: N° 2.185-ID/EMAA, "Tableaux d'effectifs de l'Inspection générale de la défense aérienne et de l'Inspection de la défense aérienne" (unpublished, Paris, September 30, 1936).

34. General [François] d'Astier de la Vigerie, *Le Ciel n'était pas vide: 1940* (Paris: Julliard, 1952), p. 38; France, SHAA, Dossier on General Féquant (unpublished, no date); Jauneaud, *De Verdun à Dien-Bien-Phu*, pp. 37ff.

35. France, MDN and G, EMA, Bureau des opérations militaires et instruction générale de l'armée; MA, EMAA, 3e Section: N° 0.2139 3-P/EMAA, "Instruction générale sur l'emploi des forces aériennes mises à la disposition de l'armée de terre, et de la DCA des armées au début des hostilités" (unpublished, July 7, 1936).

36. Pierre Cot, *L'Armée de l'air, 1936-1938* (Paris: Grasset, 1939), pp. 137, 153ff; Lt.-Col. Hayez, "Organisation du commandement, 1918-1939" (unpublished, 1961), p. 42; Jauneaud, *De Verdun à Dien-Bien-Phu*, pp. 38ff. See also David Owen Kieft, *Belgium's Return to Neutrality: An Essay in the Frustrations of Small Power*

Diplomacy (Oxford: Clarendon Press, 1972) and Brian Bond, *France and Belgium 1939-1940* (London: Davis-Poynter, 1975), pp. 17ff. For more on British attitudes see *Les Relations franco-britanniques: De 1935 à 1939. Communications présentées aux colloques franco-britanniques tenus à: Londres (Imperial War Museum) du 18 au 21 octobre 1971, Paris (Comité d'Histoire de la 2ème Guerre Mondiale) du 25 au 29 septembre 1972* (Paris: CNRS, 1975), pp. 96ff, 155, 180ff, 360ff and Patrick Fridenson and Jean Lecuir, *La France et la Grande-Bretagne face aux problèmes aériens (1935-mai 1940)* (Vincennes: SHAA, 1976), pp. 56ff., 92ff. On French airborne troops see Lt. Col. Bourdes, "La Création de l'arme aéroportée française," *Revue historique des armées* 4th year, no 2 (1977): 62ff.

37. France, SHAA, Dossier on General Gabriel d'Harcourt (unpublished, no date); France, [2ème Corps aérien, EM, 1er Bureau:] N° 280/SP, "Rapport sur l'état d'esprit du personnel en 1936" (unpublished, January 28, 1937); France, MA, EMAA, 1° Bureau: N° 1.145 1.0/EMAA-RC, Letter from General Philippe Féquant to the Air Region Commanders (unpublished, Paris, August 20, 1937); France, [2ème Corps aérien, EM, 1er Bureau:] N° 1213/SP/2CA, "Rapport sur l'état d'esprit du personnel en 1937" (unpublished, January 31, 1938).

38. Pujo's project in *DDF*, 2nd series II, pp. 464ff; France, MA, EMAA, 3e Bureau: N° 1091/3R/EMAA, "Rapport au Comité permanent de défense nationale" (unpublished, Paris, December 23, 1936).

39. Bizard, "L'Armée de l'air," pp. 18ff; France, [MA, EMAA?], "Historique des plans d'accroissement et de rénovation de l'armée de l'air" (unpublished, March 3, 1938), p. 3; Jauneaud saw things differently—Jauneaud, *De Verdun à Dien-Bien-Phu*, pp. 42ff.

40. Bizard, "L'Armée de l'air," pp. 33ff; Cot's testimony in *Événements . . . Témoignages* I, p. 275; Jauneaud, *De Verdun à Dien-Bien-Phu*, p. 428; France, MG, EMA, 3e Bureau: 3/61, "Note sommaire sur le rapport n° 1091 3R/EMA-A du 23 décembre 1936 addressé par le Ministre de l'Air au Comité permanent de défense nationale" (unpublished, January 11, 1937); France, MDN and G . . ., "Comité permanent de la défense nationale: Séance du 15 février 1937" (unpublished, Paris, February 24, 1937). See also Bond, *France and Belgium*, pp. 19ff and Ian Colvin, *The Chamberlain Cabinet: How the meetings in 10 Downing Street, 1937-1939, led to the Second World War—Told for the first time from the Cabinet Papers* [sic] (New York: Taplinger, 1971), pp. 23ff. See further *Relations franco-britanniques*, pp. 23, 119, 180ff, 359ff and Fridenson and Lecuir, *France et Grande-Bretagne*, pp. 85-97.

41. Cot, *L'Armée de l'air*, pp. 165, 190, 201, 209ff; Jacomet, *L'Armement de la France*, passim; Jeffrey J. Clarke, "The Nationalization of War Industries in France, 1936-1937: A Case Study," *Journal of Modern History* 49, no. 3 (September 1977).

42. See Eugène Angot and René de Lavergne, *Une figure légendaire de l'aviation française de 1914 à 1940: Le Général Vuillemin. Le Combattant. Le Pionnier du Sahara. Le Chef* (Paris and Geneva: La Palatine, 1965), pp. 20ff, 135ff, 183ff, 241; Cdt. André Lanceron, "Notre grand chef: Vuillemin, le 'Joffre' des aviateurs," *Les Ailes* (March 3, 1938); Gamelin, *Servir* II, pp. 319ff.

43. France, SHAA, Dossier on the Inspectorates General of the Air Force (unpublished, no date); Hayez, "Organisation du commandement," pp. 46ff.

44. Jacomet, *L'Armement de la France*, pp. 139ff; France . . ., "Mesures à prendre pour le renforcement de l'Armée de l'air au cours de l'année 1938: Rapport au Conseil supérieur de l'air" (unpublished, [early 1938]).

45. France, MA, EMAA, 1e Bureau, "Note sur la réalisation du plan d'accroissement de l'Armée de l'air établi par le Conseil supérieur de l'air au cours de ses séances des 7, 8, 9 et 15 mars 1938" (unpublished, Paris, March 18, 1938); *Événements . . . Témoignages* I, p. 302; France, [EMAA?], "Répartition des avions en ligne par catégories" (unpublished, February 18, 1938); Bizard, "L'Armée de l'air," p. 30.

46. Bizard, "L'Armée de l'air," pp. 307ff; John McVickar Haight, Jr., *American Aid to France* (New York: Atheneum, 1970). See further *DDF*, 2nd series, VIII, pp. 832ff, 786ff and 2nd series, IX, pp. 134ff, 235ff; and John McVickar Haight, Jr., "France's Search for American Military Aircraft: Before the Munich Crisis," *Aerospace Historian* 25, no. 3 (Fall/September 1978).

47. Interview with General Pierre Bodet held at the SHAA, Vincennes, February 20, 1973.

48. Quote from France, MA, EMAA, [Cdt. Pierre Bodet], *Instruction sur l'emploi tactique des grandes unités aériennes* (Paris: Imprimerie nationale, March 31, 1937), pp. 17ff, 73, 83ff.

49. France, Centre d'expériences militaires, Capt. Arsac, "Chasse. Rapport partiel. Question n° 7: Valeur du procédé éléctromagnétique de détection des avions: Précision, délais d'utilisation, application à la manoeuvre de la Chasse" (unpublished, Reims, 1938); France, MA, EMAA, 4ème Section, "Programme général de matériel de l'armée de l'air (Projet): Titre I: Avions destinés à l'armée de l'air" (unpublished, Paris, June 15, 1936); France, MA, EMAA, 3° Bureau:N° 184-3C/EMAA, Letter from Féquant to Commanders of Air Regions and Corps aériens (unpublished, Paris, November 30, 1936); Madeline Astorkia, "Les leçons aériennes de la guerre d'Espagne," *Revue historique des armées* 4th year, no. 2 (1977): 145ff.

50. France, Centre de hautes études aériennes, General Joseph Vuillemin, "Exposé sur l'aviation lourde de défense" (unpublished, December 4 and 11, 1936); France, EMAA, 4e Bureau, "Programmes 1934 et 1936: Caractéristiques Projets réalisations [*sic*] des différents types d'appareils" (unpublished, November, 1938), p. 10.

51. Vuillemin's letter dated January 18, 1938, in *Événements . . . Témoignages* II, pp. 301-302.

52. France, EMAA, 2e Bureau, "Ordre de bataille des unités de combat de l'armée de l'air allemande (Aviation et artillerie de l'air): Situation à la date du 1er janvier 1937" (unpublished, [January, 1937?]).

53. France, EMAA, 2e Bureau: N° 24 2/C/S/EMAA, "Ordre de bataille de l'armée de l'air allemande au 1er janvier 1938" (unpublished, January 6, 1938).

54. France, [EMAA, 2e Bureau], "Ordre de bataille de l'armée de l'air allemande à la date du 1er septembre 1938" (unpublished, no date); General Paul Stehlin, *Témoignage pour l'histoire* (Paris: Robert Laffont, 1964), pp. 86ff. See also *DDF*, 2nd series, X, pp. 788ff, 938ff.

55. France, [EMAA?], "Note" (unpublished, January 21, 1938) (a long record of a meeting between the Commanders in Chief designate and their aides on January 21, 1938); Gamelin, *Servir* I, p. 54, II, pp. 306ff, 472ff; Vial, "La Défense nationale," pp. 22ff; France, Présidence du Conseil, MDN and G, "Décret du 7 septembre 1938 relatif: À la direction général de la guerre. À la direction militaire de la guerre. À la

conduite supérieure des opérations'' (unpublished, Rambouillet, September 7, 1938).

56. France . . ., Letter from General Gamelin to Daladier (unpublished, Paris, March 15, 1938); France, [EMAA?]: N° 101 EMAA/S, Letter from General Vuillemin to the Air Minister (unpublished, March 23, 1938); France . . ., Letter from General Gamelin to the Minister of National Defense (unpublished, March 26, 1938).

57. France, MDN and G, Le Général Chef d'État-major général de la défense nationale et de l'armée, ''Note personnelle pour le Ministre de la défense nationale et de la guerre'' (unpublished, Paris, March 29, 1938); France . . ., ''Résumé de l'entretien du Ministre [de l'Air?] avec le Général Gamelin (21 avril 1938)'' (unpublished, no date).

58. France . . ., ''Note relative aux attributions respectives des commandements terrestres et aériens sur un théâtre d'opérations'' (unpublished, Paris, September 9, 1938).

59. René de Chambrun, *I Saw France Fall: Will She Rise Again?* (New York: William Morrow and Co., 1940), p. 27; France, Manoeuvres de l'ouest: Septembre 1937, ''Prescriptions du général directeur des manoeuvres relatives à: La Discipline de marche. La Discipline de stationnement. La Discipline de combat'' (unpublished, Strasbourg, June 14, 1937); France, Manoeuvres de l'ouest: Septembre 1937, ''Directives tactiques'' (unpublished, Strasbourg, June 14, 1937).

60. France, Manoeuvres aériennes du Sud-Est de 1937, Direction de l'arbitrage, ''Rapport d'ensemble de la direction de l'arbitrage. Fasicule III: Enseignements et conclusions'' (unpublished, Paris, October 15, 1937).

61. France, 1° Corps aérien, 3e Division aérienne, EM: N° 407/3S, ''Compte rendu relatif à la préparation aux manoeuvres d'ensemble de l'armée de terre des formations de la 3e DA'' (unpublished, Metz, August 4, 1938).

62. The core of the incipient DCR.

63. France, 1° Corps aérien, EM, 3° Bureau: N° 1168/3S/1° C.Aé., Letter from General Roger Pennès to the Colonel commanding the 4th Air Brigade (unpublished, Paris, August 23, 1938).

64. France, MDN and G, EMA, 3e Bureau: N° 5307 3/EMA-M, ''Note sur la défense contre les attaques aériennes à basse altitude'' (unpublished, Paris, April 5, 1938). Signed by Maurice Gamelin.

65. France, MA, EMAA, 3ème Bureau: N° 1727 3-IS/EMAA, Letter from the Air Minister to the Commanders of the Air Regions (unpublished, Paris, August 12, 1938).

chapter 3

SECOND CRISIS: MUNICH, 1938, AND ITS AFTERMATH

MUNICH

The remilitarization of the Rhineland and the Belgian swing to neutrality led to calls in France for further fortification, particularly behind the Ardennes. Gamelin replied in late 1936: battle in this region would be sought in Belgium—alliance or no alliance—although the line of the Meuse River would be prepared against the possibility of surprise attack by motorized forces. The Ardennes were unsuitable for major operations, and if German motorized forces reached the Meuse, they could not mount a rapid attack over it. Gamelin was more concerned with the Spanish Civil War. Italian intervention in Spain ended the spirit of Stresa; from that time France regarded Italy as a potential enemy. With the Rhineland and Belgium closed off, Gamelin turned south, seeking the vulnerable point in the forming German-Italian Axis. Germany remained the number one threat and France might have to take the offensive if Hitler turned against France's allies in eastern Europe, but hope for effective action lay in attacking Italy.[1]

In late 1937 Gamelin told the Permanent Committee of the Superior Council of National Defense that his first goal, in wartime, would be to finish Italy while holding sufficient forces to stop a German offensive and to fix some German strength on the Franco-German frontier, should Hitler menace eastern Europe. The Committee called for new arms programs.[2]

Georges reevaluated his plans. In November 1937 he warned against plans for an initial air offensive into the Rhineland. This would not stop a German land attack, and losses would render the bombers incapable ". . . of playing the *particularly important* role in the *general battle* which the army has the right to expect from them."[3] He complained that command of the fighters now seemed divided between the air armies. Nonetheless Féquant, then commander of the air force, held to his plan for an all-out air attack on the Luftwaffe at the start of a war, although insisting on the need to track the Panzerdivisionen: were they facing Czechoslovakia or France?

Mobilization Plan E, in effect from January 1938, specified the initial mission of the army: hold a front from the Meuse to Switzerland while standing ready to parry a German maneuver into Belgium, Switzerland, or both. Following mobilization, counterattacks or an offensive into the Rhineland were foreseen. The plan foresaw concentrations from Belgium to Italy and Spain—including possible offensives north of the Moselle River and against Italy—using eight armies and the Ardennes Army Detachment in line and the Seventh Army in reserve at Reims. Besides fortress troops, seventy-seven infantry divisions, two DLM's, three cavalry divisions, and seven cavalry brigades would form, plus seven infantry divisions and five cavalry brigades in North Africa.[4]

In the summer of 1938, Gamelin chose his primary army group commander, General Gaston Billotte, to command the Alpine front facing Italy. Billotte's years in the colonial forces had won him respect, particularly from Weygand who liked his style, although he had a reputation for being headstrong.[5] With Georges facing Germany and Billotte facing Italy, Gamelin would have a balanced team with himself at the center.

As the threat to Czechoslovakia grew, Gamelin asked General Gaston Prételat to prepare an offensive into the Saar to support the Czechs. The narrowness of the front would limit the offensive; the Germans might counterattack through Belgium or Switzerland—the bulk of the French army could not be committed in the Saar unless German strength was tied down elsewhere. On September 12, 1938, the Premier, Édouard Daladier, met his generals. Gamelin insisted that an offensive between the Rhine and the Moselle would lead to a "modernized Battle of the Somme."[6] Billotte agreed with Georges when he warned that the Belgian and Swiss flanks lay open. Attack plans would surely have been different had the Belgian route to the Ruhr been open.

Belgium was the key. Initially, Hitler's Rhineland coup forced Belgium closer to France. General Édouard Van den Bergen, Chief of Staff of the Belgian Army, came to Paris in May 1936. Gamelin emphasized the threat of a German attack via the Netherlands, and Van den Bergen agreed. The generals divided Belgium into areas of responsibility, the Belgians north and the French south of the Sambre River. Gamelin warned of the scale and speed that would characterize a German offensive: Belgium would have to appeal for help quickly. In October 1936, however, King Léopold III announced an "independent" foreign policy for Belgium. Belgium would abandon all alliances while reinforcing its own forces. No alliance could prevent Belgium being turned into a battleground; Belgium must therefore be strong enough to deter invasion.[7] The Belgian government felt compelled to take this step to preserve national unity. Great Britain, whose guarantee both Flemings and Walloons might have accepted, refused to make any commitment. Belgium hoped to avoid being drawn into war if Germany marched against France's allies in eastern Europe. But if Germany turned *west* toward France, it was bound by the existence of the Maginot Line to attack through Belgium. Belgium's break with France enhanced this possibility by destroying effective military cooperation between the two. Belgium could not "deter" a German attack toward France by itself; by declaring its "independence," Belgium opened a tempting maneuver ground should Hitler wish to attack west. He eventually took advantage of this option, after using Belgian neutrality to shield Germany's western frontiers while he turned east. Belgium's policy, designed to protect Belgium at the cost of the Czechs and Poles, if necessary, eventually backfired against Belgium and the West as a whole.

Gamelin warned the Belgian command that France might now replace some troops on the Belgian frontier with fortifications, although he claimed that French troops could still enter Belgium under the terms of Locarno. He reassured the Belgians that he would maintain plans to support them and expressed pleasure at the prospect of increased Belgian strength; actually Gamelin felt that Belgium could not stand up to a surprise attack by mechanized and motorized divisions supported by bombers. France would have to fortify the Belgian frontier and concentrate initially on defending its own territory.[8]

Belgium refused to recognize obligations under Locarno. By 1937 "the Palace" ordered an end to the exchange of secret information with France, although Van den Bergen assured Gamelin that the 1936 military plans remained in effect. Britain and France had little choice but to recognize Belgium's new status in April 1937.[9]

Soon after becoming Chief of Staff of National Defense, Gamelin issued a statement on the conduct of land warfare, dealing in large part with Belgium. France was menaced on its Belgian and Swiss flanks; the Belgian wing was more dangerous—its excellent communications led directly to Paris. But French forces could not move up into Belgium without the necessary tactical security. Belgium had to appeal for aid before an invasion, or gain time for French forces to arrive by resisting on the Meuse River and the Albert Canal.[10] The real hope lay in an appeal *prior* to an invasion. Otherwise, Gamelin planned to await the Germans on the French frontier, making no effort to assist Belgium beyond advancing his left wing to join the Belgian "redoubt" near Ghent.

Gamelin foresaw a single GQG serving the two theaters of operations (northeast and southeast) in France. He implied that if Belgium would not allow the French passage toward Germany, it might be better to forgo an offensive to aid Czechoslovakia, although an offensive against Italy looked promising. Thus the maneuver into Belgium, which was still being practiced until the middle of 1937—including the dispatch of DLM's into the Ardennes—changed radically. Belgium compensated by building up its armed forces, motorizing its cavalry, mechanizing some antitank guns, buying some fighters and light bombers from Britain, adapting tactics to mechanized warfare, and extending fortifications[11]—but all this was no substitute for the French maneuver force.

By September 24, 1938, French intelligence estimated that Germany had twenty-six divisions along the Czech frontier, although the Czechs could field thirty-eight divisions to face them. French planners had no intention of facing Germany without further allies and made British support a basic factor in their policy. But the British proved to be unwilling allies over the question of Czechoslovakia, to which they were not tied by treaty.[12]

After the remilitarization of the Rhineland, Britain participated in staff talks with France and Belgium but limited its promise of aid to two infantry divisions and some aircraft.[13] In early 1938 Britain still refused to prepare a major field army although it agreed on the need for further talks. Despite the attitude of the British army command that Britain would have to provide a substantial expeditionary force—that Britain could not expect France alone to bear the bloody burden of land war—Chamberlain refused to agree. He was supported by the military analyst Basil Liddell Hart and by the majority of British public opinion, which refused to contemplate a repetition of the carnage of World War I. Britain preferred to maintain its financial reserves intact in order to support a long war—a convenient rationalization—while building up its navy and reinforcing the Royal Air Force, which was beginning to receive modern fighters. Britain's air commanders so feared strategic air attack that they refused French efforts at joint air planning lest their strength be diverted to the western front of a new war. In April 1938 Vuillemin informed Gamelin that the most France could expect from England would be some bombers. Gamelin met with Leslie Hore-Belisha, the British Secretary of State for War, on April 25, 1938. Belisha explained that any British ground forces sent would be small and (despite Gamelin's request) would probably not include mechanized units at the outset. Gamelin, perhaps trying to throw a scare into his ally, implied that he expected a war to begin with an attack through Belgium. He doubted the Belgian capacity and will to resist—and claimed he could not assist Czechoslovakia. Gamelin stated that he expected Russia to remain neutral while Italy would be hostile.

As the Czech crisis intensified, Gamelin changed his position. On September 24, 1938, he informed the British attaché that Soviet air forces might intervene. Then Gamelin flew to London. There he gave an impression of confidence, asserting that he would take the offensive against Germany at once although he was worried over the situation in the air. He praised the Czech forces: he hoped that, together with Polish forces, they would form a solid front in the east.[14] Meanwhile, Gamelin tried to persuade Russia and Poland to support Czechoslovakia. He advised the Czech command to make a stand in eastern Czechoslovakia, where it might hope for aid from its neighbors: a Czech retreat would give France time to mobilize and mount an offensive.

France prepared for war: the cover force was mustered in early September; over a million men joined the colors, bringing home the danger. In the last week of September 1938, Britain promised that in case of German aggression it too would march. Europe teetered on the brink of war.[15]

France faced the prospect with a serious weakness—its air force. The Armée de l'air was outnumbered and equipped with aircraft a generation behind those of the Luftwaffe. The basis of French air strategy remained Féquant's directive of December 27, 1937, which prescribed the formation of three air armies in France: the First and Second facing Germany, the Third Italy. Féquant had intended to open hostilities with attacks on German air and land forces and bases in the Rhineland. Following operations would depend on the course of the battle: participation in the ground battle in Holland and Belgium, exploitation of a success on the ground, or an air attack to halt an enemy breakthrough.[16] By September 1938, however, Vuillemin, designated to command the Second Air Army, was Commander in Chief designate of the Air Force. He sent out an urgent amendment to Féquant's directive on September 20, 1938.

Vuillemin suppressed the Second Air Army, leaving the First Air Army alone to face Germany. The Third and Fifth Air Armies (the Fifth in Africa) faced Italy. Vuillemin concentrated his strength from the Second Air Army into the First.[17] He ordered increased defense of airfields against air attacks, underscored the need to concentrate forces to wrest command of the air from the enemy at specified times and places—even if that left the skies to the enemy the rest of the time—and renounced air offensives. Above all, Vuillemin appealed to the audacity, high morale, and professional qualities of his fighter pilots, demanding that they acquire moral ascendancy over the Luftwaffe no matter what the price. But these measures were palliatives, as he wrote to La Chambre on September 26: losses might run as high as 64 percent by the end of the second month of hostilities. Such losses could not be replaced, nor would the promised British bombers (240 planes in the first month) compensate. Land operations would be difficult. In the interior only Paris had serious protection—air attacks on France's centers might produce panic: Vuillemin anticipated the use of poison gas against the civilian populace. Would morale—and the economy—collapse under such a threat? No one knew, but the possibility haunted French and British leaders who knew how inferior they were in the air.

This knowledge was a major factor in Chamberlain's and Daladier's decision to abandon Czechoslovakia to Hitler at the celebrated Munich Conference on September 29, 1938. As the crisis grew, Daladier renounced the initiative to Chamberlain, who was a man of peace, convinced that total war would encompass the destruction of Western civilization whether Britain and France won or not: only Soviet Communism stood to gain. Chamberlain knew that France was torn between its treaty commitments and Daladier's determination to support them, and Foreign Minister Georges Bonnet's (and others like Flandin's) fears that France was too weak to fight. In the Czech crisis Gamelin urged Daladier and the British to stand firm. But Chamberlain had the initiative, and France would not act without British support. Chamberlain was determined not to go to war to keep the Sudetenlanders from joining Hitler's Reich; he would fight only if Hitler's designs went beyond that. At Munich Chamberlain conceded to Hitler the Sudetens—even if the parties directly concerned objected—but nothing more. Italy joined the Munich agreements; the Soviet Union was excluded and the Czech state, shorn of Sudetens and its border defenses, was handed a set of worthless guarantees from the parties present. But peace was saved.[18] Returning to Paris amid scenes of near delirium at the disappearance of the threat of war, Daladier moved immediately to consolidate France's unity and to prepare its defenses. Munich did not mean "peace in our time" as Daladier well knew.

EVOLUTION TOWARD WAR

The loss of Czechoslovakia forced Gamelin to reexamine his strategy. The situation was worse than in 1914.[19] Italy and eastern Europe were at a crossroads—especially Poland, whose attitude during the Czech crisis left Gamelin furious. Still, Gamelin thought, Hitler had recoiled from war; German public opinion seemed to dread the prospect. Gamelin proposed that France orient its strategy toward the Mediterranean, using the eastern Mediterranean for contact with friends in eastern Europe. The Soviet Union remained an enigma; Poland might sell out to Germany. Above all France had to bind itself to Britain. Germany now had more than 80 million people; Hitler could soon sustain a total war on several fronts. Gamelin foresaw a conflict in one of two forms: a war of attrition on fortified fronts, or a war of vast maneuvers on external fronts—the Middle East or colonial areas. France would face attack by Germany and Italy, but it had to keep strength in reserve for a long war and for an attack on the strategic resources of the enemy. France had to be ready to defeat Italy when the time came. Gamelin proposed that France's frontiers be so fortified that France could "conduct its war like England behind the Channel," while developing maneuver forces to intervene in Belgium or Switzerland. And he demanded an "exceptional augmentation" of the air force.

Gamelin invited opinions from the other services.[20] General René Keller, the Chief of the Air Force Staff, sent Vuillemin a draft reply. A British alliance was a necessity, but would mean an increase in potential strength only: Britain was not prepared for war. Keller did not think France could hold out until a coalition could build up to face Germany and Italy—the disproportion in the air was too severe. French diplomacy had to keep Italy neutral and to draw Poland away from Germany. Plan V would give the Armée de l'air a minimum of security against Germany alone; it seemed impossible for France to make any further effort except for the antiaircraft. Vuillemin passed the Keller note on, adding that if the enemy stayed within present levels, Britain and France would be in a better position by 1940.

Within the army Gamelin sought new measures.[21] His position as Chief of Staff of National Defense would be a heavy burden in wartime. He had already agreed not to command a theater of operations: there was no reason why he should continue to be Commander in Chief designate of the army. In January 1939 Gamelin pressed Daladier to promote Georges, giving him command of the armies in France with the assistance of a Chief of the General Staff and a Major-général: in wartime the former would become Chief of Staff for the Interior, the latter would command the GQG. But Daladier would not accept Georges, whose politics he suspected. Perhaps they could promote Billotte? Gamelin replied that it was impossible to push Georges aside. Thus Gamelin continued to hold both posts.[22]

Hitler tore up the Munich agreement and seized the remainder of the Czech state in March 1939. With this action Hitler made a serious mistake: convinced that he had taken the measure of the British and French leaders at Munich, he arrogantly devoured the Czech state without a word to the West. Thus he discarded the mask of Wilsonian principles; he was patently intent on foreign conquest. Even Neville Chamberlain, encouraged by a wave of outrage in the British Parliament and public opinion, recognized the German threat for what it was. Convinced at last that the West must either stand against Hitler or fall victim to him, Britain finally began preparations for war—including conscription and a belated commitment to send substantial expeditionary forces to the Continent. A new wave of determination gripped Britain and France, aided by an increase in defensive air strength in both countries. The "worms," as Hitler called them, turned. Daladier obtained powers to rule by decree on matters of national defense. In April, Britain and France gave guarantees to Poland, Rumania, and Greece against German and Italian aggression, and agreed to seek a military pact with the Soviet Union; public opinion in the two countries consolidated behind this stand. An alliance between Great Britain, France, and the Soviet Union might still deter Hitler. But Poland and Rumania stood between Stalin and Hitler, and both—particularly Poland—refused to permit the passage of Soviet forces. And Chamberlain continued to suspect Soviet intentions. Soviet leaders, in turn, excluded from the concert of powers at Munich, felt that the West wanted to embroil them with Hitler. Thus, the pact between the Soviet Union and the West hung poised in the balance between fear of Hitler on the one hand, and mutual fear and cynicism on the other.

To back up his diplomacy Daladier expanded the French arms budget. Defense spending through August 1939 rose to 37.128 billion francs, compared to 16.980 for 1938. The air force received 51 percent, the army 32 percent, and the navy 17 percent.[23] The army worked to form DCR's. On December 2, 1938, Gamelin convoked the Superior War Council: given the slow production of heavy tanks, he proposed to reduce each DCR from six to four battalions of B tanks; medium D tanks could be used provisionally to form the units as soon as possible. General Héring wanted the division to have tactical groups of two tank battalions each. But Gamelin's solution would yield three or four DCR's instead of the two originally planned. Georges and Gamelin agreed that the DCR, designed to break through enemy lines or counterattack enemy mechanized units, would work within an ordinary army corps and thus need no reconnaissance unit of its own; moreover the DCR would always be engaged with one or more DLM's. The Council approved Gamelin's proposals and ordered the formation of the 1st and 2nd DCR in Lorraine and Champagne in 1940.

Meanwhile, the doctrine of the DCR took shape. A manual appeared in early 1939 although it was so secret that the Chief of Staff of the 2nd DCR claimed he never received a copy.[24] The manual specified that the DCR was intended for deep and rapid penetration of a weak or imperfect enemy front, counterattack against enemy mechanized formations, exploitation of a breakthrough, and maneuver on a flank.

The composition of the DCR was fixed at two armored half-brigades, each with two battalions of B tanks and one of infantry in armored personnel carriers, plus an artillery regiment with two groups of towed artillery, a group of mechanized artillery, a 12-gun battery of 47 mm antitank guns, and antiaircraft. Services and a squadron of observation planes completed the unit. Tactically, the division would advance in echelon with the commander, in touch by radio, ready to mass for the attack. A first wave of two or three tank battalions would attack on a front of no more than four kilometers with a second wave of one or two tank battalions following to protect the flanks and mop up. The mechanized infantry would occupy the strongpoints of the objective. Security against enemy aircraft drew particular attention, along with security from enemy armor by DLM's, the mechanized infantry, or motorized reconnaissance groups.[25]

The manual emphasized the use of attack bombers: the further the DCR penetrated beyond its initial artillery support, the more important bombers would be to keep the attack rolling. Delays would be reduced by keeping a scout plane above the battle and having a formation of bombers in the air on call. The manual reflected Héring's notion of tactical groups and emphasized that in the exploitation of a breakthrough the greatest initiative would be given to the combatants. Tank versus tank combat would pose important problems: the advantage would lie with the side that was in a masked position against an enemy in movement. While the enemy was engaged and fixed from the front, the mass of friendly tanks would maneuver to take the enemy in enfilade, working to achieve surprise—"primordial" in a battle between tanks. Decisions had to be communicated quickly: each tank would carry radio; other units had radios down to the infantry company and the artillery battery. The tanks would carry a one-day fuel supply, armored supply vehicles a further half day's ration, and trucks of the main supply column would have a further one and one-half day's worth.[26]

The manual of the DCR closely resembled provisions on the DLM in the contemporary cavalry manual.[27] This manual added a new mission for the DLM—assault—made practical by the delivery of SOMUA tanks (although an assault mission would be exceptional). Antiaircraft defense was stressed and air firepower was to be used to reinforce and eventually replace the artillery. In the attack, tanks would be engaged in mass with a minimum of infantry accompanying them; the progression of the assault would follow the speed of the tank rather than the infantry, with the command ordering the intervention of air units as required. The mechanized infantry of the DLM would follow up in half-tracked vehicles, accompanied by armored scout vehicles, when the enemy position was shaken. Tactics against enemy tanks were identical to those specified for the DCR.

A commission led by Inspector General Dufieux wrote a new manual for infantry tanks in 1939. This published work was conservative but incorporated part of the DCR concept, although most infantry tanks were lightly armed, slow, and without radio. The commission divided tank actions into infantry support and the more independent manoeuvre d'ensemble which had inspired the development of the DCR.[28] The commission set the minimum mass of tanks in the attack at forty infantry support tanks or twenty heavier tanks (types D or B) per kilometer.

By 1939 the Army Staff College put considerable emphasis on the mobility of reserves as a counterweight to enemy numerical superiority.[29] The High Command envisaged "motorized groups"—groups of motorized and cavalry units, particularly DLM's—operating in a field army. The archetypal mission for such a "motorized group" was the maneuver into Belgium.

Modernization carried down to the lower echelons. Reconnaissance groups of motorized infantry divisions were allotted some forty-five armored vehicles, giving them striking power.[30] These groups could be detached to form sizable independent groupings or to reinforce other units, such as the DCR. By 1939 the cavalry division had seventy-five armored vehicles to complement its horse and motorized cavalry, while the DLM with its SOMUA tanks and lighter Hotchkiss combat vehicles and its older armor boasted 300 armored vehicles, plus 500 half-tracks for its motorized cavalry. The ordinary infantry regiment was to have twelve 25 mm antitank guns, and each infantry division an additional company of twelve more plus twelve heavy weapons (in principle the excellent 47 mm, although in many units 75's were substituted) along with nine armored utility vehicles per company of guns to haul and supply the weapons. Communications improved too: each infantry battalion was to have six radios with which the commander could equip his companies. Each infantry division was to have twenty-nine radios, some capable of long distance telephony. In short, by 1939—at least in principle—the French army was thoroughly modern.

By September 1, 1939, French industry produced more than 5,300 antitank guns and 1,200 antiaircraft weapons. New production plus World War I stocks yielded almost 17,000 artillery pieces, while the infantry had some 180,000 automatic weapons plus 3 million rifles. French mechanized forces counted 1,780 light infantry tanks; 172 B and 50 D2 tanks; 261 SOMUA tanks, 269 scout cars, 316 reconnaissance and 98 combat vehicles in the cavalry—plus some 3,700 armored utility vehicles. In March 1939 Gamelin planned a third DCR and demanded the constitution of a motorized maneuver force to relieve a threatened sector or to act beyond the frontiers.[31]

As the crisis in Europe intensified, the army staff circulated a note on the attack of fortified fronts, a mission the French army would face if Hitler turned on Poland, and Belgium refused passage to French troops. A heavy force of artillery would be needed. B and D2 tanks would directly accompany infantry to neutralize enemy forts. A concentration of air forces and antiaircraft would have to cover this mass.[32] This instruction offered little hope for immediate aid to Poland—but a supplement, provisions of which were being practiced in August 1939, promised quicker results. The new doctrine directed that the infantry deal with enemy works by bringing up high-velocity guns (antitank weapons, 75's, guns of accompanying tanks) to knock out the enemy weapons. Once each fort was neutralized the advance could proceed, leaving mop-up teams to finish the job.

Gamelin charged Prételat with the establishment of "defensive anchor points," fortified pivots for the maneuvers of the armies. Prételat reported that an urgent effort should be made on the Saar and Ardennes "gaps."[33] The Superior War Council approved Prételat's proposals in December 1938. But Gamelin gave priority to the Alps and the Belfort region, then the Saar, and finally the Ardennes, even though he had attended the maneuvers Prételat conducted in the spring of 1938, which demonstrated that enemy mechanized forces could launch a surprise attack and arrive at Sedan in less than three days. Gamelin apparently felt that even if the Germans broke through to the Meuse, they would still have to cross the river against resistance; that would be slow and difficult.

By the beginning of September 1939, French intelligence understood German doctrine.[34] It credited Germany in early 1939 with four Panzers, four light divisions (similar to Panzers but with half the tanks), and four motorized infantry divisions. Each Panzer had some 400 tanks, but only 48 of these were mediums—the rest were very light. In fact by fall 1939, Germany had only 200 medium PzKpfw III tanks (armed with a weak antitank gun) and 200-250 PzKpfw IV tanks with a 75 mm piece, although carrying less armor than French tanks. French intelligence also reported that Germany had at least one division of airborne troops and speculated that it would be used in combination with mechanized units.[35]

Meanwhile, Vuillemin developed the Armée de l'air. In October 1938 his principal subordinate, General Mouchard, complained that his First Air Army would have responsibility for the air defense of the armies in his zone as well as part of the defense of the interior and the conduct of bombing operations in his zone. Mouchard felt he could not handle these diverse missions while commanding and administering the air divisions, brigades, and fighter groupments (which usually had 75-100 fighters). Therefore, Mouchard decentralized his command, giving each air division, which grouped bombers and some reconnaissance groups, charge over the sector in which it would operate. But air division staffs were too small, the air division commanders too junior: Mouchard pressed Vuillemin to form two zone commands directly subordinate to the First Air Army.[36] In effect, Mouchard was proposing the restoration of two air armies facing Germany, with himself in command over them. Through the spring of 1939 Mouchard urged his solution since his "Northeastern Theater of Air Operations," as he wanted to call it, needed time to prepare.[37]

In his views on the role of air power, Mouchard was less of a maverick. In May 1939 he wrote that at the opening of a war bombers should attack the enemy air force on its bases. He also felt that strategic air war, undertaken at the right moment, might be decisive. It was in choosing such moments that Mouchard saw the proper role for the Commander of the Air Force.[38] Mouchard wrote that no land battle could be successful without air superiority at critical moments. But, given the equipment in service, battlefield "assault" missions could only be exceptional.

In July 1939 General Keller, Chief of the Air Force Staff, retired. Vuillemin chose to replace him the fifty-one-year-old General Marcel Têtu, a graduate of the École polytechnique who fought with distinction in the artillery in World War I before joining the air service. Têtu was marked out for further advancement.[39]

The air force's most serious problem remained expansion, although progress was made due in part to the purchase of American aircraft. La Chambre called Albert Caquot (the brain behind aircraft production during World War I) to direct the nationalized air industry from October 1938. With the support of Vuillemin, engineers like Émile Dewoitine designed aircraft for mass production.[40] Monthly production of warplanes increased from about forty in March 1938 to 320 in September 1939; France reached a cadence of 300 planes per month within eighteen months of the decision to increase production; in Great Britain and Germany it took three years.

Although Pierre Cot played an important part in developing the industry, the number of workers in spring 1938 was still at the same level as 1935, about 35,000; employment reached 80,000 in January 1939 and 171,000 in January 1940.

In January 1939 the Industrial Director of the Air Force, Joseph Roos, informed La Chambre that, depending on the type of aircraft, the industry could produce from 370 to 600 planes per month in 1940. La Chambre called in Roos, Caquot, Vuillemin and Keller (then still Chief of Staff) to discuss the air force's need. Roos was shocked to hear the officers respond that the air force would need only forty to sixty aircraft—assuming France remained at peace—per month. Two months later the air force staff settled on the production of 330 planes per month. This decision retarded the industry through reduced investments and purchases of raw materials.

The explanation for this decision emerged in a meeting between La Chambre, his senior commanders, and Gamelin and Georges, on March 28, 1939. La Chambre indicated that the level of 300-330 aircraft per month would be reached by September 1939; orders had to continue at that level to sustain the industry. Keller explained that Plan V would be largely complete by the middle of 1940, except for observation aircraft—a tremendous advance over the original timetable. However, General Houdemon, Inspector General of the Reconnaissance and Observation Aviation, warned that with their obsolete planes his observation units could not accomplish their missions for the army. Mouchard stressed that day bombing expeditions would need fighter escort, contrary to doctrine. The Superior Air Council agreed to the creation of five groups of heavy fighters for escort missions. Gamelin insisted that fighters would be vital to the army as well as to the defense of the interior—this led Mouchard to complain that large aircraft reserves seemed useless when the air force was so outnumbered. Mouchard's outburst brought the issue to a head: Vuillemin replied that sufficient personnel, even for Plan V, could not be trained before the middle of 1940. The air force's expansion was limited by lack of personnel, *not* by lack of planes.

A confused wrangle followed. Vuillemin claimed that everything possible was being done to train crews; it seemed dangerous to crowd units with trainees when war might break out at any moment. The Superior Air Council finally decided to maintain production at 300-330 aircraft per month, planes going first to the units and second to form reserves.[41] The problem was to have sufficient force at hand without throwing billions into unnecessary machines that would quickly become obsolete. Hitler alone would decide when to put them to use. By September 1939, of the 6,858 aircraft ordered under Plan V, 1,470 had left the factories and 1,241 had been tested and armed and were in service. Most were fighters—their arrival changed the strategic balance. Unfortunately, the situation in antiaircraft artillery and the aircraft warning network was worse. The resources stretched only so far.

The evolution of French air doctrine continued. The 1939 bomber manual took account of assault aviation—an incipient force then being planned—emphasizing that the primary mission of the regular bombers would be to operate behind enemy lines. Assault aviation and dive-bombers could intervene directly in the land battle.[42] Nonetheless conventional bombers could be called into the ground battle during crises. The air force cooperated with the army in training to respond to German air attack. But the air staff warned against using observation planes to simulate low-level attacks. Such missions were dangerous to the crews and gave a false impression of such attacks; the staff promised a larger effort in 1940 when its asault aviation would be formed.[43]

Air-ground cooperation occupied most of the 1939 manual for observation and reconnaissance units. This manual took no account of the state of the observation units, which Houdemon had underscored. It put emphasis on providing security and directing artillery fire on mobile enemy targets, assigning a crucial role to observation aircraft in armored attacks.[44] These provisions were in keeping with the demands of modern war—but the units in service lacked the means to carry them out.

With the approach of war Gamelin and Georges pressured Vuillemin to change his strategy. Traditionally French air strategy called for a bombing offensive against enemy air forces while the fighters concentrated on defending the interior. But Gamelin and Georges worried about the effects of bombing on the army during mobilization. Vuillemin responded by asking Mouchard to include the army's zones of concentration in his air defense coverage. Mouchard argued that fighters could not protect such widespread movements: he insisted the army be told just that, although he accepted the redistribution of some antiaircraft guns.[45]

Meanwhile General Aubé worked on new defense techniques. In March 1939 Britain revealed its radar system which was considerably more effective than the French DEM. Britain offered to sell enough to satisfy French needs, delivery to take place early in 1940. Aubé halted the creation of DEM units, installing the single unit already formed on a night fighter sector of the Paris warning net.[46]

By September 1939 the Armée de l'air had made considerable progress. Not all its units had received new equipment and it had not yet expanded to its planned size, but it was no longer hopelessly inferior. It had some 225 modern Morane 406 fighters plus almost 100 American Curtiss Hawk 75's in line. In 1939 the British and French air industries, with the addition of American equipment, turned out some 10,250 military aircraft against a German total of 8,295. However, French production of modern bombers was just beginning.

French intelligence credited the Luftwaffe with fifty-four single seat and twenty-one heavy fighter squadrons, one hundred and two medium and thirty-six dive-bomber squadrons, sixty-one reconnaissance and observation units and eighty-eight groups of Flak.[47] The balance still tilted heavily against France, but inferiority in the air did not weigh on French leaders as at Munich.

Meanwhile, French strategy adjusted to the destruction of the Czech state. The Superior War Council met on March 13, 1939; Gamelin concluded that without Czech forces, with the Soviet Union lacking access to Germany, with the reinforcement of the German fortifications in the west, and with Belgian neutrality, French efforts should initially be limited to tying down German forces.[48] Gamelin added that the Italians seemed unable to act, and Spain seemed to be moving toward neutrality. The army's main problem would be to aid Belgium when Germany attacked.

But the establishment of a solid British alliance offered prospects. In February 1939 British intelligence picked up signs of an impending German invasion of the Low Countries. Britain asked for serious staff talks with France; Hitler's seizure of the Czech rump state in March abolished the last of British reticence. Talks continued through the summer, yielding agreements on economic collaboration, on an interallied Supreme Council to direct the war effort, and on grand strategy.

The Allies agreed that Germany and Italy would have initial superiority on land and in the air, the Allies on the seas and in economic potential. Therefore the Allies would have to withstand initial offensives in the air against Britain, or by land and air against France. They would counterattack Italy while blockading Germany, gaining support from neutrals (particularly the United States), and building up for a final offensive against Germany. After Poland became an ally, Britain and France agreed that they could do little for Poland beyond a limited French land offensive and bombing strictly military targets in Germany—the onus of first bombing civilians would be left to the enemy.

But the Allies did not agree on how to meet the initial German offensive which each feared would be directed at itself. For France, the land-air threat was paramount. The initial British contribution on land would be small, and the British Expeditionary Force, the BEF, would be under French command. The French High Command tried to tie the RAF to its plans. Following Munich, Gamelin proposed that the Armée de l'air concentrate on cooperation with the army, leaving strategic missions to the RAF which was prepared *only* for such missions. Vuillemin responded that France needed its own strategic capability to undertake reprisal raids; the bombers in production were capable of both missions. Vuillemin appealed to Gamelin to influence Britain toward a common plan.[49] In November 1938 the air staff proposed that the RAF should furnish forces to deal with

The Allied High Command—from left to right: General Ironside, General Georges, Mr. Churchill, General Gamelin, Lord Gort.
Photo Courtesy of E. C. P. Armées

Germany while the Armée de l'air concentrated on Italy. But this was wishful thinking: Vuillemin informed La Chambre in early 1939 that the RAF had no intention of detaching fighters to France. RAF planners admitted that Allied air effort should be applied on the most decisive mission at a given moment—a German offensive through the Low Countries would constitute such a mission. But the commanders of the RAF were determined to maintain fighter strength in Britain to ward off the German strategic air threat—no matter what happened on the Continent. The response to a German land offensive should be the initiation of strategic air war over Germany. That alone, in their view, offered serious prospects for victory.

This commitment did not compensate France for the loss of Czechoslovakia as an ally. Not only were the well-equipped Czech divisions lost, but their armament and arms works fell to Germany, including about 2,000 artillery pieces, 1,800 antitank guns (better than the German model), and 600 medium tanks.[50] Britain compensated France by instituting conscription on April 24, 1939, and promising to reinforce the BEF to ten divisions—including the 1st Armoured Division—within eight months of the beginning of hostilities. But the loss of the Czechs continued to weigh on General Georges at the beginning of August 1939 when he met Winston Churchill.[51]

Sir Edward Spears, an old friend of Georges, brought together these two men who he thought would play key parts in the new alliance. Spears found Georges aged by the wounds suffered in 1934—Georges invariably wore a wool glove on his left hand—but as alert and forthright as ever. Churchill came away full of admiration for Georges and the French military.[52]

Meanwhile, France and Britain agreed that an Allied Supreme Council, consisting of the Premier and the Prime Minister and such persons as they might wish, would direct the war effort once hostilities began.[53] Gamelin objected to Chamberlain's proposal to establish a permanent military staff for the council but he accepted a military study committee as a secretariat, provided he and the other Commanders in Chief had direct access to the council itself. Gamelin foresaw that an interallied coordinator of air and land operations might be necessary, but his designation could wait until events imposed it. This vexing question remained in abeyance, but the council and its secretariat were set up. General Lelong, the French attaché in London, led the French mission.

Preparations at lower levels also went forward. Sir John Vereker, 6th Viscount Gort, the Chief of the Imperial General Staff, attended the July 14 celebration and met Gamelin and Georges. They agreed that the BEF would be subordinate to Georges on the northeastern front, with the right of appeal to the British government in case of an order endangering its existence.

The parade of July 14, 1939, included modern units of the French army and air force plus British troops and squadrons of the RAF, with Hore-Belisha and Gort joining Gamelin on the reviewing stand. The French army appeared magnificent; the crowds greeted the British warmly. This nationalist exaltation troubled one spectator: Ulrich Liss, head of the German intelligence section for the western armies. Liss found the mood of the populace exalted—it was best not to be caught speaking German![54]

Hitler's next target was Poland; the Anglo-French guarantees of April made a confrontation inevitable. The main problem facing French strategy remained Belgium. It was tempting to consider an offensive toward the Ruhr through Belgium—whether the Belgians wanted to participate or not. But the Allies stood for the defense of small nations against aggression: could they react to German aggression by invading Belgium? Could they afford to alienate the neutrals, particularly the United States which was vital to their war effort? Belgian "independence" proved a crucial aid to Hitler in his aggression in the east.

In April Georges worked out a new maneuver into Belgium. If Belgium appealed for aid prior to a German invasion, Georges proposed to intervene with an army group including the First Army in the north, the Ardennes Army Detachment in the center, and the Second Army in the south linking up with the fortifications behind Luxemburg.[55] French mechanized and motorized forces would join the Belgians on the Albert Canal and the Meuse from Liège to the French frontier; French cavalry would retard the enemy in the Ardennes, although the main resistance would rest on the Meuse. The First Army would have two DLM's and three motorized divisions, the Ardennes Army Detachment a single motorized infantry division for the Meuse south of Namur; the Ardennes Army Detachment and the Second Army would each send one cavalry division and one brigade into the Ardennes. If the Belgian appeal came *after* a German invasion, Georges intended to move only to the Escaut River in southwestern Belgium, sending cavalry and mechanized forces forward to retard the Germans.

General Mouchard prepared corresponding air operations in May 1939.[56] His offensive capabilities were weak, but he ordered air cover for the armies and the defense of the interior.

Meanwhile, Belgium developed its fortifications, and from late 1938 gave its motorized cavalry corps a mechanized punch, including thirty-six armored cars and forty-four mechanized 47 mm antitank guns; Belgium also purchased twelve Renault combat vehicles from France.[57] But these were meager resources against the German army. The Belgian Foreign Ministry considered a defensive entente with the Netherlands which faced a similar menace, but General Henri Denis, the Belgian Defense Minister, warned in March that such an entente would be an illusory gain. Dutch interests, determined by geography, drew them to concentrate north of the Waal River, abandoning hope of joint action with Belgium which had no interest in extending its dispositions north of the Albert Canal. The Dutch attitude in case of invasion remained unknown: would they resist? Certainly the Dutch government hoped that, as in 1914, the war would flow around the Netherlands. Would the Dutch risk their small, untested military strength to help Belgium? Or would they emulate the other small powers and concentrate solely on defending their own interests in the hope that the wolf would turn elsewhere for his next meal? In any case, a Belgian-Dutch entente would not be much stronger than Belgium and the Netherlands standing alone. Denis admitted that staff talks would be of interest, but felt that political accords would only endanger Belgian "independence." Léopold and his military adviser General Van Overstraeten cherished the illusion that Belgian strength might deter Hitler. They credited their army with considerable defensive potential, despite its poverty in modern heavy weapons. They had little confidence in Britain and France, whose weakness had allowed Hitler to become a menace in the first place. So Belgium and the Netherlands remained fixed in isolation.

Finally, a Polish plenipotentiary arrived in Paris on May 13, 1939. Gamelin was not pleased—in part because he had not forgiven Poland for its attitude during the Czech crisis—in part because he wanted to discuss the matter with Russia first, since prolonged Polish resistance was impossible without Soviet aid.[58] Gamelin and Georges agreed that in case of a German attack on Poland, they would commence an offensive with the bulk of the French forces on the Franco-German front from the fifteenth day following mobilization. To Gamelin's surprise, Vuillemin added that he could send bombers to operate from Polish bases. Vuillemin charged General Armengaud with command of the mission in Poland, although Armengaud considered sending air units there an "absurd pretention."

The key to the eastern theater was Russia. If Stalin could be bound into a military alliance with the West, Poland, and Rumania, Hitler might be deterred. A Franco-British military mission set out for Moscow in August 1939. But the Allies had difficulty persuading Poland to concede to the Soviets the right to move troops onto Polish soil. The Soviets were suspicious of Western intentions. Stalin pondered: he had more to gain by dividing Poland and the Baltic states with Hitler; on August 23, a Soviet-German pact was announced. Hitler's alliance with Stalin and the threat of German might convinced the vast majority of French leaders and public opinion that war was inevitable, sooner or later. The previous fall Daladier had agreed reluctantly to sacrifice Czechoslovakia to the cause of appeasement; the results of that policy became clear in March 1939. Hitler could not be appeased with anything less than total surrender. Britain and France, at last united, preferred to fight.

NOTES

1. General P[aul-É[mile] Tournoux, *Haut commandement Gouvernement et Défense des frontières du nord et de l'est 1919-1939* (Paris: Nouvelles éditions latines, 1960), pp. 271ff; *Les Relations franco-britanniques: De 1935 à 1939. Communications présentées aux colloques franco-britanniques tenus à: Londres (Imperial War Museum) du 18 au 21 octobre 1971, Paris (Comité d'Histoire de la 2ème Guerre Mondiale) du 25 au 29 septembre 1972* (Paris: CNRS, 1975), pp. 296ff, 317.

2. France, Parlement, Assemblée nationale, *Les Événements survenus en France de 1933 à 1945: Rapport de M. Charles Serre, Député au nom de la commission d'enquête parlementaire* II (Paris: Presses universitaires de France, no date), pp. 24ff; France . . ., "Measures à prendre pour le renforcement de l'armée de l'air au cours de l'année 1938" (unpublished, January 1938).

3. Quote from France, CSG, EM du Général Alphonse Georges, "Instruction personnelle et secrète aux généraux commandants d'armée aériennes: Avis du général Georges" (unpublished, Paris, November 15, 1937); France, EMAA, 2e et 3e Bureau: N°2658 3-0-S/EMAA, "Plan de renseignements" (unpublished, December 15, 1937).

4. Tournoux, *Défense des frontières*, pp. 339ff.

5. Maurice Gamelin, *Servir* III (Paris: Plon, 1946), p. 20; General [Maxime] Weygand, *Mémoires* II (Paris: Flammarion, 1957), p. 103; interview with General André Beaufre, Paris, January 23, 1973.

6. Quote from Gamelin, *Servir* II, p. 20, III, pp. 26ff; General [Gaston] Prételat,

Le Destin tragique de la ligne Maginot (Paris: Berger-Levrault, 1950), pp. 18ff; Tournoux, *Défense des frontières*, p. 299.

7. *Les Relations militaires franco-belges de mars 1936 au mai 1940: Travaux d'un colloque d'historiens belges et français* (Paris: CNRS, 1968), pp. 52ff; General [Raoul] Van Overstraeten, *Albert I-Léopold III: Vingt ans de politique militaire belge 1920-1940* ([Bruges]: Desclée de Brouwer, [1946?]), p. 220; Belgium, Ministère des affaires étrangères, *Belgium: The Official Account of What Happened 1939-1940* (New York: Didier Publishers, 1942), pp. 54ff; David Owen Kieft, *Belgium's Return to Neutrality: An Essay in the Frustrations of Small Power Diplomacy* (Oxford: Clarendon Press, 1972), pp. 102 passim, 166, 187; Brian Bond, *France and Belgium 1939-1940* (London: Davis-Poynter, 1975), pp. 23ff.

8. Van Overstraeten, *Albert I-Léopold III*, pp. 235ff; *Relations franco-belges*, pp. 65ff.

9. *Relations franco-belges*, pp. 29ff; Belgium, *The Official Account*, pp. 56ff.

10. The Albert Canal linked Liège to Antwerp; designed as a military obstacle, its completion in 1938 cast a protective screen behind Belgium's vulnerable northern frontier: General Oscar Michiels, *18 jours de guerre en Belgique* (Paris: Berger-Levrault, 1947), p. 27—Michiels succeeded Van den Bergen in early 1940 as Chief of Staff of the Belgian Army through the campaign of May 1940; France, EMA, Bureau des opérations militaires et instruction générale de l'armée: 0990 3/EMA P, "Mémento sur la conduite générale de la guerre sur terre: La France. Le Problème de l'offensive ou contre-offensive. L'Empire" (unpublished, March 7, 1938).

11. France, Centre des hautes études aériennes, 1936-1937, "Exercise sur la carte" (unpublished, [1937?]); Michiels, *18 jours de guerre*, pp. 11ff.

12. General G[aston] Roton, *Années cruciales: La Course aux armements (1933-1939). La Campagne (1939-1940)* (Paris: Charles-Lavauzelle, 1947), p. 25—Roton was on the staff of the CSG before becoming Georges' chief of staff in 1940; Gamelin, *Servir* II, pp. 468ff.

13. Keith Middlemas, *Diplomacy of Illusion: the British Government and Germany, 1937-39* (London: Weidenfeld and Nicolson, 1972); Peter Dennis, *Decision by Default: Peacetime Conscription and British Defense 1919-1939* (Durham, North Carolina: Duke University Press, 1972), pp. 66-69, 115ff; Sir John Slessor, *The Central Blue: The Autobiography of Sir John Slessor, Marshal of the RAF* (New York: Praeger, 1957), pp. 146ff; France, MA, EMAA, 3e Bureau: N° 863 3-0-S/EMAA, Letter from General Joseph Vuillemin to General Maurice Gamelin (unpublished, Paris, April 28, 1938); R[ubeigh] J. Minney, *The Private Papers of Hore-Belisha* (London: Collins, 1960), pp. 120ff; Bond, *France and Belgium*, pp. 19-40; Ian Colvin, *The Chamberlain Cabinet: How the meetings in 10 Downing Street, 1937-1939, led to the Second World War—Told for the first time from the Cabinet Papers* [sic] (New York: Taplinger, 1971), pp. 116-167; *Relations franco-britanniques*, pp. 96ff, 359ff; Patrick Fridenson and Jean Lecuir, *La France et la Grande-Bretagne face aux problèmes aériens: (1935-mai 1940)* (Vincennes: CEDOCAR, 1976), pp. 85ff; Donald Cameron Watt, *Too Serious a Business: European Armed Forces and the Approach to the Second World War* (Berkeley and Los Angeles: University of California Press, 1975), p. 47. Note the stiff criticism of British policy in N. H. Gibbs, *Grand Strategy. Volume I: Rearmament Policy* (London: H.M. S. O., 1976), pp. 798ff.

14. Great Britain, Foreign Office, *Documents on British Foreign Policy 1919-1939* (London: H. M. S. O., 1949), 3rd series, II, p. 509 (hereafter cited as *DBFP*); Oliver Harvey, *The Diplomatic Diaries of Oliver Harvey 1937-1940*, ed. John Harvey (London: Collins, 1970), pp. 199-200; Slessor, *The Central Blue*, pp. 148-149; Gamelin, *Servir* II, pp. 348ff; Pierre Le Goyet, *Le Mystère Gamelin* (Paris: Presses de la Cité, 197[6]), pp. 157ff.

15. Gamelin, *Servir* II, pp. 342 passim.

16. France, MA, EMAA, 3e Bureau: N° 2720 3-OS/EMAA, "Instruction personnelle et secrète destinée aux généraux commandants d'armée aérienne" (unpublished, Paris, December 27, 1937).

17. France, MA, EMAA, 3ème Bureau: N° 2147/30S/EMAA, "Modificatif à l'Instruction personnelle et secrète N° 2.720-3.0.S./EMAA du 27 décembre 1937" (unpublished, September 20, 1938); France, MA, EMGAA, N° 116 EMGAA/S, "Note au sujet de l'emploi de l'armée de l'air au début d'un conflit" (unpublished, September 20, 1938); France, N° 127/EMGAA/S, Letter from General Vuillemin to the Air Minister (unpublished, September 26, 1938).

18. Colvin, *The Chamberlain Cabinet*, pp. 146 passim and John W. Wheeler-Bennett, *Munich: Prologue to Tragedy*, 2nd ed. (New York: Viking Press, 1963); a different interpretation in Robert J. Young, "Le Haut commandement français au moment de Munich," *Revue d'histoire moderne et contemporaine* 24 (January-March 1977).

19. France . . ., N° 853/DN.3, "Note sur la situation actuelle" (unpublished; Paris, October 12, 1938).

20. France, EMAA, 3ème Bureau: N° 2495 3-0-S/EMAA, "Note pour M. le Général Chef d'État-major général [Vuillemin]" (unpublished, October 25, 1938); France, MA: N° 141 EMGAA/S, Letter from Vuillemin to Gamelin (unpublished, Paris, October 25, 1938).

21. Gamelin, *Servir* II, pp. 383ff.

22. Gamelin's testimony in France, Parlement, Assemblée nationale, *Les Événements survenus en France de 1933 à 1945: Témoignages et documents recueillis par la commission d'enquête parlementaire* II (Paris: Presses universitaires de France, [1950?]), pp. 399ff; Gamelin, *Servir* II, p. 388.

23. Robert Jacomet, *L'Armement de la France 1936-1939* (Paris: Éditions Lajeunesse, 1945), pp. 141ff; *Événements . . . Rapport* II, pp. 187ff.

24. Testimony of General Devaux in *Événements . . . Témoignages* V, p. 1362; France, MDN and G, Direction de l'Infanterie, Bureau technique, 3e Section: Chars de combat, *Notice provisoire à l'usage des unités de la division cuirassée* (Paris: [Presse de l'École des chars de combat], February 1, 1939), pp. 1-12, 66.

25. Battalion-sized cavalry units attached to each infantry corps and division to provide security and scouting; in motorized units the reconnaissance group was usually mechanized.

26. *Notice provisoire . . . division cuirassée*, pp. 13ff, 27, 37, 72ff, 90ff, 103.

27. France, MDN and G, EMA, *Règlement de la cavalerie. Première partie: Emploi de la cavalerie* (Paris: Imprimerie nationale, February 15, 1939), pp. 3, 21ff, 88, 100ff, 110, 123.

28. France, MDN and G, EMA, *Règlement des unités de chars de combat: 2e Partie: Combat* (Versailles: Typographie-lithographie de l'École des chars de combat, 1939), pp. 12ff, 52ff, 100.

29. France, ESG, Cours de tactique générale et d'état-major, *Notes pratiques d'état-major* ([Paris: Charles-Lavauzelle], 1939), pp. 138, 186.

30. France, ESG, Cours de tactique générale et d'état-major, *Aide-mémoire pour les travaux d'état-major: 1939* (Paris: Charles-Lavauzelle, 1939), pp. 7ff, 19ff, 55ff, 94ff, 257ff.

31. Jacomet, *L'Armement de la France*, pp. 288ff; slightly different figures in Roton, *Années cruciales*, pp. 46-47, and in the article by Raymond Surlémont in Peter Chamberlain and Chris Ellis, *Pictorial History of Tanks of the World 1915-45* (Harrisburg, Pennsylvania: Stackpole, 1972); *Événements . . . Rapport* II, pp. 257ff.

32. France, MDN and G, EMA, Bureau des opérations militaires et instruction générale de l'armée, "Note sur l'attaque des fronts fortifiées (n° 02.996-3/EMA-P du 7 juillet 1939) et Additif (n° 092 3/FT du 10 septembre 1939)" (unpublished, September 10, 1939); Col. J. D'A. Anderson, "'Coming Events?'-III: The French A Further Impression [sic]," *Army Quarterly* 46, no. 2 (August 1943): 192.

33. Prételat, *Destin tragique*, pp. 11ff.

34. France, [EMA?], "Synthèse sur l'armée de terre allemande" (unpublished; [August?], 1939); Gauché, *2e Bureau*, pp. 150ff.

35. F. M. von Senger und Etterlin, *Die Kampfpanzer von 1916-1966* (Munich: Lehmanns Verlag, 1966), pp. 63ff; France, EMAA, 2ème Bureau: N° 1519-2-C/S/EMAA, "Allemagne: Note sur les unités de chasseurs parachutistes et d'infanterie de l'air et leur emploi" (unpublished, May 9, 1939).

36. France, . . . Inspection générale des écoles: N° 54 bis 3-S, "Étude sur l'organisation du commandement à l'intérieur de la 1re armée aérienne" (unpublished, October 18, 1938).

37. France, Inspection générale des écoles de l'armée de l'air: N° 10/3S, Letter from General Mouchard to General Vuillemin (unpublished, Paris, April 3, 1939).

38. H. E. Mouchard, "Le Facteur aérien dans la guerre moderne," *Revue des questions de défense nationale* 1, no. 1 (May 1939): 148ff.

39. France, SHAA, Dossier on General Marcel Têtu (unpublished, no date).

40. General Jean d'Harcourt, "Les Chasseurs ont fait tout leur devoir," *Icare* no. 54 (Summer 1970): 44; Raymond Danel, "Histoire du Dewoitine 520" (unpublished, [Blagnac?], 1965), pp. 22ff; Engineer General Joseph Roos, "La Bataille de la production aérienne," *Icare* no. 59 (Spring 1971): 46ff.

41. France, . . ., Minutes of the meeting of March 28, 1939 (unpublished, Paris, April 8, 1939); Bizard, "L'Armée de l'air," pp. 51ff; France, MA, "Étude complète demandée par M. le Maréchal Pétain sur l'aviation et la DCA" (unpublished, October-November 1938); for data on the officer corps of the Armée de l'air, see D. Gaxie, "Morphologie de l'armée de l'air: Les officiers (1924-1974)," in SHAA, *Recueil d'articles et études: (1974-1975)* (Vincennes: CEDOCAR, 1977).

42. France, MA, EMAA, *Règlement de manoeuvre de l'armée de l'air. Livre II: Aviation de bombardement. Titre I: Organisation et emploi* ([Versailles]: École de l'air de Versailles, August 1939), pp. 12, 24.

43. France, MA, EMAA, 3° Bureau: N° 18-31C/EMAA, Letter from the Air Minister to . . . EMA, 3rd Bureau (unpublished, Paris, June 1, 1939).

44. France, MA, EMAA, 3me Bureau, *Règlement de manoeuvre de l'armée de l'air. Livre III: Forces aériennes de renseignement. Titre I: Organisation et emploi* (Versailles: École de l'air, April 1939), pp. 52, 97, 154ff.

45. France, CSG, EM du Général Georges, "Protection anti-aérienne des grands

courants de transport de concentration'' (unpublished, September 28, 1938); France, MG, EMA, Bureau des opérations militaires et instruction générale de l'armée: N° 0518 3/EMA-P, Letter from the Premier to . . . EMAA, 3rd Bureau (unpublished, Paris, February 10, 1939)—signed Gamelin; France, MA, EMAA, 3ème Bureau: N° 477 3-0-S/EMAA, Letter from General Vuillemin to General Mouchard (unpublished, [February-March, 1939]); France, Inspection générale des écoles: N° 09/3S, Letter to . . . EMAA, 3rd Bureau (unpublished, March 28, 1939)—signed Mouchard.

46. France, MDN and G, Cabinet du ministre, Section de défense nationale: N° 406/DN, Letter from Daladier to the Air Minister (unpublished, Paris, April 22, 1939); France, EMAA, 3ème Bureau: N° 2095 3-0-S/EMAA, Letter . . . to Colonel commanding the Reims Experimental Center (unpublished, August 16, 1939); Raymond Danel, ''Drôle de guerre . . . Pas pour l'aviation,'' *Icare* no. 53 (Spring-Summer 1970): 82; Danel, ''Le Bombardement dans la bataille: Un bilan qui donne à penser . . . 30 ans après,'' *Icare* no. 57 (Summer 1971): 67; *Relations franco-britanniques*, pp. 364ff; Fridenson and Lecuir, *France et Grande-Bretagne*, pp. 128, 166ff.

47. France, EMAA, 2ème Bureau: N° 1692-2-C/S/EMAA, ''Ordre de bataille de l'armée de l'air allemande à la date du 22 mai 1939'' (unpublished, May 22, 1939).

48. *Événements . . . Rapport* II, pp. 255-256.

49. France, EMAA, 3ème Bureau: N°2535 3-0-S/EMAA, Letter from Vuillemin to Gamelin (unpublished, November 4, 1938); France, [EMAA?], ''Aide à demander à la Grande-Bretagne dans le cas où nous aurions à faire face à une coalition germano-italienne'' (unpublished, Paris, November 22, 1938); France, [EMAA]: N° 32 EMGAA/S, Letter from Vuillemin to La Chambre (unpublished, February 21, 1939); Slessor, *The Central Blue*, p. 232; *Relations franco-britanniques*; Fridenson and Lecuir, *France et Grande Bretagne*; Gibbs, *Grand Strategy*, pp. 653ff; Philippe Masson, ''La Marine française et la stratégie alliée (1938-1939)'' (as yet unpublished paper for the Franco-German colloquium held at Bonn in September 1978).

50. *DBFP*, 3rd series, IV, p. 535; Dennis, *Decision by Default*, pp. 217ff; Major L. F. Ellis, *The War in France and Flanders 1939-1940* (London: H.M.S.O., 1953), p. 5.

51. Major-General Sir Edward Spears, *Assignment to Catastrophe* I (New York: A. A. Wyn, 1954), pp. 2ff.

52. Sir Edmund Ironside, *Time Unguarded: The Ironside Diaries 1937-1940* (Edinburgh: Constable, 1962), p. 90—Ironside was then Inspector General of Overseas Forces and expected to command the BEF, but command went to Lord Gort; Ironside succeeded Gort as Chief of the Imperial General Staff—J. R. Colville, *Man of Valour: The Life of Field-Marshal the Viscount Gort, VC, GCB, DSO, MVO, MC* (London: Collins, 1972).

53. Lord Hastings Ismay, *The Memoirs of General the Lord Ismay K.G., P.C., G.C.B., C.H., D.S.O.* (London: Heinemann, 1960), pp. 87, 102ff; General Sir John Kennedy, *The Business of War: The War Narrative of Major-General Sir John Kennedy G.S.M.G., K.C.V.O., K.B.E., C.B., M.C.* (New York: William Morrow, 1958), pp. 10ff; *Relations franco-britanniques*, pp. 47, 130ff, 146ff; Fridenson and Lecuir, *France et Grande-Bretagne*, pp. 149ff.

54. Minney, *Hore-Belisha*, pp. 212ff; Kennedy, *The Business of War*, p. 11;

General Ulrich Liss, *Westfront 1939/40: Erinnerungen des Feindarbeiters im O.K.H.* (Neckargemünd: Kurt Vowinckel Verlag, 1959), pp. 82ff; General Sir Kenneth Strong, *Intelligence at the Top: The Recollections of an Intelligence Officer* (New York: Doubleday, 1969), pp. 67ff and Sir Kenneth Strong, *Men of Intelligence: A Study of the Roles and Decisions of Chiefs of Intelligence from World War I to the present day* (London: Cassell, 1970), p. 77.

55. *Relations franco-belges*, pp. 71ff.

56. France, . . . Inspection générale des écoles de l'armée de l'air: 41/3S, "Note sur les opérations aériennes correspondant à l'intervention éventuelle des forces françaises en Belgique" (unpublished, Paris, May 9, 1939).

57. Van Overstraeten, *Albert I-Léopold III*, p. 314; Belgium, Ministère des affaires étrangères, *Documents diplomatiques belges 1920-1940: La Politique de sécurité extérieure* V (Brussels: C. de Visscher and F. Vanlangehove, 1964-1966), pp. 170ff; Robert Aron, *Léopold III ou le choix impossible: Février 1934-juillet 1940* ([Paris]: Plon, 1977), pp. 254-255; interview with Jean Vanwelkenhuyzen, Centre de Recherches et d'Études Historiques de la Seconde Guerre Mondiale, Brussels, June 21-23, 1978. The account by Rémy, Stanley R. Rader, trans., *The Eighteenth Day: The Tragedy of King Léopold III of Belgium* (New York: Everest House, March 1979), is biased, full of errors, and poorly translated.

58. Gamelin, *Servir* II, pp. 413ff, 426ff; General [Paul] Armengaud, *Batailles politiques et militaires sur l'Europe: Témoignages (1923-1940)* (Paris: Éditions du Myrte, 1948), pp. 92ff.

chapter 4

THE NEW WORLD WAR

On August 23, 1939, the French military chiefs and ministers met to discuss the Polish situation. La Chambre claimed that French and British fighter strength now roughly balanced that of Germany and Italy, although only Britain had offensive capability. General Aubé, the Inspector General of the Territorial Air Defense, warned that he was not ready. But Gamelin emphasized that if Poland and Rumania fell, Hitler, freed from a second front in the east, could mount an enormous surprise attack against France. Polish resistance would occupy Hitler until the following spring, by which time British forces would arrive in strength. The group agreed: France would honor its pledge to Poland.[1] The issue ran deeper: in December 1938, Gamelin analyzed Hitler's cold war strategy—failure to stand up to Germany jeopardized France's role as a great power. He added:

> Along with France the whole of humanist civilization, the civilization of all the democratic powers, is on the line.
>
> . . .
>
> . . . only an intense military effort . . . can put us in a position . . . to deter war or . . . to win. But we are no longer talking about a rapid victory, but rather a long war of endurance in which the fate of the whole world, which will be progressively drawn in, will be determined.[2]

France was fed up with the constant insecurity and preferred to confront Germany. General Prételat, who would command the Second Army Group, found that among the reservists joining the colors the motto seemed to be "il faut en finir."[3] The British ambassador confirmed what Prételat said.[4] And a Gallup poll taken in France in June 1939 showed that 76 percent of the people questioned advocated the use of force to stop Germany from seizing Danzig.

But the Allies were critically weak in the air. Vuillemin credited the Allies with 3,800 first-line and 1,900 second-line aircraft against the German-

Italian totals of 6,500 and 6,000.[5] Nonetheless, French fighters were capable of defending the interior and of protecting observation planes over the army. The antiaircraft, the reconnaissance and observation units, and the bomber force were dangerously weak. But the Allied air forces should counterbalance the enemy air forces within six months. Vuillemin explained to an old comrade that German attacks on French communications would suffer such losses from his fighters that the enemy would have to give them up.[6]

Hitler struck at Poland on September 1, 1939. On September 2, Daladier asked Parliament to vote new defense credits; the Parliament understood that if last-minute negotiations failed, this meant war.[7] On September 3 France entered the fray.

Gamelin began calling up reservists on August 21; general mobilization began on September 1.[8] The infantry divisions of peacetime split themselves to encadre three divisions: an ''active'' division with one-third its original officers, two-thirds of its enlisted cadres and some 55 percent of its original enlisted men; a ''series A'' division with 23 percent active officers and 17 percent active NCO's but only 2 percent active enlisted; and a ''series B'' division with three officers in each regiment as its *total* active personnel—all the rest were reservists.[9] These formations were of unequal value, particularly reservist units from the time of the one year's service which formed the largest element of series B divisions.

While the mobilization shuffled millions of men, Gamelin assembled the senior commanders on the morning of September 3. The Allies had decided not to initiate strategic air war; Gamelin and his associates decided to withhold air action until the army was mobilized and then to limit it to support of the land offensive. Poland thus paid the price of its isolation. Vuillemin opposed an air offensive; Georges stated that only the army's advance guards could take offensive action for the moment. The commanders supported Gamelin's desire to hold off hostilities as long as possible so that further preparations could be made, but Daladier called: he had given in to British urging and fixed the expiration of the French ultimatum for 5:00 p.m. Gamelin met with Daladier briefly, then drove to Notre Dame to pray.[10]

His next destination was the cold and dark but majestic Château de Vincennes. Gamelin chose this location midway—geographically and morally—between the government in Paris and the GQG on the Marne River at La Ferté-sous-Jouarre. With him was a small cabinet led by his longtime assistant, Colonel Jean Petibon, and a staff with two sections: one dealing with national defense matters, the other with the army, for Gamelin was Chief of Staff of National Defense *and* Commander in Chief of the Army. He took a direct interest in the GQG and the northeastern front facing Germany; not a single important order went out without his approval.[11]

Gamelin's close supervision bore directly on Georges, who set up at the Château des Bondons at La Ferté with General Bineau as head of the GQG. The system soon functioned smoothly; Gamelin and Georges both seemed in fine form. Gamelin impressed the new Chief of the British Imperial General Staff, General Sir Edmund Ironside, as a "small, dapper little man with dyed hair,"[12] while a Swiss officer sent to coordinate contingency plans in case of German aggression remarked the monastic character of Gamelin's office while noting the General's tinted hair, his "soft" handshake, and the friendly but fleeting glance. This Swiss officer, visiting Georges, was immediately impressed. He found Georges large and imposing in his buttoned-up tunic, with the slightly Asiatic cast of his face, and his expression of benevolence, perhaps even of humor. He also noted the gloved left hand, hiding the wounds received at the assassination of King Alexander of Yugoslavia in 1934. The Bondons, with its château, gardens, and walkways, was pleasantly different from the austere Vincennes.[13] Georges himself was in a quandary. In late August he told Lieutenant Colonel Paul de Villelume, liaison officer between the Quai d'Orsay and GQG, that he regretted the decision to risk war for Poland. He did not feel he could take effective offensive action—he would resign if ordered to attack the *Westwall.* After Poland's collapse, however, Georges thought the war should go on; France would never get another chance to mobilize without interference from the Luftwaffe.

Meanwhile, the French air force also mobilized. On August 28 Mouchard activated his First Air Army in Paris, Houdemon took command of the Third Air Army at Aix-en-Provence, and General René Bouscat joined the Fifth Air Army at Algiers facing Italy. Vuillemin moved to Air Force General Headquarters at Saint-Jean les deux Jumeaux (near La Ferté) where he worked in collaboration with his old comrade, General J. Mendigal. The position of Mendigal vis-à-vis Vuillemin was similar to that of Petibon vis-à-vis Gamelin:[14] both were old subordinates and comrades from World War I.

The French forces assembled following prewar directives. Georges' directive of July 24, 1939,[15] to Prételat specified offensive operations that the Second Army Group would execute. Following reconnaissances and advance guard operations, Prételat was to attack with his Third, Fourth, and Fifth Armies between the Vosges Mountains and the northeastern corner of France, beginning the twelfth day after calling up the cover force. Having reached the Westwall, he was to regroup and prepare to break through the fortifications. The air forces would cover the action and provide direct support. He was to conserve the ground won, eventually by fortifying it.[16]

Vuillemin reminded his units that civilian targets were strictly off limits.[17] At the same time, Gamelin wrote to Daladier stating his strategic views for the record. He felt that the neutrality of Spain and especially Italy left France sufficient forces for a campaign into Belgium which would secure air bases near the Ruhr and push the Allied front to the Albert Canal and Liège, perhaps even into the Ardennes. Gamelin did not have to decide to concentrate east or west of the Moselle River until September 5; the Maginot Line and Prételat's forces offered ample security in Lorraine. But this push into Belgium was impossible, and Gamelin knew it. Belgium mobilized and its initial dispositions were directed against *France*, not Germany; politically, France could not risk an invasion.

Italian neutrality deprived Gamelin of his last chance for a decisive initial offensive. Gamelin held Billotte in Paris rather than have him waste time in the southeast. The only opportunity for action lay in the northeast; Gamelin pressed Georges to aid the desperate Poles.[18] Caught in mid-mobilization, inferior in heavy weapons, and following an unrealistic strategy, Polish resistance was compromised in the first days of the war, although Polish units continued to fight bravely.

Vuillemin decided on September 4 that France would not commence offensive bombing until the enemy took that initiative, unless the situation on the ground required it. That same day Ironside came to Paris. He found Gamelin delighted at having so far completed his concentration without enemy air attacks; Gamelin hoped to reach the Westwall from Luxemburg to northeastern France by September 17. After that he could "try his experiments upon the line."[19]

Meanwhile the concentration on the northeastern front required some 5,200 trains plus 870 vehicle (road) trains; several hundred thousand civilians were evacuated from border regions and 300,000 from Paris. By September 25, France mobilized eight armies, nineteen corps, and five fortified regions in the northeast. These included fifty-three infantry divisions, twenty-two fortified sectors, two DLM's, two armored brigades—cores of the DCR's—three cavalry divisions, and five territorial divisions to keep order. The southeastern front received one army and three corps with ten infantry divisions, three fortified sectors, one cavalry brigade, and one territorial division. General reserves included forty tank battalions: twenty-eight of infantry support tanks, one of D2 and three of B tanks, and seven more in North Africa and the Levant. The High Command formed two armored brigades at mobilization, each receiving, in principle, two battalions of B tanks and one of mechanized infantry.[20]

Meanwhile the war in Poland ran its course—not at all as Gamelin had expected. Gamelin had explained to Armengaud before the latter left for Warsaw in late August that he hoped to build a permanent eastern front to tie down German strength. Rumania, possibly Yugoslavia, Greece, and Turkey might enter the war supported by a French expeditionary force based initially in the Levant. Gamelin called General Weygand from retirement to command this expeditionary force. This front could be supplied through the eastern Mediterranean, provided Italy remained neutral. But first Poland had to survive. Poland would be in a critical position until Gamelin could take effective action in the west and that would take several months. Gamelin asked Armengaud to serve as technical counselor and to give moral support to the Poles in the meantime. France could do little until the army completed its concentration.[21] But something had to be done to keep Poland in the war.

Georges drove to Prételat's headquarters on September 4 to pass on Gamelin's demand for quick action.[22] Using the 9th, 15th, and 25th Motorized Infantry Divisions, Prételat could advance the schedule forty-eight hours by limiting the area of attack. His Fourth and Fifth Armies began to move forward between the Moselle River and the Vosges Mountains from September 7; by September 11 they were meeting resistance and suffering from booby traps in the wooded terrain. On September 10 the enemy counterattacked with armored support. Prételat ordered the Fourth and Fifth Armies to retake the lost ground and engaged his Third Army with the 12th Motorized Infantry and the 2nd Armored Brigade in the Saar. It made some progress, but Prételat felt he could push no further without reinforcements which were not yet available. Georges granted him two tank battalions but could do no more; Prételat postponed further operations by the Third Army on September 11.

On September 12 the Allied Supreme Council met in Abbeville; Chamberlain urged Daladier and Gamelin to take no further action to help Poland: it was a lost cause.[23] Gamelin told Georges to halt the offensive, although the Fourth Army could consolidate its positions. Georges ordered Prételat to halt, to prepare reserve units to replace active troops, and to defend the conquered ground in depth. The whole operation cost France fewer than 500 dead and 3,000 wounded. But the offensive was a failure: French intelligence had identified twenty-five German divisions in the west on September 6, and only forty or so on September 12. The Polish collapse was too rapid, French mobilization inevitably too slow. Gamelin later maintained that since only a third of his troops were in place by September 12, it would have been folly to attack the Westwall while the enemy was free to turn his flank in Belgium.

The Polish campaign touched off a storm, the experts seeking to discern the lessons of the Polish debacle. Georges characterized the German system on September 9 as based on the assault of armored divisions with a powerful array of antiaircraft; he underscored the "primordial role" played by the air forces which disorganized the Polish rear. French troops must not allow themselves to be surprised by air attacks; security must be strictly observed—especially the use of automatic weapons and eventually field artillery to ward off air attacks.[24] French military missions in Poland forwarded volumes of information. Armengaud sent back two reports in mid-September. He emphasized attacks by German medium bombers at low level, noting the moral effect they had on troops as well as communications, air units, and industries. In the exploitation of his breakthrough, he explained, the enemy formed corps (each with two armored and one motorized divisions) which drove thirty kilometers ahead of their supporting infantry. The German light divisions had been reinforced and were comparable now to Panzers. Finally, he described the breakthrough battles, emphasizing the massive air attacks preceding massed tank assaults. These tactics often crushed Polish resistance before the Poles even saw German infantry. In Armengaud's opinion, once the front was broken, the defeated troops could not maneuver in retreat—the Panzers were too fast.[25] Nothing in this was new to French intelligence, but the demonstration of German tactics was convincing.

On September 21, Gamelin presented his system to defeat the Blitzkrieg to Georges.[26] Gamelin felt that the number of troops on the front should be reduced to the minimum necessary to halt a surprise attack, especially on the Maginot Line; reserves should be placed to launch immediate counterattacks. Reservist formations should be used for the first mission while active divisions would form two echelons of reserves: a first of infantry near the front, a second echelon of motorized infantry, DLM's, and cavalry in the rear. The nature of the German system made it likely that there would be interpenetration of the opposing forces; it was vital that units that were cut off stand fast to stop German infantry seeking to follow the Panzers. Armored counterattacks would play a major role and all major units—no matter how far from the front—had to be ready for tank attacks at any instant.

Meanwhile the Armée de l'air began to feel the effectiveness of German fighters and Flak. Mouchard asked Vuillemin for directives on the observation units which, equipped with obsolete machines, were suffering heavily. Georges, Mouchard wrote, wanted him to prepare the intervention of French bombers in support of ground operations. Mouchard warned that such missions were impossible with the old planes in service: even with fighter escort his bombers were incapable of direct support or of attacking enemy columns on the battlefield. Mouchard appealed to Vuillemin for directives.[27] Mouchard knew there was nothing Vuillemin could do about the situation, but he wanted the responsibility fixed.

French intelligence kept informed on the Luftwaffe. A note on German airborne troops appeared in late September:[28] at the start of a campaign the enemy would use airborne troops to seize river crossings and other key passage points. Mouchard drew attention to the tactics the Luftwaffe used to destroy the Polish air force; he prescribed countermeasures—especially camouflage. In late October Allied intelligence finally cracked the settings of the now famous German code machine, *Enigma.* This proved a valuable, but not decisive, source, particularly on the dispositions of the Luftwaffe.

In early October it seemed that the enemy, reinforced with units returning from Poland, would take the offensive. Meeting with senior French and British commanders on October 6, Gamelin explained that the lesson to be learned from the Polish campaign was the penetrating power and speed of German Panzers working with the Luftwaffe.[29] Gamelin noted that the enemy might be able to penetrate French fortifications west of Longwy (on the Luxemburg frontier) which consisted merely of casemates and field works. However, bypassed posts were to hold firm to cut off the Panzers from their supporting units. With the Panzers thus halted, Gamelin would counterattack. His principal fear was the Luftwaffe: he appealed for British fighters, thereby raising a question that became more and more pressing as time passed. Shortly after the October 6 meeting, the GQG issued a note stressing that antitank defense must be deep and supple, interdicting likely zones of approach and taking advantage of potential strongpoints such as woods. It was important to make use of all weapons, particularly camouflaged 75's. General Georges Blanchard, commanding the First Army on the Belgian frontier, passed this note to his subordinates warning of the "imperious necessity" of antitank defense, even in the rear echelons of his army. Intelligence warned that German Flak was effective against ground targets in Poland, firing into the embrasures of fortifications and tackling tanks.[30]

On the whole, the French command understood the Blitzkrieg system. This information was disseminated in October 1939, although the French were not certain that the enemy would try these tactics in the west. French intelligence had accurate information on German dispositions down to July 1939; after that, however, it overestimated the number of German divisions and tank units.[31]

The Polish campaign did not lead the French command to despair: the Poles had been outgeneraled as well as overwhelmed by German superiority in equipment. Things would be different in the west. Gamelin explained to a group of ministers in the spring of 1940 that Panzers might well break through his front—but they would soon be cut off from their supply columns.[32] However, it is not so clear that the High Command grasped the shock effect of the German air and ground assault on untried reservists, particularly when these troops were thinly dispersed on the ground.

On the other side, the German infantry was shocked at the ineffectiveness of its antitank gun against French armor. German intelligence discovered that French weapons were effective even against the PzKpfw IV. But the same basic question haunted the French *and* Germans: would Blitzkrieg work in the west? Opinions in the Panzer arm divided sharply. Some Germans thought the French front too strong to be broken through—although once the front was broken, an armored exploitation might succeed.[33]

German mechanized and motorized units flowed west, fresh from their

Polish triumph. In mid-September the French High Command directed air reconnaissances to watch for these units— *"the real shock force of the Reich."*[34] By late September Georges expected an attack on the Saar front with a possible flanking action through Luxemburg and the Belgian Ardennes. This had been in Georges' mind from the moment he began his own offensive; he prescribed countermeasures to Prételat and to Generals Condé, commanding the Third Army facing the Saar, and Charles Huntziger, commanding the Second Army behind Luxemburg and Belgium facing the Ardennes. Prételat was to be prepared to face armored counterattacks with D2 and B tanks.[35] To parry a German counteroffensive through Luxemburg from the area of Trier, Georges ordered concentration, as mobilization progressed, of the 3rd Cavalry Division, the 2nd Armored Brigade, and the 12th and 25th Motorized Infantry Divisions. Ultimately the regrouping of the 1st DLM and the 1st, 3rd, and 5th Motorized Infantry originally sent to the Belgian frontier would permit Prételat to face any eventuality.

Georges shifted the boundaries of his Second and Third Armies, freeing the Third Army (save the 3rd Cavalry) of the maneuver to counter a thrust through Luxemburg and laying the intervention in Huntziger's lap.[36] In case of a German offensive into Luxemburg without violation of Belgian territory, Huntziger was to secure the city of Luxemburg and the Alzette River if possible. In any case, Huntziger was to cover the iron industry in Longwy, which lay in front of the Maginot Line. To accomplish this he would receive the 1st DLM and the 1st Spahi Brigade (North African cavalry). A second mobile echelon would hold the line attained; Georges promised the 5th Motorized, followed by further units as mobilization progressed.

As German reinforcements arrived, Vuillemin ordered a fighter group from the Third Air Army to Mouchard. Georges asked Mouchard to prepare air support for his planned Luxemburg maneuver; Mouchard asked his British liaison mission for assistance.[37] Mouchard detailed five fighter groups to cover Huntziger and planned to employ the old bombers of his 6th Air Division by night over the crossings of the Our and Sauer rivers; he requested British bombers to attack enemy columns by day. On September 26 Vuillemin gave Mouchard specific directives: French bombers would work by night, British by day, maintaining the effect of the demolitions being prepared in the Ardennes by the Belgian army. However, should the enemy break the French front, French bombers would join the British to slow the enemy at all cost.

The arrival of enemy armor made Gamelin and Georges more prudent. Both agreed to withhold their mechanized strength for counterattacks: Georges informed Huntziger on September 26 that the 1st DLM would remain in reserve.[38] In mid-October air reconnaissance and intelligence signaled an impending attack. Gamelin and Georges issued orders of the day. Georges restated the measures against air and tank threats: never retreat from an assigned position without a formal order; if bypassed by the enemy, continue to hold up the second wave of the attack; detain the enemy to favor the counterattack of reserves; use camouflage and dig in deeply to escape bombs and tanks.

Georges and the GQG restructured Allied forces to face German units that took positions on the Belgian and Dutch frontiers. Georges' initial dispositions left forty-nine major units and thirteen fortress units on the Saar front, with only twenty-two units facing Belgium, three facing Switzerland and seventeen in the southeast facing Italy.[39] In October the French rail system worked to capacity to reinforce the Belgian frontier and the central reserve. By November 1, twenty-seven units (requiring some 1,450 trains) had moved, leaving forty major units in the north, twenty-five in Lorraine, five facing Switzerland, and ten in central reserve, and bringing the first units of the British Expeditionary Force onto the Belgian frontier.

In the midst of these movements the German counterattack started in mid-October, but the enemy made no effort beyond retaking what the French had captured in September. Georges and Gamelin had already decided not to seriously contest this counterattack; action then dropped to a low level. But the threat of a German onslaught through Belgium continued to grow. At the end of September Gamelin installed the First Army Group under General Billotte on the Belgian frontier, leaving the Southeast Theater in the hands of General Antoine Besson commanding the Sixth Army. In early November Gamelin created the Third Army Group under Besson. Thus there were three army groups under Georges from north to south: the First under Billotte, the Second under Prételat holding Lorraine in contact with the enemy, the Third under Besson along the Rhine River and behind Switzerland. In early December Gamelin withdrew the Sixth Army under General Robert Touchon into central reserve to replace the Seventh Army which he moved onto the northern frontier, leaving a scratch Army of the Alps under General Olry to face Italy.[40]

Vuillemin also restructured his command. He agreed to Mouchard's request that the sector of the First Air Army be divided into two zones. On September 20 the Northern Zone of Air Operations under General François d'Astier de la Vigerie took over the sector from the North Sea to the west of Verdun; General Pennès took the zone running east from Verdun.[41] On October 24 Vuillemin switched Pennès to the Fifth Air Army, replacing him with General Têtu in the Eastern Zone. Each zone corresponded to an army group, preserving the principle of an air command subordinate to an army command for the same area: d'Astier to Billotte, Pennès then Têtu to Prételat.

Obviously d'Astier, commanding the Northern Zone, would play a key role. D'Astier was born at Mans in 1886 and joined the infantry in World War I. In 1916 he became a fighter pilot, shooting down five planes and being several times wounded. He served overseas and in North Africa, then rose through successive commands before taking charge of the Northern Zone.[42]

Finally, a new force arrived: the BEF. Command of the BEF went to Lord Gort, who left his position as Chief of the Imperial General Staff in Britain to General Ironside. Gort placed his 1st Corps of three infantry divisions on the Franco-Belgian frontier at Maulde on October 3, followed by General Bernard Montgomery's 3rd Division of the 2nd Corps on October 12.[43] These divisions had motorized transport, but were not true motorized units since they lacked transport for their infantry. Gort's force included two armored reconnaissance brigades, but these units were very light. He also commanded the Air Component of scout planes and fighters, but not the RAF's Advanced Air Striking Force of bombers in France.

While these shufflings took place, the northeast front sank into that unexpected state which Roland Dorgelès dubbed the *drôle de guerre:* the Twilight or Phoney War in Britain, the *Sitzkrieg* in Germany.[44] Germany's superior strength gave Hitler the initiative, but he was unable to launch his offensive until 1940. Until then there was nothing to do but prepare and wait.

NOTES

1. *Événements . . . Rapport* II, pp. 276ff.
2. Maurice Gamelin, *Servir* I (Paris: Plon, 1946), pp. 135-136.
3. "This time we've got to finish it."
4. Great Britain, Foreign Office, *Documents on British Foreign Policy 1919-1939* 3rd series, VII (London: H. M. S. O., 1949), p. 463; George H. Gallup, general ed., *The Gallup International Public Opinion Polls: France 1939, 1944-1975* I (Westport, Conn.: Greenwood Press, 1976), pp. 1-3; Anthony Adamthwaite, *France and the Coming of the Second World War 1936-1939* (London: Frank Cass, 1977), p. 316.
5. France, n°167 /EMGAA/S [sic], Letter from General Vuillemin to La Chambre (unpublished, August 26, 1939).
6. Robert Lemaignen, "Le Vuillemin que j'ai connu," *Icare* no. 59 (Spring 1971): 58.
7. Guy Rossi-Landi, *La Drôle de guerre: La Vie politique en France 2 septembre 1939-10 mai 1940* (Paris: Armand Colin, 1971), pp. 15ff.
8. Gamelin, *Servir* II, pp. 446-448.
9. General [Gaston] Prételat, *Le Destin tragique de la ligne Maginot* (Paris: Berger-Levrault, 1950), pp. 29ff.
10. Olivier Poydenot, "Vu du P. C. de Vincennes: Quelques aspects de la campagne 1939-1940," *Revue des deux mondes* (January 15, 1968): pp. 168ff; *Les Relations franco-britanniques: De 1935 à 1939. Communications présentées aux colloques franco-britanniques tenus à: Londres (Imperial War Museum) du 18 au 21 octobre 1971, Paris (Comité d'Histoire de la 2ème Guerre Mondiale) du 25 au 29 septembre 1972* (Paris: CNRS, 1975), pp. 116ff, 145, 380ff; Patrick Fridenson and Jean Lecuir, *La France et la Grande-Bretagne face aux problèmes aériens: (1935-mai 1940)* (Vincennes: CEDOCAR, 1976), p. 127.

11. Jacques Minart, *P. C. Vincennes: Secteur 4* I (Paris: Berger-Levrault, 1945), pp. 69ff; General G[aston] Roton, *Années cruciales: La Course aux armements (1933-1939). La Campagne (1939-1940)* (Paris: Charles-Lavauzelle, 1947), p. 119.

12. Sir Edmund Ironside, *Time Unguarded: The Ironside Diaries 1937-1940* (Edinburgh: Constable, 1962), p. 101.

13. Roton, *Années cruciales*, p. 64; Bernard Barbey, *Aller et retour: Mon journal pendant et après la drôle de guerre 1939-1940* (Neuchatel, Switzerland: Éditions de la baconnière, 1967), pp. 64ff; General Paul de Villelume, *Journal d'une défaite: Août 1939-Juin 1940* ([Paris]: Fayard, 1976), pp. 8, 12ff, 29, 48ff.

14. France, "Journal de marche et des opérations du GQGAé" (unpublished, August 28, 1939 to July 1940), p. 18 (hereafter cited as *JMO-GQGAé);* Lemaignen, "Vuillemin," p. 59; Minart, *P. C. Vincennes* I, p. 70.

15. France, Théâtre d'opérations du nord-est, EM, 3e Bureau, "Instruction personnelle et secrète pour le commandant du groupe d'armées en vue des opérations initiales à conduire éventuellement entre Rhin et Moselle" (unpublished, Paris, July 24, 1939).

16. France, TONE, EM, 3e Bureau, "Note annexe à l'IPS du général commandant le TONE pour le commandant du GA en vue des opérations initiales à conduire éventuellement entre Rhin et Moselle" (unpublished, Paris, August 7, 1939).

17. France, EM des forces aériennes, 3e Bureau, Opérations: N° 14 3.0.S./ EMGFA, "Instruction générale pour les généraux commandants d'armée aérienne" (unpublished, Paris, August 29, 1939); Gamelin, *Servir* III, pp. 15ff, 56.

18. Roton, *Années cruciales*, p. 65.

19. *JMO-GQGAé*, pp. 27ff; quote from Ironside, *Time Unguarded*, pp. 101ff.

20. *La Manoeuvre pour la bataille: Les Transports pendant la guerre 1939-1940* (Paris: Charles- Lavauzelle, 1941), pp. 10ff; Jean Vidalenc, *L'Exode de mai-juin 1940* (Paris: Presses universitaires de France, 1957); Minart, *P. C. Vincennes* I, pp. 44ff.

21. General [Paul] Armengaud, *Batailles politiques et militaires sur l'Europe: Témoignages (1923-1940)* (Paris: Éditions du Myrte, 1948), p. 96; *JMO-GQGAé*, pp. 31, 40.

22. Prételat, *Destin tragique*, pp. 55ff.

23. Roton, *Années cruciales*, pp. 68ff; Prételat, *Destin tragique*, p. 65; interview with [Maurice] Gamelin, *Résistance* (Paris) June 29, 1946; Villelume, *Journal d'une défaite*, p. 68; minutes of the September 12 meeting in ED, 3DA2, Dr 2, sdr a.

24. France, Armée G [sic], EM, 3e Bureau: N° 105/3. ["Note"] (unpublished, September 9, 1939).

25. Armengaud, *Batailles*, pp. 304ff.

26. Gamelin, *Servir* I, pp. 245ff.

27. France, I° Armée aérienne, EM, 1° et 3° Bureau: N°1495/3/S, Letter from General Mouchard to General Vuillemin (unpublished; 2 QG, September 24, 1939).

28. France, Commandement en chef des forces aériennes, EM général, 2e Bureau: N° 213/2/AE/S/EMG, "Allemagne: Étude sommaire sur l'organisation et l'emploi des unités de parachutistes et d'infanterie de l'air" (unpublished, GQGA, September 24, 1939); Gustave Bertrand, *Enigma: ou la plus grande énigme de la guerre 1939-1945* ([Paris?]: Plon, 1973), pp. 76ff.

29. Ironside, *Time Unguarded*, pp. 116ff.

30. France, GQG, EMG, 3ème Bureau: N° 0486-3/FT, "Note au sujet de la

défense contre engins blindés" (unpublished, GQG, October 12, 1939); France, le Armée, EM, 3e Bureau: N° 424/3S, "Note de service" (unpublished, October 16, 1939); France, EMA, 5e Bureau: Section de recherches: N° 56/E, "C.R. [*Compte rendu*-Report] du 13 octobre 1939: Allemagne" (unpublished, October 13, 1939).

31. Dr. Gerd Brausch, "Sedan 1940: Deuxième Bureau und strategische Überraschung," *Militärgeschichtliche Mitteilungen* (no. 2 1967): 36, 86ff.

32. Charles Pomaret, *Le Dernier témoin: Fin d'une guerre, fin d'une république juin et juillet 1940* (Paris: Presses de la Cité, 1968), pp. 35ff.

33. General Ulrich Liss, *Westfront 1939-40: Erinnerungen des Feindarbeiters im O. K. H.* (Neckargemünd: Kurt Vowinckel Verlag, 1959), pp. 99ff; Graf J[ohann] A. Kielmansegg, *Panzer zwischen Warschau und Atlantik* (Berlin: Verlag "Die Wehrmacht," 1941), p. 87.

34. Quote from France, GQG, EM, 2ème Bureau: N° 43/2.NE, "Instruction particulière n° 2 pour la recherche des renseignements" (unpublished, September 17, 1939); France, GQG, EM, 2e et 3e Bureaux: N° 66/2/NE, "Instruction n° 3 pour la recherche du renseignement" (unpublished, September 27, 1939).

35. France, GQG, EM, 3e Bureau: N° 0111 3/NE, "Instruction particulière n° 9 au Général commandant le GA n° 2" (unpublished, GQG, September 10, 1939).

36. France, GQG, EM, 3° Bureau: N° 0110 3/NE, "Instruction particulière n° 8 pour les IIe et IIIe Armées" (unpublished, September 10, 1939).

37. France, 1° Armée aérienne, EM, 3° Bureau, "Note verbale pour la mission britannique n° 2" (unpublished, September 24, 1939); September 26, 1939, entry in *JMO-GQGAé*.

38. Commandant Pierre Lyet, *La Bataille de France: (Mai-juin 1940)* (Paris: Payot, 1947), p. 13; France, GQG, Le Général d'armée Georges commandant le TONE: N° 0484-3/NE, "Note pour les armées" (unpublished, October 15, 1939).

39. *La Manoeuvre pour la bataille*, pp. 19ff.

40. Roton, *Années cruciales*, pp. 80ff; France, ESG, École d'état-major, [Lt.-Col. P. Gendry] *La Guerre 1939-1940 sur le front occidental* (Paris: Société française de presse, 1947), pp. 21-25.

41. September 7 and October 24, 1939, entries in *JMO-GQGAé*; France, [GQGAé], "Ordres généraux et particuliers" (unpublished, September 4, 1939, to June 19, 1940), pp. 22ff.

42. General Martial Valin, "Le Général d'Astier de la Vigerie," *Forces aériennes françaises* (December 1956): 1307ff.

43. Lord John Gort, *Despatches* (London: H.M.S.O., 1941), pp. 5899ff; Major L. F. Ellis, *The War in France and Flanders 1939-1940* (London: H.M.S.O., 1953), pp. 11ff; Pierre Le Goyet, *Le Mystère Gamelin* (Paris: Presses de la Cité, 197[6]), p. 279.

44. On the *drôle de guerre* generally see Henri Michel, *La Drôle de guerre* ([Paris]: Hachette, 1971) and Marcel-Edmond Naegelen, *L'Attente sous les armes ou la drôle de guerre* (Paris: Martineau, [1970]).

chapter 5

THE ALL-OUT EFFORT

The armies stood on the French frontiers, waiting out the *drôle de guerre.* Patrol actions and a severe winter made life bleak. Each side sent out air reconnaissances, often accompanied by dogfights as fighters rose to the challenge. In General Prételat's Second Army Group a round of units entered and left the line, gaining a taste of battle. The infantry, spread out in isolated strongpoints, battled the cold and isolation as well as the enemy. But combat had a tonic effect on morale as mail samplings proved.[1]

The troops facing Luxemburg and Belgium missed the tang of action. Marcel Lerecouvreux was a reserve officer of what became the 2nd Light Cavalry Division, which alternated between the Second and Third Armies. Lerecouvreux's division hustled to Sedan on October 13, ready to execute Georges' maneuver. Nothing came of the maneuver, however, and his unit moved to the Chiers River where it stayed for the next seven months. Lerecouvreux was agreeably surprised at the spirit with which the troops pitched into the work of fortification. They received good intelligence reports on German tactics. His division trained with its tanks and cavalry in combined operations; courses given by the Second Army were good, but often were interrupted by alerts.[2]

Just west of Lerecouvreux, General C. Grandsard's 10th Corps, which occupied Sedan, was in the reverse condition. Almost exclusively reservist, Grandsard's troops were in poor physical condition and lacked training and equipment—including shoes![3] His air observation group could not operate in the presence of the enemy; when renovated the following spring it had three planes, of which only one was modern.

Grandsard had to fortify his front, on which little had been done in peacetime. He planned eighty-six demolitions and 60,000 antitank mines; in fact, his units planted only 1,200 mines in the Sedan sector. Grandsard ordered a defense in depth as doctrine prescribed. His siting of the defenses, however, provoked an argument with Huntziger, commanding the Second Army, who would not allow him to move his final line of resistance back to the heights dominating Sedan; thus the initial resistance would have to hold the enemy until reserves could garrison the heights. Grandsard emphasized antiaircraft defense, but there is no sign that he prepared his field artillery for an antiaircraft role. Despite complaints of laziness and lack of authority among the cadres, his units accomplished much on a front too wide for their numbers. In the spring General Billotte declared that they had obtained the best results of his whole army group.[4]

Grandsard also had to train his reservists. Only his senior officers were professionals; most of his reserve officers had lost touch with modern techniques and lacked authority. His enlisted men showed only traces of training amid general nonchalance—they apparently believed that Germany, unable to break the defenses of the West, would succumb to low morale and the ravages of blockade. Allied propaganda helped foster this delusion, against which Grandsard had to react. Only in March could two regiments go to camp for three weeks' training during which they maneuvered with artillery cadres and a few tanks. In April Grandsard ran an exercise to study the use of a DCR and two reserve divisions to counterattack enemy tanks on the plateau behind Sedan. He had difficulty with his reserve cadres—many had served in World War I—who clung to linear tactics. Grandsard felt that morale remained acceptable, but the life of his troops in isolated groups amid civilians hardly fostered the warrior spirit.[5]

His series B infantry divisions, the 55th and 71st, had low priority in equipment; they started the war with nine 25 mm antitank guns instead of the 104 required. They had only a few 75's on platforms instead of the prescribed 47 mm pieces, and were short of automatic weapons and artillery. Some of these deficiencies were made up, but they remained short of antitank armament.[6]

Gabriel Delaunay found a similar situation in the series B 61st Infantry Division. His unit was used for labor in the rear before moving to the Meuse River at Revin—north of Grandsard and in the neighboring Ninth Army created from the Ardennes Army Detachment in October 1939. Although arriving in frigid weather, the 61st got a warm welcome from the populace. It had to build fortifications: practically nothing had been done previously. Delaunay worked as a draftsman, and by late March work had begun. Generals Georges, Billotte, and André Corap, commanding the Ninth Army, came to inspect. The division commander explained the dispositions; Georges asked where the antitank casemates were to be. Delaunay's Colonel answered that none were planned. Taken aback, Georges replied,

"And why is that? Do you think the Germans incapable of crossing the Meuse with their tanks?"
"Oh, of course they could, sir."
"Well then!"
"It's just that we have no antitank guns."[7]

And the officer explained that the division had not a single piece. Corap reminded Georges that he had reported this. Georges told Corap he would settle the problem soon and ordered that every fifth casemate be built for an antitank gun. The 61st planned to complete its works on July 15. By May 10 the division still had no antitank guns at the regimental level.

To the northwest the First Army facing the Belgian plain boasted more active personnel and a higher priority. Major Narcisse Bourdon served in the 101st Fortress Division which manned the renovated works of the old fortress of Maubeuge and casemates set up to counter a mechanized surprise attack.[8] An antitank ditch covered the works, barbed wire and antitank mines doubled it; blockhouses protected the rear of the casemates. As infantry divisions developed fieldworks, the belt grew to resemble the German Westwall. More important was the bearing and equipment of the divisions superimposed on the fortified front. The 101st by itself held seventy kilometers—an impossible front for its five battalions and five garrison companies and 125 works—but the infantry divisions added 300 positions. Although a few old 37's still served as antitank pieces, Bourdon was confident of success as long as the infantry remained in place.

General Henri Aymes, commanding the 4th Corps of the First Army, would eventually see battle on the Belgian plain. Aymes commanded active units including a motorized division. He trained his well-equipped troops in antitank and antiaircraft tactics: he believed the enemy would follow Guderian's doctrine in the west. Aymes faced the Blitzkrieg with confidence.[9]

On the whole, series B units had difficulty obtaining equipment, training facilities, and the time off from digging necessary to become effective. Priority went to the more active units which would receive more difficult missions. None of the B divisions tasted combat in Lorraine. It was natural that the command should set priorities: the question was whether its choice was correct.

The air force faced different problems. Almost all units assigned to the front got some taste of combat. French bombers found no place in these battles, but some flew reconnaissances into Germany by night. French reconnaissance, observation, and fighter units were sorely tested. Guy Bougerol, a reserve officer, joined Reconnaissance Group 2/33 (Group 2 of the 33rd Wing) which included the famed writer Antoine de Saint-Exupéry. Group 2/33 served as the eyes of an air division and entered the war with thirteen modern Potez 637 and four old Potez 542 (BCR) aircraft.[10] Group 2/33 flew its first mission in September to Trier, searching for the attack Georges feared; Flak and German fighters soon took their toll. The long missions, often in frigid conditions at high altitude or at night, were hardly *drôle*.

French fighter pilots found that weapons froze at high altitude; pilots died of cold and lack of oxygen at high altitude, chasing reconnaissance aircraft.[11] The groups flying the Morane-Saulnier 406, which equipped most of France's fighter arm at the beginning of the war, were in the worst situation. Underpowered, the Morane was dangerously slow. Morane-equipped units developed a system of patrols at successive levels to protect themselves while escorting observation aircraft. But the speed of the Messerschmidt 109E which entered service during the winter was such that on one occasion the enemy brought down seven Moranes without loss.[12] Radio intercepts led Morane pilots to conclude that only the size of French fighter formations deterred the enemy. And French pilots noticed that German Flak was more effective than the French. The air activity gave pilots the chance to know each other, to prepare tactics and equipment for the decisive clash.

With the start of the war, Daladier instituted industrial mobilization, appointing Raoul Dautry (a railroad executive) Minister of Armaments. In late September Gamelin demanded production of mines—"primordial" for antitank defense—and tanks.[13] The antitank mines proved unexpectedly difficult to make in safe form. Nonetheless, enough were produced for those portions of the front that the High Command thought sensitive, particularly the "Gembloux gap." One immediate problem was the lack of submachine guns which the enemy used with effect in patrol actions. France had such a weapon, the M.A.S. 1938, intended for infantry cadres, but it was in short supply and orders had to be placed abroad; even so there were never enough of these guns.

More important were the heavy weapons, especially tanks. By May 10, 1940, General Gaston Roton figured that the army had some 2,300 light tanks (Renault and Hotchkiss), 410 SOMUA tanks, 320 B and 260 D tanks (the earlier D1 models were left in North Africa), plus 145 light combat vehicles in the cavalry.[14] A recent study counted 2,791 light vehicles (Renault, Hotchkiss and 100 FCM tanks) of which several battalions were not stationed on the northeastern front; 416 SOMUA and 384 B tanks; 864 cavalry machines; the D tanks; plus obsolete machines. Engineer General Molinié, who worked in the production program, listed a similar number. The armament of the Renault and Hotchkiss tanks varied: those with the 1938 model 37 mm gun were effective against German tanks. Molinié claimed that by May 10 some 500 vehicles had been so armed; General Louis Keller[15] claimed that only 90 such weapons were then in service, equipping tanks of platoon leaders of six battalions, presumably the battalions of the DCR's.[16]

By comparison, German forces in the west massed 2,574 tanks and 6 mechanized guns on May 10. Of these 523 were PzKpfw I's armed with machine guns only, 955 PzKpfw II's with an ineffective 20 mm cannon, 278 PzKpfw III's with a weak antitank gun, 278 PzKpfw IV's which were powerfully armed, and 334 Czech tanks with an effective Czech gun.

Germany also had 812 armored cars, but only a few had the 20 mm cannon, the rest only machine guns.[17] The preponderance of the French equipment is evident, without counting France's Allies. French tanks were better armed and armored than German, but most were less mobile and—with their one-man turrets—demanded more of their crews.

The motorization of the French army depended initially on requisitioned vehicles: of 300,000 vehicles only 30,000 were of military origin.[18] A serious production effort and imports from the United States and Italy rectified the situation. Lack of vehicles also hindered the German staff; some units in Poland lost 50 percent of their vehicles. Hitler pressed for an offensive in the west from early October 1939, but the German staff calculated that by November 10 it could muster only five Panzers, two light, and three motorized infantry divisions. Hitler had to postpone the attack; at the beginning of 1940 lack of motor vehicles remained a major problem with production filling perhaps half the requirement. Only Czech machines and the massing of petroleum reserves in April allowed Germany to mount an offensive; by May 8 German units lacked no more than 10 percent of their equipment.[19]

French industry failed in one area. By April 1940 there were still shortages of radios; production and reserves equaled less than half the requirements for larger sets, although the situation was better for smaller models.[20]

In November 1939, Gamelin approved a "Five Month Plan" for new units, proposing ten new infantry divisions, one new DLM and one DCR, several tank battalions, and the transformation of the three cavalry divisions into five "light cavalry divisions" by exchanging one of each division's two cavalry brigades for a light mechanized brigade—a minituare DLM.[21] The light cavalry division included a regiment of motorized cavalry and one of armor, although the latter had only one company of Hotchkiss combat vehicles. Manpower was essential for these new units. By March 1, 1940, there were 2,330,000 men in the armies in France (including 70,000 North Africans and 20,000 colonials) plus 150,000 in the air force and 180,000 in the navy. By June 1940, 146,000 colonials had left their home colony; 20,000 colonial laborers were in France. More than 2 million men were in service in the interior including 250,000 territorial troops on farms and 710,000 released to war industry. The release of these men affected morale in the field, but it was essential.

By May 1940 France had two new metropolitan infantry divisions; the 6th and 7th North African, and 1st and 2nd Polish Infantry Divisions (formed from refugees); five light cavalry divisions; the 3rd DLM, and the 1st, 2nd, and 3rd DCR's. As active operations began, the army was establishing two more infantry divisions, the 8th Colonial and 3rd Polish and a Czech Infantry Division, and a 4th DLM and 4th DCR.[22]

But what was to be done with the fortress troops, who included some 20 percent of the active French infantry?[23] These troops belonged in maneuver units. Prételat suggested replacing them in the fortresses with series B infantry. The problem was to make the switch without disrupting the units. Georges adopted Prételat's view and on December 24 ordered the change made by February 1, 1940. But in early February, Georges wrote to Prételat that because of "unanimous opposition" at the army group and field army levels and the threat of enemy action the transformation would take effect at command levels only. Prételat replied that he and his army commanders favored the original plan. Finally in April, months after the date originally set, the exchange began: Grandsard's series B divisions received several hundred men per regiment. But these elements were not in the units long enough to make much difference—the disorganization may have done more harm than good.[24]

A more important problem was the constitution of the DCR's. Industrial mobilization increased available equipment; still there was not enough to form a significant number of DCR's following the model specified in the 1939 manual. Nonetheless the Polish campaign persuaded the experts that these units had to form posthaste. Colonel Charles de Gaulle, the commander of the tanks of the Fifth Army, addressed a report to the High Command in January 1940,[25] demanding the formation of a mechanized corps according to his model; the present system, he claimed, simply used armor to support old style units.

In early December 1939 Billotte wrote to Georges: the Polish campaign demonstrated the use of mechanized divisions in audacious maneuvers; the enemy might attempt the same thing in the west once he broke through the Belgian defenses. Billotte credited the Germans with five Panzerdivisionen and perhaps 2,000 tanks. He added "It is vital for us . . . to parry the danger which menaces us, but also—and above all—to profit . . . in a domain in which we should, it seems, hold a certain superiority."[26] France then disposed of two DLM's and one DCR with 400 tanks, plus some forty battalions with 1,800 machines. France had technical and numerical, but not tactical, superiority since the German vehicles, unlike the French, were formed into divisions. Billotte concluded that the grouping of French tanks into three DLM's and three DCR's would give them superiority. But he underestimated the number of Panzers.

Georges discussed this reorganization with Billotte, Dufieux, and General Louis Keller in December; he agreed to the immediate constitution of two DCR's each with two battalions of B tanks, two battalions of the lighter Hotchkiss tanks—the largest number that production allowed—and a single battalion of mechanized infantry.[27] The resulting unit was weak in infantry and supporting arms, and lacked the weight and flexibility of the DCR of the 1939 manual; however, the B tanks made even this formation a threat to the larger and more balanced but lighter Panzers. The first two DCR's

Subscribe to War Bonds.
Photo Courtesy of S. H. A. A.

were formed in January 1940, the 3rd in March, and the 4th assembled on the battlefield on May 15. The 1st was under General Bruneau, the 2nd under the commander of the Armor School, General Bruché, known as an honest but uninspired leader—Bruché's executive officer, Colonel Jean Perré, a rival of de Gaulle, was expected to command the division when shooting started. The two DCR's, plus the 3rd formed in March, constituted the "1st Armored Group" commanded by General Keller and his deputy General Charles Delestraint in the Châlons area. It is not clear whether Georges intended to commit several DCR's in mass under Keller. Their use would depend on the course of the battle; the initiative lay with the enemy.

The DCR's trained to counterattack an enemy mechanized assault and to break through an enemy front.[28] The 3rd DCR began division-level training at the beginning of May; when Captain Pierre Billotte—General Gaston Billotte's son—took command of a company of B tanks in the division, its commander, General Brocard, asked him to use his connections to inform Georges that the 3rd DCR was not yet ready for action. Captain Billotte gained a poor impression of Brocard's fighting spirit. On May 10 the 3rd DCR lacked radios and armored logistics vehicles and was drained of material to fill out the 1st and 2nd DCR's which were slated for dispatch to the front. Finally, the problem of doctrine remained: only the higher command had access to the 1939 DCR manual, and the DCR's actually formed were less powerful and balanced. But the secrecy paid: German intelligence knew the location of the DCR's but practically nothing of their composition.

Gamelin meanwhile fought the increasing belief in France that the war would be won without battles, that the blockade would finish Hitler. Gamelin spread his message via an interview with Jules Romains on December 16, 1939. He warned that stabilization would give way to sudden action in which all forces would engage—an action in which the decision would be more rapid, the struggle more terrible, than people thought.[29] Gamelin concluded that the battle would come in May, almost certainly. Romains was struck by the calm confidence with which Gamelin delivered this prophecy.

The army continued to develop doctrine to face the threat. General Robert Touchon, commanding the Sixth (reserve) Army, issued a manual in January 1940 dealing with mechanized warfare and antitank defense.[30] Touchon underlined the idea of a deep defensive zone of strongpoints; command posts and artillery units were to be formed into closed strongpoints unless covered by the terrain. A text used at St.-Cyr portrayed a front with a zone of resistance five kilometers deep.

To deal with the threat of the Luftwaffe, Gamelin made his senior troubleshooter, General Joseph Doumenc, the Superior Commander of the Ground Antiaircraft Forces.[31] Doumenc called for maximum production of the 75 and 90 mm antiaircraft guns, the purchase of fifty-five batteries of similar weapons abroad, and the production of 350 batteries of 25 mm guns (3,000-3,500 tubes) for protection against low-level attacks. But the army competed with the air force for these last weapons; the latter demanded 2,100 to defend its bases. And the defense of the interior required guns too. When Doumenc yielded his post in January 1940 to General Bloch, the problem remained acute. The air force improvised defenses with light machine guns.[32]

By May 10, 1940, the DLM's and motorized divisions had at least one battery of light automatic cannon each, as did ten active infantry divisions, three North African divisions, and a colonial unit; five colonial units, two North African divisions, and three active infantry divisions received a battery during the first weeks of the battle.[33] France had a total of some 2,300 weapons against low-flying aircraft, some 1,200 with the armies, along with about 380 medium pieces. British forces in France added some 530 light guns. But Allied antiaircraft was inferior to German Flak, and the series B units again came in last in weapon provisions.

General Aubé pressed his superiors to obtain the radars ordered from Britain.[34] Only at the end of March 1940 could General Mendigal order the creation of a radar service. In May 1940 there were six radar stations from Calais to Le Cateau manned by the French air force. These stations were cumbersome, less effective over land than over water, and poorly placed for operations as they developed. In short, they apparently made little difference in the conduct of the battle.

Expansion remained the Armée de l'air's priority problem. The "Plan of 3,200 Aircraft" (for a first-line strength of 3,200) of the fall of 1939 called for 6,350 planes, including American machines.[35] Scheduled for delivery by May 1940 were 700 Dewoitine 520, 770 Bloch 152, and 210 Arsenal fighters; 1,400 Potez 63-II, 200 Amiot 351, 56 Bloch 174, and 170 Glenn Martin reconnaissance and observation aircraft; 814 Bloch 175 and 179 Breguet 696 light bombers; 322 Breguet 691 assault bombers; and 290 Amiot 352-354 and 805 Lioré-et-Olivier 451 medium bombers with heavy defensive armament including a cannon. Plan VI, approved in April 1940, eventually would have boosted the assault aviation to sixteen groups with eighteen planes and a six-plane reserve each. This force would have given the Armée de l'air a fine chance against the Luftwaffe—had the production schedule been met. In fact the air force received 2,815 new aircraft, first-line units getting 1,752. Nonetheless, from September 5 to December 1939, France and Britain outproduced Germany as shown in Table 2.[36] But Germany still had an advantage in first-line aircraft. The expansion of the French industry caused problems too, including the delivery of aircraft without vital auxiliary equipment. By May 1940, 150 planes were thus immobilized. Full-scale delivery of modern planes got under way just as operations started. Sixty-seven Dewoitine 520 fighters were delivered in April, four per day being produced in mid-May; but on May 10 only one fighter group with this machine was ready. One group fought the whole campaign of 1940 with Morane fighters, although it had been promised Arsenal fighters for six months.[37] Reconnaissance groups began to get the superb Bloch 174 in mid-March.

TABLE 2

	GERMANY	*FRANCE*	*GREAT BRITAIN*
Fighters	605	725	447
Bombers	871	129	1,072
Reconnaissance and observation planes	263	279	468
Totals	1,739	1,133	1,987

The Armée de l'air entered the war short of aircrew but more so of technical personnel. Although by the spring of 1940 there were enough to man the modern planes available (including refugee Czech and Polish pilots), the lack of personnel strained the flying crews: Vuillemin issued a warning on this on May 8, 1940, two days *before* all-out operations began in the west![38]

By May 10 the Armée de l'air had in first-line units 278 Morane, 98 Curtiss, and 130 Bloch 151-152 single seat fighters; 67 Potez 63 multiseat fighters; 257 Potez 63 and 24 Bloch 174 reconnaissance and observation machines; 54 Lioré-et-Olivier 451 and 10 Amiot 354 medium bombers; and 45 Breguet 691-693 assault bombers.[39] The navy mustered 10 Bloch 151 and 24 Potez 631 fighters, and 25 Vought 156F and 24 Loire-Nieuport 410 dive-bombers. Behind these forces other units were preparing, like the group equipped with the Dewoitine 520, to enter the line. The British contributed 416 of the RAF's 1,873 first-line aircraft, constituting the British Air Forces in France under Air Marshal Arthur Barratt, including the Air Component under Lord Gort with 64 fighters, 32 bombers, and 112 reconnaissance and Lysander observation planes; and the Advanced Air Striking Force with 32 fighters, 128 old Battle light bombers, and 32 Blenheim mediums. In Britain 112 mediums and 32 heavy bombers were on call. Finally, Belgium and the Netherlands had 301 warplanes in line on May 10; only a few were modern, including 11 Hurricanes and perhaps the 13 Battles and 24 Fiat CR42 biplane fighters of the Belgian air service, and the 26 Fokker G1-A multiseat fighters of the Dutch air service. The Dutch also had 12 older medium bombers and 44 older single seat fighters ready for action.

On May 10 the Luftwaffe arrayed Air Fleets Two and Three with some 3,500 aircraft: 850 Messerschmidt 109E single seat and 200 Messerschmidt 110C multiseat fighters; 280 Junkers, 87 *Stuka* dive and 1,100 medium bombers (Heinkel 111, Dornier 17, and Junkers 88); and 42 Henschel 123 assault biplanes. The Luftwaffe also had 591 Dorniers and old, slow Henschel 126's for reconnaissance and observation.[40] Against this more homogeneous force, under a single command, and possessing the initiative, the Allied total (modern aircraft on the Continent only) of some 635 single seat and 100 multiseat fighters, 443 reconnaissance and observation machines, 49 dive and 45 assault bombers, and 414 medium bombers stood at a serious disadvantage, further handicapped by a divided command. The determination of the RAF to hold the bulk of its strength—including its Spitfire fighters—in Britain created a serious strain.

Meanwhile, Vuillemin adapted his forces and doctrine to operations. The situation was bad in the observation groups. Only about half of these units had Mureaux 115 and 117 aircraft; the rest had completely obsolete planes.[41] Plan V specified the replacement of these planes with the Potez 63-II by April 1941; none of these had reached service when war broke out. Vuillemin had to order observation groups not to cross the front lines. The reconnaissance groups were better off, beginning the war with four groups with modern aircraft. In December 1939 Vuillemin planned fifteen reconnaissance groups with modern equipment to be ready by the end of April 1940. But on May 10 they numbered fourteen and some still lacked part of their equipment

From early September 1939 French observation aircraft ran into strong enemy opposition.[42] By the middle of October only strong fighter escort—in violation of doctrine—could guarantee observation missions; the reconnaissance groups had to take over the burden of observation flights. This largely deprived the army of the local scouting and artillery direction it counted on: Gamelin demanded that the problem be resolved.

Vuillemin diverted production of Potez 631 fighters to Potez 63-II observation aircraft and added some Glenn Martin light bombers to the reconnaissance units. By March 1940 he hoped to have seven observation groups with nine Potez each and thirty-one groups with six each plus 150 Mureaux for the remaining units. By July 1 he hoped to have thirty-eight observation groups with nine Potez and eleven with three each. But he refused Gamelin's proposal to draw nine fighter groups from the defense of the interior to escort observation planes.[43] By May 10, thirty-five observation groups each had six Potez aircraft, but lack of parts and equipment kept the proportion ready for action low. And the diversion of effort slowed the training of night fighter and assault bomber crews.

Vuillemin pressed ahead nonetheless with the assault aviation. At mobilization only a single squadron was ready, and it was still equipped with old aircraft. In early December Vuillemin ordered General Girier's 6th Air Brigade to the Midi for transformation to an assault brigade; the 54th and 51st Wings and then Group 2/35 (Group 2 of the 35th Wing) began their transformation in March 1940. Assault units trained on the Potez 633 and received the Breguet 693—a fast, armored plane equipped to attack at low level with bombs, machine gun, and cannon fire—for operations.[44]

That spring the unit divided into Groupments 18 and 19 and the whole force passed to General Gama's 11th Air Division, intended eventually to form an assault division.[45] In mid-April Air Force General Headquarters announced that two assault groups would be ready from April 25, and three bomber groups with Lioré 451 bombers from April 20. From May 1, four groups with Glenn Martin bombers would enter service, one per week. General d'Astier was to use these to support the ground battle; all operations would require fighter cover, contrary to prewar doctrine. But of the assault aviation, on May 10 only Groupment 18 was operational.

Vuillemin renovated his bomber force, almost all of which started the war with aircraft fit for night operations only. In December 1939 Vuillemin withdrew his bomber units, except those flying the sturdy Amiot 143 and the Farman 222 four-engine night bombers, sending them to train and convert to modern equipment.[46]

The problem of attacking mobile ground targets received particular attention in the 1940 bomber manual.[47] It suggested the use of a guide plane to keep contact with the target (this proved difficult in the presence of German fighters) and the development of liaison between reconnaissance planes and bomber formations on their bases—a process employed with success. Assault attacks were to be made at very low level with three-plane formations to preserve surprise, using a guide aircraft when possible. Only when the enemy was disorganized could large formations of assault bombers work in a single sector. Meanwhile the Cazaux Experimental Center developed a "semi-dive bombing" mode for the assault planes.[48]

Fighter doctrine changed too. Each fighter group had several Potez 631 multiseat fighters as "command" planes; these proved ineffective and were suppressed.[49] But the fighters perfected radio-controlled interception techniques. French air doctrine by May 10, 1940, gave serious consideration to all the technical and material problems it would face in operations against the Luftwaffe.

Part of the solution lay in British aid. Unfortunately the RAF refused to compromise its vision of strategic air war. In July 1939 the RAF agreed that the Air Component of the BEF would include one, ultimately three, fighter squadrons and some antiaircraft guns. This did not satisfy the French command. On September 20, Gamelin and Daladier met with British officials and pressed for reinforcements and cooperation in attacking German columns from the air if the enemy began his expected assault in the west. Daladier and Gamelin repeated their plea at the Allied Supreme Council meeting of September 22. They had the support of General Sir Henry Pownall, Chief of Staff of the BEF in this request. On September 23, Vuillemin met the British Chief of Air Staff, Air Marshal Sir Cyril Newall, who announced that he was temporarily holding the Blenheim medium bombers of the Advanced Air Striking Force on British bases, where they would be safer and would be at hand in case of air assault on the British Isles. On September 24, Gamelin put his request for British fighters and antiaircraft in writing; on September 27 French members of the Inter-allied Study Committee asked for ten British fighter squadrons to be stationed in France. Air Vice-Marshal Evill riposted by claiming that the 1,500 German bombers might turn on Britain first. Great Britain, he claimed, could do no more: the French would have to be satisfied with what the RAF had already promised. From its arrival in France in October 1939 the British Air Component had four fighter squadrons, although two of these went to the Advanced Air Striking Force, the Air Component receiving two squadrons of Gladiator biplanes in compensation.[50]

This certainly did not satisfy the French command. In early October General Armengaud, back from Poland, visited Vuillemin and Gamelin. Learning of the meagerness of British air support, he warned of the risk of a Polish style defeat. Vuillemin agreed but concluded there was nothing he could do. Gamelin, however, decided to send Armengaud to London to persuade the British to send more planes once the German attack began. Armengaud objected—the planes had to be in place prior to the start of operations. Gamelin simply replied that he would prepare Armengaud's orders for the trip to England.

Armengaud took it upon himself to contact the Premier. Daladier was impressed and told Armengaud he would have the support of the French ambassador in London—if the British did not send reinforcements he, Daladier, would make peace![51] Daladier had written to Chamberlain on October 1, asking that in view of the imminent battle the whole British fighter force participate. Chamberlain replied on October 3 that if a great enemy offensive began, the whole RAF would be brought forth at the decisive moment. This vague promise did not satisfy Daladier, hence his strong support for Armengaud's intervention with the British. With the threat of a German offensive looming, the strains underlying Allied unity were already beginning to show. In London Armengaud met the Chief of the Air Staff, Air Marshal Sir Cyril Newall. Newall accepted the principle of reinforcement only *after* a German offensive; there the discussion stuck. Following this meeting, Chamberlain sent his military chiefs to Gamelin to settle the matter; Armengaud's demands for a further 190 fighters and as many bombers as possible rested in suspense.

On October 8 Gamelin held conference with the British, promising

Armengaud to adopt a hard line. Charged with keeping Daladier informed, Armengaud passed a message to Gamelin to report to the Premier following his meeting. Gamelin snapped back that this was a military matter; he was satisfied with the results obtained. Daladier accepted Gamelin's assurance, but Armengaud pressed the matter further; the meeting with the British chiefs should close in Daladier's office. Gamelin was furious at this "interference" and passed word to Daladier's executive assistant that he was fully satisfied with the British participation.[52] Gamelin was the Allied Commander on the Continent, the successor to Foch. In his own way, by tact and persuasion, he would hold the Allies together and wheedle the planes from the British (without Armengaud's interference). In any case, by May 10 Britain was committed to sending a further four fighter squadrons to France when active operations began, bringing the total there to 160 fighters, 160 light and medium bombers, 60 reconnaissance machines, and 60 scout planes.

This was only a minor fraction of the RAF. Nonetheless coordination was established between the air forces on January 15, 1940, when Air Marshal Barratt and his British Air Forces in France took command of Gort's Air Component and the Advanced Air Striking Force.[53] Setting up near the GQG, Barratt was charged with coordinating his forces plus conducting missions that RAF Bomber Command would send over in support of the northeastern front.

Gamelin was also dissatisfied with the British land effort. Initial British plans called for only thirty-two divisions. Gamelin demanded a greater effort from a nation with more population and industry than France.[54] Finally, the planned British total was limited to fifty-five divisions, including forces from the Commonwealth and Empire. In November 1939 General Ironside promised the British 1st Armoured Division for the following March. It would have 300 tanks, two-thirds fast and well-armed although lightly armored cruisers.[55] But the buildup of the 1st Armoured proved slower than foreseen. At the end of April 1940 the first unit of the division was scheduled to move to France on May 13 (after active operations began). The French complained about the British effort in the Allied Supreme Council meeting in Paris on December 19, 1939; the British insisted they were doing all they could and refused to reduce the level of arms in their units to get more over to France.

Gort was unhappy about going into action without an armored division and a complete heavy tank brigade.[56] However, he did obtain the 3rd Corps with its Territorial divisions in March 1940; nine of his brigades saw combat on the Lorraine front. The 3rd Corps included General Giffard Martel's 50th Motorized Infantry Division, a welcome maneuver element. From November 1939, twelve companies of engineers came over to develop fortifications; in April 1940 the 12th, 23rd, and 46th Territorial divisions, although only partially equipped, came over to train while serving as labor.

But when the attack came on May 10, the BEF had only nine infantry divisions plus one in the Saar and the tank brigade with a single company of heavy tanks. The three Territorial divisions could be used in an emergency; the 1st Armoured Division[57] was about to move—still, this was a small and motley force for a great power to field in the ninth month of a total war! The British contribution was out of all proportion to the political and material weight of the British Empire and Commonwealth.

Despite these problems, the Allies achieved a high level of strength, principally because of French efforts. The French nation in arms had prepared itself for mechanized war. The army and air force—particularly the latter—continued to lag behind their German rivals in strength, but both had much modern material and had adapted themselves to use that material. On a unit for unit basis, the French army was more modern than the larger Wehrmacht. But Maurice Gamelin knew that more than numbers would be necessary.

NOTES

1. General [Gaston] Prételat, *Le Destin tragique de la ligne Maginot* (Paris: Berger-Levrault, 1950), p. 940.

2. Marcel Lerecouvreux, *Huit mois d'attente, un mois de guerre: (Extraits)* (Paris: Charles-Lavauzelle, 1946), 44ff, 101ff.

3. General C. Grandsard, *Le 10e Corps d'armée dans la bataille 1939-1940: Sedan-Amiens-De la Seine à la Dordogne* (Paris: Berger-Levrault, 1949), pp. 3ff.

4. Ibid., pp. 13ff, 20, 41, 50ff.

5. Ibid., pp. 24ff, 38, 58ff.

6. Ibid., pp. 26ff, 62ff; France, Ministère des armées, EMAT, Service historique, *Guerre, 1939-1945: Les Grandes unités françaises: Historiques succincts* II (Paris: Atelier d'impressions de l'armée, 1967), pp. 635, 815 (hereafter cited as *GU françaises*).

7. Quote from Gabriel Delaunay, "La Drôle de guerre sur la Meuse: Janvier-mai 1940," *Histoire de notre temps* no. 4 (Winter 1965): 118ff; *GU françaises* II, p. 699.

8. Cdt. N[arcisse] Bourdon, *Le Second drame de Maubeuge: Histoire de la 101e Division de forteresse (84e et 87e R.I.F.)* (Fontenay-le-Comte: Imprimerie Lussaud frères, 1947), pp. 14ff, 47ff.

9. General Henri Aymes, *Gembloux: Succès français. Le 4e Corps d'armée dans la bataille de la 1re armée en Belgique et en France 10 mai-3 juin 1940* (Paris: Berger-Levrault, 1948), pp. 3ff.

10. R. P. Guy Bougerol, *Ceux qu'on n'a jamais vus . . .* [sic] (Grenoble and Paris: Arthaud, 1943), pp. 25, 34ff.

11. Capt. [Jean] Accart, *Chasseurs du ciel: Historique de la première escadrille du groupe de chasse I/5* (Grenoble and Paris: Arthaud, 1941), p. 53; Col. Pierre Boillot, "Viewed from the Cockpit," *Air Enthusiast* 5, no. 4 (September 1973).

12. Capt. [Robert] Williame, *L'Escadrille des cigognes—Spa 3—1939-1940* (Grenoble and Paris: Arthaud, 1945), pp. 145, 157.

13. France, Présidence du Conseil, Section d'EM: N° 129 3/EM DN, Letter from General Gamelin to the Premier (unpublished, September 29, 1939); Capt. René Pichené, *Les Pistolets et pistolets-mitrailleurs français et étrangers (Historique sommaire des armes)* (Paris: Charles-Lavauzelle, 1952), pp. 97ff. On mines, see deposition of Colonel Jacques Humbert, Chief of Staff of GA1, before the Riom tribunal in ED, 4DA22, Dr 4, sdr e.

14. General G[aston] Roton, *Années cruciales: La Course aux armements (1933-1939). La Campagne (1939-1940)* (Paris: Charles-Lavauzelle, 1947), pp. 46ff; Peter Chamberlain and Chris Ellis, *Pictorial History of Tanks of the World 1915-45* (Harrisburg, Pennsylvania: Stackpole, 1972), pp. 24ff; Molinié, "Les Matériels blindés," pp. 859ff; beautiful illustrations, data in Pierre Touzin [et al.], *Les Engins blindés français 1920-1945. Volume I* (Paris: SERA, 1976).

15. The Inspector General of the Tanks in 1940, not to be confused with the Chief of the Air Force Staff in 1939.

16. Testimony of General Louis Keller at Riom in James de Coquet, *Le Procès de Riom* (Paris: Fayard, 1945), p. 265.

17. Hans-Adolf Jacobsen, *Fall Gelb: Der Kampf um den deutschen Operationsplan zur Westoffensive 1940* (Wiesbaden: Steiner Verlag, 1957), pp. 197ff; Molinié, "Les Matériels blindés," p. 861.

18. *La Manoeuve pour la bataille: Les Transports pendant la guerre 1939-1940* (Paris: Charles-Lavauzelle, 1941), pp. 27ff; Col. Philibert, "Les Arrières dans l'attente (De fin septembre 1939 à début mai 1940)," *Revue historique des armées* 1ère année (no. 4 1974): 94.

19. Jacobsen, *Fall Gelb*, pp. 192ff.

20. Philibert, "Les Arrières," pp. 101ff.

21. Gamelin *Servir* III, pp. 240ff; Minart, *P. C. Vincennes* II, p. 53; *GU françaises* III, pp. 313ff; Bührer, *Aux heures tragiques*, pp. 109-110.

22. Gamelin, *Servir* III, pp. 243ff.

23. Liss, *Westfront*, p. 30.

24. Ibid., p. 30; Prételat, *Destin tragique*, pp. 113ff; Grandsard, *10e Corps*, p. 63.

25. Charles de Gaulle, *Trois études: Suivies du mémorandum du 26 janvier 1940* (Paris: Berger-Levrault, 1945), pp. 168ff.

26. Quote from Billotte's note in Col. P[ierre] Lyet, "Témoignages et documents 1939-1940," *Revue historique de l'armée* (no. 1 1960): pp. 147ff; de Coquet, *Riom*, p. 262.

27. Roton, *Années cruciales*, pp. 86-87; testimony of General Bruché, commander of the 2nd DCR, in *Événements . . . Témoignages* V, pp. 1214ff; *GU françaises* I, pp. 690ff, and III, pp. 457ff; Jean-François Perrette, *Propos autour d'un général "NN": Charles Delestraint. Officier de chars. Commandant de l'armée secrète* ([Evreux]: Presses de la Cité, 1972), p. 75.

28. Bruché's testimony in *Événements . . . Témoignages* V, pp. 1214ff; General Pierre Billotte, *Le Temps des armes* ([Paris]: Plon, 1972), pp. 32ff; testimony of General Devaux, Chief of Staff of the 3rd DCR, in *Événements . . . Témoignages* V, pp. 1330ff; testimony of Col. Jean Perré in de Coquet, *Riom*, p. 289; Liss, *Westfront*, pp. 129ff.

29. Jules Romains, *Sept mystères du destin de l'Europe* (New York: Éditions de la maison française, 1940), pp. 80 passim.

30. France, Armée de terre, VIe Armée, EM, 3e Bureau: N° 260 3/S, *Note au sujet du combat avec chars* (no place or publisher given, January 31, 1940), pp. 3ff; France, École spéciale militaire, *Cours d'emploi des armes, Tome I. 2e Année. 1939-1940* (Saint-Cyr: Imprimerie de l'école spéciale militaire, no date given), pp. 24ff, 48; France, Commandement en chef des forces aériennes, EM général, 2e Bureau: N° 1303/2/EMG-AE/RS, "Renseignements sur les divisions mécanisées et motorisées allemandes" (unpublished, April 1, 1940).

31. France, GQG, Le Commandant en chef des forces terrestres: 49/ Cab., Letter from Gamelin to Daladier (unpublished, September 10, 1939); France, Commandement en chef des forces aériennes, EMG, 3e Bureau: N° 346-3/O.S./EMG, Letter from the 3rd Bureau of the EM of the Air Force to the 3rd Bureau of the EM of the DAT (unpublished, September 28, 1939).

32. France, MA, EMAA, 3e Bureau: N° 500-3/4/EMAA/S, "Instruction sur la défense aérienne à basse altitude des bases aériennes et des usines de l'intérieur (autodéfense active)" (unpublished, Paris, March 16, 1940).

33. France, "Extraits du rapport du Général Georges sur les opérations du 10 mai au 24 juin" (unpublished, no date given), annexes; Raymond Danel, "En Mai Juin 1940: *Ils* étaient les plus forts," *Icare* no. 54 (Summer 1970): 51.

34. France, Commandement en chef des forces aériennes, DAT: N° 61/IDAé/1/S, Letter from Aubé to Vuillemin (unpublished, GQGA, September 14, 1939); September 20, 1939 entry in *JMO-GQGAé*; France, Commandement en chef des forces aériennes, EMG, 3° Bureau: N° 2179 3/0 2.S./EMG, "Instruction sur le commandement du Guet de l'air" (unpublished, GQGA, March 30, 1940); France, Commandement en chef des forces aériennes, EMG, 1er Bureau: N° 2389 1/O-RS/EMG, Letter from Vuillemin to La Chambre (unpublished, May 21, 1940); *Relations franco-britanniques*, pp. 364ff; Fridenson and Lecuir, *France et Grande-Bretagne*, pp. 169ff.

35. France, [EMAA], "Plan des 3.200 avions" (unpublished, [October 1939?]); Danel, "Drôle de guerre . . . Pas pour l'aviation."

36. Roos, "Bataille de la production," p. 52; Danel, "Drôle de guerre . . . Pas pour l'aviation," and "Historique du Dewoitine 520," pp. 48ff and "L'Aviation d'assaut en mai-juin 1940: Gouttes d'eau sur un brasier," *Icare* no. 80 (Spring 1977): 14; slightly different figures in General [Charles] Christienne, "L'Industrie aéronautique française: De septembre 1939 à juin 1940," in France, SHAA, *Recueil d'articles et études: (1974-1975)* (Vincennes: [CEDOCAR], 1977), pp. 150-153.

37. Williame, *L'Escadrille des cigognes*, p. 191; Bougerol, *Ceux qu'on n'a jamais vus*, p. 58.

38. Christienne, "Industrie aéronautique," p. 150 and "L'Armée de l'air française de mars 1936 à septembre 1939" (as yet unpublished paper delivered at the Franco-German colloquium in Bonn, September 1978), pp. 20-21; P. Buffotot, "Le Moral dans l'armée de l'air française: De septembre 1939 à juin 1940," in France, SHAA, *Recueil d'articles et études*, pp. 170, 175-176; more optimistic interpretation in report on personnel attached to Vuillemin's deposition to the Riom tribunal in ED, 4DA23, Dr 3, sdr b; Williame, *L'Escadrille des cigognes*, p. 171.

39. Danel, "Drôle de guerre . . . Pas pour l'aviation," p. 82; Christian-Jacques Ehrengardt, "Bilan et chronologue de l'Aéronavale en guerre," *Icare* no. 61 (Autumn-Winter 1971): 56; Danel, "En Mai Juin . . .,'" pp. 50ff; higher French figures given

in Patrice Buffotot and Jacques Ogier, "L'Armée de l'air française dans la campagne de France (10 mai-25 juin 1940): Essai de bilan numérique d'une bataille aérienne," *Revue historique des armées* (no. 3 1975); "1939-40/La Bataille de France. Volume VII: L'Aéronautique militaire belge. Première partie," *Icare* no. 74 (Autumn 1975); Willy Coppens de Houthulst, "Les 18 jours de l'aviation belge: 10 mai 28 mai 1940," *Icare* no. 76 (Spring 1976): 66ff; Raymond Danel, "La Conquête de la Hollande: Opération secondaire?," *Icare* no. 79 (Winter 1976-1977): 22ff.

40. Danel, "En Mai Juin . . .," p. 50.

41. Lt.-Col. Pierre Paquier and Cdt. Crétin, *L'Aviation de renseignement française en 1939-1940* (Paris: Berger-Levrault, 1947), pp. 6ff, 12ff.

42. Ibid., pp. 62ff; France, Commandement en chef des forces aériennes, EMG, 3e Bureau: N° 2047 3/IS/EMG, Letter from Vuillemin to Gamelin (unpublished, December 21, 1939).

43. Paquier, *Aviation de renseignement*, p. 16 and both citations in previous note.

44. General Fleury Seive, *L'Aviation d'assaut dans la bataille de 1940* (Paris: Berger-Levrault, 1948), pp. 58ff; "1939-40/La Bataille de France. Volume X: L'Aviation d'assaut: La 51e escadre. Première partie," *Icare* no. 80 (Spring 1977).

45. Seive, *Aviation d'assaut*, pp. 80ff, 100ff; Particular Instruction of April 12, 1940 in France, SHAA, "Instructions générales et particulières" (unpublished, September 3, 1939 to August 29, 1940).

46. General Order No. 16 of December 4, 1939, in France, SHAA, "Ordres généraux et particuliers" (unpublished, September 4, 1939, to June 19, 1940.)

47. France, MA, EMAA, *Règlement de manoeuvre de l'armée de l'air: Livre II. Aviation de bombardement: Titre II. Instruction pratique: Première partie. Règles et procédés d'exécution des missions* (Paris: Imprimerie nationale, 1940), pp. 25ff, 91ff.

48. France, MA, Direction générale technique et industrielle, Centre d'essais n° 372, Cazaux (Gironde), "Étude BA-461: Bombardement en semipiqué sur avion Breguet 691 entre 1500 m. et 600 m." (unpublished, Cazaux, January 19, 1940).

49. Williame, *L'Escadrille des cigognes*, pp. 75ff; Henri Menjaud, *Un groupe de chasse au combat* (Grenoble: Arthaud, 1941), p. 32; General Pierre Bodet, "La Doctrine de l'armée de l'air," *Icare* no. 53 (Spring-Summer 1970): 63ff.

50. France, Commandement en chef des forces aériennes, EMG, 3e Bureau, "Projet de historique de la collaboration aérienne franco-britannique" (unpublished, GQGA, no date given), pp. 2ff; Armengaud, *Batailles*, pp. 160ff; documents and discussion in Fridenson and Lecuir, *France et Grande-Bretagne*, pp. 184ff; minutes of the meeting of September 20 between Daladier, Belisha, Gamelin, and Lord Hankey and minutes of the Supreme Council meeting of September 22 in ED, 3DA2, Dr 2, sdr b.

51. Armengaud, *Batailles*, pp. 166ff; Fridenson and Lecuir, *France et Grande-Bretagne*, pp. 187ff.

52. Armengaud, *Batailles*, p. 180; France, SHAA, "Historique succint [sic] des opérations aériennes sur le front du nord-est du 10 mai 1940 à l'armistice" (unpublished, no date), pp. 1ff.

53. Jean Lecuir and Patrick Fridenson, "L'Organisation de la coopération aérienne franco-britannique (1935-mai 1940)," *Revue d'histoire de la deuxième*

guerre mondiale no. 73 (January 1969): 69; France, SHAA, "Historique succint" pp. 1ff; Ellis, *War in France and Flanders*, p. 27.

54. James R. M. Butler, *Grand Strategy. Volume II: September 1939-June 1941* (London: H.M.S.O., 1957), p. 32; Ironside, *Time Unguarded*, p. 162.

55. General R. Evans, "The 1st Armoured Division in France," *Army Quarterly* 46, no. 1 (part 1 of 3 articles) (November 1942): 55ff; minutes of the December 19 Supreme Council meeting in ED, 3DA2, Dr 2, sdr d.

56. Gort, *Despatches*, pp. 5906ff; Ellis, *War in France and Flanders*, pp. 20ff; Brian Bond, *France and Belgium 1939-1940* (London: Davis-Poynter, 1975), p. 40.

57. Evans, "1st Armoured Division," p. 61.

chapter 6

A STRATEGY FOR VICTORY (OCTOBER 1939-MARCH 1940)

The Polish collapse left the Allies alone facing Germany; numerical superiority gave Hitler the initiative. Where would he strike? The defenses of the West declined in strength west of the Maginot Line: in this area—ideal for the Blitzkrieg—the Allies could not rely on fortifications. An initial defeat here would carry mortal danger: Paris lay only a few days' drive away. On the other side of Belgium lay the Ruhr. Caught in the middle, Belgium and the Netherlands strove to maintain their neutrality while preparing their defenses.

Maurice Gamelin plotted his maneuver into Belgium in late September 1939. Should the Germans attack, the Allies would await them on their frontier fortifications, except on their extreme left, where Gamelin intended to push to the Escaut River in southwestern Belgium. This strategy became known as the Escaut Plan. However, if the Belgian army could be supported before the enemy broke through, Gamelin might go farther provided he could avoid an encounter battle.[1] This prospect came up in Gamelin's interview with General Armengaud on October 3. Armengaud warned that a thrust into Belgium would be possible only until German forces regrouped in the west. After that, the maneuver would be contrary to the lessons of the Polish campaign.

Gamelin discussed Armengaud's warning with senior Allied officers on October 6. He was sure that the Germans would soon strike, perhaps via Switzerland or Belgium; the main attack must come in the north. This offensive might sweep the whole of Belgium, or wheel through Luxemburg and the Ardennes to outflank the Maginot Line, then push south.[2] Gamelin felt the Belgian plain was the more likely target because the Ardennes were poor tank country and there were strong French fortifications facing Luxemburg. Only on the plain could the enemy obtain a quick, decisive success. Gamelin expected the Germans to feint in the Saar, deliver a preliminary attack through Luxemburg and the Ardennes, and finally launch a mechanized and air assault through Holland and Belgium. Ironside argued that the enemy would make his main effort through the Ardennes and then along the Franco-Belgian frontier: could the Allies push forces into Belgium to attack the German spearhead from the north while reserves attacked from the south? Whatever the German attack plan, Gamelin claimed that if the Allies were beaten in France the war would be lost: he pressed Ironside for more British fighter planes. To Gamelin it was obvious that the danger lay in a German air-ground offensive; if France went under, what could Britain do alone against Hitler and his allies Mussolini and Stalin? But to the leaders of the RAF, the danger lay in strategic air war, which could be fatal to Britain *and* to France if essential fighters were lost supporting an indecisive ground battle.

Georges feared a holding attack on the Maginot Line, combined with the Ardennes flanking stroke and possibly a maneuver through Switzerland, threatening a double envelopment of the Maginot Line.[3] The First Army Group faced Belgium to meet the threat in the north; Georges concentrated on his center. He intended to hold the Maginot Line with minimal force, shifting strength to the wings of the fortified zone. He planned to halt the enemy on the Meuse River and the Montmédy bridgehead, disputing the advances with cover forces. Georges called for an aggressive defense: hinder the enemy approach by artillery and air attacks; near the main position, use woods and built-up localities as bases for armored raids to disorganize enemy preparations.

To execute his maneuver Georges counted on General Gaston Billotte, commander of Army Group One which included the Second Army behind the eastern Ardennes and Luxemburg, the Ardennes Army Detachment—soon the Ninth Army—behind the western Ardennes, and the First Army facing the Belgian plain. To Billotte's left, the BEF held the sector next to the First Army; the French Seventh Army, later stationed to the left of the BEF, completed the lineup to the sea. Georges wanted Billotte to throw mobile forces onto the Meuse from Namur in Belgium to Mézières in France to block a German advance through the Ardennes. But Billotte was to concentrate his forces on the sector of the Second Army which covered the western flank of the Saar. Using cavalry to retard the enemy, he was to conduct operations with economy so that when circumstances permitted he could counterattack from the Belgian Meuse. Georges promised Billotte two divisions for the Second Army, two or three (one motorized) for the Ardennes Army Detachment, and from one to eight for the First Army including three motorized divisions and one or two DLM's. The First Army would move to Namur to block the enemy in the Ardennes. But the German attack, when it came in mid-October, was limited to the Saar.

Actually, Hitler was eager to take Holland and Belgium to protect the Ruhr, to conquer economic resources and bases for a long war, and to

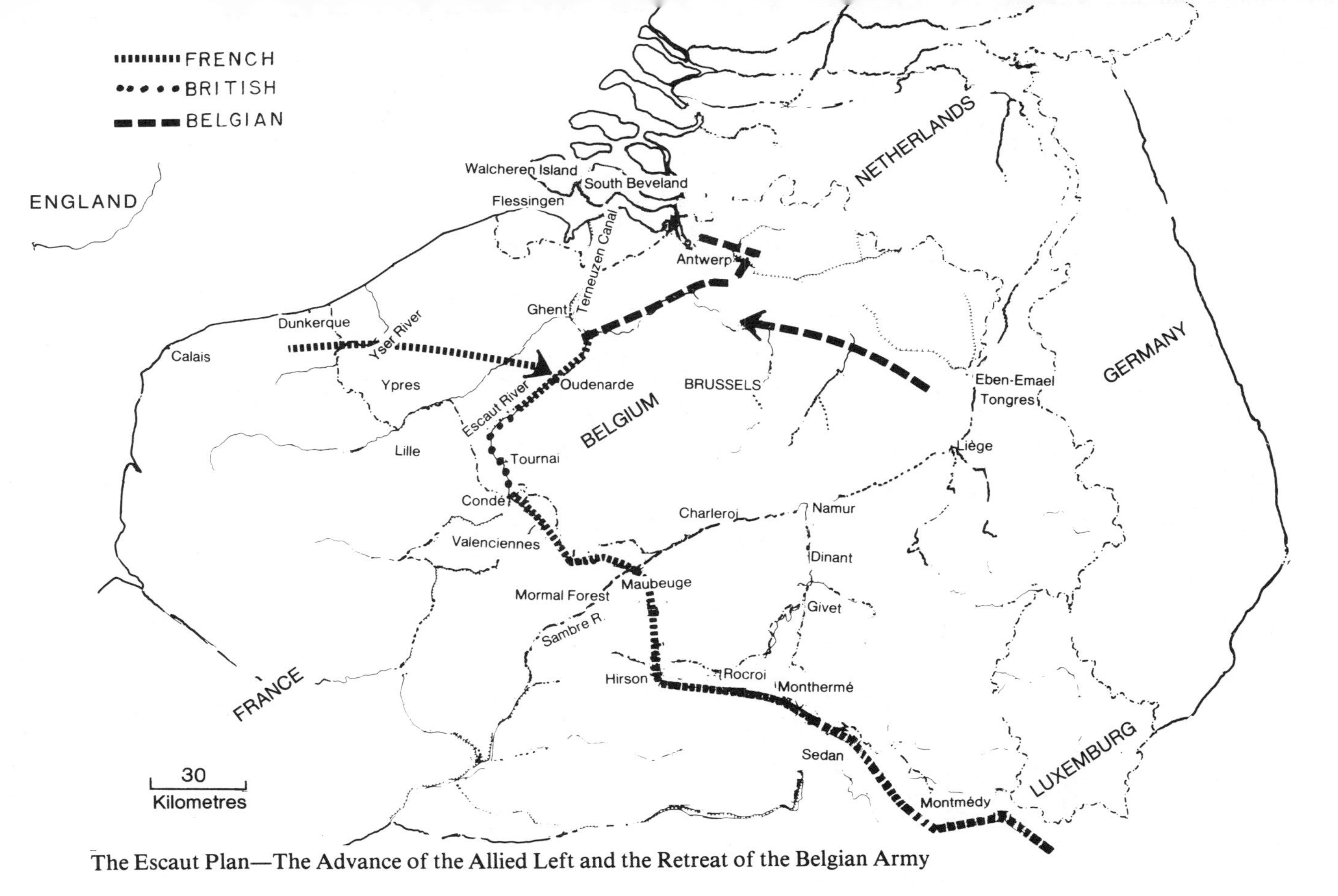

The Escaut Plan—The Advance of the Allied Left and the Retreat of the Belgian Army

destroy French strength before the British arrived in force.[4] But the German army was unable to attack immediately. Hitler initially favored a pincer stroke north and south of Liège to finish the Belgian army—a strategy the Belgian command expected—then a mechanized exploitation to Antwerp. He would then deal with Allied counterattacks before taking the initiative again.

The French command admitted the possibility of an offensive embracing Belgium, the Netherlands, and Luxemburg, but part of the command continued to ponder a potential envelopment of the Maginot Line.[5] General Augereau, commanding air units of the Ninth Army, ordered surveillance of routes penetrating the Ardennes when operations began. Intelligence on enemy mechanized and motorized units in that sector would be of "capital interest."

By this time, Gamelin's and Georges' strategic thinking was developing in different directions. Gamelin had dropped his hope of holding the Arlon and Garnich road junctions in the southern Ardennes (a hope expressed as late as April 1938);[6] but he told the chiefs of the other services on September 23, 1939, that he regretted holding up the offensive into the Saar.

On October 23 and 24 Gamelin and Vuillemin met Air Vice-Marshal Evill to try to settle the role of the British Bomber Command when the German offensive began. Evill argued that Bomber Command should attack the Ruhr. Vuillemin insisted that French industry was more vulnerable to strategic air attacks than German industry was; neither Gamelin nor Vuillemin thought attacks on German industry could stop a German drive into Belgium. This French contention caused "consternation" in London.[7] The issue of the role of the British bombers remained unresolved.

Gamelin began to seek a more positive strategy. Intelligence showed that a German invasion of the Netherlands was likely, threatening the flank of Belgian defenses at Liège. Gamelin had seen this area as a danger zone from the early 1930s. Now perhaps he could take advantage of Allied awareness of the danger there: the Ruhr lay close to Dutch bases if they could be seized and held by the Allies. Here Gamelin, the Allied commander on the Continent, found a focus for his interallied strategy. The essential interests of Britain and France—and Belgium and the Netherlands when they were finally forced into alliance—all converged on northeastern Belgium and the southeastern Netherlands. If the Allies established a front there, each would see it as the cornerstone of its own defense—and the base for an offensive against the Ruhr, Germany's industrial heart. Allied air bases in the area would stand between Germany and Britain, and the area would attract air and ground forces forward from British bases. An Allied position there would also threaten Germany's existence: the enemy would have to divert strength to protect the Ruhr, lessening pressure on the population centers of Holland to the northwest and Belgium to the southwest. Thus, it was also in the Belgian and Dutch interest to establish a front in that area. For France, a solid front in the Netherlands and Belgium would shelter France's northern industries while keeping the Luftwaffe comfortably distant from Paris. Every Allied step eastward in northern Belgium and the southern Netherlands would solidify Allied unity; every step south and west would reinforce Allied divergence. The closer the enemy drove toward the North Sea, the more planes and troops the British command would want to hold at home. The farther west the enemy drove, the more Belgians, Dutch, and French would be inclined to pull back toward their threatened population centers—*away* from each other, *away* from a common strategy. But Belgium and the Netherlands could not erect a solid front in this pivotal area. Only France had the necessary means, and to establish French forces there would be dangerous given German proximity, mechanized strength, and air superiority. Allied disunity and above all Belgian and Dutch neutrality and mutual mistrust would further endanger such a plan. Gamelin lacked the forces to mount this operation with any certainty of success, but he began to work on the maneuver, using the left-hand unit of the French army, General M.B.A. Fagalde's 16th Corps, mobilized on the Jura and then shifted to the northwest at the end of September 1939.[8] On October 19 Billotte instructed Fagalde to prepare a maneuver to link up with the "Belgian redoubt" near Ghent, along the Escaut River. This was the basic Escaut Plan.

On October 11 Gamelin decided to bring General Henri Giraud's Seventh Army out of reserve, inserting it over the 16th Corps, although Giraud did not take effective command in the area until November 10.[9] On October 28 Fagalde got the order to prepare to push a motorized division behind the Belgians into Antwerp. This extension of responsibilities led Gamelin to move the Seventh Army into the sector.

But Hitler was also at work. On October 25 he changed plans: there would be two "centers of gravity" of his offensive; one on the Belgian plain, the other in the northern Ardennes. Which offensive Hitler would pursue would depend on Allied reactions. Hitler also considered using airborne troops to secure crossings over the Albert Canal. In late November he decided that General Heinz Guderian's 19th Corps with two Panzers would attack Sedan. This would divert strength from the pincers around Liège, but offered the chance of a rapid breakthrough and exploitation which might cut off Allied strength in Belgium. Hitler originally set November 12 for his attack, but the weather—a vital factor for the Blitzkrieg—remained bad forcing repeated postponements.[10]

French intelligence struggled to keep up with German plans. In late October, German tank and air forces were detected opposite the Netherlands, suggesting an air and naval threat against Britain linked with an invasion of Holland.[11] In mid-November, however, the air observation group of the 1st Cavalry Division of the Ninth Army was still concentrating on the Ardennes: the command wanted immediate warning should German tanks reach the Meuse in Belgium. By late November, higher French headquarters focused on the Dutch-Belgian frontier covering the Belgian plain. General Gaston Roton gave priority to this region: it was vital to have warning before the enemy "Lightning War" got under way. The appearance of German mechanized and motorized units on the frontier would indicate an attack. Roton thought the enemy would likely try one of two plans: an action toward the Belgian plain via the Netherlands and northern Belgium with a diversion on the Meuse between Liège and Namur (this was in fact the German plan)—Roton noted that the German deployment seemed to fit this plan—or an action on the Meuse west of the Ardennes aimed to flank the Maginot Line, possibly combined with a diversion in northern Belgium. The location of German armor would reveal which plan the enemy had chosen.

THE POSITION OF THE NEUTRALS

Belgium and the Netherlands lay in the center of all the planning. Belgian and Dutch leaders knew that the threat to them lay in the east. The massing of German troops on their borders was no surprise, but the threat could no longer be stayed by talk of neutrality. On November 6 General Raoul Van Overstraeten, adviser to Léopold III, King of the Belgians, asked the French attaché how much aid the Belgian army could count on along the Albert Canal within forty-eight hours, then within four days, of a German offensive.[12] Van Overstraeten accompanied Léopold on a quick trip to meet the Dutch Queen that same day. Belgian and Dutch leaders discussed a common defense effort, but the Dutch government forbade concerted operations. The Dutch leadership was determined to avoid anything that might offend Hitler. They would fight only if actually invaded; they would turn a blind eye to aggression so long as Hitler left them alone. Hitler's cold war strategy paid dividends.

The Dutch government decided in early November to resist an invasion and prepared (according to French information at the time) two plans: Plan Orange, concentration of Dutch forces in Limburg, south of the great rivers which covered the heart of the country, and Plan Brown, concentration north of the rivers. The first plan offered the hope of linking up with Belgium and eventually the Allies, but it left the center of the country weakly defended and in case of defeat offered the specter of a Dutch retreat out of Dutch territory.[13] From September on, General Izaak Reynders, the Dutch Commander in Chief, argued with his government—principally the Minister of Defense, General Adriaan Dijxhoorn—over strategy. Reynders staunchly backed the idea of concentration south of the rivers along the

"Peel-Raam line" in the southeast along the German frontier, hoping to hold there until Allied forces could arrive. Reynders proposed to add the 3rd Corps and the Light Division to local units there. Dijxhoorn thought the Peel-Raam line indefensible—and neither he nor the government wanted to go beyond a defense of the heart of the country. Reynders' assertion that the Dutch would have obligations toward their allies-to-be left the government unimpressed. But for the time being Reynders disposed his troops as he saw fit.

As of November 10 the French command had indications that of the nine Dutch divisions formed from the 400,000 men mobilized—a force larger than the BEF—seven occupied the Peel-Raam line along the border canals and marshes covering Dutch Limburg, while only two covered the heart of Holland. As the crisis grew, Reynders prepared sealed instructions for his attaché in Paris, to be opened only in case of a German invasion, requesting Allied aid in holding the Peel-Raam line. However, information passed unofficially through the attachés: the Dutch command inquired about Allied help in arranging Belgian-Dutch cooperation, and asked for British troops to garrison Walcheren and South Beveland in the mouth of the Escaut River and French troops to hold North Brabant. In mid-November Gamelin let Reynders know that he hoped Dutch resistance on the Peel-Raam line would cover the arrival of the Seventh Army on the line Willemstad - Rosendaal - Antwerp. The Seventh Army would link the Belgian and Dutch fronts together. The Belgian command knew of Dutch plans but was unwilling to commit forces north of the Albert Canal and had no faith in a Dutch defense of the Peel-Raam line.

From November 8 the Belgian command took precautions against airborne attacks on the Albert Canal bridges and fortifications; French warnings on this possibility came as well. On November 11 Gamelin informed the Belgians that, given the Polish lesson, the Allies would move only to the Dyle River covering Brussels and would thrust beyond Antwerp into the Netherlands. After that, they would see about further advances. This news came as an unpleasant surprise to Van Overstraeten. Gamelin added that it would be "hazardous" to push forces into the Belgian Ardennes: the Belgians would have to accept German advances there. On November 13 Colonel Petibon told the Belgian attaché that Allied forces could be on the Albert Canal in four to eight days. This more forward strategy reflected Gamelin's realization that Belgium and perhaps the Netherlands would resist. Their resistance would be a real gain: Belgian and Dutch forces were three times the size of the BEF, although they were largely reservist and lacked modern equipment, especially the Dutch. But every division counted.[14]

Gamelin told Hore-Belisha on November 20 that the Germans had 130 divisions and would have 30 more the following spring.[15] The Allies had only 110. Belgian and Dutch forces thus would fill a real need. The alert and Belgian and Dutch interest triggered a rethinking of Allied strategy which filled the first three weeks of November with conferences and decisions that played a great part not only in strategy, but also in the personal relations between commanders. These decisions and these relationships would play a crucial role in the battle.

THE CRUCIAL DECISIONS OF LATE 1939

On November 4 Winston Churchill, the First Lord of the Admiralty, asked Gamelin what he would do if Hitler struck the Netherlands alone, leaving Belgium as a buffer.[16] The next day Ironside wrote to Gamelin in the same vein. Gamelin responded with a note to Georges stating his strategic plans: assuming the Belgians would call for Allied intervention if the enemy attacked the Netherlands alone, Gamelin would order an operation to secure the mouth of the Escaut River with motorized forces. Later, French troops could occupy Walcheren and South Beveland, keeping the port of Antwerp open, and preventing the enemy from outflanking the Allies along the sea; Gamelin proposed the Seventh Army for this maneuver. Further, Allied forces should push forward to the front Antwerp-Dyle River-Namur-Meuse River: the Dyle Plan.

On November 8 Georges put out the new directive. A German invasion of Holland would threaten Britain; the Allies would move forward to the Escaut, and possibly the Dyle. The aim was to hold Antwerp while gaining as much ground as possible in central Belgium to install air forces to counter the enemy in Holland. Georges based his maneuver on his directive of October 24, which covered an advance to the Belgian "redoubt" at Ghent.[17] The operation would depend on French and British forces only: the Belgian army would be integrated as events permitted. Georges envisaged the immediate insertion of the Seventh Army, its mission to include the occupation of Walcheren and South Beveland with cooperation from the navy and airborne infantry from the Armée de l'air.

On November 9 Gamelin met with the British and French service chiefs. He thought an attack on Holland likely. The Allies should move into Belgium and the Netherlands but should not risk being caught in a vulnerable position if the enemy moved more quickly than expected. The group agreed that the Dyle line would do if the Belgians fortified it, particularly in the "Gembloux gap," the twenty-five miles of open plain between Namur and Wavre where the Dyle River fell off to the southwest. The Seventh Army, with two motorized divisions, would secure the mouth of the Escaut River, and Vuillemin suggested an airborne expedition to take Flessingen; if the Dutch were defeated their remnants could join the Allies through Antwerp. Gamelin again pressed the British for more divisions: Ironside responded that equipment was lacking. Gamelin offered to disband ten reserve units and place their old and meager equipment at Ironside's disposal; Ironside refused. Gamelin then asked for more RAF strength in France. Air Marshal Newall again proposed bombing the Ruhr in case of a German offensive, but Gamelin demanded that air action focus on the advancing German columns. The RAF agreed to use its light and medium bombers in the latter role, but refused to release heavy bombers against anything but the Ruhr. Georges, "soldierly and impressive" as he seemed to Sir John Slessor, stressed gaining ground in Belgium to secure air bases for eventual attacks on the Rhineland and the Ruhr. Slessor raised the Ruhr issue again with Gamelin, Vuillemin, and Mendigal, but the French would not budge. The matter had to be referred to the governments. "As we broke up, little Vuillemin fired the usual Parthian shot about cooperation of British fighters in the battle. . . ."[18]

On November 10 Giraud's Seventh Army took its post on the left flank, bringing General Théodore Sciard's 1st Motorized Corps to add to Fagalde's 16th. Giraud called a conference of his subordinates the next day; no doubt setting records for staff work, he issued orders on November 12.[19]

On November 11 Gamelin considered pushing directly to the Dyle position. He asked the Belgians for information on defenses in the Gembloux gap; a move that far forward would be risky.[20] But in a meeting with the British at La Ferté he finally decided on the Dyle Plan, issuing a new directive on November 15. The First Army Group would hold between the Belgian redoubt at Ghent and the French Meuse while receiving the retreating Belgians. Gamelin removed the Seventh Army from Billotte's control and gave it the further mission of concentrating in the Antwerp area to stand ready to link up with the Dutch. That would be a difficult operation and would depend on how long the Dutch, perhaps with Belgian aid, could retard the enemy. And this project would hand most of the motorized reserve to Giraud, cutting down the mobile reserves left to Georges. Thus there was little enthusiasm at La Ferté for the idea of concentrating the Seventh Army near Antwerp, coming as it did on top of the added risks of the Dyle Plan. On November 17 the Allied Supreme Council met to finally settle the issue of bombing the Ruhr. Chamberlain warned that a German occupation of Belgium would pose a direct air threat to Britain; the RAF wanted to respond by launching a "knock-out blow" against the Ruhr. Daladier agreed that strategic air war might prove decisive—but the Allies were still too weak. In case of a German invasion, Gamelin would initiate the Dyle Plan to push forward to the line Antwerp-Namur; the RAF should cooperate by attacking the columns and logistics of the German invasion force. The meeting closed with the dispute over the use of the RAF still unresolved.

On November 17 Georges issued new orders to Billotte and Gort. The Allies would move in a single push to the Dyle, fitting the retreating Belgians into the sector from Antwerp to Louvain; the BEF would hold from Louvain to the Gembloux gap; Billotte's First Army Group would have its

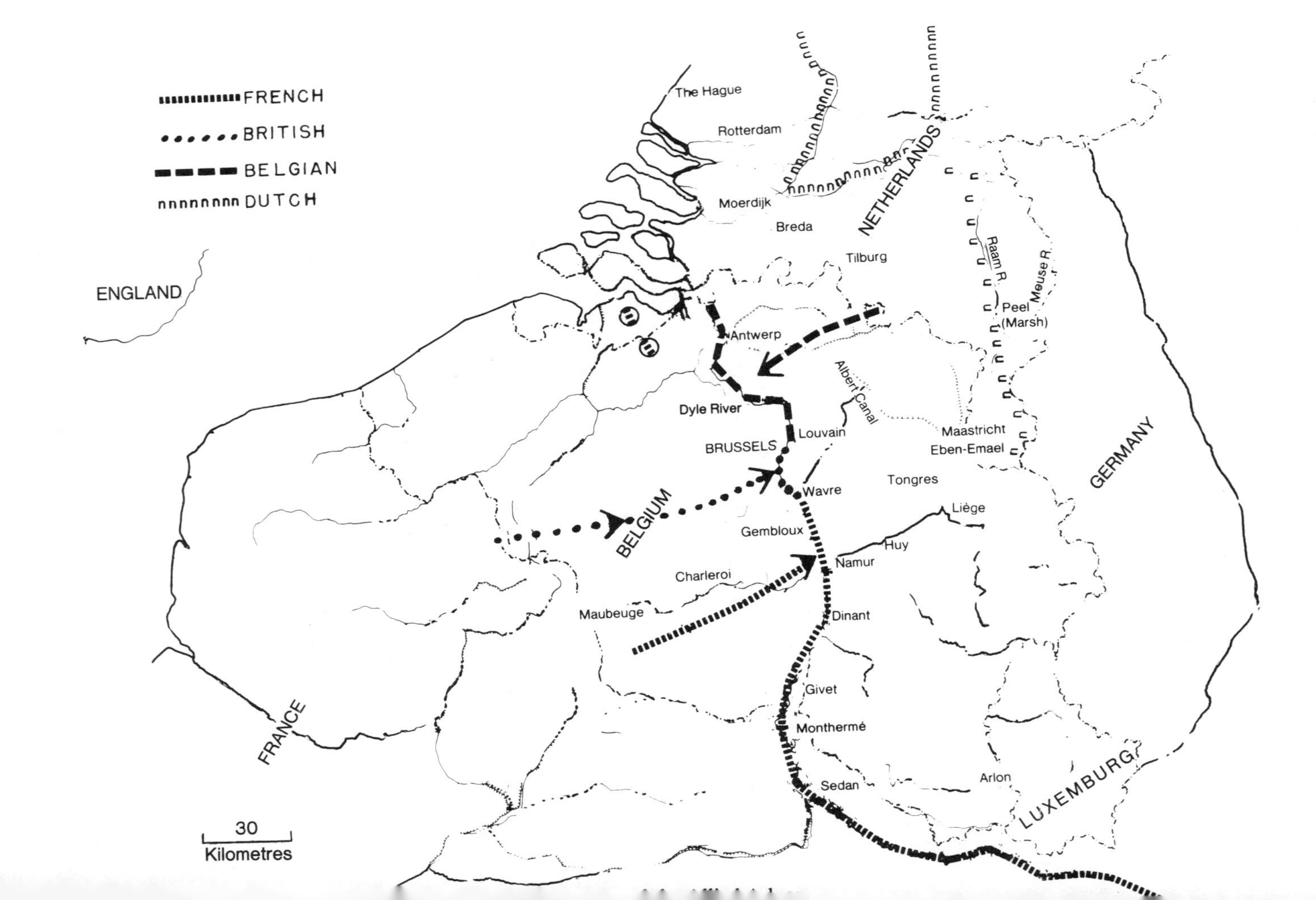
FRENCH
BRITISH
BELGIAN
DUTCH
ENGLAND
The Hague
Rotterdam
Moerdijk
Breda
Tilburg
NETHERLANDS
Raam R.
Meuse R.
Peel
(Marsh)
Antwerp
Albert Canal
Dyle River
Louvain
BRUSSELS
Maastricht
Eben-Emael
Tongres
Wavre
Liège
GERMANY
BELGIUM
Gembloux
Huy
Namur
Charleroi
Maubeuge
Dinant
Givet
Monthermé
Sedan
Arlon
LUXEMBURG
FRANCE
30
Kilometres

First Army in the gap, its Ninth Army on the Belgian and French Meuse, and the Second Army from Sedan to the Maginot Line. The armies would leave garrisons behind on the frontier fortifications; Georges promised a series B infantry division each to the First and Ninth Armies for that purpose. But he softened Giraud's mission: the Seventh Army was to be "placed in GQG reserve west of Antwerp" to support the Belgians and block an enemy flanking movement via the mouth of the Escaut.[21] Georges made no mention of a linkup with the Dutch, as Gamelin had in his directive.

The Dyle Plan touched off a controversy. It was a cardinal point of French strategy that an encounter battle at the start of a campaign was to be avoided. The Dyle Plan called for the movement of four armies into the Belgian plain. The risk of meeting enemy mechanized forces before the Allies could get forward was substantial; Gamelin did not have enough motorized units to conduct the whole maneuver rapidly. The issue boiled down to how long Belgians and Dutch could hold the German vanguard. The issue was complicated by the strength of the Luftwaffe, which led the French command to plan on making the main movements by night, doubling delays. Timing was critical to General Georges Blanchard, whose First Army would have to fill the Gembloux gap. Blanchard felt it essential to have eight days before the enemy arrived on the Dyle.[22] Billotte was aware of the possibility of a German Blitzkrieg on the Belgian plain, but he wrote to Georges on November 20 supporting the Dyle Plan.

Georges was less sure. From his first reading of Gamelin's latest directive he showed his unhappiness. Writing in the margins of the paper, he noted that everything would depend on the duration of Belgian resistance. The decision to adopt either the Escaut or the Dyle Plan would have to be made from the start of the German offensive. Ordinarily that decision would belong to the theater commander—Georges. But, given the inter-Allied importance of the choice, it would be made by Gamelin: Georges knew what that meant.[23]

Meanwhile, Gamelin forged ahead. On November 19 he dispatched "suggestions" to the Belgian command to prepare a retreat to a sector between the Seventh Army and the BEF. The evacuation of the population and resources of Belgium east of the Meuse should be canalized so as to leave routes free for the Allied advance; provision should be made to extend Allied railroad movements along Belgian rails.[24] But Gamelin was not deaf to the opposition of his subordinate. Although he had a reputation for tact and even "pliability," he felt that the role of the commander was to fix his line of conduct and hold to it, no matter what the obstacles. Georges' opposition constituted an obstacle: very well then—he would cut Georges out of the circuit!

On November 23 Gamelin called his senior commanders—except for

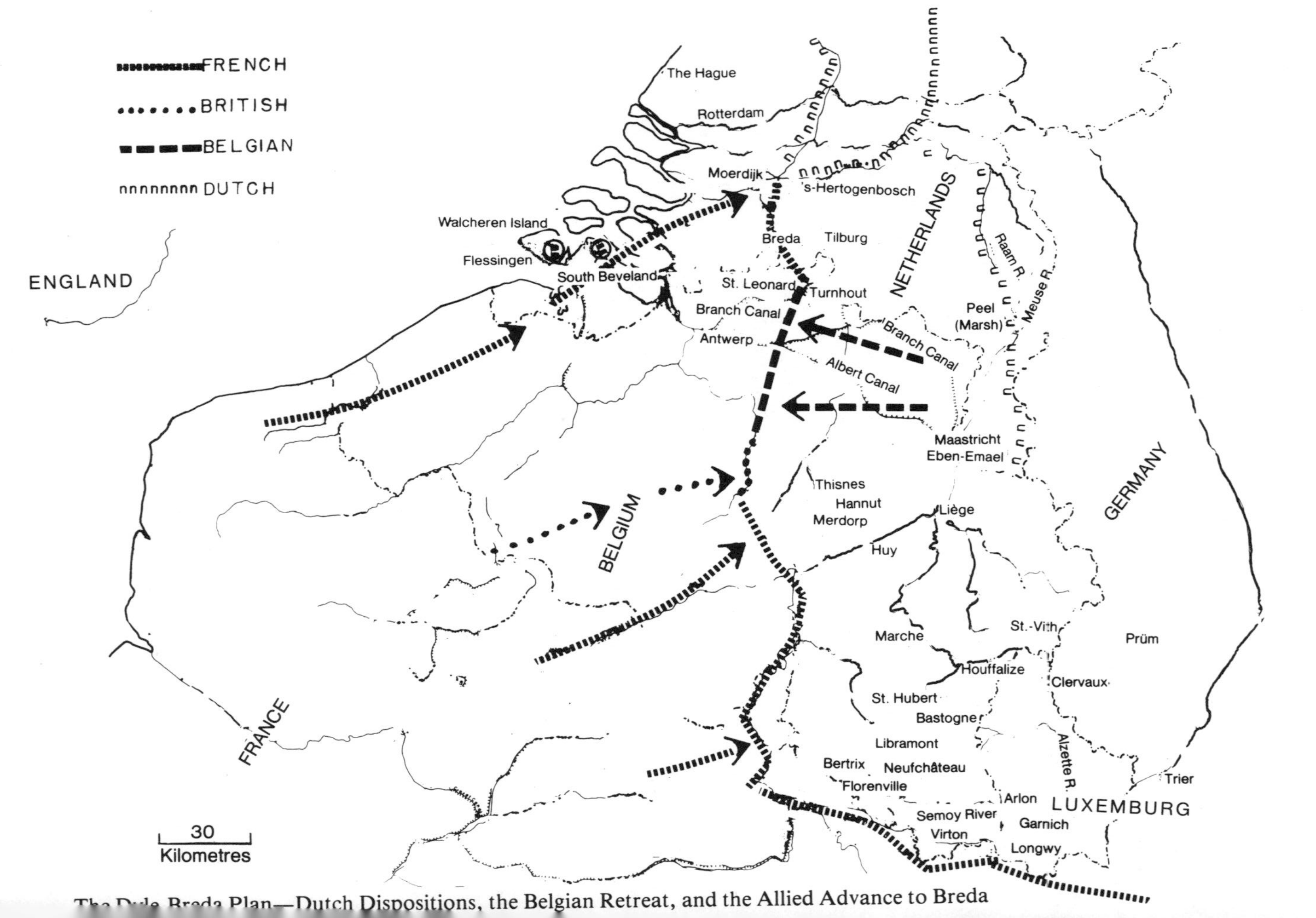

The Dyle-Breda Plan—Dutch Dispositions, the Belgian Retreat, and the Allied Advance to Breda

Georges—to Arras. Gamelin ordered Billotte, who seemed favorable, to plan operations for the Seventh Army in the Breda area of Dutch Brabant, and the eventual advance of the Allied armies to the Albert Canal once the move to the Dyle was complete.[25] Gamelin went north on November 29 to Dunkirk to meet Billotte, Giraud and Giraud's two corps commanders, Admiral François Darlan (Commander in Chief of the Navy), and General d'Astier (commanding the Northern Zone of Air Operations). Georges again was absent. Gamelin noted that the enemy was in a position to invade Belgium and to strike through Dutch Limburg toward Rotterdam. Belgium promised to call for help in case of invasion but, Gamelin claimed, Léopold refused to place his troops under Georges. In that eventuality, Gamelin added, he himself would have to direct operations on this theater. To do so would be a violation of his prewar promise to Vuillemin to forgo command of a theater, and would preempt most of Georges' authority.

Gamelin hoped that Belgian resistance on the Albert Canal would permit the Allies to reach the Dyle, the Seventh Army, at a minimum, holding the outlets of the Escaut and supporting the Belgians. The navy would prepare an expedition to the islands in the mouth of the Escaut, and supply the Seventh Army via Antwerp. Following the conference of November 9 British leaders expressed reluctance to send forces to Holland, but before Gamelin's determination they consented to assist the French navy's expedition to Walcheren and South Beveland.[26]

On November 30 Billotte delivered the studies Gamelin had requested to his superior, Georges, who thus discovered what was going on behind his back. Whatever his personal feelings, he was particularly unhappy over the direction Gamelin had chosen, noting in the margin of Billotte's study that the project to send forces into the Netherlands, ". . . is the very archetype of an adventure. If the enemy masks Belgium, he can maneuver freely elsewhere. Therefore let us not throw our strength into this business. Cast aside this dream."[27] Billotte's study called for five or six French divisions to hold 55 kilometers inside the Netherlands between the great rivers (the Waal and the Meuse) and Antwerp. Billotte figured that it would take the force from three to twelve days to reach its positions—only part of the Seventh Army was motorized. Unfortunately, the area was closer to Germany than to France. A Dutch-French-Belgian front could form only if the Dutch and Belgian defenses delayed the enemy until Giraud arrived. Giraud reached similar conclusions. In a study of December 3, he emphasized that a unified command for the three nations could not be improvised at the last moment.

These plans gravely disturbed Georges, who always paid more attention to the center of the front than did Gamelin and Billotte; even if Gamelin's Dutch maneuver were successful, it would cost almost all the mobile reserves. Georges wrote to Gamelin on December 5:

> . . . our defensive maneuver into Belgium and Holland must be conducted with care to avoid . . . engaging on that part of the Theater, before a German action which might be no more than a feint, the major part of our available forces. For example, in the case of an enemy attack . . . in the center of our front between the Meuse and the Moselle, we could find ourselves lacking the means necessary for a riposte. It is therefore necessary to act . . . with prudence.[28]

Georges believed that a move to the Albert Canal could only be attempted once the Dyle position was secured; Billotte agreed with this.

Gamelin, however, had no intention of turning back on his plan. On December 3 he sent more "suggestions" to Belgium. He emphasized preserving a land link to Holland. French troops would have to push north to Breda, but advance guards could not reach it until the third day of operations; reinforcement could only be gradual. The Belgian and Dutch forces should prepare a front connecting their positions to retard the enemy.[29] Two days later the French attaché reported that the Dutch command was planning on Belgian and Allied assistance. But the Dutch government feared compromising its neutrality by conducting discussions with Belgium. Nonetheless, the Dutch command did garrison the islands of the Escaut and considered a position in the Breda-Tilburg area. Dutch concern centered on how long it would take the French to arrive.

PLANNING FOR AIR OPERATIONS

On November 9 Vuillemin instructed Mouchard to prepare for the maneuver into Belgium and the Netherlands, following the wishes of General Billotte. His fighters were to provide daytime cover over Allied movements, and he was to prepare the airborne intervention on Flessingen.[30] On November 13 Mouchard sketched the action: he would give cover to the advancing troops while using his bombers to retard the enemy, reserving minimum strength to defend his airfields, Paris, and the Seine River oil route. Any remaining bomber units would hit the bases of the enemy attack aviation. Mouchard left the conduct of the airborne operation to d'Astier, warning that it would require strong fighter escort: if the enemy defense were too strong, the operation would be canceled. Vuillemin stripped the interior to provide fighters for Mouchard: only two fighter groups covered Paris.

In late December d'Astier sent Mouchard his plan. Noting the Dutch garrison in the Escaut islands, d'Astier dropped the airborne operation for a seaborne movement. The principal effort of the Dyle Plan lay in the center and north of Belgium and southern Holland; d'Astier envisaged five fighter groups under Groupment 25 covering the Seventh and First Armies. Groupment 23, attached to the Ninth and Second Armies facing the Ardennes, would have three fighter groups. D'Astier asked that British fighters replace the two groups of Groupment 21 in the lower Seine.[31]

COMMAND CRISES

Amid the developing strategies a crisis was brewing between Gamelin and Georges. Georges, commanding the northeastern front, had to accept a strategy he thought dangerous and in the development of which he had no voice. Gamelin felt it intolerable that an opponent of his plan should control the GQG which would prepare the maneuver, although Billotte's small army group staff could produce studies. In December Gamelin asked Daladier to name Georges "Commander in Chief on the Northeastern Front." Georges wished to command the whole "theater"—a position giving him direction of strategy in the northeastern sector. But, Gamelin claimed, an Italian front might open, and France would then constitute a single theater requiring Gamelin's coordination; he had also to coordinate operations with the Allies.[32] He thought it likely that external theaters would open; active operations would begin in the west in the spring, and he wanted to replace the chief of the GQG, General Bineau.[33] Daladier approved Georges' new title and Gamelin's proposal to split the GQG: Georges kept that part of the GQG that dealt with the northeastern front, taking General Gaston Roton as his chief of staff; the remainder of the GQG reformed into a separate body at Montry, halfway between La Ferté and Vincennes, under General Joseph Doumenc. Thus Gamelin reduced Georges' influence on the GQG and reaffirmed his own authority to direct Allied strategy.

From early December, when Gamelin pressed the reorganization, Georges bitterly objected. Until then, Georges claimed later, his relations with Gamelin had been correct, sometimes even cordial. But "a grave disaccord" opened between them when Gamelin reorganized the High Command. Letters passed back and forth until Gamelin ended the exchange on December 10, telling Georges that his intention was to relieve him of extraneous matters and leave him free to direct operations. He offered to meet Georges but added, ". . . in the name of the army, I ask you to reflect. The higher one is placed, the more one has the duty to sacrifice his personal conceptions. My intention is to aggrandize you . . . and, if you should one day succeed me, as I have up till now hoped, I am certain to have rendered you a service in doing what I have done."[34] On December 13 they met. Georges, feeling it his duty, yielded.

Georges had already vented his discontent at limitations on his authority to Sir Edward Spears on November 1, portraying Gamelin as an intriguer who used Daladier to hold him (Georges) down.[35] When Spears saw Georges in January 1940, things were worse. Captain André Beaufre, who joined the GQG as an aide to Doumenc, had served under Georges in North

General Weygand in the Levant—Age seventy-two-years-old.
Photo Courtesy of E. C. P. Armées

Africa and paid a courtesy call in February. He found Georges aged—both physically and morally—by the wounds suffered in 1934. Georges immediately launched into a bitter account of his troubles with Gamelin. The new command structure raised questions over the subordination of the BEF; Gamelin assured Spears that the BEF remained under Georges. General Sir Henry Pownall, the Chief of Staff of the BEF, came to reassure Georges of this but found him bitter.

The new system went into operation in mid-January. Georges complained that it confused responsibilities and deprived him of freedom of action.[36] Bineau gave way to Doumenc, one of the originators of mechanization in the army. But, like many graduates of the École polytechnique, Doumenc had a reputation for overoptimism and impracticality. The reorganization left Georges with a "super army group" staff interposed between the GQG under Doumenc and the army groups in the field, thus depriving Georges of the autonomous staff necessary for the interallied command in Belgium—or so Roton later claimed. Doumenc felt that the new system worked well. Since Georges no longer submitted each decision to Gamelin, Georges gained independence.

The breach between Gamelin and Georges remained open. On March 20 a new government came to power under Paul Reynaud; senior commanders from external theaters of operations were called back, including General Maxime Weygand, who led French forces in the Levant. Weygand, as vigorous as ever, returned in early April. He was upset to discover the rift between Georges and Gamelin, and took advantage of his senior status to call them to accounts. He told the two that the problem arose from the lack of clear responsibilities. Gamelin, as Chief of Staff of National Defense, should keep high authority over all fronts while Georges occupied himself with the army. They discussed this without reaching conclusions, but Weygand noticed that Gamelin, "ordinarily so cool, seemed rather stirred up. . . ."[37]

Gamelin claimed that he supported Weygand's solution and that with Reynaud in power something might be done, although Daladier remained Minister of National Defense and War and thus presented a constant obstacle.[38] Unfortunately, the dispute between the two generals was rooted in the divergence of their strategic views: as long as the question of attributions bore on the strategy adopted, neither would give way. The alternative was to dismiss one of them.

Meanwhile, a similar split opened in the command of the Armée de l'air. Vuillemin found himself preempting Mouchard's duties. Thanks to Mouchard's own suggestion, the zones of air operations handled day-to-day operations. Further, Mouchard was a graduate of the staff college while Vuillemin had risen from the ranks. A certain rivalry developed. The focus of attention of Mouchard's supporters was General Mendigal, Vuillemin's old comrade and chief of staff. Mendigal was the target of repeated attacks; Vuillemin's personal staff had to work to keep Vuillemin from resigning. The issue must have come to a head in January 1940 when Vuillemin fell ill and relinquished his post temporarily to Mendigal.[39]

La Chambre talked with Gamelin, urging the dissolution of Mouchard's First Air Army. Gamelin opposed this and Georges was unhappy to lose Mouchard, but Gamelin finally agreed.[40] La Chambre then got government approval to disband the unit and retire Mouchard. In late February Vuillemin, back at his duties, abolished the First Air Army; the air and antiaircraft forces attached to the northeastern front passed to a new command. The same order replaced the Third Air Army with the Alps Zone of Air Operations, and similarly replaced the Fifth Air Army in North Africa. General Têtu took command of the new Cooperation Air Forces on the Northeastern Front; General Bouscat took the Eastern Zone of Air Operations; General Picard became Chief of the Air Force Staff of the Interior. Têtu's new command differed somewhat from Mouchard's; the staff of the old First Air Army was broken up. Vuillemin reserved the right to intervene in the conduct of air operations on the northeastern front, and prescribed new measures of secrecy. The compromising of his plan notably if interallied operations were involved. Têtu was soon established next to Georges, and with Barratt to coordinate with the RAF, Georges could draw on all available air support.

THE MECHELEN INCIDENT

Through the middle of January 1940 Hitler projected three main attacks: one north and one south of Liège and a third toward Sedan.[41] Alert followed alert as he sought to launch his offensive, only to be checked by the weather. The tension suddenly grew to a crisis.

On the morning of January 10 two German officers set out in a light plane. The pilot, Dr. Erich Hoenmanns, a flier in World War I, and now a reservist, was anxious for flying time. When he met a young paratrooper, Major Helmuth Reinberger, in Münster and learned that Reinberger needed to get to Köln in a hurry, Hoenmanns offered to fly him. Reinberger accepted. Over the Ruhr Hoenmanns ran into fog; soon after he caught sight of a great river and was content to follow the Rhine. Then the engine died. The pilot had to pick a landing field as best he could; it was only with luck that they escaped uninjured.

Badly shaken, the two waited for help. They spotted a peasant who spoke to them in French: Hoenmanns had been following the Meuse, not the Rhine—they were in Belgium! Reinberger, livid with anger, told his pilot that he was carrying secret documents. Ducking behind a hedge Reinberger tried to burn them—igniting one sheet with his last match—while Hoenmanns attempted to distract Belgian sentinels who came up on the run.[42] The two were interned with Reinberger's documents spread out before them. The paratrooper made a desperate bid to save the situation: he thrust the documents into a nearby wood stove. But the Belgian interrogator rescued the flaming papers and packed the remains off to Brussels. They showed that a German attack, extending from the Moselle to the North Sea, was in the offing and that the German Sixth Army was charged with a major effort against Belgium after driving through the Netherlands in the Maastricht area, as the Belgian command had expected. But there was an unexpected twist—a second German thrust was to penetrate the northern Ardennes to exploit an airborne seizure of bridges on the Meuse between Namur and Dinant. The basic intention was clear: a pincers attack north and south of Liège. Belgian experts debated whether the incident could be a ruse, then in the morning of January 11 passed the information on as genuine to Van Overstraeten.

Van Overstraeten gave it to the Allied attachés,[43] and that evening he ordered alert measures. Considering that French troops were in strength from Longwy to Givet on the Belgian border, he had begun a week before withdrawing troops from the southern Ardennes; he now drew these forces farther north to reinforce the Chasseurs ardennais between the Sambre and

Meuse rivers to counter the airborne threat. In the morning of January 12 Gamelin called a meeting to discuss these developments. He read the material received, underscoring the role of air strikes on Allied air forces and armies as they moved forward, as well as the plan to seize the Meuse crossings. The senior commanders decided to take the intelligence seriously. Mendigal, taking Vuillemin's place while the latter was ill, reported these events to his chief and detailed the alert measures ordered. However, Mendigal thought the Belgian information a bit too pat. After all, Van Overstraeten did not divulge the source, and French intelligence had not detected the enemy moving up to the frontier.

The crisis edged up a notch on January 13 when the Belgian attaché in Berlin warned that the German command knew of the fate of the documents.[44] Mendigal wrote again to Vuillemin noting nervousness in Belgium; intelligence detected only sporadic German movements toward the frontiers. Nonetheless, the alert remained in effect; information indicated January 15 as the critical date.

In the night of January 13-14 General Van den Bergen, Chief of Staff of the Belgian Army, ordered the frontier barriers facing France lowered; at the same time Léopold passed a message through a British representative asking if Britain would guarantee Belgian territory in case Belgium appealed for assistance.[45] This request was telephoned to Churchill, but there was a mixup: Churchill thought Léopold was calling for Allied intervention. He passed the word to the French command.

At 3:30 p.m. on January 14 Gamelin announced to Georges that Léopold intended to ask for intervention; the French government had given its assent. Fifteen minutes later Billotte reported the Belgian frontier open.[46] One hour later Georges called Gamelin after talking with his air commander: perhaps it would be best not to provoke the enemy. Gamelin lost his temper —a rare event! He snapped back that the decision had already been made, and then reviewed the arguments one by one until Georges gave in and ordered the highest alert. As Allied troops marched through the snow to the frontier, Gamelin called on the Belgian command to garrison the Meuse bridges until French troops could arrive. He asked for reports of airborne landings there or in the Ardennes. And then everyone waited . . . .

Obviously, there had been a misunderstanding. No appeal came from Belgium, and the frontier barriers went back up as soon as Van Overstraeten discovered their removal. Allied troops stood in the snow, exposing their dispositions to enemy intelligence. Soon after this fiasco General Oscar Michiels replaced Van den Bergen.[47] A split opened in Belgium as the government began to think a German invasion inevitable; Léopold and Van Overstraeten, however, continued to believe in neutrality.

But the affair was a fiasco for Germany too. It was not certain how much the Belgian command had learned from the Mechelen documents, but Hitler, unable to launch his offensive because of the weather, was furious added impetus toward new ideas; more important was his decision to reduce the period of alert prior to the offensive to only twenty-four hours.[48] This would make it difficult for Allied intelligence and air reconnaissance to detect the buildup before the blow fell—Hitler's order made that buildup permanent.

MORE PLANS

By this time Georges had given up hope of defeating the Dyle Plan, which, in any case, would give the Allies greater depth for operations in Belgium along a shorter front than the frontier position or the Escaut Plan, while rescuing the Belgian army. But the Dutch operation—generally known as the Breda Plan since the Seventh Army was to center on that Dutch city—was another question, for it siphoned off almost all the mobile reserves.[49] Georges raised this issue at the end of January, when the pending arrival of the British 3rd Corps made it possible to consider extending the front of the BEF. He proposed to Gamelin that the BEF replace the Seventh Army on the Allied left (except for one French corps with its flank on the sea), thus freeing the Seventh and its mobile units for the central reserve. Gamelin rejected this proposal on February 6. He argued after the campaign that he had only tied down perhaps three—out of over 100—French divisions in the Breda maneuver. However, they were precious mechanized and motorized divisions.

Gamelin went on to consider an advance to the Albert Canal; such a move would create a salient formed on the east by the Meuse from Namur to Liège and on the north, facing Dutch Brabant and Limburg, by the Albert Canal. Because of the threat of German airpower to their communications, the Allies would have to widen this salient, operating in the north beyond the Albert Canal and in the south in the Ardennes. The northern operation would require a full army that would have to reach the area from the start of operations, since it would be very difficult to pass a major force through the rear areas of the BEF and the Belgian army once these forces were on the Dyle.[50] Antwerp would be vital for the logistics of this operation: it would be necessary to secure it and the islands in the mouth of the Escaut.

A study by Billotte's staff, prepared in late February, calculated that the enemy might attack in force on the Albert Canal west of Liège by the fourth or fifth day of his offensive, and on the Meuse south of Liège by the fifth day.[51] This delay seemed sufficient for the Dyle Plan as Georges, Billotte, and Blanchard agreed. As Georges later testified, the French counted broadly on six or seven days, besides which the forward movement would be preceded by two echelons of security. The initial wave would consist of DLM's, a second of motorized advance guards.

Gamelin meanwhile submitted his "1940 War Plan" to Daladier on February 26, 1940. Gamelin forecast that in April, when a German offensive might be expected, Allied forces would suffer from a 2.3 to 1 inferiority in bombers but would enjoy a 1.6 to 1.4 advantage in fighter strength. Thus the Allies could inflict such losses that the enemy would have to renounce, at least in part, daylight air attacks. He expected Germany to field 170 to 175 divisions but none of the new units would be Panzers—of which, he knew, Germany had 10. The enemy could try to force a decision in 1940. But no Allied offensive could be contemplated before 1941 when the British buildup would make itself felt. Gamelin forecast a German stroke through the Low Countries possibly combined with an attack through Switzerland. But an enemy attack would allow the Allies to "'pass advantageously to the counteroffensive, for the enemy would offer himself . . . on open terrain.'"[52] Meanwhile, the Allies could only adopt an expectant attitude on the northeast front, taking the initiative perhaps in the Balkans or northern Europe. But Gamelin was eager for the Germans to drive forward in the west. These conclusions were identical to those seen by General Pownall in a late December 1939 study.

The British command, like Georges, was reticent about pushing to the Albert Canal. Gamelin dealt with this reticence in a directive to Georges in late February; he insisted that while the main objective was to hold from Antwerp to Namur, the Seventh Army linking with the Dutch, the Allied command could not ignore the chance of reaching the Albert Canal and the Meuse from Liège to Namur, ". . . while our Seventh Army, progressing to the area of Tilburg, would render the position of the troops thus engaged between the Albert Canal and the Meuse less delicate."[53] If the BEF chose to remain on the Dyle, then the First Army Group would have to tackle the mission alone, taking command of Belgian elements in place as it advanced. Gamelin directed Georges to consult the BEF, reminding him that operations in Scandinavia (as will be discussed later) made it likely that the British would not be reinforced for some time. It might be "of interest" to substitute the BEF for the Ninth Army which could thus replace the British in the advance to the Albert Canal. Apparently Gamelin had decided that—contrary to French doctrine—the risks of an encounter battle were smaller than the gains his plan offered. His troops had been under arms for months, lack of equipment was no longer a fatal handicap, even in the air. In fact, the French command was sure that its heavy weapons were superior to those of the enemy.

In late February Gamelin insisted that the logistics be prepared for the Seventh Army to come by sea through Antwerp. He pursued the theme in a study of an Allied offensive on the Antwerp-Namur front addressed to Georges on March 5. He warned Georges that the BEF was to remain under his—Georges'—orders alone and not to be handed to an army group commander; in any case, the final command structure in Belgium would depend on the course of operations. It might be possible to return to the precedent of 1918, giving Léopold titular command of the Belgian army and the Seventh, with a French chief of staff, and perhaps bring up the reserve Sixth Army to fill in on the Belgian right. Gamelin thought the most favorable zones for an offensive would be along the Meuse toward Tongres in the zone of the First Army and in the zone of the Seventh toward Helmond. The attacks would move forward on successive lines "save for the possibility of a deep action by mechanized forces . . . ."[54] In early March Billotte sent out a corresponding study to his subordinates projecting an offensive from the front Antwerp-Namur. He emphasized that an Allied threat to the east in Dutch Brabant would not only menace the communications of any German force attacking south over the Albert Canal, but would offer excellent terrain for mechanized exploitation of a success. Billotte and Gamelin saw alike on the Breda maneuver.

In mid-March Gamelin ordered that the Breda Plan was to be executed not only in case of an advance to the Albert Canal but also under the Dyle Plan. The Seventh Army was to reach either Breda-St. Leonard, or better yet Tilburg-Turnhout, to gather in as many Dutch and Belgian forces as possible. And beyond that:

> The further east the Seventh Army and the forces it will gather in are established, the safer it will be for us to come up to reinforce the Belgians, if possible, on the Albert Canal and the Meuse from Liège to Namur.
>
> . . .
>
> Obviously, this sort of maneuver cannot be mounted in advance for lack of the ability to associate the Dutch and Belgians in its preparation—something I am trying to obtain progressively. It will be up to the General commanding the Seventh Army to carry out this maneuver as best he can.[55]

Georges had to issue corresponding orders, which he did on March 20. Designating the Dyle Plan as the most probable, he followed Gamelin's order on the mission of the Seventh Army: should circumstances be favorable, the advance would continue to the Albert Canal. The Belgian defense would be reinforced from the right flank westward by moving up toward Huy on the Meuse north of Namur, then gradually shifting the whole Allied force onto the Albert. Georges ordered garrisons left in key sectors of the frontier fortifications: the Ninth Army would leave a series B division in the "Oise gap" on the frontier on both sides of the Oise River, the First Army would leave its 101st Fortress Division at Maubeuge and the Fortified Sector of the Escaut in place, while the BEF would leave one division each in the Tournai and Audenarde areas. Allied air forces would retard the enemy advance, extend demolitions left by the Belgians, and cover the advance of the DLM's and the main forces. Priority would go to the First Army which had to occupy the Gembloux gap. This was Georges' final directive before the opening of operations.

What did Gamelin have in mind? He had reason to believe that the Allies had the upper hand in defensive air strength, although the British refusal to send more fighters to France would leave his troops vulnerable, at least at the opening of the campaign. Gamelin sought to use the open terrain of the Netherlands and Belgium to seize bases and edge toward the Ruhr. By swinging the Seventh Army onto the Dutch plain, he committed most of Georges' mobile reserve in advance. But by doing so he avoided having the Seventh's movement paralyzed from the air during the decisive moments of the battle, and also having to move it through Antwerp after the Belgian army and the BEF were in place. Once on the plain, Giraud, his most impetuous commander, would make the most of the terrain, the DLM, and the two motorized divisions allotted to him. Giraud would be acting in a sensitive area—within striking distance of the Ruhr and the weak fortifications protecting it. Giraud's force was too weak for decisive operations but strong enough perhaps to divert German strength from the vulnerable Dutch and Belgian fronts and thus to open the way for the First Army Group to thrust to the Albert Canal and the Meuse from Namur to Liège.

With a little imagination one can picture the Panzers crashing through Dutch and Belgian frontier defenses only to be stymied on the lower Meuse and Dyle lines and checked by the powerful First Army. As German infantry struggled forward through the fortresses left behind by the Panzers Giraud's force would appear in their right rear, threatening their communications and the Ruhr. At that moment, the Allies would launch a powerful counteroffensive from Gembloux. . . .

But what if—as Georges suggested—the enemy attacked between Meuse and Moselle? Gamelin, no doubt, felt that the Maginot Line and the Rhine provided ample security on his right; in the center the fortifications and the lower Meuse would hold up the enemy—assuming German forces broke through Belgian demolitions and the Allied retarding maneuver in the Ardennes—long enough for reinforcements to arrive.

Did Gamelin's subordinates understand his plan? René Chambe, who commanded the air units of the Seventh Army, later wrote that the Seventh Army was, circumstances permitting, to "press a vast menace of encirclement in the direction of Liège on the German right wing." But the uncertainties of this long thrust through two states weighed on Giraud. As General d'Astier put it, the mission of the Seventh Army was to "hold . . . the German right wing under its menace. General Giraud at first saw in this mission the occasion for a lightning maneuver offering great perspectives, in accord with his temperament. But, as events approached, he became less sure. . . . Forward anyway!"[56]

General Blanchard determined that his First Army could carry through to the Dyle; he had reservations about pushing farther. The British command approved the Dyle Plan but refused to commit itself to advance to the Albert Canal. But General André Corap's Ninth Army was in a difficult position. Corap had to swing his left wing forward to the Belgian Meuse as far as Namur while lining the French Meuse. He had a much longer front than the other Army commanders but only seven infantry divisions, of which two series B and one a static fortress unit, plus two light cavalry divisions, and a brigade of Spahis, to cover it. Corap never ceased protesting the weakness of his force. He regarded the units initially under his command as a cover force whose resistance would permit the arrival of reinforcements if the enemy made his main effort on the Meuse.[57]

Yet Georges had a reservoir of units on the Maginot Line where the opposing forces were already in contact. Sensitive about his center and concerned at his small reserve, he met with senior officers of Army Group Two in March. He ordered plans to pull six divisions from the Maginot Line into reserve, although by May 10 only three had left the front. Georges later deplored this excessive strength behind the Maginot line,[58] but there was always a chance the enemy might strike there. At the time, however, Georges offered a different explanation. Discussing the situation with General Hassler on May 2, he agreed that the impenetrability of the Ardennes was a myth as Corap claimed, and sympathized with Hassler's shock at the weakness of the French center. When Hassler criticized the mass of forces behind the Maginot Line, Georges agreed but claimed there was nothing he could do—the commanders there had political influence, and used it to thwart his wishes. Despite the pessimistic tone Hassler found Georges "smiling, his visage serene, with that power of attraction so natural to him which puts one at ease. . . ."[59] Georges did not raise the claim of "political influence" after the war.

Thus the High Command completed its preparations. The coming months would be hard.

NOTES

1. *Les Relations militaires franco-belges de mars 1936 au mai 1940: Travaux d'un colloque d'historiens belges et français* (Paris: CNRS, 1968), pp. 83ff; General [Paul] Armengaud, *Batailles politiques et militaires sur l'Europe: Témoignages (1923-1940)* (Paris: Éditions du Myrte, 1948), p. 164; Gamelin's explanation to Daladier, Belisha, and Lord Hankey in minutes of their meeting of September 20 in ED, 3DA2, Dr 2, sdr b.

2. Sir Edmund Ironside, *Time Unguarded: The Ironside Diaries 1937-1940* (Edinburgh: Constable, 1962), pp. 117 ff.

3. France, GQG, EM, 3° Bureau: N° 0403 3/NE, "Instruction n° 3 pour les groupes d'armées et la VIIIe Armée" (unpublished, October 8, 1939).

4. Hans-Adolf Jacobsen, *Fall Gelb: Der Kampf um den deutschen Operationsplan zur Westoffensive 1940* (Wiesbaden: Steiner Verlag, 1957), pp. 18ff, 32; Hans-Erich Volkmann, "Autarkie, Grossraumwirtschaft und Aggression: Zur ökonomischen Motivation der Besetzung Luxemburgs, Belgiens und der Niederlande 1940," *Militärgeschichtliche Mitteilungen* no. 19 (1/1976).

5. France, 9e Armée, Commandement des FA et FTCA, 3° Bureau: N° 1163 3/S, "Ordre d'opérations n° 2" (unpublished, October 19, 1939).

6. Maurice Gamelin, *Servir* III (Paris: Plon, 1947), pp. 23ff; General X [Bührer], *Aux heures tragiques de l'empire (1938-1941)* (Paris: Office colonial d'édition, 1947), p. 129.

7. Sir Charles Webster and Noble Frankland, *The Strategic Air Offensive Against Germany 1939-1945* I (London: H.M.S.O., 1961), pp. 136ff.

8. France, Ministère des armées, EMAT, Service historique, *Guerre, 1939-1945: Les Grandes unités françaises: Historiques succincts* I (Paris: Atelier d'impressions de l'armée, 1967), pp. 316ff; General Fagalde, "L'Affaire des îles de Zélande: (Walcheren et Sud Beveland). Mai 1940," *Revue militaire suisse* nos. 11 and 12 (November and December 1953; November article): 603.

9. *GU françaises* I, p. 318; Fagalde, "L'Affaire des îles," November article, pp. 603ff.

10. Jacobsen, *Fall Gelb*, pp. 38ff, 53ff; Guenther Blumentritt, *Von Rundstedt: The Soldier and the Man*, trans. Cuthbert Reavely (London: Odhams Press, 1952), p. 63.

11. France, GQG, EM, 2ème Bureau: N° 114—NE, "Instruction n° 6 pour la recherche du renseignement" (unpublished, [late October 1939]); France, Commandement des FA 25: 1151/CFA 25, "Ordre d'opérations n° 1" (unpublished, November 9, 1939); France, GQG, EM, 2ème Bureau: n° 130/2NE, "Plan de renseignements" (unpublished, November 24, 1939).

12. General [Raoul] Van Overstraeten, *Albert I-Léopold III: Vingt ans de politique militaire belge 1920-1940* ([Bruges]: Desclée de Brouwer, [1946?]), pp. 410ff; Brian Bond, *France and Belgium 1939-1940* (London: Davis-Poynter, 1975), passim.

13. France, SHA, Section contemporaine, Cdt. Patrick De Ruffray, "Document A/155: Relations franco-hollandais 1939-40" (unpublished, April 1956); complete documentation, testimony, and rather shallow commentary on Dutch defense in [The Netherlands, Staten-Generaal, Tweede Kamer], *Enquêtecommissie Regeringsbeleid 1940-1945: Verslag Houdende de Uitkomsten Van Het Onderzoek. Deel I^{A} en I^{B}: Algemene Inleiding/Militair Beleid 1939-1940 (Punt A Van Het Enquêtebesluit)* (The Hague: Staatsdrukkerijen Uitgeverijbedrijf, 1949), pp. 35ff, 51ff (hereafter cited as *Enquêtecommissie*) and *Enquêtecommissie I^{B} /Bijlagen*, pp. 25ff, 34ff, 42ff, 58ff and I^{C}, pp. 1ff, 25ff, 54ff, 595ff.

14. *Relations franco-belges*, pp. 90ff; Van Overstraeten, *Albert I-Léopold III*, pp. 415ff; General Oscar Michiels, *18 jours de guerre en Belgique* (Paris: Berger-Levrault, 1947), pp. 53ff; Jean Vanwelkenhuyzen, *Neutralité armée: La Politique militaire de la Belgique pendant la "drôle de guerre"* (to be published by Renaissance de la livre), p. 30.

15. R[ubeigh] J. Minney, *The Private Papers of Hore-Belisha* (London: Collins, 1960), p. 258.

16. *Relations franco-belges*, pp. 87, 148ff; General Sir John Kennedy, *The Business of War: The War Narrative of Major-General Sir John Kennedy G.S.M.G., K.C.V.O., K.B.E., C.B., M.C.* (New York: William Morrow, 1958), p. 29; General Louis Koeltz, "Les Plans français et la Belgique en 1939-1940," *Revue générale belge* (May 1960): 67; France, Marine nationale, EMG: Service historique, Hervé Cras, *Les Forces maritimes du Nord (1939-1940)* I (no place given, 1955), p. 14.

17. Georges' directive of October 24 in Hans-Adolf Jacobsen, *Dokumente zur Vorgeschichte des Westfeldzuges 1939-1940* (Berlin and Frankfurt: Musterschmidt Verlag, 1956), pp. 208ff; France, GQG, EMG, 3° Bureau: N° 0682 3/NE, "Hypothèse 'Hollande'" (unpublished, November 8, 1939); Russell D. Jacobson, "French Airborne Operation During World War II," *Aerospace Historian* 22, no. 1 (March 1975): 14ff; P[aul]-É[mile] Caton, *1939-1940: Une guerre perdue en 4 jours* I (1969), pp. 81ff, 99 and II (Blainville-sur-Mer: Éditions l'amitié par le livre, 1974), pp. 107ff, 617ff, 708ff.

18. Minutes of November 9 meeting in ED, 3DA4, Dr. 2, sdr b; Ironside, *Time Unguarded*, pp. 148ff; quotes from Sir John Slessor, *The Central Blue: The Autobiography of Sir John Slessor, Marshal of the RAF* (New York: Praeger, 1957), pp. 250ff; Malcolm Smith, "The RAF and Counter-Force Strategy before World War II," *RUSI: Journal of the Royal United Service Institute for Defence Studies* 121, no. 2 (June 1976): 68ff for background on British air strategy.

19. Brian Bond, ed., *Chief of Staff: The Diaries of Lieutenant-General Sir Henry Pownall.* I *1933-1940* (Hamden, Conn.: Archon Books, 1973), pp. 361ff—Pownall was Chief of Staff of the BEF; [Marcel] Lerecouvreux, *L'Armée Giraud en Hollande: (1939-1940)* (Paris: Nouvelles éditions latines, 1951), pp. 18ff, 39ff; Fagalde, "L'Affaire des îles," November article, pp. 604ff; France, SHAT, General [René] Lehr, "16ᵉ C.A.: 1939 1940" (unpublished, no place or date), passim.

20. Koeltz, "Les Plans," pp. 69ff; France, GQG, Cabinet du Général chef d'état-major général de la défense nationale, Commandant en chef des forces terrestres: N° 180/Cab/FT, "Instruction personnelle et secrète n° 8" (unpublished, November 15, 1939); minutes of the November 17 meeting of the Supreme Council in ED, 3DA2, DR 2, sdr c.

21. France, GQG, EMG, 3° Bureau: N° 0773 3/NE, "Instruction personnelle et secrète n° 8 pour le général commandant le Groupe d'armées n° 1 et le général commandant en chef la 'BEF'" (unpublished, November 17, 1939).

22. Commandant Pierre Lyet, *La Bataille de France: (mai-juin 1940)* (Paris: Payot, 1947), pp. 20ff.

23. General G[aston] Roton, *Années cruciales: La Course aux armements (1933-1939). La Campagne (1939-1940)* (Paris: Charles-Lavauzelle, 1947), p. 94.

24. *Relations franco-belges*, p. 158.

25. Lerecouvreux, *L'Armée Giraud*, pp. 44ff; Roton, *Années cruciales*, pp. 96ff.

26. Cras, *Forces maritimes* I, pp. 15ff, 23ff.

27. Georges' notes in Roton, *Années cruciales*, pp. 96ff; Lyet, *La Bataille de France*, pp. 21ff, 96ff; Jacques Minart, *P. C. Vincennes: Secteur 4* I (Paris: Berger-Levrault, 1945), p. 101; Lerecouvreux, *L'Armée Giraud*, pp. 45ff.

28. Georges' note in Roton, *Années cruciales*, pp. 97ff; Lyet, *La Bataille de France*, p. 22; Minart, *P. C. Vincennes* I, p. 103.

29. *Relations franco-belges*, pp. 159ff.

30. Particular Instruction No. 16 in "Instructions générales et particulières";

France, I° Armée aérienne, EM, 3° Bureau: N° 4969-3S, "Instruction générale n° 8 pour les zones d'opérations aériennes" (unpublished, November 13, 1939); France, Commandement en chef des forces aériennes, EMG, 3° Bureau: N° 2047 3/IS/EMG, Letter from Vuillemin to Gamelin (unpublished, December 21, 1939).

31. France, ZOAN, EM, 3° Bureau: N° 1148 S/3-0, Letter from d'Astier to Mouchard (unpublished, December 27, 1939).

32. Gamelin's testimony in France, Parlement, Assemblée nationale, *Les Événements survenus en France de 1933 à 1945: Témoignages et documents recueillis par la commission d'enquête parlementaire* II (Paris: Presses universitaires de France, [1950?]), pp. 401ff.

33. Maurice Gamelin, *Servir* I (Paris: Plon, 1946), pp. 64ff; Daladier's manuscript notes on the change in ED, 4DA24, Dr 6, sdr d; Georges' reaction in his deposition before the Riom tribunal in ED, 4DA14, Dr 5.

34. Georges' testimony in *Événements . . . Témoignages* III, pp. 639, 675ff; quote from Gamelin's letter in Gamelin, *Servir* III, p. 258.

35. Major-General Sir Edward Spears, *Assignment to Catastrophe* I (New York: A. A. Wyn, 1954), pp. 47ff, 72ff; interview with General André Beaufre, Paris, January 23, 1973; Bond, *Chief of Staff*, pp. 285ff.

36. Georges' testimony in *Événements . . . Témoignages* III, pp. 677, 690; interview with General Beaufre; Roton, *Années cruciales*, pp. 119ff; Doumenc's deposition in Gamelin, *Servir* I, pp. 73ff.

37. Jacques Weygand, *Weygand mon père* (Paris: Flammarion, 1970), pp. 267ff; quote from General [Maxime] Weygand, *Mémoires* III (Paris: Flammarion, 1957), p. 69.

38. Gamelin, *Servir* III, pp. 319ff.

39. Robert Lemaignen, "Le Vuillemin que j'ai connu," *Icare* no. 59 (Spring 1971): 61ff; interview with General Pierre Bodet at SHAA, Vincennes, February 20, 1973; France, SHAA, Letter from Mendigal to Vuillemin (unpublished, January 12, [1940]).

40. Lemaignen, "Vuillemin," p. 62; February 23 and 24 entries in France, "Journal de marche et des opérations du GQGAé" (unpublished, August 28, 1939, to July 1940); France, "Extraits du rapport du général Georges" (unpublished, no date given), pp. 5ff; General [François] d'Astier de la Vigerie, *Le Ciel n'était pas vide: 1940* (Paris: Julliard, 1952), p. 73.

41. Jacobsen, *Fall Gelb*, p. 87.

42. Jean Vanwelkenhuyzen, "Le 10 Janvier 1940 à Mechelen-sur-Meuse: Le Plan de Hitler aux mains des belges," *Revue générale belge* (January 1955): 5ff.

43. Van Overstraeten, *Albert I-Léopold III*, pp. 445ff; General Louis Koeltz, "Les Plans français et la Belgique en 1939-1940," *Revue général belge* (May 1960), p. 72; France, SHAA, Letter from Mendigal to Vuillemin (unpublished, January 12, [1940]).

44. *Relations franco-belges*, p. 104. France, SHAA, [GQGA], Letter from Mendigal to Vuillemin (unpublished, January 13, 1940).

45. *Relations franco-belges,* pp. 104ff; Vanwelkenhuyzen, *Neutralité armée,* pp. 50ff.

46. Roton, *Années cruciales*, p. 99; Minart, *P. C. Vincennes* I, p. 128; Gamelin, *Servir* III, pp. 157ff; Van Overstraeten, *Albert I-Léopold III*, pp. 461ff.

47. Philippe Marnay (pseudonym for Jean Vanwelkenhuyzen), "Neutralité et

défense nationale: La Politique militaire de la Belgique en 1939-1940," *Revue générale belge* (May 1960): 41; Robert Aron, *Léopold III ou le choix impossible: Février 1934-juillet 1940* ([Paris]:Plon, 1977), p. 265.

48. Jacobsen, *Fall Gelb*, pp. 90ff, 100ff.

49. Lyet, *La Bataille de France*, p. 24; Roton, *Années cruciales*, pp. 101ff; Gamelin's "Mémoire n° 8" given to the Riom tribunal in ED, 4DA27, DR 1, sdr a.

50. Gamelin's note in Gamelin, *Servir* III, pp. 166ff.

51. Lyet, *La Bataille de France*, pp. 24ff; *Événements . . . Témoignages* III, p. 743.

52. Quote from Lyet, *La Bataille de France*, pp. 26ff; Bond, *Chief of Staff*, p. 272.

53. *Relations franco-belges*, pp. 170ff.

54. Cras, *Forces maritimes* I, pp. 17ff; quote from Gamelin's note in Gamelin, *Servir* III, pp. 173ff; France, SHAT, GA 1, EM, 3ème Bureau: N° 1744 S/3, Letter from Billotte to generals commanding First and Seventh Armies (unpublished, March 8, 1940) covering enclosed "Manoeuvre offensive à partir du front ANVERS-NAMUR" (unpublished, no date).

55. Quote from France, GQG, Le Général commandant en chef, Chef d'EMG de la défense nationale, Commandant en chef les forces terrestres, N° 393/3 FT, "Instruction personnelle et secrète n° 11 pour le général commandant en chef sur le front du nord-est (pour les forces terrestres françaises)" (unpublished, March 12, 1940); France, Commandement en chef du front nord-est, EM, 3° Bureau: N° 790 3/Op., "Instruction personnelle et secrète n° 9 pour le général commandant le Groupe d'armées n° 1 et le général commandant en chef la BEF" (unpublished, March 20, 1940).

56. Quotes from René Chambe, *Équipages dans la fournaise: 1940* (Paris: Flammarion, 1945), p. 79 and d'Astier, *Le Ciel n'était pas vide*, p. 69.

57. Georges Beau and L. Gaubusseau, *Dix erreurs une défaite* (Paris: Presses de la Cité, 1967), p. 59.

58. Georges' testimony in *Événements . . . Témoignages* III, p. 687.

59. Hassler's diary entry in General P[aul]-É[mile] Tournoux, "Pouvait-on prévoir l'attaque allemande des Ardennes de mai 1940? Un général avait dit 'oui'," *Revue historique de l'armée* (no. 2 1971): 136ff.

chapter 7

THE FINAL TOUCHES (MARCH-MAY 1940)

The question of intelligence became pressing as the campaigning season approached. Gamelin reminded Vuillemin in late February that "The invasion of Luxemburg, Belgium and Holland . . . poses a problem . . . for the Germans . . . of speed. . . . It is therefore infinitely probable that the entry . . . into these neutral countries will take the form of a brutal onrush by mechanized and motorized divisions. . . ."[1] The focus of the air search was, therefore, to be the enemy mechanized and motorized force.

The effort paid off. In early March, air reconnaissance signaled strong enemy armored and motorized forces near Trier, east of the Ardennes; if this "slipping" of enemy dispositions to the south could be confirmed, "it could be the indication of a possible action against the Maginot Line with a flanking maneuver through Luxemburg."[2] It was vital to determine if this grouping was aimed west toward Luxemburg or south toward the Saar. On March 15 Air Force General Headquarters ordered the Eastern Zone to survey the Trier area to identify the armored divisions whose density north of the Moselle seemed to have increased. The Ninth Army, in instructions to its air units on March 15, again emphasized locating and tracking enemy armor in its sector. In early May General Augereau, the air commander for the Ninth, issued an emphatic warning to watch for enemy airborne actions near the Meuse, and for signs of enemy tanks moving toward Givet and Namur, toward Mézières and Sedan, or toward the Meuse at Huy, north of the Ninth's sector in a likely direction for the southern arm of a German pincers attack on Liège.[3]

In mid-April Georges was thinking of a German attack either through Holland and Belgium in the north, or against the Maginot Line with a flanking maneuver through Luxemburg and southern Belgium.[4] General Ulrich Liss, the German expert on the West, concluded later that French intelligence had a fair idea of the balance of German strength although it mistakenly thought Germany might invade Switzerland.

The French staff was not dependent on air reconnaissance alone. French agents brought in a number of alleged German plans, including one that caught the attention of Colonel Baril, chief of the intelligence section at La Ferté. This plan, received in April, specified a thrust through the Ardennes and over the Meuse to the English Channel to cut off Allied forces in Bel-Gium. Unfortunately, until operations began it was impossible to determine which "German plan" was authentic.[5]

Belgian intelligence also noted a shift in the German deployment, which it fixed at thirty divisions north and fifty south of Liège. In early March Van Overstraeten, concerned over rumored French weakness on the lower Meuse, directed the Belgian attaché to warn Gamelin of the German deployment. Colonel Petibon responded that:

> 'the position from [Mézières-] Charleville to the Moselle has benefited from the particular attention of the High Command. Especially strong in its most exposed parts [those not covered by the Meuse], backed in other areas by important natural obstacles, difficult to invest, supported by old fortresses of which one [Verdun] proved itself in the course of the last war, it is capable, if need be, of assuring the pivot for the maneuvers which will take it as a base.'[6]

The French command had confidence in its Meuse front.

THE SHIFT IN GERMAN STRATEGY

In fact, French and Belgian intelligence had detected a profound shift in German strategy as Hitler continued to look for a plan to crush the Allies before they became too strong. By March German intelligence had an accurate picture of Allied dispositions, although it mistakenly concluded that Giraud's Seventh Army would command the entire Allied mechanized and motorized vanguard.[7] It had no idea of the contacts between the Allies, Belgium, and the Netherlands, nor had it any inkling that Giraud intended to drive all the way into Duth Brabant. But German intelligence knew of the excessive French strength in the Maginot LIne and of the weakness of the Ninth Army.

In February Hitler met General Erich von Manstein, formerly General Gerd von Rundstedt's chief of staff in Army Group A facing the Ardennes. Manstein had an audacious plan; on February 18 Hitler decided to adopt most of it. The plan called for the staff to reassign one army from General Fedor von Bock's Army Group B, in the north facing Belgium and the Netherlands, to Rundstedt's group; the bulk of the Panzers would move in the same direction. These were the changes detected by French and Belgian intelligence. By the end of March, German plans were complete and, as Baril's document claimed, called for an attack through the Ardennes and over the Meuse before the Allies could reinforce their weak defenses there,

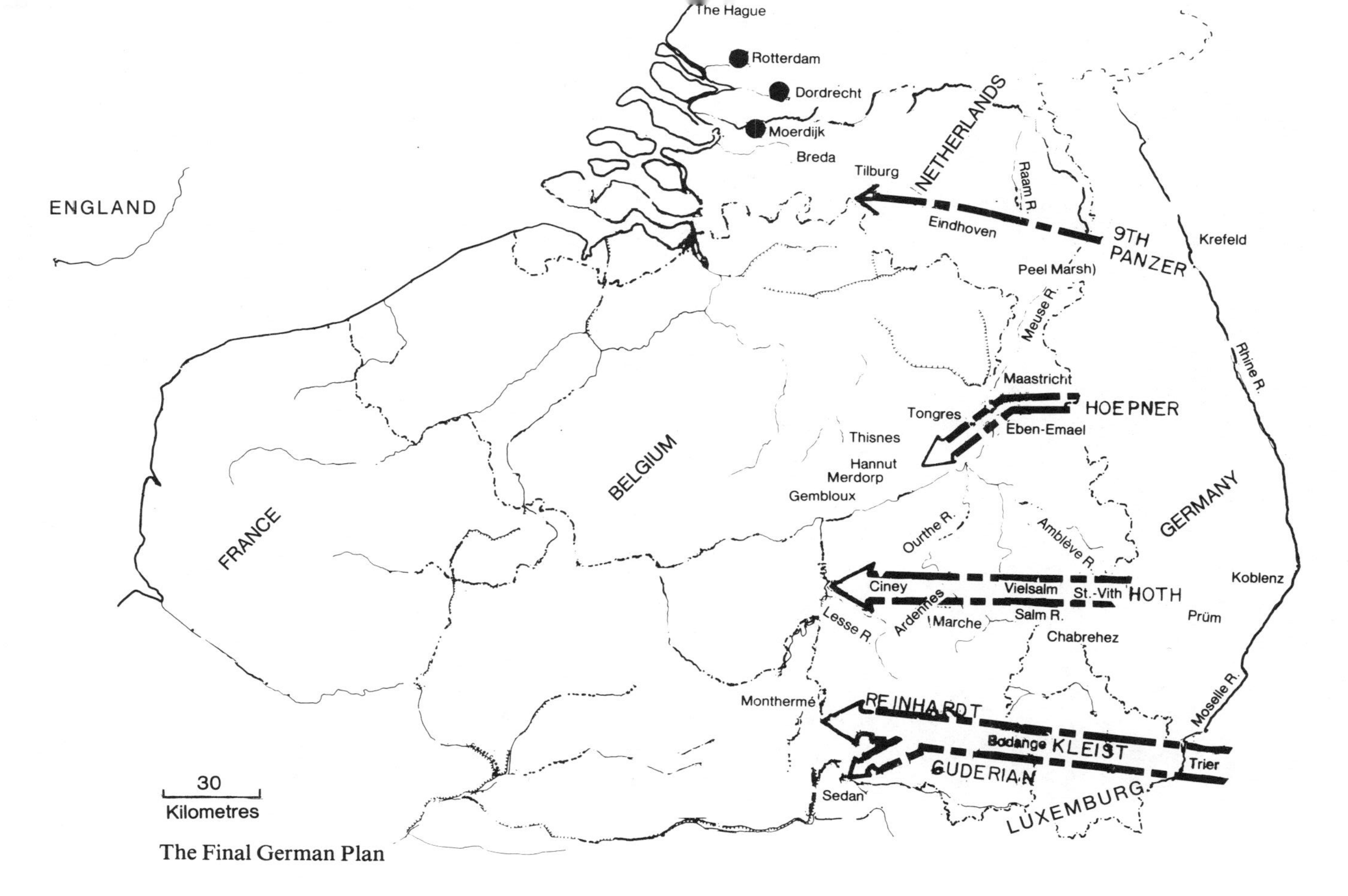

The Final German Plan

and then an exploitation to the sea to cut off the Allied armies in Belgium.[8] Two of the ten Panzers were to strike central Belgium and one Holland to convince the Allied command that the German target was still the Belgian plain. Hitler himself conceived an airborne operation against the heart of the Belgian defense of the Albert Canal—the fortress of Eben Emael and the bridges lying under its guns—and a larger scale operation to open the way into Holland for mechanized and motorized forces.

Hitler could count on the initiative, on air superiority, and on a more homogeneous and above all more experienced force. But this was still a daring plan. What would happen if the Panzers could not cross the Meuse before Allied reinforcements arrived? Could they sustain an advance of several hundred kilometers to the sea without being cut off by counter-attacks?[9]

THE POSITION OF THE NEUTRALS

By mid-December 1939 French intelligence listed Dutch strength at 400,000 men, forming four corps with two infantry divisions each plus the motorized Light Division, whose striking power was limited to three squadrons of armored cars. The Dutch army also had reserve infantry employed as sentinel troops. The weakness of the force lay in its lack of heavy weapons, the inexperience of its cadres, and its reservist character. Nonetheless, the Netherlands had a force larger than the BEF, plus several hundred anti-aircraft weapons.[10] The alert in November 1939, then the news passed on by Van Overstraeten on January 12, 1940, that the Germans intended to move through Dutch territory, convinced the Dutch government to resist the Germans. The question of strategy remained.[11] This question came to a head in February 1940 when the Dutch Commander in Chief, General Izaak Reynders, lost his post. Part of Reynders' problem lay in his lack of personal connections in the governmental milieux, part in clashes with the government over his desire to impose a state of siege and strict discipline on the armed forces: after all, the country was not yet at war. But it was the dispute over strategy that proved fatal. The government wanted the defense effort concentrated in the populous heart of the country, regardless of the fact that withdrawal from North Brabant meant opening the gate to a German invasion of Belgium from the north, and thus would injure the Allied cause. The Defense Minister, General Dijxhoorn, insisted that the Peel-Raam line was untenable, at least without a linkup with Belgian defenses. In selecting General Henri Winkelman to replace Reynders on February 6, Dijxhoorn took care to select a man who shared his views. Thus, like the Belgian Chief of Staff General Van den Bergen, Reynders was fired for "threatening" a neutrality that those in power knew might well be only temporary. The West suffered another defeat.

Winkelman was immediately handicapped in office: it was too late to construct new fortifications to rearrange the Dutch deployment. He dispersed some infantry in sentinel positions on the frontiers and in the garrison of Walcheren, but concentrated most of his forces in the heart of the country. The Peel-Raam line, based on a continuous row of casemates behind canals and marshes along the German frontier, absorbed one Dutch corps of two infantry divisions, plus the Light Division, and three infantry regiments along a front of seventy kilometers. But the Belgian defense did not begin until the Albert Canal and some branch canals farther north: there was a gap *inside Belgium* between the southern edge of the Dutch defense and the northern edge of the Belgian lines. As long as this gap remained, Winkelman had an excuse for not risking major forces there. The problem was to form a continuous front with the Belgians.[12] In January 1940 the Dutch and Belgians had begun talks to deal with this problem. Reynders offered to add another corps to the Peel-Raam line if the Belgian command would extend its dispositions north to join them. But the Belgian command thought the Peel-Raam position too close to the frontier, too weak in the flanks, and vulnerable to airborne landings in its immediate rear. The Belgian staff would send troops north only if the Dutch corps was stationed in the Tilburg area, back from the frontier. This proposal coincided with the ideas of the commander of the Dutch Field Army, General Jan Baron Voorst tot Voorst, who wanted a new front erected on the "Oranjestelling" running from Goirle to Tilburg to 's-Hertogenbosch. Further, a position here would have been available to the French Seventh Army which planned to move into the area, expecting to find positions waiting for it. But no fortifications existed in this area, and there was no time to construct them. The attempt at joint planning collapsed. Another factor worth noting is that the Belgian commanders, with their record in World War I, looked down on the Dutch military which had not fought on the Continent for a century.

Winkelman took no account of French troops in his planning, nor is it clear whether he was aware of the suggestions that Gamelin had made in November 1939 to his predecessor. He decided that without a Belgian linkup the Peel-Raam line was untenable. Therefore, he informed the Dutch commander in the area in March that he would leave the 3rd Corps and most of the Light Division there so as not to reveal the change of plans, but once the shooting began they would immediately withdraw leaving the local forces to delay the Germans as best they could. As for the French, Gamelin would have had to communicate a more detailed plan earlier to have influenced Dutch decisions.[13]

Gamelin sensed this when he talked with the Dutch attaché on April 5. Gamelin told the officer that he hoped the Dutch would cover the arrival of the Seventh Army on a north-south line in the Tilburg area and link up with Belgian cover forces on a branch canal north of the Albert Canal at Turnhout. For the first time Gamelin revealed his plan: Giraud would advance with one DLM and two motorized infantry divisions followed by three ordinary divisions. But this information came too late to influence Dutch strategy.[14]

Nor was the eventual executor of this French maneuver entirely happy with the plan. In March, when the availability of a third DLM at last made the Breda Plan practical, Giraud drafted orders for its execution. Giraud pointed out that the enemy was 100 kilometers from Tilburg and had seven routes available; the Seventh Army was 250 kilometers away and had only four. The operation was risky. If the Belgians could not hold the Albert Canal, the Seventh might find itself cut off with its back to the sea. But if the Breda maneuver was to be attempted, it ought to be done from the start of operations; detailed French-Dutch-Belgian plans would be necessary. Billotte supported Giraud's conclusions. On April 14 Georges, noting the Dutch decision to pull back from the Peel-Raam position, asked again that the Seventh Army be replaced by a single corps and that its ambitious mission be dropped. Gamelin replied that the maneuver was to be maintained regardless of Dutch moves. By April 30 the French command knew that the Dutch army had only fifteen battalions without artillery on the Peel-Raam line, although Winkelman promised to send reinforcements when Allied troops arrived. On May 10 most of the Dutch army was in Fortress Holland or in covering positions to the east; a whole corps was in reserve in the Hague area with three battalions assigned to guard airfields—a task they shared with a motorized regiment and two squadrons of armored cars from the Light Division. The Dutch command took the German airborne threat seriously after its demonstration in April in Norway.[15]

By mid-February the Belgian command had worked out its participation in the Dyle Plan. The Belgian government decided to evacuate a minimal proportion of the population in the areas threatened with invasion so as not to flood the roads with refugees. This was an unrealistic decision, and when the invasion came perhaps millions of Belgians jammed the roads, as they had in 1914.

On February 21 the French attaché in Brussels sent back to France the Belgian plan for operations in the Ardennes. General Maurice Keyaerts had three groups of motorized Chasseurs ardennais in the Ardennes: two battalions around Arlon, two around Bastogne, and three at Vielsalm. A second division of Chasseurs held the Meuse between Namur and Liège, including a bridgehead east of the Meuse at Huy covering the southern flank of Liège. The Belgian command had scouts with radios emplaced in the Grand Duchy of Luxemburg to provide early warning. As the enemy advanced, Belgian forces would set off extensive demolitions in the forests, while the Chasseurs would retreat to Huy to make a stand. Only those at Vielsalm were to engage and retard the enemy; the others would retreat at full speed. The Belgian command calculated that the enemy would reach Huy in two to four days from the start of operations. Georges passed this information to his subordinates, adding that the problem of evacuation raised fears among the Walloons whose land would largely be abandoned; Georges preferred an immediate evacuation, but the Belgian government had not confronted the problem.[16]

On March 26 Van Overstraeten and Léopold directed maneuvers in which a cavalry division dealt with simulated airborne landings.[17] On April 23 Van Overstraeten warned General Michiels again of an airborne coup against the Meuse and Albert Canal bridges—it would be *"impardonnable"* if the enemy captured the crossings. On May 10 the Belgian army had, besides the forces in the Ardennes, nine infantry divisions on the Albert Canal, and a cavalry screen behind branch canals north of the Albert; within twenty-four hours a further nine infantry divisions would be on the Belgian sector of the Dyle line.

The Belgian army was a weighty force: four active corps with twelve infantry divisions, two reserve corps with six, the 7th Corps and two motorized cavalry divisions plus two divisions of light mechanized Chasseurs ardennais, five artillery, and two antiaircraft regiments. Each active infantry division had one company of mechanized and one of motorized 47 mm antitank weapons; each active regiment had a further motorized company of 47's.[18] But the majority of Belgian troops were reservists. Above all, however, the memories of 1914 and 1918 were an inspiration to this force—which was twice the strength of the BEF.

But who would command the Allied armies in battle? Gamelin seemed to intend Georges to command in the field. The matter could not be settled until King Léopold accepted Gamelin's delegation of authority to Georges, and this could not happen until operations began—or so Gamelin claimed. Georges was to keep personal control over the Seventh Army and the BEF,[19] leaving Billotte with the First, Ninth, and Second Armies in the center of the northeastern front. When the Belgian army entered the line between the Seventh and the BEF, Léopold could be given titular command of another army group with a French chief of staff. This vital question of command remained unsettled until the fighting began. Of course that was the worst possible time to search for a solution.

ALLIED PLANNING AT THE LOWER LEVELS

Assuming the Belgian army would secure the Albert Canal and the branch canal north of it to Turnhout, Giraud's vanguard—the 1st DLM, the 25th and 9th Motorized—would have to drive through Belgium into Dutch territory under the threat of air attack. Giraud planned to transport his tanks, those of the 1st DLM and two battalions of infantry tanks forming the 510th Tank Groupment, by rail, thereby saving their tracks. His most ambitious idea called for the tanks to move all the way into Dutch territory by rail. The motorized reconnaissance groups of his army could be added to the 510th Groupment to form, in effect, a second armored division.[20] Whether this plan could be accomplished would depend on the circumstances of the moment. The conditions under which Giraud's army reached the area would depend on Belgian and Dutch preparations to expedite the movement *and* to cover his flanks once he arrived. If the Belgians and Dutch did not comply, Giraud by himself would be unable to accomplish his mission.

The composition of the seaborne expedition to the islands in the mouth of the Escaut was fixed on May 9: a series B infantry regiment with artillery, communications, and antiaircraft units would land at the mouth of the Escaut. Because of the danger of air attack, the operation would be conducted at or near nightfall in Dutch waters with cover from the multiseat fighters of the French naval air arm.[21] Fagalde's 16th Corps would enter the area overland.

The 25th Motorized had the longest distance to go; it had to remain on constant alert. Because of the air threat, its main movements would have to be made at night. Two groups of 75's, two batteries of 25's plus four companies of machine guns (drawn from the reserved 4th Infantry) would form its antiaircraft screen; a network of aircraft warning posts would be erected as the advance proceeded.[22]

The problems of the BEF and the French First Army were similar but less demanding since the distances they had to cover were smaller while the Belgian defenses covering them were stronger. And Blanchard's army would have General René Prioux's Cavalry Corps with the 2nd and 3rd DLM in front of it.

But General André Corap's Ninth Army faced a trying mission. Corap's left wing, his 2nd Motorized and 11th Corps, had to move to the Belgian Meuse on a front as wide as that covered by the whole First Army; his 41st Corps—installed on an even longer front on prepared positions behind the French Meuse—consisted only of the series B 61st and the static 102nd Fortress Infantry Divisions. The most delicate part of Corap's mission was the movement into Belgium as far north as Namur, so Corap placed his best units on his left—including the 2nd Corps' 5th Motorized, and the series A 18th and 22nd Infantry Divisions of General Julien Martin's 11th Corps. Corap planned to hold the active 4th North African Infantry in reserve behind his left wing; he intended the series B 53rd Infantry to garrison the frontier position his left would leave behind. But he was worried about the weakness of his army, as he confided to General Hassler on May 8.[23]

To Corap's right, General Huntziger's Second Army extended from Sedan to the Montmédy bridgehead, the westernmost bastion of the Maginot

Line. Huntziger's front was shorter than Corap's and he had, on the whole, better troops. However, he placed the series B 55th Infantry at Sedan since it was protected there by the Meuse River. The rest of his front was covered only by the small Chiers River and farther east the Maginot Line.

To Huntziger's right, in turn, General Condé's Third Army (constituting the left wing of Prételat's Second Army Group) faced Luxemburg. Condé held the Maginot Line except for the bridgehead covering Longwy, which lay in front of it. The Ninth, Second, and Third Armies were to dispatch cavalry into the Ardennes to join Belgian forces there and retard the enemy advance—particularly in the northern Ardennes where the advance of the Ninth Army would take time. This combined cavalry force consisted of five light cavalry divisions, each with a light mechanized brigade with a single squadron of light battle tanks, plus two Spahi brigades, and the independent Cavalry Brigade. The Ninth Army would have, from north to south, the 4th and 1st Light Cavalry and the 3rd Spahis. The Spahis would link up with the 5th Light Cavalry, the Cavalry Brigade, and then the 2nd Light Cavalry of Huntziger's army. Further east, the 1st Spahis of the Third Army would link Huntziger's force to Condé's 3rd Light Cavalry, which was to retard the enemy advance in Luxemburg. Corap's cavalry was to push east to Ciney in the western Ardennes, if possible to Marche in the central Ardennes, to form a front between the Ourthe and Lesse rivers. The rest of the cavalry would move into the Belgian province of Luxemburg "to act in the flank and on the rear of the [German] motorized troops rushing toward the Meuse."[24] But if the enemy attacked in force in the southern Ardennes as well as in the north, Huntziger's cavalry would be unable to assist Corap's.

Corap wanted to get a force onto the Belgian Meuse quickly and keep it there until his left wing could come up—only one of his infantry divisions was motorized. His Spahis would move to the Semoy to join Huntziger's cavalry, but his light cavalry divisions would stay on the Belgian Meuse until the river was "solidly enough held." Only then would he order them into the Ardennes. General d'Arras, the commander of the 1st Light Cavalry, would coordinate the cavalry action.[25] This cavalry maneuver violated Georges' directive of March 14 which specified that the cavalry was to move as rapidly as possible to aid the Belgian cover force and retard the enemy, but he agreed to let Corap keep his cavalry on the Meuse until infantry advance guards reached the river.[26]

Huntziger, in the meantime, varied the mission of his cavalry. On March 15 he considered two hypotheses: an enemy attack in force against the Second Army or an attack directed farther north with a cover force toward the Second Army. In the first case Huntziger proposed to leave his cavalry on the Semoy River just inside Belgium. In the second case his cavalry would push to Libramont and Neufchâteau in the midst of the Ardennes.

New instructions from GQG on March 27 decided on the second maneuver. Most of Huntziger's cavalry was to reach Libramont; motorized elements would, if possible, reinforce the Belgian defense at Bastogne and Arlon.[27] This order took no account of Belgian plans—known to the French command—to withdraw without a fight from Bastogne and Arlon. Perhaps the French thought the Belgians would not quit the battlefield just as their Allies came up.

Huntziger faced another problem in March. A parliamentary committee led by M. Taittinger inspected the fortifications at Sedan—and was shocked. The defenders counted too heavily on the Meuse and the Ardennes for protection; Taittinger warned of a possible disaster: "There are fields of misfortune for our arms." Huntziger responded to the criticism on April 8 to Georges. His troops had more than doubled fortifications in the area. Huntziger agreed that the air and antiaircraft units in the sector were weak, but two batteries of 25 mm guns had recently arrived; the air defenses shot down eight enemy planes, including three in the first week of April. Huntziger thought no urgent reinforcement necessary and expressed his confidence in Grandsard and his troops. Further, he had faith in "the . . . resistance of the Belgians, the difficulties . . . in crossing the Ardennes, the effectiveness of the demolitions and finally the value of the Meuse as an obstacle. . . ."[28] Obviously Huntziger's superiors shared his feeling.

Georges' entire force on May 10 included eighty-nine divisions plus fortress units equal to a further thirteen. There were five light cavalry divisions, three DLM's, three DCR's; thirty-one active—seven motorized—infantry divisions, twenty series A, sixteen series B, ten British, and one Polish infantry divisions. Georges' chief of staff, General Gaston Roton, calculated that Billotte's First Army Group had thirty-seven divisions including four of light cavalry, a Spahi brigade, and three DLM's.[29] Prételat's Second Army Group had twenty-six divisions including one of light cavalry and a Spahi brigade; Besson's Third Army Group facing the Rhine and Switzerland had five divisions and a Spahi brigade; Georges had eighteen infantry divisions and three DCR's in reserve. Three divisions remained at Gamelin's disposal for possible use in the Alps. Five of the divisions in central reserve, including the 3rd DCR, were not yet ready; Georges' central reserve was already largely committed as a function of the maneuver adopted. Thus, a Belgian intervention group stood behind Billotte with a first "lot" of three motorized infantry divisions and one DCR committed in advance—the 1st DCR going to the First Army—and a second lot of two divisions. Billotte assumed that the enemy would make his main effort in the Gembloux gap; to parry this enemy effort he asked Georges to commit the 1st and 2nd DCR under General Louis Keller's 1st Armored Group. Billotte felt this force was the minimum necessary to counterattack the massed enemy armor hitting the First Army at Gembloux or possibly the

BEF. That such a force might hit his Ninth or Second Armies apparently did not occur to him. Georges, however, mindful of other threats, refused to commit the 2nd DCR in advance. Five divisions stood ready to face a German invasion via Switzerland; the central reserve in Lorraine and Champagne held eight infantry divisions—only one motorized—and two remaining DCR's: only these ten divisions remained uncommitted.[30] To these French and British totals may be added eight Dutch infantry divisions and the Light Division, eighteen Belgian infantry divisions, two Belgian motorized cavalry divisions, and two divisions of Chasseurs ardennais, for a total on May 10 of ninety-six conventional infantry divisions. The Allied force also included at least eight motorized infantry divisions, thirteen division-sized fortress units, six armored divisions plus the British tank brigade, five Dutch and Belgian motorized cavalry divisions, five French light cavalry divisions, and four French cavalry brigades. The Germans mustered 124 infantry divisions of which seven were motorized, ten Panzers, one airborne division, and a horse cavalry division. The Allied force was superior except for armored divisions, and the British 1st Armoured and the French 4th DCR joined the battle within two weeks of the start of operations.

The question remains as to why Georges did not draw forces from the Maginot Line. Prételat's army group was well endowed with tank battalions, although it had no armored divisions. Giraud's Seventh Army had two infantry tank battalions, Blanchard's First had four, Corap's Ninth had only three—one equipped with FT's from 1918—and Huntziger's Second had three. But Prételat had seventeen tank battalions in his three armies, and although five had obsolete machines, one had powerful D2 mediums. Another four battalions were with Besson's army group (two with obsolete machines); one battalion of obsolete tanks was in the Alps.[31] Georges' reasoning in leaving so many active infantry divisions and tank units on a fortified front remains shrouded in doubt. Georges complained to Gamelin in March that Prételat always found pretexts to keep forces, but he refused Gamelin's offer to intervene—he preferred to handle it himself. But Georges failed to impose his will.

FINAL PLANS FOR AIR OPERATIONS

By January the RAF was committed to engage the ten squadrons of the Advanced Air Striking Force and some or all of the twenty-five squadrons of Bomber Command in Britain in support of land operations. Marshal Barratt was to coordinate these operations.[32] From mid-April d'Astier had three groupments of French bombers, each with twenty to thirty aircraft, but these were old planes fit only for night operations. On April 20, however, d'Astier received Groupment 6 with its modern Lioré 451 medium bombers for daylight operations, plus Assault Groupment 18 on April 25. In May, Groupment 1, equipped with modern American machines, would begin to arrive: the long gestation of the modern French bomber force was ending. In late March Vuillemin directed that Georges, or Têtu under Georges' authority, would choose where to apply the assault aviation.[33] But as the assault units trained, there were ominous warnings that low-level missions might suffer heavily from small caliber Flak, especially if they did not secure the element of surprise.

The British air staff never gave up hope of strategic air war over the Ruhr; it remained hostile to the use of bombers over the battlefield. In mid-April Barratt saw Gamelin again on this matter, but failed to move him. Under "severe" British pressure, the Allied Supreme Council finally agreed on April 23 to sanction the bombing of the Ruhr once active operations began, on a retaliatory basis. Then, unexpectedly, the British army staff withdrew support for the Ruhr plan and demanded instead that the bombers concentrate on communication lines supporting the enemy offensive. This shift threw RAF planners into a counterattack which Slessor was drafting on May 10. The French, however, found a friend in Barratt, who supported calls for more British air strength in France. But the chief of Fighter Command, Sir Hugh Dowding, put all his prestige into keeping his force in Britain. And Air Marshal Portal, who took charge of Bomber Command in April, wrote on May 8 that the use of medium bombers in support of the armies was "'fundamentally unsound'" and would have "'disastrous consequences on the future of the war in the air.'"[34]

The Dyle Plan brought renewed appeals for air support from the ground commanders. Billotte met d'Astier and his army commanders on April 6 to settle the issue. D'Astier credited the Germans with 1,200 fighters and 3,000 bombers (this last double the actual number). His Northern Zone had 432 fighters (72 British) and 314 bombers (192 British). D'Astier reallocated fighter Groupment 23 to the First, Ninth, and Second Armies; Groupment 25 to the Seventh Army; and Groupment 21 to Paris, although it could be drawn on to reinforce the first two. His bomber strength was in the 1st Air Division, which by May 10 had two day and three night bomber groupments. These groupments were to work primarily for the First Army; Bomber Command in Britain would serve the BEF and the Seventh Army; the British Advanced Air Striking Force, based in Champagne, would support the Ninth and Second Armies. The presence of Barratt at d'Astier's headquarters at Chauny would secure Allied coordination. French antiaircraft was concentrated in the armies facing the Belgian plain and behind the Maginot Line opposite Germany. The Ninth Army had only nine mobile batteries of medium and three of light weapons; only the Ninth and Second Armies had to emplace field artillery as antiaircraft.[35]

THE SCANDINAVIAN INTERLUDE

The stalemate was first broken in November 1939 when Stalin attacked Finland to improve the Soviet strategic position on the Baltic. The Finnish struggle aroused strong sympathy in the West, which saw the Soviet Union as a totalitarian power and an ally of Germany, supplying Hitler with strategic raw materials. In the winter, Allied leaders planned to dispatch an expeditionary force to Finland; British leaders further suggested cutting off Swedish iron ore which, coming through the Baltic and the Norwegian port of Narvik, was essential to German war industry.[36] On February 5, 1940, Daladier put the issue to the Allied Supreme Council, which decided that the expeditionary force was to be ready in mid-March.

Gamelin also considered air attacks from the Middle East on Russian oil fields in the Caucasus which, it was thought, were supplying Germany. This farfetched idea never went beyond the planning stage; the Swedish iron ore seemed the most vulnerable resource the Allies could attack to reinforce their blockade and open a second front.[37] But on March 13 Finland made peace with Stalin.

The Finnish collapse and the stalemate on the western front brought down the Daladier government on March 20. The public demanded more energetic prosecution of the war: the call rose for Paul Reynaud. Known as a patriot and anti-Nazi from the early 1930s, Reynaud's flamboyant personality symbolized the hard line toward Germany.[38] Lacking a major party to support him, Reynaud had to compromise in forming a government, retaining Daladier as Minister of National Defense and War, and accepting the presence of a number of "soft" ministers: his new government was shaky from its inception. Reynaud recast the government as the War Cabinet and added a permanent secretary—a position originally meant for Charles de Gaulle. He signed a pact with Britain agreeing that neither party would make a separate peace, and persuaded labor and management organizations to issue a declaration urging national unity and a vigorous prosecution of the war. He looked north for opportunities to demonstrate his vigor.

The end of Finnish resistance temporarily halted planning, but the Allies were still eager to stop the supply of Swedish iron ore to Germany. From late March they considered mining Norwegian waters to cut off the German coastal trade.[39] But on April 8 intelligence reported German shipping moving north: landing troops from merchant ships, seizing airports with airborne troops, and pouring in reinforcements by air and sea; German forces snapped up most of Norway under the nose of the Royal Navy, while occupying Denmark by land. Gamelin agreed with Admiral François Darlan that the first wave of the French expeditionary force should embark for Norway, but it could not move before April 12.

On April 9 the French military chiefs attended a meeting chaired by the President of the Republic himself. Discontent was evident. Unable to act immediately in the north, Darlan proposed that they demand that Belgium invite Allied intervention to preempt the German invasion. All present agreed; Belgium refused the demand.[40]

Meanwhile, the expeditionary force slowly formed. Reynaud was particularly unhappy at the delays, and he found Gamelin's calm manner and his blaming of the British command, which had authority in the north, annoying. Reynaud began to think seriously of replacing Gamelin. On April 12 another high-level meeting took place; Reynaud delivered an unparalleled attack on Gamelin in an attempt to force him from his post. For Gamelin, April 12 and 13 were among the "most painful days" of his life.[41] But the issue at stake was more than personal, as were the issues between Gamelin and Georges. Reynaud, influenced by his principal military adviser, Lieutenant Colonel Paul de Villelume, disagreed with Gamelin's grand strategy. Gamelin believed that victory would come from an offensive toward the Ruhr which the Allies should be able to mount in the spring of 1941, provided Belgian and perhaps Dutch neutrality was negated. To this end, he was eager to see the enemy attack in the west. But Villelume and Reynaud feared that Germany was too strong. According to Villelume, the Allies could never mount a successful offensive without numerical superiority, and that was unattainable unless another great power like the United States took the field.

Villelume's solution was to use the Allies' one superiority: seapower. Germany must be penned up by land and in the air and stifled by blockade. The Germans depended on foreign iron ore and oil: these were weak links that the Allies must strike. Given this conception, the Norwegian operation was vital; Gamelin's failure to treat it as such, combined with his strategy centering on the western front, were grounds—to Villelume—for dismissal. It was this disagreement over grand strategy between Villelume and his wavering master Reynaud, and Gamelin, that burst into the open on April 12.

As the War Cabinet sat in embarrassed silence, Reynaud attacked Gamelin's conduct of the Norwegian crisis. No one at first responded. Finally, Daladier defended Gamelin; he would not accept Gamelin's dismissal. The meeting broke up with the government divided on this vital issue.[42] Gamelin drafted a letter of resignation, but Daladier would not accept it. However, the cabinet meeting of April 13 was much more calm: Reynaud left the question in abeyance. Afterwards, Jean Fabry, an old friend of Gamelin's and a member of the senate, visited Gamelin to tell him that his quarrel with Georges was leading the senate to interpellate the government. Gamelin replied that he had always favored giving Georges command of the army while he concentrated on the national defense level; Fabry spread this information. The senate dropped its interpellation on April 18. The Command issue remained temporarily in suspense.

On April 16 Allied landings began in Norway, but the Allies soon found their supply lines disrupted by the Luftwaffe. The blow came on April 26 when Ironside told Gamelin that a major decision on Norway had to be made soon. Gamelin flew to London to discover that Ironside proposed to evacuate central Norway. Gamelin knew that such a loss would probably end his career; he pressed the British to hold on and got agreement for a meeting of the Allied Commanders in Chief followed by the Supreme Council. Gamelin convinced the Supreme Council to accept his views but the next morning Ironside informed Gamelin that he had ordered the evacuation of central Norway the night before.[43] The more strategically significant operation against the Germans at Narvik continued (Narvik fell to the Allies on May 26), but the Allied withdrawal proved fatal to Neville Chamberlain's government—Winston Churchill became Prime Minister on the evening of May 10—and the withdrawal's political impact on France was grave.

On the morning of May 9 Reynaud drove the cabinet to vote on the replacement of Gamelin. Daladier would not yield; Reynaud declared the government fallen. The news, however, was kept secret while the President of the Republic selected another Premier—expected to be Reynaud himself with a new cabinet.[44] Reynaud decided to put Weygand in Gamelin's place (although he later claimed that Georges had been his choice).[45] Weygand combined experience in the High Command, prestige, and passionate patriotism. General Pownall heard him speak at La Ferté in December 1939, ". . . [Weygand] hardly looks 55 [he was actually 72] and seems fit and fresh. He cuts a lot of ice still in France. . . ."[46]

But this change was not to be. Hitler—finally favored with exceptionally good weather—picked this moment, when both Allied governments were in disarray and the High Command in unprecedented crisis, to launch his offensive against the West. As the news reached Paris, Reynaud resumed office, writing to Gamelin, "General, the battle has begun. Only one thing matters: to win it. We will all work toward that end in the same spirit." Gamelin replied, "Monsieur le Président, I see only one response to your letter of this day: France alone counts."[47] Two armies, each numbering some 3 million men, rumbled toward a collision. By a narrow margin the hopes of the West remained tied to the plans of Maurice Gamelin. The next days would be decisive.

NOTES

1. France, GQG, Le Général commandant en chef, Chef d'EM de la défense nationale, Commandant en chef les forces terrestres: N° 275 Cab/DN, Letter from Gamelin to Vuillemin (unpublished, February 24, 1940).

2. Quote from France, Commandement en chef sur le front du nord-est, EM, 2ème Bureau: N° 424/2S, "Ordre particulier de recherches de renseignements" (unpublished, March 7, 1940); "Instruction particulière n° 18" of March 15, 1940, in "Instructions générales et particulières"; entry of March 15 in France, "Journal de marche et des opérations du GQGAé" (unpublished, August 28, 1939 to July 1940).

3. France, IX° Armée, Commandement des FA et FTAA, 3° Bureau: N° 2829 3S, "Ordre d'opérations n° 5" (unpublished, March 15, 1940); France, IX ° Armée, EM, 3° Bureau: N° 3893/3, "Instruction particulière n° 7 pour l'emploi des forces aériennes en cas d'exécution la [sic] Manoeuvre *Escaut* ou de la Manoeuvre *Dyle*" (unpublished, May 2, 1940).

4. France, Commandement en chef sur le front du nord-est, EM, 2 ème Bureau, "Instruction particulière N° 9 pour la recherche du renseignement par les forces aériennes" (unpublished, April 10, 1940); General Ulrich Liss, *Westfront 1939/40: Erinnerungen des Feindarbeiters in O.K.H.* (Neckargemünd: Kurt Vowinckel Verlag, 1959), p. 133.

5. Col. Michel Garder, *La Guerre secrète des services spéciaux français 1935-1945* (Paris: Plon, 1967), pp. 153ff; interview with General André Beaufre, Paris, January 23, 1973; General André Beaufre, *Le Drame de 1940* (Paris: Plon, 1965), p. 231.

6. General Oscar Michiels, *18 jours de guerre en Belgique* (Paris: Berger-Levrault, 1947), pp. 18ff; quote from General [Raoul] Van Overstraeten, *Albert I-Léopold III: Vingt ans de politique militaire belge 1920-1940* ([Bruges]: Desclée de Brouwer, [1946?]), p. 522.

7. Liss, *Westfront*, pp. 113ff, 123ff.

8. Hans-Adolf Jacobsen, *Fall Gelb: Der Kampf um den deutschen Operationsplan zur Westoffensive 1940* (Wiesbaden; Steiner Verlag, 1957), pp. 107ff, 133ff, 143ff, 155ff; General Louis Koeltz, *Comment s'est joué notre destin: Hitler et l'offensive du 10 mai 1940* (Paris: Hachette, 1957), passim.

9. Guenther Blumentritt, *Von Rundstedt: The Soldier and the Man*, trans. Cuthbert Reavely (London: Odhams Press, 1952), p. 64.

10. France, EMAA, 2ème Bureau: Échelon lourd: N° 10.397 2-C/S/EMAA, "Dossier de campagne: *Hollande*" (unpublished, December 13, 1939); The Netherlands, Ministerie van Oorlog, Hoofdkwartier van de generale Staf, Krijgsgeschiedkundige Afdeling, Generaal-Major Tit. B.D.V.E. Nierstrasz et al., *De Strijd op Nederlands grondgebied tijdens de Wereldoorlog II: Hoofdeel III: Nederlands Verdediging tegen De Duitse Aanval van 10-19 Mei 1940. Deel I: Inleiding en algemeen Overzicht van de Gevechtsdagen van 10-19 Mei 1940* (The Hague: Staatsdrukkerijen Uitgeverijbedrijf, 1957), p. 9 (hereafter cited as *Overzicht*); interview with Jean Vanwelkenhuyzen, June 21-23, 1978, Brussels.

11. General V. E. Nierstrasz, "L'Evolution du plan d'opérations néerlandais en 1939-1940," *Revue générale belge* (May 1960): 79ff; for testimony of the Dutch principals and documents and commentary, see [The Netherlands, Staten-Generaal, Tweede Kamer], *Enquêtecommissie Regeringsbeleid 1940-1945: Verslag Houdende de Uitkomsten Van Het Onderzoek. Deel I^A en I^B: Algemene Inleiding/Militair Beleid 1939-1940 (Punt A Van Het Enquêtebesluit)* (The Hague: Staatsdrukkerijen

Uitgeverijbedrijf, 1949), pp. 51ff, 95ff, 99ff and *I^B/Bijlagen,* pp. 25ff, 42ff, 58ff and *I^C*, pp. 1ff, 25ff, 54ff, 64ff, 272ff, 520ff.

12. Nierstrasz, "Évolution du plan," pp. 84ff; *Enquêtecommissie I^B/Bijlagen,* pp. 25ff and *I^C*, pp. 75ff.

13. Nierstrasz, "Évolution du plan," pp. 84ff; *Enquêtecommissie I^C*, pp. 64ff, 272ff, 520ff.

14. *Overzicht*, pp. 49ff.

15. France, SHAT, GA 1, EM, 3ème Bureau: N° 1854 S/3, Letter from Billotte to Giraud (unpublished, March 12, 1940); France, SHAT, GA 1, EM, 3 ème Bureau: N° 2401 S/3, "Instruction personnelle et secrète n° 11" (unpublished, March 27, 1940); France, SHAT, VII° Armée, EM, 3ème Bureau: N° 5764 S/3, "Note sur l'emploi éventuel d'une D. L.M. par la VII° Armée" (unpublished, March 13, 1940); France, SHAT, VII° Armée, EM, 3° Bureau: N° 6329 S/3, Letter from Giraud to Billotte (unpublished, March 19, 1940); France, SHAT, VII° Armée, EM, 3me Bureau: N° 6.918 S/3, "Instruction personnelle et secrète n° 5 . . ." (unpublished, March 25, 1940); France, VII° Armée, EM, 3° Bureau: N° 7374 S/3, Letter from Giraud to Billotte (unpublished, March 29, 1940); France, SHAT, [GA 1, EM, . . . N°] 2785, Letter from Billotte to Georges (unpublished, April 6, 1940); [Marcel] Lerecouvreux, *L'Armée Giraud en Hollande: (1939-1940)* (Paris: Nouvelles éditions latines, 1951), pp. 53ff; *Les Relations militaires franco-belges de mars 1936 au 10 mai 1940: Travaux d'un colloque d'historiens belges et français* (Paris: CNRS, 1968), pp. 186ff; *Overzicht*, pp. 22ff; France, SHAT, N° 799 Cab/FT, Letter from Gamelin to Georges (unpublished, April 15, 1940).

16. *Relations franco-belges*, pp. 176ff; France, Commandement en chef sur le front du nord-est, EM, 2° Bureau: N° 394/2S, "Note sur la situation militaire en *Belgique*" (unpublished, March 3, 1940).

17. Van Overstraeten, *Albert I-Léopold III,* pp. 533ff, 557ff; Michiels, *18 jours de guerre*, pp. 40ff.

18. Michiels, *18 jours de guerre*, pp. 319ff.

19. Roton, *Années cruciales*, p. 121; interview with M. Vanwelkenhuyzen cited above.

20. Lerecouvreux, *L'Armée Giraud*, pp. 58ff and citations in note 15 above.

21. Cras, *Forces maritimes* I, pp. 41ff; General Fagalde, "L'Affaire des îles de Zélande: (Walcheren et Sud Beveland). Mai 1940," *Revue militaire suisse* nos. 11 and 12 (November and December 1953): November article, pp. 608ff.

22. France, ESG, Études générales, ler Cycle, Cours d'histoire, Lt.-Col. d'Ornano, "La 25me DIM dans la marche à l'ennemi: (Étude de la préparation et de l'exécution des transports opérationnels)" (unpublished, November 1955), pp. 1 passim.

23. General P[aul]-É[mile] Tournoux, "Pouvait-on prévoir l'attaque allemande des Ardennes de mai 1940? Un général avait dit 'oui'," *Revue historique de l'armée* (no. 2 1971), p. 139.

24. Van Overstraeten, *Albert I-Léopold III*, p. 544.

25. France, IX° Armée, EM, 3° Bureau: N° 3326/3, "Instruction particulière n° 11 pour l'action de la cavalerie au delà de la *Meuse* et de la *Semoy*" (unpublished, March 28, 1940).

26. France, IX ° Armée, EM, 3° Bureau: N° 3893/3, "Instruction particulière n°

7 pour l'emploi des forces aériennes en cas d'exécution la [sic] Manoeuvre *Escaut* ou de la Manoeuvre *Dyle*" (unpublished, May 2, 1940); Georges' directive in General A. [Joseph] Doumenc, *Histoire de la neuvième armée* (Grenoble and Paris: Arthaud, 1945), p. 43; Georges' report on the inquiry on the Ninth Army in ED, 3DA9, Dr 1, sdr c, pp. 7-8.

27. General C. Grandsard, *Le 10e Corps d'armée dans la bataille 1939-1940: Sedan-Amiens-De la Seine à la Dordogne* (Paris: Berger-Levrault, 1949), pp. 78ff.

28. A reference to the disaster at Sedan in 1870. Quotes from France, Parlement, Assemblée nationale, *Les Événements survenus en France de 1933 à 1945: Rapport de M. Charles Serre, Député au nom de la commission d'enquête parlementaire* II (Paris: Presses universitaires de France, no date), pp. 359ff.

29. These totals included the Seventh Army and the BEF which at the time were not under Billotte's command.

30. Roton, *Années cruciales*, pp. 124ff; Jacobsen, *Fall Gelb*, p. 258; on the DCR's see France, SHAT, GA 1, EM, 3ème Bureau: N° 1853 S/3, "Note: Objet: Emploi de divisions cuirassées" (unpublished, March 12, 1940) and France, SHAT, GA 1, EM, 3° Bureau: N° 2717 S/1, Letter from Billotte to Georges (unpublished, April 4, 1940).

31. *Événements . . . Rapport* II, p. 306; General [Gaston] Prételat, *Le Destin tragique de la ligne Maginot* (Paris: Berger-Levrault, 1950), pp. 120ff, 129; Maurice Gamelin, *Servir* III (Paris: Plon, 1947), p. 318.

32. France, [I° Armée aérienne, EM,] "Action de l'aviation de bombardement britannique en cas d'intervention en Belgique-Hollande" (unpublished, [January, 1940?]); Particular Instruction no. 20 of April 12, 1940, in "Instructions générales et particulières."

33. France, Commandement en chef des forces aériennes, EMG, 3° Bureau: N° 1931 3/OS/EMG, "Instruction sur l'organisation du commandement dans les opérations combinées des forces aériennes d'assaut, de bombardement et de chasse" (unpublished, GQGA, March 21, 1940); Charles Eugène, "En opérations avec le groupe I/51 du 18 mai au 24 juin 1940," *Icare* no. 80 (Spring 1977): 81.

34. Sir John Slessor, *The Central Blue: The Autobiography of Sir John Slessor, Marshal of the RAF* (New York: Praeger, 1957), pp. 253ff; Sir Charles Webster and Noble Frankland, *The Strategic Air Offensive Against Germany 1939-1945* I (London: H.M.S.O., 1961), p. 143; Poydenot, "Vu du P.C.," p. 181; Portal's remarks in Denis Richards and Hilary St. George Saunders, *Royal Air Force: 1939-1945* I: *The Fight at Odds* (London: H.M.S.O., 1953), pp. 62ff, 109; minutes of the Supreme Council meeting of April 23 in ED, 3DA5, Dr 5, sdr b.

35. General [François] d'Astier de la Vigerie, *Le Ciel n'était pas vide: 1940* (Paris: Julliard, 1952), pp. 71ff, 86; "Extraits du rapport du général Georges," *annexe* 2.

36. Gamelin, *Servir* III, pp. 189ff, 201; Roton, *Années cruciales*, pp. 103ff.

37. General X [Bührer], *Aux heures tragiques de l'empire (1938-1941)* (Paris: Office colonial d'édition, 1947), pp. 137ff; Charles O. Richardson, "French Plans for Allied Attacks on the Caucasus Oil Fields January-April, 1940," *French Historical Studies* 8, no. 1 (Spring 1973).

38. Guy Rossi-Landi, *La Drôle de guerre: La Vie politique en France 2 septembre 1939-10 mai 1940* (Paris: Armand Colin, 1971), pp. 55ff; Gamelin, *Servir* I, p. 6;

Pomaret, *Le Dernier témoin*, pp. 46ff; pact with British in minutes of the Supreme Council meeting of March 28 in ED, 3DA5, Dr 4, sdr b.

39. Gamelin, *Servir* III, pp. 214ff, 313.

40. Ibid., p. 314; Cras, *Forces maritimes* I, pp. 93ff.

41. Paul Reynaud, *Mémoires* II: *Envers et contre tous: 7 mars-16 juin 1940* (Paris: Flammarion, 1963), pp. 322ff; Jacques Weygand, *Weygand mon père* (Paris: Flammarion, 1970), pp. 267ff; Roton, *Années cruciales*, p. 107; quote from Gamelin, *Servir* III, pp. 336ff; General Paul de Villelume, *Journal d'une défaite: Août 1939-Juin 1940* ([Paris]: Fayard, 1976), pp. 216, 250-263, 275ff, 288ff, 303ff, 314, 319ff; Reynaud's remarks in Supreme Council meeting of April 22 in ED, 3DA5, Dr 5, sdr b.

42. Édouard Bonnefous, *Histoire politique de la troisième république* VII (Paris: Presses universitaires de France, 1967), pp. 162ff; Gamelin, *Servir* III, pp. 336ff.

43. Gamelin, *Servir* III, pp. 356 passim.

44. Ibid., pp. 382ff; Bonnefous, *Histoire politique* VII, pp. 164ff; Paul Baudouin, *Neuf mois au gouvernement (avril-décembre 1940)* (Paris: Éditions de la table ronde, 1948), pp. 37, 44ff.

45. France, Parlement, Assemblée nationale, *Les Événements survenus en France de 1933 à 1945: Témoignages et documents recueillis par la commission d'enquête parlementaire* VIII (Paris: Presses universiaires de France, [1950?]), pp. 2385ff; testimony of Col. Villelume in IX, p. 2796; Oliver Harvey, *The Diplomatic Diaries of Oliver Harvey 1937-1940*, ed. John Harvey (London: Collins, 1970), p. 355; Sir Edmund Ironside, *Time Unguarded: The Ironside Diaries 1937-1940* (Edinburgh: Constable, 1962), p. 301.

46. Brian Bond, ed., *Chief of Staff: The Diaries of Lieutenant-General Sir Henry Pownall.* I *1933-1940* (Hamden, Conn.: Archon Books, 1973), p. 268.

47. Gamelin, *Servir* I, pp. 6ff.

chapter 8

THE "DIABOLIC" DEFEAT (MAY 10-16, 1940)

THE RACE TO THE DYLE

The timing of Hitler's offensive took the Allies largely by surprise, although a member of the German counterespionnage service had warned the Dutch attaché in Berlin. French intelligence passed this news to Paris on May 6. On the night of May 9 the Dutch got urgent warning from the same source.[1] But there had been so many alerts. . . . Nonetheless, the French air force alerted its fighters on May 7 and issued instructions for the protection of bases from airborne assault on May 9. Key units of the armies went on alert: the 2nd DLM stood to in the afternoon of May 9. But French air reconnaissances from the Moselle to Bavaria on the nights of May 8-9 and 9-10 found nothing unusual; similar reports came in from British planes farther north.[2] No general alert went out.

Late on May 9 German irregular troops crossed into Luxemburg with the aid of a few locals of German extraction—a rare case of the "fifth column"—and clashed with the Luxemburg militia.[3] French intelligence in Luxemburg passed the news by radio. The offensive was almost as great a shock to the German troops in the field as it was to the Allies: the 1st Panzer, spearhead of Guderian's corps, received only sixteen hours' notice to prepare!

May 10: The View from the Top

From the first hours Gamelin's headquarters issued information on German crossings into neutral territory. By 5:30 a.m. enemy airborne landings and air attacks were reported. Georges ordered alert 1.[4] Alert 3 followed at 6:30 a.m., as Belgium demanded Allied aid. Gamelin telephoned Georges; the conversation was brief:

> 'Well General,' he [Georges] said to me, 'it's the Dyle maneuver I suppose?'
> 'Since the Belgians are appealing to us, do you see anything else we can do?'
> 'Evidently not.'[5]

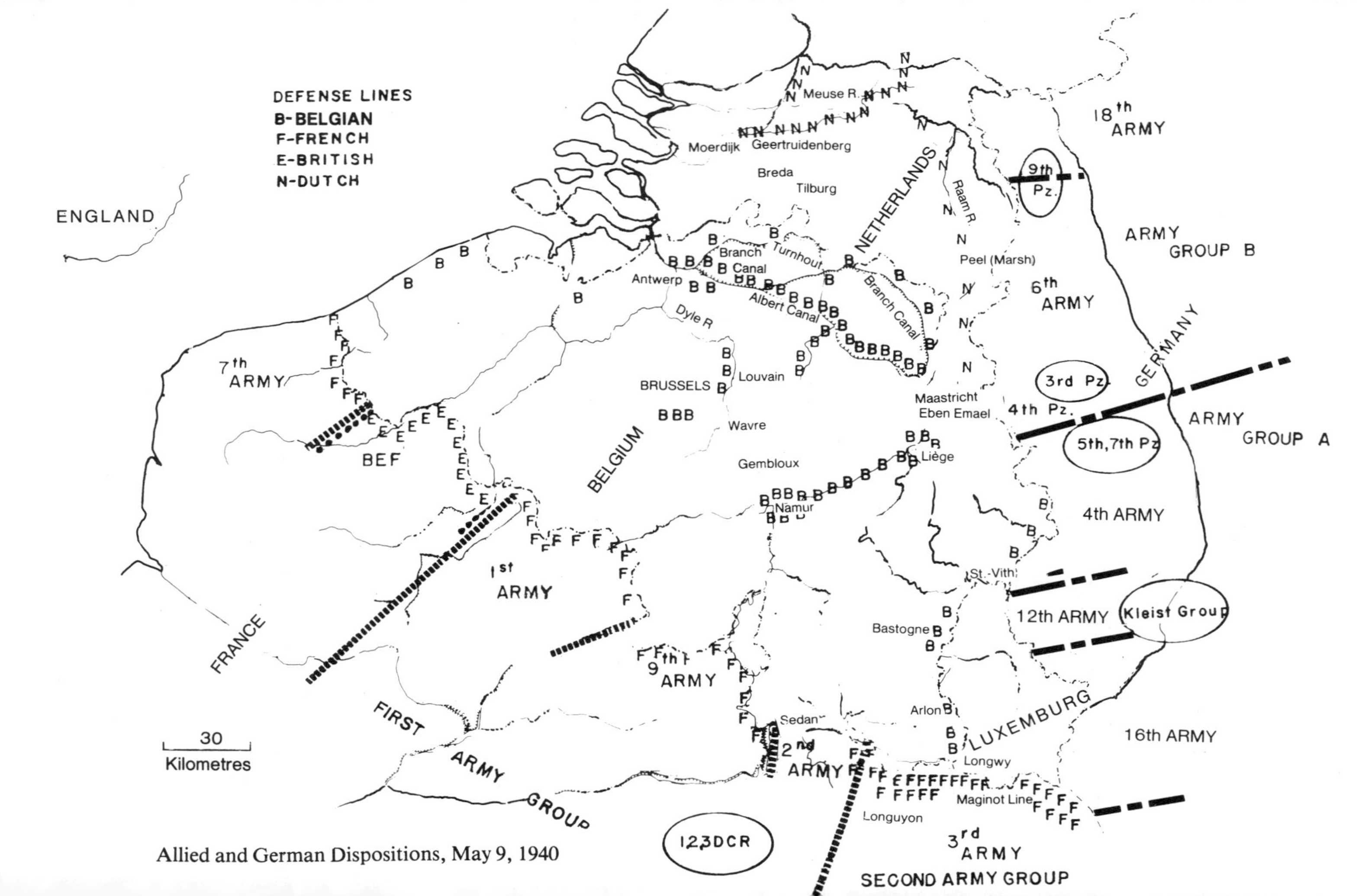

Allied and German Dispositions, May 9, 1940

Georges passed the order to Billotte to enter Belgium and to General Condé to send his cavalry into Luxemburg. Gamelin ordered a mission led by General Champon to assist the Belgians; Champon was to press them to retreat only under pressure, particularly to keep troops south of the Meuse at Huy as long as possible: Gamelin feared a pincers attack on Liège.

Gamelin maintained a calm front before his staff,[6] but one of Doumenc's aides, arriving at Vincennes at 6:30 a.m., saw him pacing the corridor "humming to himself with a martial and satisfied air that I had never before seen in him." Gamelin had first to organize the interallied command: he asked Léopold to accept the authority of Georges. Gamelin talked twice with the Dutch attaché, detailing his plans for the Seventh Army and asking that Dutch troops on the Peel-Raam line join Giraud when pressed. He also spoke with General Winkelman, who asked for French help in retaking the vital Moerdijk causeway. But since the alert of the previous night the Dutch 3rd Corps and Light Division were already abandoning the Peel-Raam position: opening the gate to the enemy even before the Germans crossed the frontier. However, it is not certain that Winkelman told Gamelin this. But by the evening of May 10, it was clear that the Dutch were in retreat toward Holland, where the heart of their country was under massive airborne assault from first light. Thus, in the first day of operations, one member of the improvised coalition was already forsaking joint action and falling back on an isolated defense of its own population centers.

In the Field

German SS units in Dutch uniforms attempted to seize the Meuse bridges at Maastricht. The Dutch guards alertly destroyed the bridges; but this operation and the airborne landings fed the wildfire "fifth column" panic that quickly gripped the West.[7] The weak training of the Dutch cadres, the long period of routine, and the suddenness of the attack sapped Dutch resistance. German airborne troops seized the Moerdijk causeway linking North Brabant to Holland; the Dutch defense there had not been alerted. German forces seized bridges at Dordrecht and Waalhaven too, but an attempt to land a force near the Hague to capture the Dutch government met disaster: Dutch antiaircraft brought down eleven of the thirteen troop-carrying planes. Dutch counterattacks followed and the Germans fell back on Rotterdam, losing roughly two-thirds of the troops engaged. The effort cost the German airborne troops some 4,000 casualties, including 1,600 taken prisoner, plus some 224 transport aircraft which failed to return to base—but the vital bridges remained in their hands despite counterattacks, and the Dutch reserve of three infantry divisions was tied down. These events and the rapid and disorganized withdrawal of Dutch troops, just as Giraud's force began to arrive, made a bad impression on the French, who were further disillusioned to find no positions prepared in the Breda area.

Belgian Troops on the Move—Seventh Army Sector.
Photo Courtesy of E. C. P. Armées

Giraud hustled his units forward as best he could. He knew of German landings in the Netherlands, but not their targets. He therefore decided to switch several reconnaissance groups from their original assignment north of Breda and send them into Dutch Zeeland, leaving only two groups to cover the left flank of the 1st DLM which he ordered up between Breda and the Belgian canals. The seaborne expedition to Walcheren began that evening. Giraud's columns reached Antwerp on May 10—shocking the German Eighteenth Army, charged with reducing Dutch resistance, which had not expected French troops so far north.[8] Officers of Giraud's 1st DLM confided to a Belgian officer that their mission was to reach Breda and break the point of the German offensive by a southward movement.

But more important events took place farther south, where the Belgian 7th Infantry, a first reserve division, held eighteen kilometers of the Albert Canal with the fortress of Eben Emael on its right. To the east the Dutch had antiaircraft units and five battalions garrisoning the "Maastricht appendix." It was this knot, the northern bastion of the Liège complex, which Hitler chose to cut with an airborne attack followed by two Panzers, trying to reach the Belgian plain before Belgians and Allies could react. However, Dutch sentinels destroyed the Maastricht bridges, leaving the Panzers stacked up behind the Meuse. But glider troops neutralized Eben Emael and took the Albert Canal bridges despite the Belgian alert and the precautions taken.[9] Belgian headquarters knew of this at 6:00 a.m.; by 8:30 the Belgians knew of German landings in the Ardennes. By afternoon it was clear that the 7th Infantry, under intense air attack, could not retake the bridges. With an enemy mechanized exploitation threatening, the Belgian command prepared to withdraw toward its assigned positions under the Dyle Plan, leaving the forts of Liège to hold out alone—as some did until the Belgian armistice. This initial disaster shook the confidence of King Léopold, who never fully recovered.

News of the Belgian disaster reached French headquarters in the early afternoon, but it was not clear whether the enemy had a foothold over the Albert Canal. German columns struggled with the Maastricht bottleneck but the Dutch forces there surrendered easily once the bridges were blown. Although the Belgians fought well, they failed to mount effective counterattacks.[10] Meanwhile, the advance of the BEF and the French First Army, covered by the Belgians, met no obstacles.

Farther south, Corap's cavalry reached the Meuse that afternoon and stopped; Georges ordered them into the Ardennes, to Marche, that night. Corap replied that he would move the troops early the next morning.[11] Corap's advance left a fifteen kilometer gap in the frontier fortifications at Anor: reinforcements would have to arrive before a continuous screen stood behind Corap's left. The three infantry divisions of Corap's left wing found their sectors on the Belgian Meuse running to some fifteen kilometers each; the heights on the east bank of the river dominated those on the west; almost no defenses had been prepared. The situation on Corap's center and right was not much better. His 41st Corps had the series B 61st Infantry along twenty-five kilometers of the French Meuse; the 102nd Fortress Infantry held *thirty-five*!

Corap's right wing was stretched so thin it was hard for General Grandsard, commanding the adjoining 10th Corps of the Second Army, to maintain liaison with neighboring headquarters sixty kilometers away. Grandsard was preoccupied with the series B 71st Infantry, given to him by the Second Army, which was to move so that by the next morning it would be one day's march from the lines, ready to enter at the most threatened point. Grandsard ordered his corps reserve, the 213th Infantry Regiment, to a similar stance. The cavalry of the Second Army, meanwhile, pushed into Belgium amid a countercurrent of fleeing refugees. The 2nd Light Cavalry reached Arlon but met German tanks before noon and was thrown back that night to Florenville, its elements filtering back after being bypassed by Panzers. The division's single squadron of combat tanks lay unused in reserve at Virton with the battalion of infantry support tanks which Huntziger ordered to its support. The encounters of the 2nd Light Cavalry came to the attention of GQG shortly after noon, along with a report that some one thousand enemy tanks lay a few kilometers from the southeastern corner of Luxemburg.[12]

The force that met the 2nd Light Cavalry came from Guderian's corps which sped through Luxemburg and pitched across the Belgian frontier before 9:00 a.m. Guderian's 1st Panzer then ran into Chasseurs ardennais at Bodange; two Belgian platoons held it up for six hours. Farther north, at Chabrehez, another small unit of Chasseurs stopped General Erwin Rommel's 7th Panzer, the northern prong of Rundstedt's drive, until night. Again the tortuous terrain allowed a small force to contain German armor, but Corap's cavalry, reaching the area late that night, was blocked by Belgian demolitions and could not reach the favorable positions of Houffalize and St.-Vith or reinforce the Belgians, by then in retreat.[13]

The German armor in Luxemburg drew Allied air attacks: RAF units sent four waves of eight Battle bombers each. But the Flak was formidable. The British lost thirteen aircraft; the rest were damaged.[14] By day's end Huntziger knew that two enemy motorized forces were advancing, but whether toward Sedan, or Carignan, or both was unclear.

What of the cavalry of the Third Army which was to retard the Germans in Luxemburg? Before dawn German aircraft landed small groups of troops which barricaded the routes into Luxemburg from France; motorized troops would reinforce these groups to secure the south flank of Guderian's advance, *if* they could arrive before French units.[15] General Condé knew that German operations had begun; he had authority to order forces into Luxemburg on his own initiative. But Condé did not order an advance until 6:55 a.m., too late to forestall German reinforcements. The French cavalry was blocked on the frontier, its armor halted by the terrain and German mines. Only the 1st Spahi Brigade—not ordered forward until 7:50 a.m.—made progress, and it was soon dangerously far in front of its neighbors and was forced to stop. Despite Allied air superiority there, and the wounding and temporary capture of the commander of the German operation, German reinforcements secured Guderian's flank. The house-to-house fighting against a largely unseen foe left French troops (and Germans too!) with the impression that the "fifth column" was at work; this impression was unfounded.[16]

In the Air

The great trial of strength in the air began. General d'Astier had 350 single seat and 70 heavy fighters: Groupment 21 assigned to Paris with five

Bloch 152 Fighters.
Photo Courtesy of S. H. A. A.

fighter groups and four night fighter squadrons; Groupment 25 to the Seventh Army with two groups; and General Jean Romatet's Groupment 23 to the First, Ninth, and Second Armies with five groups and one squadron of heavy fighters.[17] The Eastern Zone had 160 single seaters under Groupment 22. The seven remaining fighter groups of the Armée de l'air in France were reequipping and were not immediately available. D'Astier's bomber strength was in General Philippe Escudier's 1st Air Division which included Groupment 6 with twenty-two Lioré 451's, General Girier's Groupment 18 with twenty-nine assault bombers, and Groupment 9 with thirty-eight old Amiot 143's. The Eastern Zone had General Valin's 3rd Air Division with Groupment 15 (six Farman 222 four-engine night bombers) and Groupment 10 with Amiot 143's; these passed to d'Astier's disposition. Thus d'Astier had some 420 fighters and 95 bombers (51 modern). The bulk of the French bomber force—thirteen groups—was still reequipping and was not available for immediate action. The RAF had 135 bombers in France; three squadrons of Hurricane fighters arrived to bring the British total in France to 160 fighters.[18]

Much of the Luftwaffe was initially directed into airborne operations; the rest attacked Allied air bases. Bombing of Dutch and Belgian bases racked up quick successes; the small neutrals lacked space to disperse their air units.[19] During the morning of May 10 Belgium lost fifty-three aircraft, including many modern ones; by May 12 the Belgians had seventy to eighty planes left from the original 230. The Dutch lost sixty-two planes—half their total—but claimed 230 German aircraft, mostly Junkers 52's used to transport airborne troops. After the first combats, only sixteen old single seat and two multiseat fighters remained to defend Dutch skies. In French territory the enemy raided air bases, seventeen rail targets, sixteen military bases and forty-five localities. This dispersal of effort proved to be an error; the Luftwaffe destroyed all twelve of a French naval squadron's dive-bombers and damaged half the Morane fighters of one of Groupment 23's groups; but in d'Astier's whole force, enemy bombing cost only four planes destroyed and thirty damaged—a poor return for almost 1,000 German attack sorties.

Vuillemin placed the strategic reconnaissance groups, the modern medium and assault bomber groups, and the fighters in the northeast (except those covering Paris) at the disposition of General Têtu. Reinforcement of the Northern Zone's fighters, underway since May 9, continued. Têtu received permission to install direct liaison between his headquarters and the zones of air operations (forbidden since the dissolution of the First Air Army).[20] Late in the morning, Têtu freed d'Astier to employ medium and assault bombers against military objectives, according to the wishes of General Billotte; he added that d'Astier would receive one to three more fighter groups. Vuillemin and Georges, however, forbade the use of bombers over cities—putting the onus of first attacking civilian targets on the enemy— ruining d'Astier's plan, which called for "cuts" to be made along enemy advance routes, many of them in or near inhabited areas. Nonetheless, d'Astier agreed with Barratt that the RAF should carry out its planned night operations. Air reconnaissance searched the mouth of the Escaut, Luxemburg, and particularly the enemy rear north of the Saar where the large enemy forces reported threatened either the Saar or the Ardennes. Independently, three Dutch bombers attacked the enemy bridgehead at Maastricht; afterward, remaining Dutch bombers operated against Dutch airfields captured by German airborne troops. Four Dutch reconnaissance planes also attacked the enemy-held fortifications at Moerdijk.

Allied fighters, meanwhile, defended their bases. Romatet's Groupment 23 put up 316 sorties with 110 single seat and 10 heavy fighters, losing four pilots killed and five wounded but claiming thirty-two "certain" kills and seventeen "probables."[21] The missions of Captain Jean Accart's squadron of Group I/5, operating over the Second Army, were typical. Accart's first patrol ran into enemy bombers and heavy fighters, his second covered a Potez 63 scouting for French cavalry in the Bastogne-Arlon area, discovering enemy columns—much sooner than expected. A third mission took off on alert and intercepted twenty-one Dornier bombers, escorted by heavy fighters, trying to hit Accart's base: bombs hit the town of Suippes, killing forty-seven and wounding one hundred civilians. The enemy lost eight bombers, one to antiaircraft. Captain Robert Williame's squadron in the Eastern Zone flew the same type of missions; like many in the Eastern Zone, these were Williame's only missions for the next several days.

While the fighters ran up kills, the 368 reconnaissance and observation planes of the Armée de l'air tried to bring back intelligence on enemy movements.[22] They suffered more heavily on the ground than the rest, although they lost under 10 percent of their strength. Some units were hard hit: the observation group of the 1st Light Cavalry lost all of its planes; that of the 2nd DLM lost six of nine modern aircraft. Nonetheless, they did good work. A plane from the 2nd Light Cavalry, working over Martelange, shot down a German Henschel 126 and brought word of the German advance in the Ardennes. That evening a reconnaissance from the 1st Air Division found Belgian troops pulling back from the Ourthe River; French cavalry was still to the west. That night the commander of a bomber group saw enemy columns from Euskirchen to Prüm rolling with all their lights on, but the Air Division maintained plans to attack air bases in the Rhineland. Only on the three following nights were bombing missions, followed by strafing runs, flown against the advancing columns.

French observation groups, unlike the enemy and despite their more modern planes, were handicapped by strong enemy defenses. A pilot from one group of the Seventh Army reported he could never execute the slow,

low-altitude cruise necessary for proper observation; his group furnished only liaison and communications flights.[23]

The Allied command authorized bombing too late for day attacks, except for those over Luxemburg; the effort began that night. Bomber Command in Britain furnished thirty-six heavy bombers to hit the enemy-occupied airfield at Waalhaven; nine bombers attacked communications in the Wesel area; eleven Amiot 143's hit air bases in western Germany and communications in the Aachen area.[24] Nonetheless, at 11:55 p.m. Gamelin sent Georges a message that bombers would no doubt be "very useful" on the front of the Third Army facing Luxemburg. The matter would be settled the next day.

Georges' first order for reconnaissance was to determine if the enemy's principal aim was Holland, operations farther south serving as a diversion, or if "this offensive is aimed at bringing on a decisive battle against the allied forces in Belgium. . . ."[25] Georges wanted to know if German forces were driving toward Utrecht, inside Holland, or farther south, and if the German effort in Belgium was directed toward Brussels and the Gembloux gap. As for the Ardennes, Georges wanted to know if the enemy aimed at Huy to turn the defenses of the Albert Canal from the south, or the general direction of St.-Vith-Dinant, Malmédy-Sedan, and Bitburg-Luxemburg "with the aim of flanking the organizations of the Maginot Line."

By early next morning, May 11, reconnaissances revealed numerous German columns heading toward St.-Vith and Clervaux in the Ardennes. Enemy convoys were in the Libramont and Florenville clearings and in the Maastricht area. By 6:00 a.m., the Northern Zone deduced that the enemy was making a "big effort" in the Maastricht area and "seems to be pushing rather energetically" in Luxemburg. "The general impression seems to be: . . . principal enemy effort in the region between Maastricht and Nimegen . . . secondary but rather violent effort toward the west in Luxemburg. . . ."[26] Unfortunately, it was at just this crucial moment that the enemy changed the code settings of his Enigma code machines, depriving Allied intelligence of potentially vital command and supply intercepts until the new settings were cracked on May 20.

The overall impression at Vincennes that first night was favorable, despite the troubles in Holland and the situation at Eben Emael. Actually, the enemy had dropped one parachute and one airborne division into Holland, sending the 9th Panzer and motorized formations to link up with them. Farther south the operation against Eben Emael had succeeded, but General Hoepner's 16th Corps with the 3rd and 4th Panzers and a motorized infantry division had not yet reached the airborne troops.[27] Established in or heading toward Luxemburg Guderian's 19th Corps, General Hans Reinhardt's 41st Corps, and the 14th Motorized Corps with two motorized infantry divisions formed a huge force under General Ewald von Kleist.

Guderian had the 1st, 2nd, and 10th Panzers and the elite Grossdeutschland Infantry Regiment; Reinhardt had the 6th and 8th Panzers and a motorized infantry division. This spearhead had 1,230 tanks, 362 armored cars, and 134,370 men. Hoepner's corps was the vanguard of Army Group B; Kleist's force was the first wave of Army Group A. Between the two, under Army Group A, General Hermann Hoth's 15th Corps controlled the 5th and 7th Panzers racing through the upper Ardennes for the Belgian Meuse, linking the two main thrusts into a coherent wedge. Hoth, temporarily held up at Chabrehez, later passed the Ourthe River without meeting the resistance he feared. Belgian demolitions hemmed in his columns, but the advance circumvented the undefended obstacles without losing time. And the German forces as a whole greatly benefited from the withdrawal of Dutch forces from Limburg and Brabant, and Belgian forces from the Ardennes: gates opening wide just as the main columns of the invasion arrived. These withdrawals were the fruit of Hitler's cold war strategy—and of the Belgian and Dutch failure to face up to the inevitablity of a German attack.

On May 10 German forces succeeded—at heavy cost—in seizing crossing points into Holland and Belgium with airborne units, but their mechanized vanguard was tangled up at Maastricht. German forces in the Ardennes met some delays, but the area proved passable: Allied airpower did not intervene effectively. Guderian's Panzers shoved aside Huntziger's cavalry at Arlon; the German flank in Luxemburg was secure. On the other side, the Allied air forces survived the threat of annihilation on the ground and inflicted heavy loss on the Luftwaffe. The Allied advance started—particularly on the left where Giraud made excellent time—without a problem, except for Corap's holding his cavalry on the Belgian Meuse. But it was too early to judge the coming battle.

May 11: The View from the Top

May 11 dawned hot and clear, as would the next few days—fine Blitzkrieg weather! Around 7:00 a.m. a report from Georges reached Vincennes. The enemy had a foothold over the Albert Canal at Eben Emael. The gravity of the news was apparent: a large German mechanized force on the Belgian plain before the Allies could settle into position would mean disaster! At 9:30 a.m. Gamelin asked Vuillemin to bring airpower into this critical area. Georges ordered Têtu and Barratt to retard the enemy columns "as long as the menace lasts."[28]

At 11:00 a.m. a message reached Vincennes from the Dutch command: the vital Moerdijk causeway linking North Brabant to Holland was still in German hands—could Belgian motorized troops retake it?[29] It would be dangerous to push Giraud's mechanized and motorized elements onto the Dutch plain when their communications might be threatened by a German exploitation from Eben Emael: Gamelin sent a message to Giraud at 1:20 p.m., ordering him not to push beyond Breda, from which he would help retake Moerdijk and thus gain contact with Holland. The survival of the northern extremity of the Allied front was already in jeopardy: Giraud had to reopen the route into Holland if the Dutch were to be kept in the war. Gamelin's ambitious plan was foundering.

Georges, meanwhile, parceled out his reserves. The first lot, including the 1st DCR intended for the First Army, moved as the Dyle Plan went into effect. Georges called up the second lot, ordering the active 1st North African Infantry and 43rd Infantry Divisions to the Maubeuge area to backstop Blanchard; these movements were to begin the next day. Considering German pressure in the Ardennes, Georges decided to reinforce the hinges between the Ninth, Second, and Third Armies. He envisaged two or three active infantry divisions behind the junction of the Second and Third Armies, reinforcing the Second Army with the reserve 21st Corps and the 1st Colonial Infantry which were already in the area. The Ninth Army would get disposition of the series B 53rd Infantry, already in its area. The 2nd and 3rd DCR, the reserve 23rd Corps plus three active infantry divisions—including the 3rd Motorized—and the 87th African Infantry would reinforce the junction of the Ninth and Second Armies. These units were to move from May 11 to 13, as transport became available.[30] Georges ordered the 6th Infantry to the Third Army and General Jean Flavigny's 21st Corps to immediately join the Second Army. Finally, anxious to get the First and Ninth Armies into position and considering the lack of German air activity over them, Georges confirmed Billotte's decision to move by day as well as by night.

In the afternoon Léopold agreed to accept Georges' authority. Gamelin drove to La Ferté to finalize command arrangements. He got a rude shock —Georges had already decided to make Billotte coordinator of Allied forces in the north. Georges, whose responsibilities extended from Dunkirk to Lake Geneva, felt he could not concentrate on operations in Belgium when the offensive might spread to new sectors, including Switzerland— "I cannot at the same time command the whole and one part."[31] As Georges had already promised Billotte, Gamelin confirmed the decision, although he observed that it seemed a heavy responsibility for an army group commander. Georges agreed; he would take charge of the Second Army himself. Georges' attention had never centered on Belgium as had Gamelin's; Gamelin could not force Georges to change his mind in the midst of battle. For the first time Georges had his own way. The establishment of a real interallied command was now more vital than ever: Gamelin had expected Georges to fill the role, but Georges' decision to hand "coordination" in the north to his subordinate Billotte—the third echelon of the French command—gravely weakened the command structure. How could Billotte dominate Lord Gort, much less the Belgian sovereign? And Léopold's commitment to the Allied cause had no agreed political basis beyond the fact of invasion by a common enemy. Gamelin, paralyzed perhaps by his antagonistic relationship with Reynaud, took no effective action to enforce unity of command over the patchwork coalition. The Allies would pay heavily for this.

Meanwhile, General René Prioux, commander of the Cavalry Corps pressing toward the Albert Canal, scouted the weak and incomplete defenses in the Gembloux gap. Considering the strength of the Luftwaffe, the weakness of the Belgian defenses, and the collapse of resistance on the Albert Canal, Prioux wanted to revert to the Escaut Plan. He passed this suggestion to Blanchard, who sent it to Billotte and then up to Georges, the point coming up at La Ferté while Gamelin was present. The decision was unanimous: there was no turning back now.[32]

Georges issued a general instruction that afternoon. He described the enemy attack, preceded by airborne landings "or by German detachments constituted in place" (the "fifth column").[33] He noted the German bridgehead over the Albert Canal and the precipitous retreat of the Chasseurs ardennais from the Ardennes, adding that the French cavalry there had begun its retarding maneuver. He concluded that the enemy effort "seems to be working to the north and south of Liège." The Allied armies were to hold on the line Antwerp-Namur-Mézières-Longuyon; they must reach that position as quickly as possible. To gain time he prescribed a "powerful retarding action" to cover the Gembloux gap, Dinant, and Carignan, using air forces, DLM's, and light cavalry. The air forces were to act in mass against bottlenecks along the enemy's route, with priority to Maastricht; the DLM's would deliver "brutal" braking attacks as would the armor of the light cavalry.

In the Field

The Dutch army continued to counterattack German airborne pockets in Holland, pulling remaining troops south of Holland (save in Zeeland) back to the heart of the country. Giraud's advance guards raced into the Breda area, suffering light casualties but no significant delays from air attack thanks to their antiaircraft system. The tanks of the 1st DLM, however, had to detrain south of Antwerp because of the bombing.[34] German air attack caused serious losses to one column of the 25th Motorized once it moved beyond the Seventh Army's antiaircraft screen. On the whole, however, the advance guard of the 25th was in place 200 kilometers from the French frontier within twenty-four hours—quite a performance! Enemy bombing slowed the seaborne force on its way to Walcheren but caused no damage.

Two major events took place: General Picard, commander of the 1st DLM, decided to hold his tanks south of the Belgian canals lest they be left stranded by the Belgian forces, in whom he had no confidence. Second, the single French reconnaissance unit assigned to Moerdijk found the enemy installed in Dutch fortifications and the *polders* flooding—the Dutch had opened the sluices. The small French force pulled out when German bombers arrived. French cavalry could have reached Holland farther east, but this was not known at the time.[35] Thus Holland remained isolated, and French forces in North Brabant lacked the armor to defeat the enemy. The lack of interallied cooperation was proving fatal to the Netherlands.

The pressing danger at Eben Emael led Léopold, despite French protests,[36] to withdraw the 1st Division of Chasseurs ardennais from the Ardennes and move it toward Tongres, southwest of Eben Emael. Before noon came news of the surrender of the fort and the urgent threat of an enemy exploitation. Van Overstraeten proposed immediate withdrawal to the Dyle; it was so ordered. Meanwhile, the most powerful unit of the Belgian army, the company of battle tanks, stood in reserve against "parachutists."[37] Prioux's Cavalry Corps was rushing toward the threatened area; however, liaison between French and Belgians was poor, and Prioux decided, despite Billotte's urging, not to directly support the Belgians. He halted and organized his motorized cavalry into strongpoints behind which he posted his tanks for counterattacks. Prioux's air strength was six scout planes; as he told Billotte at 8:00 p.m., it was risky to rush into an encounter battle with an enemy superior in air and mechanized strength. Actually his mechanized force was at least equal to that of the enemy, although he was not aware of it. In fact, due in large part to Allied air attacks, the German command held back the 4th Panzer on May 11 until the 3rd Panzer could cross the Albert Canal. On the evening of May 11 the Panzers bore down on Prioux's forty kilometer front. General Champon asked that Belgian units submit to Allied command as Allied and Belgian forces moved together. But Van Overstraeten refused, except for the corps holding Namur which might be "coordinated" with the French armies which would encadre it.

Farther south indecisive clashes took place in the northern Ardennes. German armor threatened to break through the 4th Light Cavalry at Marche; General Barbe, commanding the cavalry, led a counterattack to restore the situation.[38] Despite air attacks and tank and infantry assaults, French cavalry held all day on the Homme River.

But in the southern Ardennes Guderian's Panzers ran full tilt into the 5th Light Cavalry. In maneuver battles in the Neufchâteau and Bertrix clearings, the Germans drove the overmatched 5th all the way back to the Semoy River by noon, forcing the entire line of French cavalry to recoil.[39] That evening the 3rd Spahi Brigade, linking the 5th to Corap's cavalry, lost a post on the Semoy; the Spahis retreated, opening a gap in the front. This ripple of withdrawal spread along the line of Corap's cavalry until, at 11:30 p.m., he ordered the cavalry to withdraw to the Meuse. At 7:00 p.m. Huntziger ordered his cavalry to stand on the Semoy; later he released the 71st Infantry to Grandsard for insertion into line during the next two nights. Grandsard felt there was no need to rush, so he moved the 71st mostly by night, aiming to insert it on May 13.

In the Air

Billotte's decision, at 11:00 a.m., to advance to the Dyle by day led him to stress fighter cover for the First Army, the BEF, and the Seventh Army which had the longest distances to cover.[40] This mission took the bulk of Groupment 23's fighters, although d'Astier left one group each to the Ninth and Second Armies. Billotte's attention remained riveted to Tongres and Gembloux; at 10:30 p.m. he set priorities for the following day: air cover first for the First Army and Tongres, second for the Seventh Army and perhaps the BEF.

The fighter strength of the Northern Zone dropped to 387 on May 11. French fighters took a larger part in covering ground troops as the push to the Dyle spilled over into daylight. That morning two Belgian squadrons with nine Battle bombers took off to knock out the bridges over the Albert Canal; they scored hits. But their light bombs were ineffective and six planes failed to return. This was the only bombing mission attempted by the Belgian air service during the campaign.[41] Dutch planes concentrated on German bridgeheads into Holland, losing several planes to their own antiaircraft and ground troops, who fired at everything in the air.

Gamelin's decision to launch the bombing campaign enabled d'Astier to lend a strong hand to the Belgian effort. Two expeditions of twelve British mediums hit Maastricht, followed by a similar force of Lioré 451's. These attacks delayed German forces crossing the waterways. The RAF continued to bomb occupied Dutch airfields, while bombers of the Advanced Air Striking Force hit German columns in the Ardennes. Fourteen Allied bombers failed to return.[42]

Air reconnaissance during the night of May 11-12 again spotted German columns in the Ardennes with their lights on. At 10:00 p.m. on May 11 the GQG sent its estimate to Vincennes. The axes of the enemy attack seemed to be the "Bastogne gap" and the area north of Liège. An instruction for air reconnaissance from Georges' headquarters early on May 12 pointed out German attacks in the direction of Tilburg, Tongres, and finally Mézières by "important forces including at least two armored divisions and an important number of active divisions."[43] The main thrusts seemed to be the second and third, although it was not clear where the bulk of the enemy infantry was. The note concentrated on the possibility of a flanking maneuver against the Maginot Line via the Ardennes combined with a similar movement through Switzerland, on the situation of enemy units north of the Aachen-Liège line, and on the situation in the Ardennes—particularly the location of enemy armor.

May 11 was a good day for the Germans as they broke through the Peel-Raam position into the Brabant plain, although the commander of Army Group B was disturbed to find French columns moving into the same area. The Maastricht bottleneck imposed delays; gasoline for the Panzers beyond the waterways had to be flown in.[44] Still, the invasion was progressing faster than the Allied command had expected, endangering its plans.

May 12: The View from the Top

Georges worked to settle the command system, a problem which demanded a solution as the Allied and enemy forces closed. Doumenc arranged an interview with Léopold at the Château de Casteau. Georges left that morning for Billotte's headquarters in Belgium where he met Pownall in the absence of Lord Gort who was "sick."[45] Pownall asked for four squadrons of fighters from Britain; he got one—"That will leave thirty-four squadrons at home where there is no attack. . . ." Georges secured Pownall's agreement to delegate command to Billotte, then, meeting Daladier who was inspecting in the north, got his support. The whole group moved to meet Léopold at 3:00 p.m. Pownall told the conference of the RAF's refusal to give him the fighters he requested. "The general sense of the meeting was that it was imperative that adequate reinforcement of fighter aircraft should be available. . . ."

Speaking in Gamelin's name, Georges declared that the latter's intention was to "fight all out" on the Antwerp-Namur-Meuse position. Georges continued:

> 'Unlike the *moral* offensive toward the Netherlands, the Belgian maneuver could have a decisive effect. The battle will be hard because we will have to conduct it without agreeing on plans beforehand; but it must be fought without thought of retreat in spite of the certain superiority of the enemy air force.
>
> Events have moved faster than expected. Besides that, a parallel battle has flared up in the Ardennes, where the Germans are using very heavy tanks, and in Luxemburg.
>
> Good coordination is essential. Given the extent of the front under my command, I ask that the Belgian and British armies accept General Billotte as the eventual coordinator of operations by delegation [from me].'[46]

Georges' headquarters was distant; it would be relatively easy for Billotte to coordinate the Belgian, British, and northern two armies of the First Army Group since these were close together. Georges apparently intended to give Giraud's army to Billotte too, although this is not clear. Daladier

General Billotte.
Photo Courtesy of E. C. P. Armées

and Pownall supported Georges; Léopold agreed. Van Overstraeten asked Billotte in an aside for a larger front, given the size of the Belgian force. Billotte was skeptical, replying "'comes the battle, everyone proclaims his front too wide!'" Billotte then took the floor:

> "The coming battle may be decisive, certainly difficult. We must expect that Belgium will be the theater of the principal German effort. Wisdom requires that we envisage the worst. We must prepare a withdrawal to a position farther back, without openly saying so, at the same time remaining resolute to fight to a finish [on the Dyle]."[47]

On that note the meeting broke up. Georges returned to La Ferté completing his first—and last—visit to Belgium during the battle. Léopold remarked to Van Overstraeten that "'confidence in success appears limited'"; Van Overstraeten was more impressed by the Allies' avowed inferiority in the air. For his part, Daladier noticed Léopold's sadness and discouragement.

Thus Billotte assumed command in Belgium, although his rank and the size of his staff would necessarily limit his ability to "coordinate." Georges imposed this solution in the midst of battle on three Allied nations whose strengths and interests in the theater were unequal. It must have given him a certain satisfaction to cut Gamelin out, just as Gamelin had done to him the preceding November—Gamelin, titular Commander in Chief, was conspicuously absent from the Casteau meeting. Responsibility now lay on Billotte, whose optimism had begun to fade in the glare of the initial German successes.

That same morning Colonel de Villelume spoke to Gamelin about his fear that the enemy was drawing the Allies into a trap in Belgium: otherwise, why did the enemy not bomb Allied columns as they moved forward? Gamelin replied that perhaps the Luftwaffe was occupied elsewhere. Gamelin clearly did not take the threat of entrapment seriously. He told Georges at 9:00 a.m. that the cavalry, following its retreat from the Ardennes, should "side slip" north behind the First Army and the Gembloux gap.[48] This would have deprived Corap of his mobile reserves just as the enemy came up. But Georges paid no attention to this "suggestion." The initial dispositions of Georges' force had been imposed on him, but now command was his and he did not intend to share it.

Gamelin ordered air effort concentrated on enemy columns at Tongres and in the Ardennes.[49] Georges, however, switched priorities at about 3:00 p.m., asking that the British Air Component bomb in support of the BEF, and that French bombers operate at Bouillon and Bertrix in the Ardennes. The bombers were to work for Prioux as a second priority. This switch caused quite a stir.

The probable cause of this shift was an alarming report at 3:00 p.m. from the Second Army. Roton and Doumenc ordered three divisions to the junction of the Second and Ninth Armies: the 3rd DCR and the 3rd Motorized Infantry—the last motorized units left—and General Jean de Lattre de Tassigny's active 14th Infantry. General Flavigny's 21st Corps would encadre these units. Huntziger got free disposition of the 1st Colonial Infantry which lay behind his right flank.[50] Georges later added the series A 28th (Alpine) Infantry. The 3rd DCR, relatively close to the Second Army, and the 3rd Motorized got under way that night. De Lattre's 14th Infantry in Lorraine began to move by rail the next day. The 28th could not begin its journey until May 15. French doctrine ruled that such railroad transports required four days or so—a long time! Having committed his last motorized reserves, Georges had to figure that further long distance reinforcements would involve considerable delay.

In the Field

On the Seventh Army front the 510th Tank Groupment debarked north of Antwerp and was held in reserve by the 25th Motorized Infantry behind the Breda position. But between Breda and the Waal and Meuse rivers only scattered Dutch forces and French reconnaissance troops stood guard; the northern column of the 9th Panzer shoved this screen aside and reached the open rear door into Holland, sealing the fate of the Netherlands.[51] Billotte ordered Giraud at 1:35 p.m., *before* the conference at Casteau, to abandon the Dutch venture. All that remained was to redeploy Giraud's force, which lay so far north.

To the south the Belgian command reacted to the breakthrough at Eben Emael by ordering its motorized Cavalry Corps onto the Gette River between the enemy and the Belgian sector of the Dyle line.[52] The key action on May 12 was near Hannut, where the 4th Panzer, exploiting the Eben Emael bridgehead, ran into the 3rd DLM. The Germans enjoyed air superiority, but French artillery compensated with heavy and accurate fire. The 3rd Panzer was still struggling over the waterways. By evening a German battlegroup broke into a French strongpoint at Thisnes; but German infantry could not follow and French armor counterattacked. The commander of the Panzer regiment had his tank knocked out; but by night German infantry moved forward, and in the first hours of May 13 the French cavalry fell back.

In the northern Ardennes Rommel's 7th Panzer roared into the relatively open area just east of the Meuse. He massed his tanks; the 1st Light Cavalry could not stand against such force for long.[53] With the 1st Light Cavalry thrown back during the morning, the 4th Light Cavalry fell back in step, using its mechanized elements to hold off pursuit; the cavalry crossed the Meuse that afternoon, leaving Corap's infantry in the front line. General Hermann Hoth, commanding the German 15th Corps, criticized the command of the 4th Light Cavalry for failing to assist its neighbor; Corap could have gained another day if he had pushed his cavalry onto the Ourthe River from the start of operations rather than holding it on the Meuse. Corap ordered the artillery of the cavalry divisions to reinforce the infantry in line: only the 75's of those divisions had reached their positions; they had not had time to coordinate fire plans or install communications. Even the 5th Motorized, the only such unit in Corap's army, had not had time to lay barbed wire or minefields.[54] Corap ordered motorized cavalry from the 1st Light Cavalry into line, regrouping the rest farther west. That night his 5th Motorized held sixteen kilometers as did its neighbor to the south, the series A 18th Infantry. Corap's only infantry reserve in the area was the 4th

North African Infantry which, scheduled to reach Philippeville on May 15, was still well to the rear.

Behind his right flank Corap had only the series B 53rd Infantry, which moved to the southeast of Mézières from the night of May 11 in response to the threat coming through the southern Ardennes. This left him nothing with which to garrison the frontier fortifications behind his left wing. On the morning of May 13 the Ninth Army had only nineteen of twenty-seven battalions on the Meuse or in immediate reserve. To fill the holes Corap drew on lower echelon reserves; he ordered part of the reserve 39th Regiment of the 5th Motorized to fill a gap between the 5th and 18th Divisions. But the company ordered to hold the Houx basin failed to move to the riverbank, instead remaining on heights to the rear, leaving a chink in the line. As darkness descended so did riflemen of the 5th Panzerdivision who infiltrated this gap and carved the first pocket into the French position on the Meuse.[55]

In the southern Ardennes Guderian turned south on the morning of May 12, leaving the routes leading west open for Reinhardt. But Reinhardt, starting from east of the Rhine and following Guderian over the steep and winding roads, was terribly hampered by German infantry cutting across his march. His units, delayed by the infantry and Allied demolitions, became fractionated beyond radio range, threatening his attacks on Monthermé and Nouzonville which were scheduled to coincide with Guderian's at Sedan. Guderian's force ran into resistance from French cavalry on the Semoy and was harassed by artillery fire from Sedan and by three bombing attacks which hindered bridge building. Nonetheless, he was pushing toward the Meuse by nightfall.[56] Grandsard did not think an immediate attack likely, for the enemy had not had time to bring much artillery into position. As for the Luftwaffe, the Second Army's fighter group gave an impressive display that morning in defense of the cavalry. Five Curtiss of Group I/5 intercepted twenty Stukas; French pilots claimed at least twelve and two antiaircraft batteries claimed two more bombers east of Sedan.[57]

Huntziger placed two infantry tank battalions at Grandsard's disposal that night and warned him to maintain liaison with the neighboring Ninth Army: his reconnaissance groups were to hold the Bar River between the two armies. During the afternoon, General Keller, the Inspector General of the Tanks, approved the movement of the 3rd DCR in two nights behind the junction of the Ninth and Second Armies. There was no urgency in the unit's movement:[58] the armor could easily have made the trip that day.

Farther east Condé's cavalry, back from Luxemburg, had to move into line to shore up the series B 58th Infantry in the Longwy bridgehead. Despite this move, Prételat informed Georges that morning that German operations east of the Moselle aimed only at tying down French troops.[59]

In the Air

The Northern Zone mustered 345 fighters on the morning of May 12; German attacks on French territory slackened. Remaining Dutch aircraft attacked German columns in the Frise and Arnhem areas, and continued to harass the German airborne bridgeheads; this last mission occupied them until the Dutch capitulation. The Allied effort concentrated, from the early morning, on the Eben Emael area. Nine Blenheims hit the area at 7:00 a.m., two returned; five Battles tried it at 9:15, all were lost; finally twenty-four Blenheims made the run, ten were lost. The Flak and the eighty-five Messerschmidt 109E's of *Jagdgeschwader* 27, which flew 340 sorties, were deadly. By day's end the Advanced Air Striking Force, which had had 135 bombers on May 10, was down to 72. The Chief of the British Air Staff signaled his concern to Barratt, warning that nothing would be left "'when the critical phase comes. . . .'" Barratt decided to withhold his Blenheims from daylight action.[60]

Twelve Lioré 451's hit the same area at 6:30 p.m.; all returned. But an afternoon expedition of eighteen Breguet 693 assault bombers—the maiden action of the assault aviation—ended in tragedy. Operating at low altitude over the straight Belgian roads in single file, the bombers delivered bombs and shells onto the German columns snaking out from Tongres. Some of the three plane sections escaped with only a plane or two lost; several were destroyed by Flak; senior officers were lost. Eight failed to return, thus calling the concept of this elite force into question.[61]

Georges' decision that afternoon to switch priority in the air to the Second Army came after fifty British bombers attacked Bouillon to slow Guderian's Panzers (eighteen planes lost); Georges' order resulted in night attacks on German communications in the Saint-Hubert area and farther north over Aachen.[62] Georges' decision also left Billotte "astonished." Despite Georges' order, Billotte directed two-thirds of the air effort to the First Army, one-third to the Second. But Billotte's decision made little difference: the Second Army failed to request a bombing mission—the fifty Blenheims went out at d'Astier's initiative. Billotte's interference with Georges' order indicates the confusion in command responsibilities resulting from Billotte's preoccupation with Belgium and Georges' preoccupation with the Second Army.

On the night of May 12 Ninth Army headquarters warned that the enemy had at least two armored divisions on its front. General Thierry d'Argenlieu, Corap's chief of staff, thought the enemy could bring two to three infantry divisions up that night: they could mount assaults beginning in the afternoon of May 13.[63] But at that moment German riflemen were infiltrating across the Meuse at Houx.

DISASTER ON THE MEUSE

May 13: The View from the Top

In Georges' opinion the key to the German attack and the Allied defense seemed to be the center of his front at Sedan. He took direct charge of the Second Army. Gamelin visited Georges that morning, then issued a general order: "It is time now to stop the onrush of the mechanized and motorized forces of the enemy. The hour has come to fight to a finish on the positions fixed by the High Command. We no longer have the right to retreat. If the enemy makes a local breach, don't just seal it off, but counterattack and retake it."[64] Gamelin seemed astonished at the speed with which the enemy made contact with the main Allied positions—but it was too late for second thoughts.

Around noon Vincennes learned of the crossing at Houx. This caused the first stir of emotion; Gamelin had calls placed directly to the Ninth Army. Thierry d'Argenlieu reported that he was watching the Monthermé area toward which Reinhardt's Panzers were racing, while Generals Julien Martin commanding the 11th Corps and Bouffet commanding the 2nd Motorized Corps were dealing with the situation at Houx.[65] Georges focused on Sedan: he directed the active 36th Infantry and the new 44th Infantry toward the right rear of the Ninth Army, but they were far from the front and could not move until the next day. At 1:00 p.m. Georges ordered the 2nd DCR, waiting in Champagne for heavy railroad wagons for its transport, to move as quickly as possible behind Corap's left flank, beginning that evening. For reasons that are not clear, at 7:30 p.m. Doumenc changed the unit's destination to the First Army. The 2nd DCR began embarking that evening, but lack of railroad cars and air attacks prolonged the process into the next night; its elements on wheels set off at 9:00 p.m. on May 13.[66]

Georges lunched with Villelume, Reynaud's adviser. Georges admitted the situation was serious. The Allies were fighting against two to one odds—worse in the air (this was a gross exaggeration). The Belgians had given up the Albert Canal in forty-eight hours instead of the eight days expected, and had failed to fortify the Dyle positions. Further, Georges said, Giraud's army had been wasted on a useless adventure just as he (Georges) had predicted, although it was being recovered. But the worst was in the south where violent attacks, with heavy reinforcements following, were hitting the Meuse and Sedan. French infantry (he mistakenly thought) had given way under air bombardment and had allowed a German battalion across the river at Houx. Corap, however, would counterattack with a DCR (presumably the 2nd). Villelume repeated his fear that the enemy was trying to trap them in Belgium; Georges replied that he was giving the matter his full attention. Georges also felt that most of the troops stood up well to air attack and the SOMUA tanks were superior to those of the Germans.

At 4:00 p.m. Roton issued a directive for strategic reconnaissance: "The enemy seems . . . to be preparing to increase his pressure in the immediate future in the general direction of Sedan, where the center of gravity of his offensive may be directed."[67] Roton wanted to know if the enemy was reinforcing Sedan or, farther east, Longwy. Georges, no doubt, was still concerned about a flanking attack against the Maginot Line. Colonel Baril, head of the intelligence section at La Ferté, concluded that the enemy effort was moving in the direction of Mézières; recalling the plan acquired by espionnage for a German advance to the Channel, he decided that this was what the enemy had in mind. But there is nothing to suggest that he convinced his superiors that this was the German plan.

Meanwhile, Guderian's troops began their assault on the Sedan position and Hoth's forces won lodgements on Corap's left flank. Guderian pushed his men to capture the heights dominating Sedan, giving him room to bring Panzers over the Meuse. At 9:45 p.m. Georges ordered a counterattack toward Sedan to be led by the 3rd DCR. But word came back that the enemy had tanks over the Meuse—a false report. Although La Ferté reported to Vincennes at 11:45 p.m. that "here we are calm," a cloud of foreboding hung over the French command that night. As the midnight shift took over at Vincennes and most of the officers went to bed, the light in Gamelin's office remained on.[68]

Billotte visited Corap that afternoon and instructed him to regain the Meuse at Houx that same day. When the attempt failed, Billotte renewed his order for the next day and alerted the 1st DCR, behind the First Army, for a possible move to support Corap. With his first lot of reinforcements, the 1st North African and 43rd Infantry, arriving behind the First Army and the 32nd Division in Blanchard's immediate rear, Billotte had sufficient forces to defend the Gembloux gap. But he hesitated. He held the series A 4th Infantry of Giraud's army at Ghent for transport south and ordered Giraud's two motorized divisions and the 1st DLM ready in three or four days to follow. Billotte's hesitation to commit his available reserves cost precious time.[69]

In the Field

Grandsard spent the morning of May 13 hurrying his 71st Infantry into line east of Sedan and shifting the series B 55th into more compact dispositions at Sedan. German air activity was heavy; Grandsard had to comfort General Baudet, the commander of the 71st, who was reluctant to enter the line under such conditions.[70] Grandsard phoned Huntziger for more air support; the latter, who had no more to give, replied that the troops "'had to receive their baptism of fire.'" The relief of parts of the 55th left some confusion in the front. By 3:30 p.m. Grandsard had ordered his two reserve infantry regiments and two battalions of tanks to take stations five kilometers behind the front before nightfall, at which time he would direct their intervention. Most of the night of May 12-13 his artillery, demolitions, and rearguards retarded the German advance; the French fire was "outstandingly accurate" and the German situation "anything but pleasant." To the rifle regiment of the 1st Panzer the situation in the morning of May 13 seemed "ominous"; the unit commander, Colonel Balck, sent word that "the attack could not hope to succeed unless the French artillery was eliminated."[71] Guderian's answer was a sustained assault by all available units of the Luftwaffe.

Huntziger had always taken the Luftwaffe seriously: after the Polish campaign he issued a directive warning that every precaution against air attack must be taken "with application, even with passion, to battle successfully against dangerous low level attacks."[72] But the series B troops at Sedan could not withstand the bulk of the attack strength of the Luftwaffe. The onslaught and the screen of smoke and dust it blew up silenced many French batteries, especially the heavier artillery—with "remarkable effect" on German morale. Under this cover the 1st Panzer assembled antiaircraft, tanks, eight artillery groups, and eleven battalions of infantry and assault engineers to attack the eight companies holding the 55th Infantry's center. The Germans brought high-velocity guns to bear at close range with devastating effect.[73] The 2nd and 10th Panzers attacked Donchery to the west and Wadelincourt to the east of Sedan.

As the assault troops crossed, some French bunkers resisted and some French artillery opened fire. At Sedan the Germans broke into the position; French infantry—contrary to orders—began to fall back.[74] As some of the French, dazed by the four-hour air bombardment, gave way, the commander of the corps artillery in the rear panicked and ordered a retreat; that night the rear of the 10th Corps was clogged with fleeing troops, although senior officers organized a weak stop line south of the heights. The rumor that German armor was over the Meuse began to circulate.

The attacks on Donchery and Wadelincourt stuck fast before French fire, but as the French center gave way, riflemen of the 1st Panzer took many posts of the 55th from the rear, opening the way for their neighbors. The flood of fugitives and the impression left by the air attack delayed the arrival of Grandsard's reserves. None were in position at nightfall; Grandsard was unable to reinforce the main position or to counterattack on the 13th.

That morning the 3rd Motorized Infantry had debarked thirty kilometers south of the Second Army, arriving on foot. Why the unit detrained so far south is not clear; only late that night could the 3rd move to support Grandsard.[75] The 3rd DCR spent the day parked some distance from Sedan; it moved at 8:00 p.m. Huntziger ordered his 5th Light Cavalry to the Bar River to link Grandsard's left with the Ninth Army; he improvised a force under General Roucaud, commander of the 1st Colonial Infantry, including the 1st Colonial, the 2nd Light Cavalry, and Huntziger's last battalion of infantry tanks. Huntziger ordered Roucaud to shore up Grandsard's right flank.

While Huntziger lost the Battle of Sedan, Corap's army clung to the Belgian Meuse with its left flank, outnumbered two to one.[76] Corap was almost caught in an encounter battle as Hoth's Panzers appeared before the defenders were fully installed on the Meuse. The Germans who crossed at Houx found the active 5th Motorized and the series A 18th Infantry tenacious: the French defended their strongpoints, retreating only when ammunition was exhausted and suffering heavy loss.[77] The 1st Light Cavalry filled in the line, then counterattacked with armor, driving the enemy to the edge of the water; but French infantry was delayed by air attack and did not follow up to hold the ground. When General Erwin Rommel, commander of the 7th Panzer, visited the area that night, he found senior officers of the rifle unit dead or wounded, the unit itself "severely mauled"; Rommel redoubled efforts to get tanks across in the night of May 13.

During the day Rommel directed an attempt to cross the Meuse near Dinant; French artillery and flanking fire caused heavy casualties and repeatedly halted the crossing. Rommel brought up tank and artillery support and, taking personal command—heavy losses had left the officers "badly shaken"—managed to get the operation going.[78] As Rundstedt put it, the 5th and 7th Panzers and the infantry facing Corap had to fight "dourly" to get across, and had to fight off counterattacks; the crossings at Sedan were much easier.

One other German force crossed the Meuse: Reinhardt managed to push enough of his 6th Panzer over the cliffs at Monthermé to meet his obligation to attack simultaneously with Guderian. Supported weakly in the air and with only half his artillery in place—and some of that was destroyed, he claimed, by his own bombers—his troops could secure only a thin lodgement against weak infantry but strong French artillery fire. His attack on Nouzonville did not take place: the motorized infantry was stuck on the roads miles to the east. Reinhardt was checked.

Near the Gembloux gap, meanwhile, a mechanized battle developed as General Hoepner flung his 16th Corps beneath heavy air support against Prioux's Cavalry Corps. The Panzers attacked near Hannut. As the concentrated tank units of the German corps thrust into the zone of French strongpoints, local French armored reserves of the 3rd DLM counterattacked. The 4th Panzer attacked toward Merdorp, drawing the reserve SOMUA tanks of the 2nd DLM.[79] German riflemen infiltrated between the defenses; the ineffectiveness of their tank guns and antitank weapons shocked them, but 88 mm Flak fended off the French armor. As night fell the Panzers conquered a key strongpoint, forcing the French to retreat.

French tanks shouldered through the German antitank barrage to bring off most of their garrisons; Prioux made good his retreat. Here, near the Gembloux gap, the Germans had the advantage of air superiority and the initiative; Prioux was unable to mass as many tanks in the crucial sector. The French lost some of the garrisons of their strongpoints; the 3rd DLM lost half its Hotchkiss tanks and thirty of its eighty SOMUA tanks. German losses were substantial, particularly among antitank units. But Prioux still stood between the Panzers and Gembloux; the Germans had to fight his cavalry again, a prospect that the bloodied German tank crews did not relish.

To the west Lord Gort prepared a defense in depth with three divisions along the Dyle, two more in support, another two farther back with his tank brigade, and yet another two divisions on the Escaut River.[80] That same afternoon the Belgian Cavalry Corps and 14th Infantry fighting on Prioux's left began to feel the pressure; the Belgian army took its place on the Dyle line. Except for its 7th Infantry, mauled in the Eben Emael fighting, and parts of the 14th and some of the cavalry, the Belgian army was intact. In Holland, part of the 9th Panzer and some SS troops pushed the French south of Breda, hampering the withdrawal of the French 25th Motorized which was ordered back on the night of May 12; the French retreated to the northern edge of the Antwerp fortress. The northern column of Panzers drove into Fortress Holland—the hours of Dutch resistance were numbered. Giraud ordered the 1st DLM south of Antwerp to support the Belgians. Some of its Hotchkiss tanks saw action that morning routing German infantry out of Belgian defenses northeast of Antwerp, but by May 13 it was clear that the destiny of Giraud's units lay to the south.

In the Air

General Vuillemin released two fighter groups from the Paris air defense to d'Astier, and added Group I/3, the first equipped with Dewoitine 520's, and the four Paris night fighter squadrons for strafing attacks against ground targets. He also began to draw on pilots and planes from his flying schools: through May 22 well over 100 planes and crews joined the battle from this source.[81] Vuillemin ordered up Groupment 1 armed with Glenn Martin light bombers, but they were not ready for action for several days; finally he ordered Groupments 9 and 10, flying the old Amiot 143, to support ground operations by day if the enemy broke through.[82] Despite these reinforcements d'Astier had only 314 fighters on the morning of May 13; the situation was aggravated by Barratt's refusal to commit British bombers to daylight action, although one small force of Battles raided Breda. On the other hand, the equivalent of two more squadrons of Hurricanes flew to France in response to pressing appeals from Gort and Barratt. Attrition cut into the Luftwaffe too: the Second Air Fleet operating over Belgium and Holland was down to 30-50 percent strength. But with their numerical advantage, the Germans could afford to pay a higher price. Meanwhile, the remaining Dutch bombers tried one last time to save Holland by glide bombing the vital Moerdijk causeway: one scored a direct hit, but the bomb failed to explode.

At 9:40 a.m. Billotte gave air priority to the Second Army: he expected a general mechanized and air attack—in two or three days! D'Astier then ordered Romatet to commit fighter Groupment 23 to the Second Army. At noon the Second Army reported large numbers of enemy tanks but did not request air strikes since the targets lay under artillery fire. Nonetheless, d'Astier sent an expedition with the remaining French day bombers to Sedan, then another small group to Dinant when, at 4:20 p.m., Billotte switched priority to the Ninth Army whose line gave way before Rommel. Meanwhile, the enemy massed 310 medium bombers, 200 Stukas, and some 200 fighters over Sedan. Despite the resistance of the outnumbered French fighters, the Luftwaffe took command of the air. In a typical incident Captain Accart's eight Curtiss ran into forty enemy mediums escorted by as many fighters: there was little Accart could do. By nightfall French fighters had flown 250 sorties over the Ninth and Second Armies, losing twelve planes and claiming twenty-one victories, but there was no stopping the onslaught on Sedan. That night Billotte and Georges ordered an all-out air attack against enemy pontoon bridges at Sedan for dawn, when Grandsard was to counterattack. As Billotte put it, "'victory or defeat rides on those bridges.'"[83]

May 14: The View From the Top

As midnight passed tension peaked at La Ferté. A false report came in that German tanks were across the Meuse at Sedan and pushing south. Georges telephoned to send Doumenc to La Ferté. Doumenc arrived toward 3:00 a.m.: the atmosphere at La Ferté was that of a family wake. Georges described the situation—"'Our front has caved in at Sedan! It was a rout . . . ,'" and the Commander in Chief on the Northeastern Front fell back into an armchair, choking back a sob. Doumenc reacted instantly: "'Sir, this is war, and in war there are always such incidents!'" But Georges, pale and fighting back tears, was not to be consoled. Doumenc pulled him to a map and sketched out a concentric counterattack from the north, west, and south by the 1st, 2nd, and 3rd DCR toward the German bridgeheads over the Meuse. Georges accepted the idea, but his confidence and that of his staff had collapsed, leaving behind an air of hopelessness. Perhaps the wounds Georges suffered in 1934 had destroyed his nerve. But there was more to it: Sedan was the last in a series of reverses which fell like the blows of a triphammer. First Gamelin's insistence on the Breda maneuver, then the German landings in Holland, the loss of Eben Emael, the premature loss of the Ardennes, the crossing of the Meuse on Corap's front and the failure to throw the enemy back, and now—the defenders of Sedan routed and German tanks across the river before reinforcements could arrive. Gamelin's plan had forced him to divert strength to the north; now the enemy had broken his center and was pushing on: and Gamelin hung back and watched him—Georges—take the responsibility! It was too much to bear. "The rupture of our front seemed [literally] diabolic, therefore believable. The news was like the apparition of the pale face of inexorable destiny."[84]

A chillingly similar scene took place at Billotte's headquarters, where he, d'Astier, Barratt, and their aides met. As one British witness described it, "The conference was a tragic affair. Most of the French officers were in tears, some quite openly sobbing at having to admit the shame they felt in acknowledging the appalling fact that the French had walked out of their fortified positions without any attempt at genuine resistance. This is a very bad affair."[85] Although the breakdown at the front was not so complete as this report suggested, it revealed the mood at Billotte's command post.

Doumenc immediately reported to Gamelin.[86] Colonel Petibon suggested that Gamelin might begin taking lunch with Georges, "'who would be happy to feel himself in constant contact with and supported by you.'" Should Gamelin have replaced Georges? This he could not do. Gamelin's own position had been undermined by the attacks of Paul Reynaud and by the collapse of his Breda maneuver. If anyone were to dismiss a senior commander it would have to be the Premier.

Later that morning Georges issued a general order. He reaffirmed the mission of the First Army Group and the Second Army to hold from Antwerp to Namur and the Meuse. The situation on the Meuse was to be "reestablished," and the "hinge" from Revin to Carignan to be defended "energetically" to prevent the enemy from exploiting to the south and west: "The operations mounted during the day of the 14th will be conducted with extreme energy in order to reabsorb the localized pockets made by the enemy as soon as possible. No faltering [*aucune défaillance*] will be tolerated."[87] The armies were to organize a barrage on their reserve positions to prevent a mechanized exploitation, using reconnaissance groups, light cavalry, fortress troops, and reserves. The Second Army Group was to free reserves by abandoning advanced positions such as Longwy. Priority in fighter and bomber forces was to go to the Dinant and Sedan areas. Early that morning Billotte finally ordered the 1st DCR to Corap to counterattack on his left flank. Meanwhile, Reinhardt's Panzers struck the center of Corap's front at Monthermé and Nouzonville, but the defense held firm and "the enemy did not seem to be in force" at these points.

Shortly after noon Vincennes heard that the 5th Light Cavalry on the Bar had panicked—the enemy had opened the way into Corap's weak right rear. Later that afternoon word came that the enemy had tanks across the Meuse on Corap's left. The staff, meanwhile, was distracted by the threat of a German attack via Switzerland.[88] Gamelin kept up his "serene" appearance, but the gravity of the situation reached him as he worked with Georges amid a constant coming and going of officers.

At 2:00 p.m. Georges ordered the 2nd DCR to move on Signy-l'Abbaye in Corap's right rear. Unfortunately, the staff seems to have thought the 2nd DCR was at Charleroi, where previous orders had directed it. Actually it was still moving, partly by road and partly by rail, and could not march on Signy "'battalions of B tanks at the head.'"[89] The officers of the road columns of the unit received this order late in the afternoon; confusion followed. It was only after 5:00 p.m. that the GQG discovered its error and ordered the 2nd DCR to regroup as quickly as possible in the Signy area. But precious time had been lost. That afternoon Billotte visited Léopold. Léopold later told Van Overstraeten that Billotte was worried about Sedan and had declared anxiously that "'the Germans have prepared a means [*outil*] to win this war: we have no such means'"; Billotte had added (mistakenly) that the Luftwaffe had acted so violently on Corap's left that the bulk of his divisions had been unable to reach the Meuse. Georges was equally dismayed: he had never thought the enemy could take a position such as Sedan "at a single stroke." Certainly the German performance had been superb—and terribly demoralizing to the French command which had as yet scored no success worth mentioning.

That evening Georges decided to replace Corap with the prestigious and energetic Giraud who, with the end of the Breda maneuver, was available. Hearing from the Second Army that the counterattack by the 3rd DCR had not gone in, Georges curtly reminded Huntziger that he had given him the armor for an attack: "that is the way to regain dominance over the enemy and paralyze any progression of the enemy pocket to the west and south."[90] Georges ordered the bombing effort for the next day to concentrate on the same targets that d'Astier was hitting on the 14th. D'Astier was to maintain permanent fighter cover "no matter how weak it might be" over Sedan on the morning of May 15 to raise the morale of the troops. Finally, Georges began to draw on the reserves of the Second Army Group. By the end of the day he withdrew one corps and one infantry division, two antiaircraft groups, and a tank battalion. But this was a minor measure given the critical situation.

In the Field

At midnight on May 13-14 Huntziger ordered General Jean Flavigny, commanding the 21st Corps, to seal off the pocket south of Sedan with the 3rd Motorized Infantry, then attack behind the 3rd DCR. Meanwhile, the Roucaud group with the 1st Colonial Infantry, the 2nd Light Cavalry, and a tank battalion would attack on Flavigny's right. Huntziger added "'this action must be fought with the most brutal energy without regard to losses.'"[91] Grandsard gave his two reserve infantry regiments and two tank battalions to General Lafontaine, commander of the 55th Infantry, for a dawn counterattack independent of Flavigny. One regiment and one tank battalion finally moved out at 7:00 a.m., a critical three hours late. At first the advance went well, artillery and antitank units knocking out some enemy armor and the infantry moving forward—then masses of German tanks that had just crossed the river appeared. The infantry support tanks, outnumbered and outgunned, stood their ground and were decimated; then the Panzers were loose against the series B French infantry. The remains of the 55th Division fell back; Flavigny's units took over.

Allied bombers began to work over the German crossings; the staff of the 1st Panzer rated the French counterattack strong but noted that it did not involve large units. Considering this, Guderian made the daring decision to rely on the French reputation for methodical action and turned his forces immediately toward the west, into the rear of the weak Ninth Army, leaving only the elite Grossdeutschland Infantry Regiment to hold the south flank of the pocket.[92]

Guderian swung his 1st and 2nd Panzers west, leaving the Grossdeutschland to hold Flavigny until the 10th Panzer, tied up in the French position on the Meuse, could struggle forward.[93] Guderian's first two Panzers took the bridges of the Bar River and the Ardennes Canal by surprise, routing elements of the 5th Light Cavalry. But resistance stiffened: Corap's series B 53rd Infantry and 3rd Spahi Brigade were west of the Bar with the 5th Light Cavalry. The 53rd spent the night countermarching between the Meuse facing north and the Bar facing east as Corap received conflicting reports about the threat. By the afternoon of the 14th, the 53rd defended the Bar to the south of the 102nd Fortress Infantry on the Meuse; Corap's Spahis linked it to the 5th Light Cavalry farther south. But the units were intermixed and thinly spread.

The infantry and cavalry locked themselves into the woods and towns. The defense in the Vendresse area stopped the Panzers until late that afternoon. The 2nd Panzer spent most of the day attacking—from the rear—the 148th Fortress Regiment on the Meuse. The 148th was scattered in works on a wide front, but the tanks operating by themselves had great difficulty neutralizing the casemates. That evening, however, the defenders ran out of ammunition and gave way, opening the rear of the 102nd Division. Similarly, the defense farther south inched back; a gap opened between the 53rd Division and the cavalry farther south, although the arrival of some of de Lattre's 14th Infantry helped. As the night of May 14 fell, the

Panzers had not yet conquered French resistance west of the Bar. German losses—unlike those on May 13—were substantial; both sides were exhausted. But Georges' hopes for Sedan rested on counterattacks from the 3rd DCR and the 3rd Motorized. By 4:00 p.m. May 14, they were on the south edge of the German pocket, after a day in which parts of the 3rd DCR stood waiting, champing at the bit, for orders.[94] This division lacked radios and logistics tractors; its lack of training also made itself felt. As his tanks plowed forward through refugees and retreating fragments of frontline units, Captain Billotte itched to match his powerful B tanks against the Panzers. Billotte found the terrain strangely empty. Guderian had left his flank open to Georges' counterstroke!

The commander of the counterattack, Flavigny, had long led the crack 1st DLM in peacetime. He was unfavorably impressed with the clumsy manner in which General Brocard maneuvered the 3rd DCR; he knew of the unit's weak equipment and training. Despite Brocard's insistence, Flavigny decided to call off the attack. The 55th Division no longer existed, his left flank was threatened west of the Bar, and he felt—incorrectly—that the enemy had had time to reinforce the pocket. His attack would be overtaken by nightfall; a failure might compromise his defense. He cancelled the attack and, worse, split up the 3rd DCR—in violation of doctrine—to support his infantry: dispositions that Huntziger approved.[95] Although bitter fighting later developed, the chance for a decisive advance was lost. Despite pressing orders from Georges (repeated that evening) and urgings from Brocard, Flavigny and Huntziger fulfilled Guderian's prophecy that the French would act cautiously. Flavigny and Huntziger wanted primarily to contain the enemy. Georges saw the threat of an exploitation to the west, but he was not there to impose his will.

The final piece in the Sedan mosaic was the series B 71st Infantry which, installed to the east of the 55th Division on May 13, held the eastern flank of the pocket. Warned of German tanks south of the Meuse, the 71st threw out a screen on its left. But the division commander, nervous at the threat, pulled his command post back and left the screen without direction and artillery support. Grandsard's remaining reserves joined it but the 71st, left without direction and facing infiltrations, gave way. Grandsard met General Berniquet, commanding the 2nd Light Cavalry which was coming up into the area (Berniquet was under Roucaud's orders) and urged him to order his cavalry to join the 71st. But Berniquet feared an enemy attack in strength and declined. That evening most of the 71st either fled or retreated under orders, although some units stood in place and then fought their way out that night.[96] The 2nd Light Cavalry dug in quietly amid wrecked German aircraft and, like Billotte of the 3rd DCR, wondered why it was not pushed to contact.

The collapse of the 71st led Huntziger to pull the eastern flank of the

Sedan pocket back to Inor in the afternoon of the 14th.[97] This meant abandoning key terrain east of Sedan, although the enemy was not pressing. Worse, the longer front absorbed the remnants of the 71st and the Roucaud group which was intended to counterattack, thus tying them to a defensive mission and giving enemy infantry time to arrive. Thus Flavigny and Huntziger tied the reinforcements Georges sent—against orders—to defensive tasks even though they were not under enemy pressure. The inexperience of the French command at corps and army level made itself felt.

Farther north Corap faced disaster: by evening his right flank, the right of the overextended 102nd Fortress Infantry, shattered after resisting Guderian's Panzers. The center of the same division resisted Reinhardt's Panzers which had won a toehold over the Meuse at Monthermé where the river made a peninsula of the French bank, dominated by heights on the east bank. The 102nd had almost no reinforcements to send but, taking advantage of the terrain and fortifications, the outnumbered defenders penned Reinhardt's riflemen into the peninsula.[98] Reinhardt attempted to swing a second force across at Nouzonville. His motorized infantry was still blocked in the Ardennes, so he laid hands on a regiment from another corps which had marched into the area. But the thin line of the 102nd, posted in casemates and covered by artillery fire, stopped the crossing cold. Reinhardt was checked again, leaving the riflemen of his 6th Panzer, as he later wrote, in a "bad spot" (*ernsten Lage*). Indeed they almost collapsed before a weak French counterattack and were barely able to hold their positions in Monthermé.

The situation on the rest of Corap's front was more serious. The German 32nd Infantry hit the French 22nd Infantry at Givet on May 14 and forced it back from the Meuse. The 22nd, whose commander, General Hassler, had not yet rejoined the unit from convalescent leave, fell back in disarray under the weak guidance of General Beziers-Lafosse—who pulled back his command post three times in twelve hours! Corap intervened to demand a counterattack. He sent out a general order demanding that cadres set the example for their men, threatening "pitiless sanctions" on leaders who failed; but his troops were in a perilous situation and they knew it.[99] Meanwhile, the only uncommitted unit in the Ninth Army's right rear, the 2nd DCR, struggled to regroup at Signy. Its commander, General Bruché, was with the First Army, unaware that he was to go instead to the Ninth Army; he did not see Corap until evening. The division's road columns moved toward Signy that afternoon; then they heard of enemy armor west of the Bar. The commander of the road echelon decided to shelter his unarmed vehicles south of the Aisne River. At the same time the division's fighting vehicles detrained to the west, unaware of what had happened to their support units: the pieces moved in divergent directions, cut off from their commander. The 2nd DCR was unable to join the day's fighting.

General Corap.
Photo Courtesy of E. C. P. Armées

On Corap's left flank, the morning of May 14 started off well as reserves from the 5th Motorized and the 4th Light Cavalry counterattacked, but enemy air attacks and artillery fire and tanks halted them. The commander of the 18th Infantry Division then decided to abandon the Meuse and pulled back, establishing his troops in woods and villages. But the disparity in strength was too great; that evening the French gave ground, covered by mechanized cavalry which took a heavy beating.[100]

The 1st Light Cavalry held off Rommel's force in Onhaye until surrounded on three sides. As the afternoon faded the cavalry pulled out onto the hastily formed front of the 4th North African Infantry. This unit, Corap's infantry reserve on his left flank, was to counterattack with the 1st DCR, but it went to ground before Philippeville, halfway between the Meuse and the French frontier, and rebuffed the Panzers. Rommel himself was slightly wounded and had to be rescued.[101]

The 1st DCR moved that afternoon through a welter of refugees across the Sambre River while General Bruneau, its commander, met General Martin, commander of Corap's 11th Corps (and prewar Inspector General of Tanks). They decided to push the 1st DCR as far east as possible to attack the next morning. The combat elements of the division, moving by daylight, reached their assigned positions; the supply columns moved by night at a snail's pace. Bruneau set his tanks in mass facing east, his mechanized infantry and artillery in the rear. His combat echelons did not have their logistics tractors with them—contrary to doctrine—and thus most of his tanks sat at nightfall waiting for gasoline. Nor was the unit ready the next morning.[102]

Meanwhile, Martin, on his own initiative, sanctioned the retreat from the Meuse that night, deciding not to await the counterattack of the 4th North African and the 1st DCR. This withdrawal, combined with the threat of Guderian on the Ninth Army's other flank, forced Corap at the end of the day to ask Billotte for permission to retreat. The two had a stormy conversation; Billotte finally let Corap withdraw to the frontier position in the north and a second position in the south where Guderian's Panzers had penetrated. But Billotte told him to hold one more day on an intermediate position so he could reinforce the frontier defenses. Billotte was highly displeased; shortly after Giraud replaced Corap.[103]

Farther north, on May 14, General Prioux's armor finally fell back to the Gembloux gap. Among the men of the cavalry morale was high; they had accomplished their mission. Leaving the tanks and artillery near the front, the cavalry regrouped in the rear.[104] German tanks raced forward, despite "terrible" French artillery fire and occasional air attacks, on their heels. Hiding amid the refugees, elements of the 4th Panzer broke into the front of the 1st Moroccan Division of General Aymes' 4th Corps; the Moroccans were not yet fully installed. Despite German air superiority (Aymes got a single air mission to observe for his artillery), a battalion of Moroccans and a battalion of infantry tanks restored the position.

On the British and Belgian fronts German infantry made contact; farther north the 25th Motorized Infantry of the Seventh Army clashed with SS troops north of Antwerp. General Molinié's troops held twenty-two kilometers—four times what doctrine advocated—but had organized strongpoints in depth. At 9:00 a.m. armor from the SS Germania Division broke into his position followed by infantry attempting to reduce the isolated strongpoints. English fighters fended off German air attacks during the morning and French artillery took a heavy toll, but by afternoon several garrisons had fallen. Then Molinié released two battalions of infantry tanks in a mass of eighty vehicles: the Renaults bowled over the German armor, which was overextended between the French strongpoints, and routed the SS infantry. The French lost only a few machines (but well over 500 infantrymen) and claimed some 100 enemy vehicles from a force of 150 engaged.[105] This counterattack impressed the German command, but the 25th was needed elsewhere and withdrew that night.

To the north the German advance cut off some of the French reconnaissance troops still in Brabant, then pushed toward South Beveland and Walcheren. There was little cooperation between Dutch forces there and the French seaborne expedition.[106] The French commander had to be replaced by General Deslaurens, commander of the series B 60th Infantry. Dutch morale was low: the Dutch government had fled the country before the German tanks and, goaded by threats to bomb Rotterdam, General Winkelman surrendered all his forces except those fighting in Zeeland. Thus the bulk of the Dutch army, having prepared to fight in isolation, capitulated in isolation. The German strategy of divide and conquer, prepared by Hitler's cold war and abetted by the failure of the Netherlands and Belgium to join together to face the common threat, bore fruit.

In the Air

The feeling of crisis dominated air operations on May 14. The Dutch capitulated, closing out five days in which Dutch planes flew 332 missions and claimed thirty-six victories in the air (thirty-two "certain") and lost eighty-one aircraft. The Germans lost between 325 and 350 planes in the Netherlands, most to antiaircraft fire during the airborne assault. But one Ally was out of the war. Vuillemin, meanwhile, pressed for more British fighters, and Gort appealed to the Secretary of State for Air, who sent two more squadrons.[107] Given the breakthrough at Sedan, Barratt again took an active part in the bombing effort. D'Astier's strength that morning reached 330 fighters and 47 bombers; the Eastern Zone had 33. With British aid he engaged 152 bombers and 250 fighters over Sedan, losing 11 percent of the planes. Two small expeditions of Battles hit the area early, followed at 9:00 a.m. by eight Breguet assault bombers, operating at higher altitude this time. Vuillemin ordered d'Astier—his first direct order —to send the old Amiot 143's over: a number went in, taking heavy losses from fighters and Flak, accompanied by eight Lioré 451's and followed by the remaining British bombers. German fighters flew 814 sorties to oppose the Allied effort.[108] The Meuse bridges, under heavy Flak protection, were not knocked out; the German advance was not halted; but German troops became very conscious of Allied airpower.[109] From May 13 Guderian's corps reported heavy Allied fighter activity and evening air attacks; requests for German fighter protection brought no result. Allied air attacks and artillery fire slowed bridge building. And air observation—a critical component of the Blitzkrieg—was severely impeded. These complaints goaded the Luftwaffe to extraordinary measures. But the Allies lacked the numbers to transform partial air superiority over Guderian's spearhead into paralysis on the ground.

By the end of May 14 the bare bones of disaster glared at Allied commanders as they followed the invasion on their maps. The reinforcements Georges ordered to his weak center from May 11 began to reach the Second Army, but only the scattered 2nd DCR and the advance guard of de Lattre's

14th Infantry lay behind the Ninth Army's right wing, with a thin screen of cavalry and reservist infantry, facing Guderian's Panzers. In Belgium the Ninth Army yielded the Meuse; there another Panzer group was over the river. Could the three DCR's slow the enemy until reinforcements arrived? In the Gembloux gap another Panzer group threatened to break into the Belgian plain, although the Moroccans halted an initial probe, as did the 25th Motorized north of Antwerp. But success in the north meant nothing if Panzers broke loose in the center. Georges had nothing immediately at hand to send the Ninth Army save a new commander. Giraud would bring along the mobile parts of his Seventh Army, but could they arrive in time?

May 15: The View from the Top

From the early hours of May 15 Gamelin pressed the RAF for more support, and dispatched a liaison officer to the Ninth Army, which he found in critical straits. Georges meanwhile pressed Huntziger to strike toward Sedan.[110] At 5:30 a.m. Gamelin "suggested" (as Georges later put it) that the mechanized cavalry gather at the right of the First Army and thrust over the Sambre River into the flank of the Panzers that had crossed the Belgian Meuse. Georges telephoned this plan to Billotte. But Billotte thought Prioux's cavalry was needed in the Gembloux gap; the SOMUA tanks of the 1st DLM, also ordered to Gembloux, had not yet arrived; the 1st DCR was not yet in place with the Ninth Army. Nothing could be done until the next day. Giraud, taking over from Corap, had similar notions but did not think his maneuver could begin before the evening of the 16th. No plan came out of these discussions, thus wasting precious time while French armor idled before the German feint at Gembloux.

Meanwhile, GQG assembled Colonel de Gaulle's 4th DCR from odds and ends in the Ninth Army's right rear. De Gaulle had a brief interview with Georges, finding him "calm, cordial, but visibly overwhelmed."[111] But on the 15th the "4th DCR" was no more than some artillery, some gunners fighting on foot—found in place—and a battalion of infantry support tanks coming up that night.

At 7:15 a.m. Georges ordered Huntziger to hold his front with forces at hand. An Army Detachment, soon the Sixth Army, under General Robert Touchon was to take the front from Huntziger's left through the right wing and center of the Ninth Army; the Ninth Army's front would now stop at Givet. Georges gave Touchon the reserve 23rd Corps, de Lattre's 14th Infantry, the 2nd DCR and some training battalions, and the troops of the Ninth Army already engaged: the 41st Corps with the 53rd, 61st Infantry, and 102nd Fortress Divisions and the Spahi Brigade. Georges promised Touchon three further divisions, the 44th, 28th, and 87th, which would arrive from May 16 to May 18. Touchon was to hold the frontier position

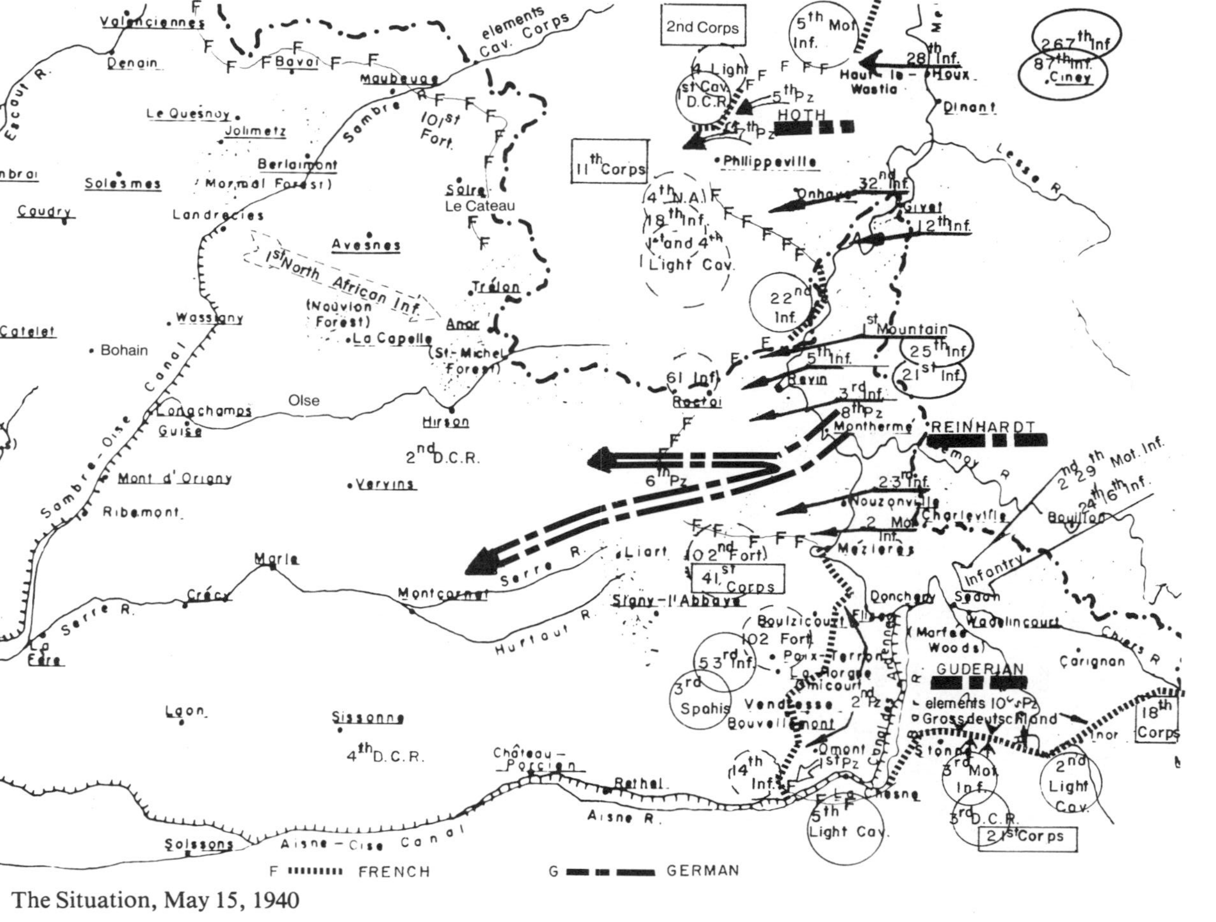

The Situation, May 15, 1940

on his left, then the planned second line behind the frontier on his center and right where, conforming to Corap's and Billotte's orders, the retreat of the 41st Corps had begun.[112] Georges assigned the weight of Allied bombing to Mézières where Guderian threatened to break into the open; he gave priority for fighters to the same area, second to Sedan, third to Dinant where Hoth's Panzers pressed. Georges also withdrew three more infantry divisions and two tank battalions from Prételat.

Billotte also mustered reinforcements for the decisive front. In the early morning he ordered the 9th Motorized and the series A 4th Infantry from the Seventh Army to stand ready, and ordered the 4th toward Maubeuge to reinforce the frontier defense. He gave Blanchard permission to pull back the First Army's right flank, exposed by the Ninth Army's retreat, to the Charleroi Canal. Thus, while warding off Panzers in the Gembloux gap, Blanchard had to plan the retreat of his right and organize a new line in the rear. To prepare that line Blanchard called on the Cavalry Corps and the reserve 32nd Infantry Division.[113]

Billotte felt he had little choice but to retreat: he felt he could not gather his armor on the right flank of the First Army to counterattack toward Dinant because of the threat to Gembloux. The mechanized and motorized troops of the Seventh Army were too distant to be of help on the 15th; Billotte made no attempt to draw on nearby British and Belgian forces. Unless Giraud could reestablish the Ninth Army on or near the Meuse—unlikely once Panzers were across—Billotte could only sanction the Ninth's withdrawal to the frontier position. Once that was accepted there was no choice but to pull back the exposed First Army. Once the Ninth was on the frontier and reinforcements from the Seventh Army arrived, he could reestablish his front while Georges worked in the south to firm up the center with Touchon.

Billotte's defects as interallied "coordinator" showed to the full. Faced by an unexpected crisis, his reaction was to lay hands on French forces. But substantial British and Belgian forces were available, and they were much closer. Had the British and Belgian reserves been *French*, Billotte would surely have used them. He might have requested, for example, the motorized British 50th Infantry and the tank brigade, some of the Belgian mechanized cavalry, followed by conventional Belgian and British infantry. Unfortunately, Billotte was merely the "coordinator" of operations in the north. And the allies, particularly Belgium, had no commitment beyond the agreement to defend the Dyle position. But this was an emergency: Billotte could have appealed to his Allies for help just as General Joffre had appealed to the British commander just before the Battle of the Marne in 1914. However, such initiative comes more easily to a Commander in Chief like Joffre than to a lower echelon "coordinator" like Billotte. Gamelin and Georges must share the blame with Billotte for this critical failure.

As the day wore on the situation seemed calmer with no more breakthroughs reported. Churchill called his friend Georges who "seemed quite cool, and reported that the breach at Sedan was being plugged";[114] Gamelin wired Churchill explaining that the situation was serious but that he viewed it with calm.

Then, suddenly, everything went to pieces: in the late afternoon reports came in of an enemy breakthrough in Touchon's sector. Georges ordered an antitank barrage on the Aisne, Oise, and Marne rivers behind the danger zone, but after 8:00 p.m. came crushing news that German tanks had reached Montcornet—the Panzers had broken into the clear. Georges thought the tanks were Guderian's coming from Sedan—actually they were Reinhardt's from Monthermé.[115] Panzers were loose with only pieces of formations between them and the vital centers of France. Gamelin called General Pierre Héring to become Military Governor of Paris to set its defense in order, impressing Héring with his self-control and lucidity: qualities he would soon need.

In the Field

Huntziger did not order a counterattack until pressed by Georges at 6:00 a.m.[116] Flavigny decided that the 3rd DCR was incapable of operating as an armored division; its tanks would support the 3rd Motorized. But the enemy, reinforced as the 10th Panzer finally came up, attacked first, drawing elements of the 3rd DCR and the 3rd Motorized into bitter fighting around Stonne. The counterattack toward Sedan was reduced to a raid by part of a tank battalion that evening. Lacking communications and spread out by Flavigny's order, the 3rd DCR left most of its armor idling uselessly on May 15. Upset over the delays, Flavigny replaced Brocard.[117] To Flavigny's right the 2nd Light Cavalry repulsed German tank and infantry attacks while Allied fighters downed several enemy planes.

To the west the 53rd Infantry, supported by a battalion of old FT tanks, the 3rd Spahis, elements of de Lattre's 14th Infantry, and the 5th Light Cavalry, clung to the rugged country west of the Bar River, staving off Guderian's corps. The Spahis at La Horgne finally gave way at nightfall after losing 30 percent of their strength including their senior officers, thus allowing the Germans, who were at the end of their tether, to turn the French positions and overrun them during the night. But Guderian's troops had been held all day and were completely exhausted, allowing many of the French to slip south over the Aisne.[118]

The great German success of the day belonged to Reinhardt. His spearhead, held by French and Malgache defenders on the Monthermé peninsula, burst through in the first hours of May 15 just as the 41st Corps ordered the defense back in accord with Billotte's retreat order.[119] By 9:30 a.m. Reinhardt's Panzers cleared the thin French defenses which had so long stymied them, turned to open the way for the crossing at Nouzonville which was still stuck fast, then burst into the clear. Only their disorganization, plus delays imposed by Allied bombs which temporarily cut the Monthermé bridge, slowed Reinhardt's advance. The French 41st Corps, already thin on the ground, abandoned most of its heavy weapons for lack of transport —the 102nd Fortress Infantry was a static unit—and when German tanks broke into pursuit, the troops were forced to surrender or disperse. The other division of the corps, the 61st Infantry, left the Meuse that morning to occupy defenses in the Rocroi area. Hustled back and forth as the command tried to erect a front before the ubiquitous enemy, most of the demoralized reservists were overrun. The 61st Infantry was finished. The overextended center and right of the Ninth Army, now of Touchon's army, left without reinforcement, was lost. Reinhardt's, and not Guderian's force, as the French command thought (ignoring what had happened at Monthermé), tore a huge gap in Georges' front and raced on to Montcornet, touching off the explosion of despair at La Ferté. The GQG had to order upcoming reinforcements debarked behind the shelter of the Aisne River. Only units already in place stood between the Panzers and the sea.

Hope lay with the 2nd DCR, elements of which lay squarely in Reinhardt's path. Early that morning Bruché learned that he was at the disposal of General Touchon. Meanwhile the Inspector General of Tanks, General Keller, arrived on the scene from GQG and ordered Bruché to form a front from Signy-l'Abbaye to the Aisne River. Leaving Colonel Perré to form the division, Bruché set off to talk with Touchon and then de Lattre, whose 14th Infantry was arriving. As the day progressed and Reinhardt's Panzers appeared, Perré, unable to contact Bruché, withdrew his command post farther south. In the afternoon some of the division's mechanized infantry was driven from Montcornet; that evening parts of the division were fighting on the Aisne at Rethel where de Lattre requisitioned them. Later that night the first sizeable portion of the division's combat strength—Commandant Bourgin's 15th Battalion of B tanks—reached Giraud's Ninth Army. Bourgin talked with Giraud, who seemed enthusiastic about so desperate a situation, determined to hold out "'to the bitter end'" and "'extremely confident.'"[120] Giraud ordered Bourgin to clear Montcornet; Touchon gave similar orders to Bruché, placing Bruché under General Libaud, commander of the 41st Corps—who, however, was not to be found. Thus the 2nd DCR got orders from Keller, Giraud, and Touchon; its commander was out of touch with his own headquarters; support elements of the division were south of the Aisne, and its combat elements were fighting in separate groups near the Aisne or were still debarking farther west. In short, the confusion was total. Although Georges intended to centralize command over the breakthrough area in Touchon's hands, the single available force, instead of being regrouped—at a cost in time—was grabbed up by commanders on the spot without regard for any overall plan. Touchon had neither time nor means to contact his subordinates, conceive a plan, and communicate it. In the end all he could do was to order remaining units back over the Aisne, blocking Guderian's route south.

Farther north Giraud worked to get the Ninth Army back to the fortified frontier. The backbone of that line was the 101st Fortress Infantry Division which, by itself, garrisoned *seventy* kilometers around Maubeuge. The morale of the 101st, so high when it had been reinforced by field troops, dropped steadily as it saw the refugees and retreating units, and suffered from the "menace of the Fifth Column."[121] On the evening of the 14th the division had to garrison a further fifteen kilometers of fortifications left behind by Corap's troops in the Anor area to the south. The 4th Infantry was on the way from the Seventh Army, but in the chaos of evacuation the Belgian railroads were slow; no elements of the 4th arrived until May 17. On May 15th, however, General Tarrit, commander of the reserve 1st North African Infantry of the First Army, arrived to hold Anor. But few of these troops were in place on the 15th: the defense of the frontier hung on the brink of disaster.

Just east Hoth's Panzers pressed their advance. General Martin's 11th Corps retreated, leaving Bruneau's 1st DCR behind to counterattack to buy time.[122] Martin knew that the DCR was not meant to fight independently—as Inspector General of the Tanks he had criticized this limitation before the war. Thus he was ordering a suicide mission. But Bruneau did not execute the order. Many of his tanks had not yet refueled; the positions Martin ordered attacked were well behind enemy lines: Bruneau decided instead to report to Martin while waiting for supplies.

The 1st DCR that morning was in touch with French reconnaissance units to the north; to the south there was open terrain. At 9:30 a.m. a cannonade began on the open terrain as Rommel's 7th Panzer made contact. Before noon Bruneau visited the scene, finding that unsupported tank units were being fed piecemeal into an indecisive but costly action; toward 2:00 p.m. he pulled the division back, then received orders from Martin to divide his armor into two forces to back infantry divisions farther west, leaving his mechanized infantry and artillery in reserve—prescriptions that violated doctrine. Bruneau thought it impossible to carry out this mission and tried to reach Martin to discuss the situation. But the crowds on the roads were too thick, and Rommel's Panzers, turning aside from the 1st DCR to pursue their exploitation, now stood between him and Martin's headquarters. Bruneau ordered a retreat on his own initiative.

While Bruneau careered around the rear, his division engaged in a deadly slugging match with the 5th Panzer, supported by aircraft and artillery that Hoth rushed up as Rommel resumed his pursuit to the southwest.[123] After an hour's fight the 31st Panzer Regiment lost a battalion commander, and

The French First Army in Action. *Photos Courtesy of E. C. P. Armées*

its PzKpfw IV's, the only vehicles capable of engaging B tanks, had exhausted their ammunition. More French tanks joined battle as the units of the 1st DCR, some finally getting fuel, drove toward the cannonade. German supply vehicles were still on the east bank of the Meuse; the situation was becoming critical—the French had an open route into the rear of Rommel's 7th Panzer. In desperation the Panzer Regiment commander personally led a last charge. And the French tanks gave way, retreating under Bruneau's orders as evening approached. Although the French armor fought bravely and well, as Hoth later wrote, many tanks had to be abandoned for lack of gasoline when the retreat began; more armor was lost during the nocturnal withdrawal. The tank strength of the 1st DCR dropped catastrophically; most of the vehicles lost were B tanks. Nonetheless, the action of the 1st DCR gave pause to General Hans Günther von Kluge, Hoth's superior and commander of the German Fourth Army; he held Hoth back until the afternoon of May 16, giving the French time to establish their defense on the frontier.

May 15 was a critical day for Billotte farther north: Hoepner's Panzers hit the Gembloux gap. The 3rd and 4th Panzers attacked the French 3rd and 4th Corps, principally near Gembloux itself. The Panzers were harrassed the preceding night by French artillery, but at first light the attack went in under a heavy Stuka and artillery barrage. Panzers fell on the 1st Moroccan Division, which fought from strongpoints in villages and from a railway embankment; German riflemen pushed forward with direct tank and air support, mopping up resistance and clearing minefields under artillery fire. Two Moroccan reserve battalions and a battalion of infantry tanks counterattacked; German tanks intervened: seventeen of the French machines were knocked out, but the Germans suffered heavily and their ammunition ran low.[124] The Moroccans filled in the gap but lost up to 50 percent of their strength; that evening they pulled back a few kilometers. General Mellier, commanding them, did a fine job of handling his artillery (with assistance from that of the 15th Motorized), aided by a corps spotter plane. His intervention helped restore the situation when one of his battalion commanders ordered a retreat, contrary to orders. Arriving by motorcycle, Mellier rallied the troops, who held the enemy along the stop line of their position. The Germans too, under constant artillery fire, pulled their tanks and most of their riflemen back during the night. Heavy German attacks also pushed into the front of the 1st Motorized and the 2nd North Africans of the French 3rd Corps, forcing the French back that evening with substantial losses. But again the Germans were too battered to capitalize on their success.

Meanwhile, the Panzers facing General Alphonse Juin's 15th Motorized Infantry in Gembloux fared far worse. Here the German "tank-plane team" charged into minefields, barricades, artillery, and antitank guns established in proper strength. French fire took a heavy toll of the advance;

the Panzers could not find an opening in the obstacles and minefields, and tank reinforcements could not get forward. The Panzer Brigade commander's tank was knocked out, and he lost contact with his subordinates, who decided on their own to pull back. But as the Panzers withdrew the rifle units panicked—staff officers had to turn out to stem the retreat.[125] The 4th Panzer was content to form a defensive front. Losses in the German units were high: one rifle regiment lost a third of its officers. But this success did little for the French First Army except allow it to retreat in peace the next morning.

Farther north the British and Belgian armies held off German infantry attacks. General Pownall complained, however, of being caught between the French and Belgians and also of the lack of central direction of the Allied force, since Billotte was "shy of interfering."[126] Of course Billotte had other things on his mind.

In the Air

On the morning of May 15 d'Astier had only 284 fighters and 43 bombers. Georges had ordered air priority the previous evening for the Second Army, but d'Astier promised to do something for the Ninth; receiving intelligence from General Augereau, the air commander of the Ninth, at 8:00 a.m., d'Astier sent 12 Blenheims over Dinant before noon and had 150 fighters over the same area.[127] At 6:30 a.m. Georges ordered Têtu to split bombing and fighter cover between Mézières, Sedan, and Dinant. But at the same time Billotte ordered 60 percent of the fighter cover to Touchon's new army, 30 percent to the Second Army, and 10 percent split between the First and Ninth Armies. D'Astier concluded that Billotte had given up the Ninth Army and was pinning his hopes on Touchon. Thus Billotte, who had no authority over the Second and the new Sixth Armies, was nonetheless in charge of the air unit covering them—and favored them over his own hard-pressed units despite Georges' order. The command echelons of the air force and army no longer corresponded to the situation; d'Astier did much as he saw fit. He received early warning of the critical situation at Monthermé, and ordered sixteen Blenheims and then nine Breguet and six Lioré bombers there that afternoon and evening. The apparition of Panzers at Montcornet led the command to demand immediate reconnaissances in the area then bombing attacks; d'Astier was warned to pull back air units whose bases were exposed by the breakthrough.

By the end of May 15 the Germans had lost 539 planes destroyed and 137 damaged, not counting transport or reconnaissance and observation aircraft, while the RAF lost 248 planes of which 205 were based in France, including 71 fighters and 125 bombers.[128] French losses are not fully known but must have totaled two to three times as many fighters as the RAF, perhaps a fourth as many bombers. These losses were catastrophically high, demonstrating an effort without regard to the price paid—save of course for the RAF in Britain. That this battle might well be decisive had not escaped the RAF commanders in London: Dowding requested a meeting with the British War Cabinet on May 15. Pessimistic about the outcome of the struggle on the Continent, Dowding already foresaw Britain standing alone, its defense resting on his precious fighters. He recognized that a crisis was at hand in France and proposed to resolve it by initiating strategic air war. The enemy had bombed Rotterdam: Bomber Command should retaliate over the Ruhr, provoking the Luftwaffe into strategic air war over Britain where his Spitfires, which had taken no part in the battle, would knock out enemy strength under favorable conditions. That night some 100 "heavies" of Bomber Command hit the Ruhr, attacking again the next night. The plan failed: there was no retaliation over Britain, and no serious damage in the Ruhr. Within a few days Bomber Command went to work hitting communications behind the Panzers; Dowding's Spitfires continued to sit on the sidelines. British cooperation hit a further low on the evening of the 15th as d'Astier prepared to evacuate his exposed headquarters. After some hesitation Barratt decided to leave d'Astier and move toward his own units in the Coulommiers area, severing the effective link between British and French air units.

May 15 was a disastrous day for the French High Command. Panzers crashed into the open through the center of its front with only a scattering of regional units and armor between them and wherever they were going. Would the enemy march on Paris? Would he advance west into the rear of the First Army Group? It was a question now of whether the Allied armies could pull themselves together on a coherent front before losing either a fatal proportion of their strength or the vital centers of France. If France and Belgium followed the Netherlands down, Britain might be able to survive in isolation, as Dowding and others began to consider. But Britain alone could never defeat Hitler if he were master of the Continent—and what would happen to the British Empire while Britain was preoccupied in Europe? Those like Dowding, who withheld strength for the defense of Britain alone, paid little heed to the fact that the collapse of the coalition threatened to end Britain's role as a great power. Even if the United States and the Soviet Union finally helped crush Hitler, Britain could hardly emerge as the power it had been in 1939. The same thing was true for the rest of the coalition: France, Belgium, the Netherlands. Failing to stand together on the Continent, they risked being individually beaten and shorn of their empires.

May 16: The View from the Top

Gamelin attended a cabinet meeting at 3:00 a.m.: Paris was ordered ready to defend itself. Signs of panic appeared at Vincennes as Colonel Petibon moved a 75 into the courtyard of the old Château—Gamelin's headquarters prepared to make its stand! Daladier and Gamelin visited La Ferté before 11:00 a.m.; Daladier recorded the "deplorable impression" he received—Georges had collapsed; only Doumenc seemed to be reacting. In the panic-stricken atmosphere Doumenc told him that Gamelin himself would have to go north to direct operations. But for the moment nothing happened. Gamelin by then was convinced that Georges had lost control of the situation and was exhausting himself on details, paying insufficient attention to strategy. He later blamed Georges' wounds of 1934 for his exhaustion, but Georges denied that, complaining that the command system under which Doumenc alternated between La Ferté and Montry deprived him of the "close and constant collaboration which the situation rendered necessary."[129] Gamelin made arrangements to relocate his headquarters if necessary and then disposed of some personal matters, convinced that he would soon have a critical part to play. Was the enemy aiming at Paris? Gamelin considered that danger less ominous than other possibilities, but as a Frenchman he had to consider it the most pressing.

That morning GQG dispatched a general order Georges had prepared the previous afternoon, abandoning the Dyle position for a new line from Antwerp to Charleroi, then along the Sambre River to the frontier position at Anor, then south to the second position in the rear of the old Ninth Army front (Liart-Signy-l'Abbaye-Omont-Inor). This order may have corresponded to reality when drafted, but it was out of date by the morning of May 16 since Panzers had already driven beyond this position to Montcornet.[130] New orders soon followed. After the loss of Montcornet the staff at La Ferté worked all night to throw a new front together; desperate decisions were taken: at 4:00 a.m. Roton allowed a transport officer to use elements of the 2nd DCR to guard bridges over the Oise River west of the breakthrough area. This was contrary to doctrine but "necessity ruled." Later, the GQG secured Giraud's agreement—the 2nd DCR was switched from Touchon to Giraud during the night—to place General Delestraint, General Keller's deputy, in charge of the 2nd DCR in the absence of General Bruché who, no doubt, was searching for his units. Mismanagement, confusion, and contradiction piled on top of crisis!

Billotte threw his French reserves toward his threatened right flank. He ordered the 1st North African to the Anor gap and the 1st DLM and 9th Motorized from the Seventh Army to secure Giraud's flank facing south along the lower Oise River, north of the 2nd DCR.[131] Billotte saw Delestraint late that morning and ordered him to check on the 1st DCR, about which he had no information. It was only that afternoon that Billotte learned what had happened to that unit. Meanwhile, he took a major decision: the Allied armies in Belgium were to begin a four-day retreat which would take them to the Escaut River position. Georges approved this. Billotte thus took measures to keep a coherent front and reinforce his right wing, but he was counting on Georges to fill the gap in the French center. He might have taken different steps had he thought that Georges might not succeed. And again Billotte made no attempt to draw on British and Belgian strength.

Georges ordered bombing of the Montcornet area, giving the bombers priority in fighter cover to accomplish their mission.[132] Barratt's separation from d'Astier forced Têtu to go through Vuillemin to obtain British air intervention. Georges withdrew another two infantry divisions and the 3rd Light Cavalry from Prételat. But the infantry moved by rail; the Luftwaffe concentrated on isolating the battlefield. The French railway service performed magnificently, however, and lost little time to bomb damage. The decision to debark units south of the Aisne had a greater effect. But the French command could not transport reinforcements by rail at the pace at which the Panzers drove. Once the front was broken and reserves failed to close the breach, Georges felt he could only build another front in the rear, relying on mechanized units to buy time for the new defense to crystallize.

Georges supplemented his last general order, noting that "an enemy exploitation based on mechanized forces seems to be under way between the Aisne and the Oise."[133] He ordered that exploitation halted. French mechanized forces were to sweep the region followed by a counterattack from Rethel where de Lattre's infantry was assembling. Westward extension of the pocket would be limited by holding the passages of the Aisne and Oise up to their confluence. At 1:50 p.m. Giraud called the GQG: his right wing was secure up to the Forest of St.-Michel, but not beyond. Assuming that the 1st DCR was behind the frontier, Giraud proposed to direct that unit south, adding the tanks of the 1st DLM which were coming up and the 9th Motorized Infantry, beginning the next morning.[134] This was just the response Georges needed; he drafted a new order putting the 1st and 2nd DCR and the tanks of the 1st DLM, reinforced by the reconnaissance group of the 9th Motorized, under Giraud to counterattack into the Marle-Signy area. De Gaulle's 4th DCR would join the action from the south under Touchon's direction. If the initial attack were successful, infantry would follow up toward Signy and Poix-Terron just west of the Bar River. In case of failure the units would retard the enemy and link Giraud's right to the 3rd Light Cavalry, which had just joined Touchon. Têtu ordered the air forces to concentrate fighter and bomber support over this action "because of the decisive importance the High Command attaches to the success of this counterattack." But Georges had no idea of the state of the three armored divisions he ordered southward; it is reflective of his state of mind that he gave the order without determining whether it was feasible. Finding later that only de Gaulle's force would be ready, he let Giraud act as he chose, surrendering all hope of a coherent counterattack for the moment.

In the Field

From first light bitter but indecisive fighting broke out at Stonne as elements of the French 3rd DCR and 3rd Motorized Infantry clashed with the 10th Panzer and the Grossdeutschland Infantry Regiment.[135] To the west Guderian's 1st Panzer broke the last French resistance to reach Montcornet that afternoon, then Marle (halfway between Montcornet and the Oise) that night. However, Commandant Bourgin's battalion of B tanks from the 2nd DCR swung into action. Setting out that morning from Marle, the French tanks rumbled east, suffering more from breakdowns than enemy resistance.[136] The two companies of tanks (the third was still debarking) advanced along the Serre River followed by some mechanized infantry, reaching Montcornet by 10:00 a.m. and throwing the headquarters of the 1st Panzer into an uproar. German resistance was ineffective, but gasoline ran low and mechanical troubles took a constant toll of the French. Without support units, the French armor had to pull back to Marle to resupply, crossing to the west bank of the Oise that night after covering some 160 kilometers in action in twenty-one hours and suffering heavy loss from breakdowns. That night elements of the 2nd DCR held *sixty* kilometers of the Oise River.

To the north Giraud struggled to establish his army on the frontier position while gathering forces to protect his right from Reinhardt's and Guderian's corps. His reinforcements ran a race with the enemy: a reconnaissance from the German 12th Infantry found defenses at Anor unoccupied that morning, but when the division arrived that afternoon bitter fighting broke out.[137] The French defense was "dented" but held firm that night.

North of Anor Bruneau raked together some tanks to support the 18th Infantry on the frontier position; that night parts of the artillery and mechanized infantry of the 1st DCR lay behind Solre-le-Château which was held by elements of the 101st Fortress Infantry.[138] As Martin's 11th Corps retreated, Giraud ordered most of it into the fortifications, withdrawing some cavalry to cover his right flank on the lower Oise River facing south.[139] General Didelet, commanding the 9th Motorized arriving from the north to garrison the Oise, ordered reconnaissance elements to that river, but failed to order them to stand in place. Despite the help of some French armor, they allowed the enemy, presumably from Reinhardt's corps, to cross the river that night. News of this crossing in his right rear reached Martin, and he made the fateful decision—on his own—to abandon the frontier position. And further disaster struck Giraud that night.

Rommel's 7th Panzer reached Solre-le-Château that afternoon. Rommel tried to take the French works by surprise but his troops' assault was stopped. He resolved to try a night attack.[140] The defense consisted of crews of the 101st Fortress Division with some elements of the 1st DCR in reserve. The fortress troops and a battery of artillery from the First Army warded off Rommel's Panzers that afternoon, but the artillery ran out of shells. At that point the defense had only the antitank weapons in the casemates: on four kilometers of front, the defense mustered four 25's and four old 37's! Working with engineers and infantry, German tanks edged up in the dark, aided by a smokescreen. A few French 75's arrived, but they soon fired off their ammunition; the first tanks broke through, followed by eighty more and some motorcyclists at about 10:00 p.m. Shortly before, the elements of the 1st DCR received orders to regroup at Avesnes although some of the mechanized infantry joined combat—but the 7th Panzer was through and soon raising havoc in the French rear.

On Giraud's far left, still retreating toward the frontier position, the 5th Motorized dissolved in confusion on the refugee-crowded roads, edging with its back along the Sambre River to the south. The French retook Fosse in Hoth's right rear with the aid of mechanized cavalry sent as a liaison from the First Army. But the 2nd Corps commander, General Bouffet, and a number of his staff were killed in an air attack that afternoon; his forces barely made it to Maubeuge. Similarly the 4th North African Infantry was deprived of direction when its headquarters was cut off and disappeared.[141]

Thus Giraud's right wing hung open and wavered toward the west where only elements of the 9th Motorized were at hand. In his center Rommel's Panzers ran roughshod over the battered elements trying to regroup; his left was tangled up and deprived of leadership attempting to reach the frontier. Giraud's situation was desperate.

Meanwhile, Blanchard fell back from Gembloux onto two fresh infantry divisions plus elements of the Cavalry Corps.[142] The BEF, pressing Billotte for orders that morning, withdrew unimpeded that night. But news of the retreat broke like a tidal wave over the Belgian troops, who had had success defending their front and were dismayed to abandon the heart of their country because of events to the south; King Léopold began to ponder capitulation.[143] Low morale was also apparent on the islands in the mouth of the Escaut, where elite German troops threw back Dutch and then French series B troops. The Netherlands had already capitulated except for units in Zeeland, while the French were in a strange country whose soldiers they often mistook for the enemy. Despite support from French naval dive-bombers, fighters, and escort craft in nearby waters, the Allied defense of the Escaut islands fell apart.

Thus the Allies retreated, their essential strategic interests diverging with each step back. Léopold abandoned the heart of his country and with it his reason for fighting; Gort abandoned Belgian soil from which the enemy could attack Britain; Georges and Billotte failed to knit together a coherent Allied front which alone might have the strength to preserve France from invasion. The Allies lacked central direction, lacked a plan for a counteroffensive to weld their efforts together. Every hour lost before a counteroffensive was imposed lessened the chances for the survival of the West.

In the Air

Direction of the air war fell largely to Têtu on May 16 as d'Astier pulled back to Chantilly, losing contact with Barratt and with Billotte. D'Astier persuaded Vuillemin to rescind his order sending obsolescent bombers over the lines by daylight; his forces were further cut when some ten air units had to withdraw from the path of the Panzers.[144] On May 16 the Northern Zone had at least 162 fighters and the Eastern Zone another 60, plus 24 modern and 20 old bombers. But the pilots were exhausted. General Jean Romatet of fighter Groupment 23 had to draw on up to three fighter groups to gather a viable patrol. The British Advanced Air Striking Force all but dropped from the picture, taking only a minor part in further bombing missions, mainly at night. Most of the observation and reconnaissance units of the Ninth, Seventh, and First Armies had to pull back to refit. Fighters in the Eastern Zone began flying missions for d'Astier, but the pilots there felt they were being wasted.[145] However, the Armée de l'air did effective work at Montcornet where reconnaissance planes delivered intelligence directly to the bombers, bringing them immediately into play. Assault bombers operated effectively at low level against enemy columns and German observation planes caught on an airfield. Eighteen medium bombers attacked in two missions in the morning, twenty-six machines in the afternoon. But these interventions were too small and sporadic to halt the enemy.

Late in the day d'Astier received reinforcements: two groups of old bombers and one of Lioré 451's, a new fighter group, and a squadron of naval dive-bombers.[146] But real hope for reinforcement lay with the RAF. That morning Vuillemin spent an hour pleading with Barratt for another ten squadrons of fighters. Barratt agreed. Georges went so far as to phone directly to No. 11 Group RAF in England to complain about the failure to send its Spitfires into battle. The RAF decided to send some four more squadrons of Hurricanes; the final decision came that evening when Churchill met Reynaud and Gamelin at the Quai d'Orsay amid clouds of smoke from burning archives. The British staff agreed to a further six squadrons working on a rotating basis from French airfields. This scheme took effect in the next three days.

The fighter question was a major issue at the Quai d'Orsay meeting—but Gamelin had more on his mind. Gamelin was "no optimist" but he thought the battle "might yet be saved." He planned to gather forces to strike at the flanks of the German "bulge," but he could not yet say when and where. This seemed sound to Churchill, but "I was conscious . . . that it carried no conviction in this small but hitherto influential and responsible company":[147] too much had happened too suddenly. In a week's time all the old issues shrank into irrelevance. The West was fighting for existence now, and doing badly. The old confidence in the French army was shattered. Daladier's prestige went with it, leaving Reynaud in control of the French war effort. Reynaud had never liked Gamelin, had never trusted his smooth nonchalance. Facing a crisis unparalleled since August 1914, Reynaud put no faith in Gamelin. At 9:20 p.m. a telegram went out to General Maxime Weygand, reaching him at 8:00 the next morning. Weygand was to return to Paris as quickly as possible.[148] Perhaps the man whom the dying Foch had commended to his country for a time of crisis could perform another Miracle of the Marne.

NOTES

1. France, SHA, "Document A/184" (unpublished, December 5, 1947); May 7 and 9, 1940, in France, "Journal de marche et des opérations du GQGAé" (unpublished, August 28, 1939 to July 1940).

2. Bersaucourt, *Sous la croix de Lorraine en 39-40: La 2e DLM* (Fontenay-le-Comte: Imprimerie Lussaud frères, 1949), p. 19; France, [EMAA?], "Historique succint [sic] des opérations aériennes sur le front du nord-est du 10 mai 1940 à l'armistice" (unpublished, no date given), *Titre* II, p. 1.

3. Henri Koch-Kent, *10 Mai 1940 en Luxembourg: Témoignages et documents* (Mersch, Luxemburg: Faber, 1971), pp. 23ff, 69ff; Lt.-Col. Archen, *Missions spéciales au Luxembourg* (Paris: Éditions France-Empire, 1969), pp. 7ff; Lt.-Col. E. T. Melchers, *Kriegsschauplatz Luxemburg: August 1914 Mai 1940* (Luxemburg: Sankt-Paulus-Drückerei, 1963), pp. 239ff; Graf J[ohann] A. Kielmansegg, *Panzer zwischen Warschau und Atlantik* (Berlin: Verlag "Die Wehrmacht," 1941), pp. 97ff.

4. The lowest of three levels of alert.

5. France, Marine nationale, EMG: Service historique, Hervé Cras, *Les Forces maritimes du Nord (1939-1940)* II (no place given, 1955), pp. 21ff; quote from Maurice Gamelin, *Servir* III (Paris: Plon, 1947), p. 389; Pierre Bourget (presentation and commentary), "Les 'communications sécrètes du grand quartier général (10 mai-25juin 1940),'" *L'Aurore* (November 5-6 to December 6, 1949), issue of November 5-6, p. 4 (hereafter cited as "Communications sécrètes"); France, "Extraits du rapport du général Georges" (unpublished, no date given), *Titre* V, pp. 1ff; Jacques Minart, *P. C. Vincennes: Secteur 4* II (Paris: Berger-Levrault, 1945), pp. 104ff.

6. Minart, *P. C. Vincennes* II, p. 101; quote from General André Beaufre, *Le Drame de 1940* (Paris: Plon, 1965), p. 230; Gamelin's testimony in France, Parlement, Assemblée nationale, *Les Événements survenus en France de 1933 à 1945: Témoignages et documents recueillis par la commission d'enquête parlementaire* II (Paris: Presses universitaires de France, [1950?]), p. 424; Maurice Gamelin, *Servir* (Paris: Plon, 1946-1947), I, p. 335, III, p. 390; The Netherlands, Ministerie van Oorlog, Hoofdkwartier van de generale Staf, Krijgsgeschiedkundige Afdeling, Generaal-Majoor Tit. B.D.V.E. Nierstrasz et al., *De Strijd op Nederlands grondgebied tijdens de Wereldoorlog II: Hoofdeel III: Nederlands Verdediging tegen de*

Duitse Aanval van 10-19 Mei 1940. Deel I: Inleiding en algemeen Overzicht van de Gevechtsdagen van 10-19 Mei 1940 (The Hague: Staatsdrukkerijen Uitgeverijbedrijf, 1957), pp. 63ff, 76; France, SHA, Section contemporaine, Cdt. Patrick De Ruffray, "Document A/155: Relations franco-hollandais 1939-40" (unpublished, April 1956), p. 8; [The Netherlands, Staten-General, Tweede Kamer], *Enquêtecommissie Regeringsbeleid 1940-1945: Verslag Houdende De Uitkomsten Van Het Onderzoek. Deel I^A en I^B: Algemene Inleiding/Militair Beleid 1939-1940 (Punt A Van Het Enquêtebesluit* (The Hague: Staatsdrukkerijen Uitgeverijbedrijf, 1949), *I^B/Bijlagen,* pp. 42ff, 61ff, and I^C, pp. 71ff; Gamelin's suggestions to the Belgians in ED, 4DA27, Dr 2, sdr a.

7. Eelco Nicolaas van Kleffens, *Juggernaut over Holland: The Dutch Foreign Minister's Personal Story of the Invasion of the Netherlands* (New York: Columbia University Press, 1941), pp. 118ff; Walter Melzer, *Albert-Kanal und Eben Emael* (Heidelberg: Kurt Vowinckel Verlag, 1957), pp. 34ff; Louis de Jong, *The German 5th Column in the Second World War*, trans. C. M. Geyl (Chicago: University of Chicago Press, 1956), pp. 184ff; *Overzicht*, pp. 58ff, 150. See also Danel, "La Conquête de la Hollande," pp. 24ff and testimony of Col. Leonhard Schmidt, the Dutch territorial commander in North Brabant in *Enquêtecommissie* I^C, pp. 272ff, 520ff.

8. [Marcel] Lerecouvreux, *L'Armée Giraud en Hollande: (1939-1940)* (Paris: Nouvelles éditions latines, 1951), p. 139; France, Marine nationale, EMG: Service historique, Hervé Cras, *Les Forces maritimes du Nord (1939-1940)* II (no place, 1955), p. 43ff; France, ESG, Études générales, ler Cycle, Cours d'histoire, Lt.-Col. d'Ornano, "La 25me DIM dans la marche à l'ennemi: (Étude de la préparation et de l'exécution des transports opérationnels)" (unpublished, November 1955), p. 9; Col. Léon Paulet, "Mai 1940: Mission impossible," *Icare* no. 74 (Autumn 1975): 51.

9. A Belgian commander refused to believe an attack was under way, delaying the blowing of the bridges until the garrisons were overcome—General [Raoul] Van Overstraeten, *Albert I-Léopold III: Vingt ans de politique militaire belge 1920-1940* ([Bruges]: Desclée de Brouwer, [1946?]), pp. 575ff, 736ff; General Oscar Michiels, *18 jours de guerre en Belgique* (Paris: Berger-Levrault, 1947), pp. 62 passim; Melzer, *Albert-Kanal*, pp. 26 passim; Col. Rudolf Witzig, "Coup from the Air; the Capture of Fort Eben-Emael," *History of the Second World War* I, no. 7 (1966); interview with M. Jean Vanwelkenhuyzen, Brussels, June 21-23, 1978. For an honest if opinionated account of the Belgian campaign, see de Fabribeckers, *La Campagne de l'armée belge en 1940*, 2nd ed. (Brussels and Paris: Rossel, [1978?]). On Léopold see Robert Aron, *Léopold III ou le choix impossible: Février 1934-juillet 1940* ([Paris]: Plon, 1977), p. 26. See also Jean-Louis Lhoest, *Les Paras allemands au Canal Albert: Mai 1940* (Paris: Presses de la Cité, 1964) and Col. James E. Mrazek, *The Fall of Eben Emael: Prelude to Dunkerque* (Washington and New York: Luce, 1970).

10. Melzer, *Albert-Kanal*, pp. 70ff, 102ff, 120ff.

11. General A. [Joseph] Doumenc, *Histoire de la neuvième armée* (Grenoble and Paris: Arthaud, 1945), pp. 46ff; "Extraits du rapport du général Georges," *Titre* V, p. 3; Cdt. N[arcisse] Bourdon, *Le Second drame de Maubeuge: Histoire de la 101e Division de forteresse (84e et 87e R.I.F.)* (Fontenay-le-Comte: Imprimerie Lussaud frères, 1947), p. 68; Gamelin, *Servir* I, pp. 326ff.

12. General C. Grandsard, *Le 10e Corps d'armée dans la bataille 1939-1940: Sedan-Amiens-De la Seine à la Dordogne* (Paris: Berger-Levrault, 1949), pp. 98ff; Lerecouvreux, *Huit mois d'attente*, pp. 140ff; General Edmond Ruby, *Sedan: Terre d'épreuve. Avec la IIe Armée. Mai-juin 1940* (Paris: Flammarion, 1948), p. 79; "Communications sécrètes," November 5-6 issue, p. 4.

13. Graf J[ohann] A. Kielmansegg, *Panzer zwischen Warschau und Atlantik* (Berlin: Verlag "Die Wehrmacht," 1941), pp. 102ff; Belgium, Ministère de la défense nationale, EMG-Force Terrestre: Direction générale du renseignement et de l'historique: Section historique, *L'Armée belge dans les deux guerres mondiales:* No. 1: Cdt. [Georges] Hautecler, *Le Combat de Bodange: 10 mai 1940* (no place given: Imprimerie des FBA, 1955); Belgium, Ministère de la défense nationale, EMG-Force Terrestre: Direction générale du renseignement et de l'historique: Section historique, *L'Armée belge dans les deux guerres mondiales:* No.2: Cdt. Georges Hautecler, *Le Combat de Chabrehez: 10 mai 1940: Chasseurs ardennais contre Rommel* (no place given: Imprimerie des FBA, 1957).

14. Major L. F. Ellis, *The War in France and Flanders 1939-1940* (London: H.M.S.O., 1953), p. 54; entry of May 10 in Anonymous, *The Diary of a Staff Officer: (Air Intelligence Liaison Officer) at Advanced Headquarters North B.A.F.F. 1940* (London: Methuen, 1941), p. 4; Ruby, *Sedan*, p. 84.

15. Paul Berben and Bernard Iselin, *Les Panzers passent la Meuse (13 mai 1940)* (Paris: Laffont, 1967), pp. 73ff; Claude Gounelle, *Sedan: Mai 1940* (Paris: Presses de la Cité, 1965), pp. 50ff.

16. Melchers, *Kriegsschauplatz*, pp. 374ff, 409ff; General P. Jouffrault, *Les Spahis au feu: La 1re Brigade de Spahis pendant la campagne 1939-1940* (Paris: Charles-Lavauzelle, 1948), pp. 27, 40, 47ff; Koch-Kent, *10 Mai 1940 en Luxembourg*, pp. 69ff; Pierre Ordioni, *Les Cinq jours de Toul* (Paris: Laffont, 1967).

17. Raymond Danel, "En Mai Juin 1940: *Ils* étaient les plus forts," *Icare* no. 54 (Summer 1970):50ff; Lt.-Col. Salesse, *L'Aviation de chasse française en 1939-1940* (Paris: Berger-Levrault, 1948), pp. 191ff; France, [ZOAN], "Situation des avions disponibles: 10-31 mai 1940" (unpublished, no date given); Col. Pierre Paquier, *L'Aviation de bombardement française en 1939-1940* (Paris: Berger-Levrault, 1948), pp. 205ff. Robert Jackson provides a popular account of Allied air operations with excellent photos in *Air War over France: May-June 1940* (London: Ian Allan, 1974).

18. Richards, *Fight at Odds*, pp. 113, 119ff.

19. Danel, "En Mai Juin . . .," p. 52; Jean Delaet, *Escadrilles au combat* (Brussels and Paris: Les Écrits, no date), pp. 30ff, 87ff; table of German attacks, May 27 entry, *JMO-GQGAé*; "1939-40/La Bataille de France. Volume VII: L'Aéronautique militaire belge. Première partie," *Icare* no. 74 (Autumn 1975); Raymond Danel, "La Conquête de la Hollande: Opération secondaire?," *Icare* no. 79 (Winter, 1976-1977):38ff.

20. France, [EMAA?], "Historique succint [sic] des opérations aériennes," *Titre* II, pp. 2ff; France, FACNE, EM, Section d'opérations: 810-0, Message from Têtu to the ZOAS and Bouscat (unpublished, May 10, 1940); France, FACNE, EM, Section d'opérations: 812-0, Message from Têtu to d'Astier (unpublished, May 10, 1940); General [François] d'Astier de la Vigerie, *Le Ciel n'était pas vide: 1940* (Paris: Julliard, 1952), pp. 86ff; entry of May 10 in *JMO-GQGAé*; Danel, "En Mai Juin . . .," p. 54; Danel, "La Conquête de la Hollande," pp. 38ff.

21. General Jean Romatet, "Le Groupement de chasse 23 dans la bataille," *Icare* no. 54 (summer 1970): 80ff; Capt. [Jean] Accart, *Chasseurs du ciel: Historique de la première escadrille du groupe de chasse I/5* (Grenoble and Paris: Arthaud, 1941), pp. 75 passim; Capt. [Robert] Williame, *L'Escadrille des cigognes—Spa 3—1939-1940* (Grenoble and Paris: Arthaud, 1945), pp. 194ff.

22. Danel, "Au service de l'armée de terre," *Icare* no. 59 (Spring 1971): 78ff; R. P. Guy Bougerol, *Ceux qu'on n'a jamais vus* . . . (Grenoble and Paris: Arthaud, 1943), pp. 85ff; General Raymond Brohon, "Le Groupement de bombardement n° 10: D'Après les cahiers du lieutenant-colonel Aribaud," *Icare* no. 57 (Summer 1971): 89.

23. General Michel de Lesquen et al., "Historique de Groupe aérien d'observation 501: 1939/1940," *Icare* no. 59 (Spring 1971): 136ff.

24. Danel, "En Mai Juin . . .," p. 53; Pierre Le Goyet, *Le Mystère Gamelin* (Paris: Presses de la Cité, 197[6]), p. 305.

25. France, Commandement en chef sur le front du nord-est, EM, 2ème Bureau, "Instructions particulières pour la recherche des renseignements stratégiques par les forces aériennes" (unpublished, May 10, 1940).

26. Quotes from France, General Têtu, "Evennements [sic] survenus pendant la nuit du 10 au 11/5/40 [sic]" (unpublished, no date); Minart, *P. C. Vincennes* II, p. 108; Gustave Bertrand, *Enigma: ou la plus grande énigme de la guerre 1939-1945* ([Paris?]: Plon, 1973), pp. 78ff.

27. Hermann Zimmermann, *Der Griff ins Ungewisse: Die ersten Kriegstage 1940 beim XVI. Panzerkorps in Kampf um die Deylestellung, 10.-17. Mai* (Neckargemünd: Kurt Vowinckel Verlag, 1964), pp. 19ff; General Kurt Zeitzler, "Die Panzer-Gruppe v[on] Kleist in Westfeldzug 1940," *Wehrkunde* 4-7 (April-July 1959), April article, p. 182—Zeitzler was Kleist's chief of staff; Hermann Teske, *Bewegungskrieg: Führungsprobleme einer Infanterie-Division im Westfeldzug 1940* (Heidelberg: Kurt Vowinckel Verlag, 1955), pp. 20ff.

28. Minart, *P. C. Vincennes* II, pp. 108ff; quote from France, Commandement en chef du front nord-est, EM, 3° Bureau: N° 1399 3/Op., Message from Georges to Barratt and Têtu et al. (unpublished, GQG, May 11, 1940).

29. Minart, *P. C. Vincennes* II, pp. 112ff; *Overzicht*, p. 166.

30. "Extraits du rapport du général Georges," *Titre* V, pp. 7ff; General G[aston] Roton, *Années cruciales: La Course aux armements (1933-1939). La Campagne (1939-1940)* (Paris: Charles-Lavauzelle, 1947), pp. 146ff.

31. Quote from Georges' report in Paul Reynaud, *La France a sauvé l'Europe* II (Paris: Flammarion, 1947), pp. 91ff; Gamelin, *Servir* I, p. 386; Gamelin's testimony in *Événements . . . Témoignages* II, p. 424.

32. General René Prioux, *Souvenirs de guerre: 1939-1943* (Paris: Flammarion, 1947), pp. 62ff; Georges' testimony in *Événements . . . Témoignages* III, p. 724; General A. [Joseph] Doumenc, *Dunkerque et la campagne de Flandre* (Paris: Arthaud, 1947), p. 40. On incomplete Belgian defenses see Jean Vanwelkenhuyzen, *Neutralité armée: La Politique militaire de la Belgique pendant la "drôle de guerre"* (to be published by Renaissance de la livre), pp. 84-85.

33. France, Commandement en chef du front nord-est, EM, 3e Bureau: N° 1404 3/Op., "Instruction générale n° 12" (unpublished, May 11, 1940 [at about 4:20 p.m.]).

34. D'Ornano, "La 25me DIM," pp. 18ff, 28ff; Cras, *Forces maritimes* II, pp. 50ff.

35. *6e Régiment de cuirassiers: Journal des marches et opérations pendant la campagne contre l'Allemagne du 2 septembre 1939 au 25 juin 1940* (Bergerac: Imprimerie générale du sud-ouest, 1940), p. 16; Lerecouvreux, *L'Armée Giraud*, pp. 130ff, 160ff, 303.

36. Doumenc, *Histoire de la neuvième armée*, p. 53; Van Overstraeten, *Albert I-Léopold III*, pp. 582ff.

37. Cdt. Georges Hautecler, "Chars belges en 1940," *L'Armée La Nation* no. 4 (April 1, 1957): 18; Michiels, *18 jours de guerre*, p. 100; Prioux, *Souvenirs*, pp. 42ff, 60ff; Zimmermann, *Griff ins Ungewisse*, pp. 40ff; Van Overstraeten, *Albert I-Léopold III*, p. 582.

38. Doumenc, *Histoire de la neuvième armée*, p. 50; Richecourt, *La Guerre de cent heures: 1940* (Paris: Flammarion, 1944), p. 129; Capt. de Bellescize, "Carnet de route du Capitaine de Bellescize du 5e Régiment de dragons portés (10 mai au 18 mai 1940)," *Revue de l'armée française* no. 1 (October 1941): 18.

39. Grandsard, *10e Corps*, pp. 105ff; Lerecouvreux, *Huit mois d'attente*, pp. 145ff; Kielmansegg, *Panzer zwischen Warschau und Atlantik*, pp. 106ff; France, Ministère des armées, EMAT, Service historique, *Guerre, 1939-1945: Les Grandes unités françaises: Historiques succincts* III (Paris: Atelier d'impressions de l'armée, 1967), pp. 384ff, 550ff; Doumenc, *Histoire de la neuvième armée*, pp. 51ff; de Bellescize, "Carnet," p. 18.

40. France, [ZOAN?], Capt. Puget, "Historique des opérations menées par la zone d'opérations aériennes nord" (unpublished, no date), Chap. 2, p. 27; "Historique succint [sic] des opérations aériennes," *Titre* II, Chap. 1, pp. 6ff; d'Astier, *Le Ciel n'était pas vide*, pp. 90ff.

41. "Situation des avions disponibles"; Delaet, *Escadrilles*, pp. 37ff; Michael Terlinden, "Mission with No Return," *Aerospace Historian* 20, no. 1 (March 1973); "1939-40/La Bataille de France. Volume VIII: L'Aéronautique militaire belge. Deuxième partie," *Icare* no. 76 (Spring 1976); Danel, "La Conquête de la Hollande," pp. 41ff.

42. Paquier, *Aviation de bombardement*, pp. 33ff; Danel, "En Mai Juin . . .," p. 55.

43. Col. Henri Alias, "Le II/33 avait *vu* les Allemands percer sur la Meuse," *Icare* no. 57 (Summer 1971): 73ff; Minart, *P. C. Vincennes* II, p. 119; quote from France, Commandement en chef sur le front du nord-est, EM, 2° Bureau, "Instruction pour la recherche du renseignement stratégique par les forces aériennes" (unpublished, May 12, 1940). There was skepticism at lower levels of the Ninth Army staff about reconnaissance reports of German tanks in the Ardennes—see Alias, "Le II/33," and General Max Gelée, "La Percée des Ardennes vue d'en haut," *Icare* no. 57 (Summer 1971): 68ff.

44. Hans-Adolf Jacobsen, ed., *Dokumente zum Westfeldzug 1940* (Göttingen: Musterschmidt Verlag, 1960), pp. 14ff; France, SHAT, Baron Ernest Gedult von Jungenfeld, *So kämpften Panzer!* (French translation, no other information given), pp. 24-25.

45. "Communications sécrètes," November 7 issue, p. 4; Georges' report in Reynaud, *La France a sauvé l'Europe* II, pp. 91ff; quotes from Brian Bond, ed.,

Chief of Staff: The Diaries of Lieutenant-General Sir Henry Pownall. I: *1933-1940* (Hamden, Conn.: Archon Books, 1973), pp. 311ff; Van Overstraeten, *Albert I-Léopold III*, p. 590.

46. Quotes from Van Overstraeten, *Albert I-Léopold III*, pp. 590ff; Bond, *Chief of Staff*, pp. 312ff.

47. Quotes from Van Overstraeten, *Albert I-Léopold III*, pp. 592ff; Le Goyet, *Le Mystère Gamelin*, p. 313; Daladier's impressions in ED, 3DA8, Dr 1, sdr a.

48. General Paul de Villelume, *Journal d'une défaite: Août 1939-Juin 1940* ([Paris]: Fayard, 1976), p. 333; Lt.-Col. [Pierre] Le Goyet, "La Percée de Sedan (10-15 mai 1940)," *Revue d'histoire de la deuxième guerre mondiale* no. 59 (July 1965): 38; Georges' testimony in *Événements . . . Témoignages* III, p. 690.

49. Minart, *P. C. Vincennes* II, p. 123; France, "Demandes de bombardement exprimés par le général Georges, le 12 mai à 15 h 19" (unpublished, May 12, [1940]).

50. Roton, *Années cruciales*, p. 149; "Extraits du rapport du général Georges," *Titre* V, p. 15; *GU françaises* II, pp. 36ff, 190ff, 390ff, III, pp. 498ff; France, ESG, Cours de tactique générale et d'état-major, *Notes pratiques d'état-major* ([Paris]: [Charles-Lavauzelle], 1939), p. 216.

51. Lerecouvreux, *L'Armée Giraud*, p. 303; d'Ornano, "La 25me DIM," p. 33; Billotte's order in *Overzicht*, p. 168; Lerecouvreux, *L'Armée Giraud*, pp. 206, 212.

52. Van Overstraeten, *Albert I-Léopold III*, p. 593; Zimmerman, *Griff ins Ungewisse*, pp. 50ff; reports of Chef d'Escadron Vignes, Capt. Hardouin, Capt. de Beaufort of the 3rd DLM in ED, 4DA7, Dr 4; Jungenfeld, *So kämpften Panzer!*, pp. 26-27.

53. De Bellescize, "Carnet," pp. 18ff; Richecourt, *La Guerre de cent heures*, pp. 144ff; Doumenc, *Histoire de la neuvième armée*, pp. 53ff, 68; Hermann Hoth, "Das Schicksal der französischen Panzerwaffe im I. Teil des Westfeldzuges 1940," *Wehrkunde* 7 (July 1958): 369ff.

54. General Pierre Bertin, "Un régiment d'infanterie sur la Meuse en 1940: Le 129e R. I. en Belgique," *Revue historique de l'armée* (no. 4 1972): 79; *GU françaises* II, pp. 908ff.

55. Doumenc, *Histoire de la neuvième armée*, pp. 78ff; testimony of General Vallet of the Ninth Army staff and of General Véron, Deputy Chief of Staff of the Ninth, in *Événements . . . Témoignages* V, pp. 1377, 1290ff; Bertin, "Le 129e R.I.," pp. 83ff.

56. Kielmansegg, *Panzer zwischen Warschau und Atlantik*, pp. 107ff; Grandsard, *10e Corps*, pp. 112ff; Hans Reinhardt, "Im Schatten Guderians," *Wehrkunde* 3rd year no. 10 (October 1954): 334ff.

57. Accart, *Chasseurs du ciel*, pp. 112ff; Henri Menjaud, *Un groupe de chasse au combat* (Grenoble: Arthaud, 1941), pp. 82ff; "Bulletins d'homologation d'un avion allemand abattu" nos. 99 and 100 in France, [EMAA?], "Bulletins d'homologation" (unpublished, October 1939 to June 1940).

58. Ruby, *Sedan*, pp. 117ff; testimony of General Devaux, Chief of Staff of the 3rd DCR in *Événements . . . Témoignages* V, pp. 1334ff.

59. Jouffrault, *Spahis*, pp. 67ff; General [Gaston] Prételat, *Le Destin tragique de la ligne Maginot* (Paris: Berger-Levrault, 1950), p. 135.

60. "Situation des avions disponibles"; May 27 entry of *JMO-GQGAé*; Danel, "En Mai Juin . . . ," pp. 55ff; quote from Richards, *Fight at Odds*, p. 119; Danel, "La Conquête de la Hollande," pp. 41ff.

61. General Fleury Seive, *L'Aviation d'assaut dans la bataille de 1940* (Paris: Berger-Levrault, 1948), pp. 103 passim.

62. Paquier, *Aviation de bombardement*, p. 40; d'Astier, *Le Ciel n'était pas vide*, pp. 96ff.

63. France, IXe Armée, EM, 2e Bureau: N° 27/2, "Bulletin de renseignements n° 127 (jusqu'au 12 mai-21 heures)" (unpublished, May 12, [1940]).

64. France, Commandement en chef du front nord-est, EM, 3° Bureau: N° 1451 3/Op., "Ordre particulier n° 90" (unpublished, GQG, May 13, 1940); Gamelin, *Servir* I, p. 336; France, Le Général Commandant en chef, Chef d'EMG de la défense nationale, Commandant en chef les forces terrestres, "Ordre général" (unpublished, GQG, May 13, 1940); Van Overstraeten, *Albert I-Léopold III*, p. 595.

65. Minart, *P. C. Vincennes* II, pp. 135ff; "Extraits du rapport du général Georges," *Titre* V, pp. 20, 27; *GU françaises* II, pp. 488ff, 544ff; France, ESG, École d'état-major, [Lt.Col. P. Gendry], *La Guerre 1939-1940 sur le front occidental* (Paris: Société française de presse, 1947), p. 62.

66. Le Goyet, "Dans la tourmente de mai 1940: L'Engagement de la 2e division cuirassée française," *Revue historique de l'armée* (no. 1 1964): 148; *GU françaises* III, pp. 478ff; Villelume, *Journal d'une défaite*, pp. 334ff.

67. Quote from France, Commandement en chef sur le front du nord-est, EM, 2° Bureau: N° 1434/2S, "Instruction pour la recherche du renseignement stratégique" (unpublished, May 13, 1940, at 4:00 p.m.); General André Beaufre, *Le Drame de 1940* (Paris: Plon, 1965), p. 231.

68. Georges' order in Commandant Pierre Lyet, *La Bataille de France: (Mai-juin 1940)* (Paris: Payot, 1947), p. 54; "Extraits du rapport du général Georges," *Titre* V, pp. 18ff; Minart, *P. C. Vincennes* II, pp. 138ff.

69. Doumenc, *Dunkerque*, pp. 74ff.

70. Ruby, *Sedan*, p. 103; quote from Grandsard, *10e Corps*, pp. 126ff.

71. Kielmansegg, *Panzer zwischen Warschau und Atlantik*, pp. 109ff; quotes from Balck's account in General F. W. von Mellenthin, *Panzer Battles 1939-1945: A Study of the Employment of Armour in the Second World War*, L. C. F. Turner, ed., trans. H. Betzler (London: Cassell, 1955), pp. 13ff.

72. Quote from France, II° Armée, EM, 3° Bureau: N° 395/3, "Note de service au sujet de la lutte contre les avions volant bas par les armes de l'infanterie (Mitrailleuse-Fusil-mitrailleur-Fusil)" (unpublished, October 1, 1939); Grandsard, *10e Corps*, pp. 136, 153; Mellenthin, *Panzer Battles*, pp. 13ff; Le Goyet, "La Percée de Sedan," pp. 36ff.

73. More than thirty years later almost all the works in the Sedan area bore multiple impact markings from high-velocity guns; almost none showed signs of air attack.

74. Grandsard, *10e Corps*, pp. 159ff; Kielmansegg, *Panzer zwischen Warschau und Atlantik*, pp. 111ff; Ruby, *Sedan*, pp. 130ff.

75. Le Goyet, "Contre-attaques manquées: Sedan 13-15 mai 1940," *Revue historique de l'armée* (no. 4 1962): 117ff; *GU françaises* II, pp. 36ff, III, pp. 12ff, 332ff, 384ff, 498ff; Lerecouvreux, *Huit mois d'attente*, pp. 157ff.

76. Jacobsen, *Dokumente zum Westfeldzug*, p. 22; testimony of General Vallet in *Événements . . . Témoignages* V, p. 1377.

77. Bertin, "Le 129e R.I.," pp. 84ff; J[ean] Dalat, *Les 66me et 90me R.I. au combat en 1939-1940: Carnet de route d'un officier* ([Poitiers]: P. Oudin, 1961),

pp. 50ff; de Bellescize, "Carnet," p. 20; Hoth, "Schicksal," p. 369; B[asil] H. Liddell Hart with Lucie-Maria and Manfred Rommel and Gen. Fritz Bayerlein, eds., *The Rommel Papers*, trans. Paul Findlay (New York: Harcourt, Brace and Co., 1953), pp. 10ff.

78. *The Rommel Papers*, pp. 8ff; Blumentritt, *Von Rundstedt*, pp. 68ff; Hautecler, "Rommel contre Corap: La Bataille de la Meuse (12-15 mai 1940)," *Revue générale belge* (November 1962): 98; Reinhardt, "Im Schatten Guderians," pp. 336ff; Heinz Maassen, *Par-dessus la Meuse: Comment fut forcé le passage à Monthermé*, trans. J. Jamin (Paris: Payot, 1943), pp. 77-102.

79. Zimmermann, *Griff ins Ungewisse*, pp. 65 passim; Bersaucourt, *La 2e DLM*, pp. 35ff; reports of Chef d'escadron Vignes, Capt. Hardouin and Capt. de Beaufort in ED, 4DA7, Dr 4; Jungenfeld, *So kämpften Panzer!*, pp. 28-35.

80. Major L. F. Ellis, *War in France and Flanders 1939-1940* (London: H.M.S.O., 1953), pp. 39ff; Van Overstraeten, *Albert I-Léopold III*, p. 598; *GU françaises* II, pp. 340ff; *Overzicht*, p. 101; Lerecouvreux, *L'Armée Giraud*, pp. 214ff.

81. "Historique succint [*sic*] des opérations aériennes," *Titre* II, chap. 2, p. 18; Salesse, *Aviation de chasse*, p. 93; study on personnel appended to Vuillemin's deposition at Riom in ED, 4DA23, Dr 3, sdr b.

82. Paquier, *Aviation de bombardement*, p. 43; "Situation des avions disponibles"; Richards, *Fight at Odds*, pp. 119ff; Albert Kesselring, *Soldat bis zum letzten Tag* (Bonn: Athenäum-Verlag, 1953), p. 77; Danel, "La Conquête de la Hollande," p. 44.

83. D'Astier, *Le Ciel n'était pas vide*, pp. 104ff; Puget, "Historique des opérations," chap. 2, p. 31; Danel, "En Mai Juin . . .," p. 56; Accart, *Chasseurs du ciel*, pp. 117ff; Menjaud, *Un groupe de chasse*, pp. 85ff; "Historique succint [sic] des opérations aériennes," *Titre* II, pp. 21ff.

84. Quotes from Beaufre, *Le Drame de 1940*, pp. 233ff; interview with General André Beaufre, Paris, January 23, 1973.

85. *The Diary of a Staff Officer*, p. 10.

86. Interview with General Beaufre; Petibon's remarks in Gamelin, *Servir* III, p. 397.

87. Quotes from France, Commandement en chef du front nord-est, EM, 3° Bureau: N° 1465-3/Op., "Ordre général n° 13" (unpublished, May 14, 1940); Roton, *Années cruciales*, p. 165; "Extraits du rapport du général Georges," *Titre* V, p. 24.

88. Minart, *P. C. Vincennes* II, pp. 141ff.

89. Quote from Gendry, *La Guerre 1939-1940*, pp. 62ff; Billotte's remark in Van Overstraeten, *Albert I-Léopold III*, pp. 600ff; Georges' testimony in *Événements . . . Témoignages* III, p. 688.

90. "Communications sécrètes," November 7 issue, p. 4; quote from France, Commandement en chef du front nord-est, EM, 3° Bureau: N° 1490 3/Op., "Ordre particulier n° 91 pour la II° Armée" (unpublished, GQG, May 14, 1940, at 9:30 p.m.); d'Astier, *Le Ciel n'était pas vide*, p. 130; France, FACNE, EM, Section d'opérations: 898-0, Message from Têtu to d'Astier (unpublished, May 14, 1940); Prételat, *Destin tragique*, p. 258.

91. Huntziger's order in Le Goyet, "Contre-attaques manquées," pp. 110ff; Grandsard, *10e Corps*, pp. 165ff.

92. Mellenthin, *Panzer Battles*, p. 15; Kielmansegg, *Panzer zwischen Warschau und Atlantik*, p. 119; General Heinz Guderian, *Erinnerungen eines Soldaten* (Heidelberg: Kurt Vowinckel Verlag, 1951), pp. 94ff.

93. Kielmansegg, *Panzer zwischen Warschau und Atlantik*, pp. 118ff; Georges Beau and L. Gaubusseau, *Dix erreurs une défaite* (Paris: Presses de la Cité, 1967), pp. 163ff, 206 passim; *GU françaises* II, pp. 616ff; Gérard Simond, *Décrochages: Sedan 10 mai Saint-Valéry-en-Caux 12 juin 1940* (Annecy: Gardet, 1975), pp. 69-79—Simond was an officer of the 5th Light Cavalry.

94. General Pierre Billotte, *Le Temps des armes* ([Paris]: Plon, 1972), pp. 32ff; Le Goyet, "Contre-attaques manquées," p. 119.

95. Letter from Flavigny in *Événements . . . Témoignages* V, pp. 1253ff; Le Goyet, "Contre-attaques manquées," pp. 120ff.

96. Grandsard, *10e Corps*, pp. 172ff; Ruby, *Sedan*, pp. 139ff; *GU françaises* II, pp. 820ff; Lerecouvreux, *Huit mois d'attente*, pp. 159ff.

97. Ruby, *Sedan*, p. 154; Hanns Wiedmann, ed., *Die grüne Hölle von Inor* (Munich: Zentralverlag der NSDAP, 1941); General Rollot, "La Bataille de Sedan: Le Repli de la IIe Armée (14 mai 1940)," *Revue d'histoire de la deuxième guerre mondiale* no. 32 (October 1958): 28ff.

98. *GU françaises* III, pp. 626ff; Reinhardt, "Im Schatten Guderians," pp. 337ff; Maassen, *Monthermé*, pp. 118-126.

99. *GU françaises* II, pp. 292ff; Teske, *Bewegungskrieg*, pp. 26ff; testimony of General Bruché in *Événements . . . Témoignages* V, pp. 1218ff; Le Goyet, "Dans la tourmente de mai 1940: L'Engagement de la 2e division cuirassée française," *Revue historique de l'armée* 1 (1964): 148ff; Corap's report in ED, 3DA9, Dr 1, sdr b, p. 16 and report on Ninth Army by General Dufieux in ED, 3DA9, Dr 1, sdr d, p. 32.

100. Bertin, "Le 129e R.I.," pp. 94ff; *GU françaises* III, p. 380.

101. De Bellescize, "Carnet," pp. 20ff; *The Rommel Papers*, pp. 11ff; *GU françaises* II, pp. 908ff.

102. Bruneau's testimony in *Événements . . . Témoignages* V, pp. 1166ff; testimony of Capt. Barbeau in ED, 4DA7, Dr 3, "Fiche N° 164," p. 3.

103. Testimony of General Véron in *Événements . . . Témoignages* V, pp. 1294ff; Roton, *Années cruciales*, p. 166; Corap's account dated June 9, 1940, in ED, 3DA9, Dr 1, sdr b, p. 18.

104. Prioux, *Souvenirs*, pp. 70ff; Doumenc, *Dunkerque*, p. 81; Zimmermann, *Griff ins Ungewisse*, pp. 95ff; General Henri Aymes, *Gembloux: Succès français. Le 4e Corps d'armée dans la bataille de la 1re armée en Belgique et en France 10 mai-3 juin 1940* (Paris: Berger-Levrault, 1948), pp. 17ff; *GU françaises* I, pp. 116ff, II, pp. 968ff; quote from Jungenfeld, *So kämpften Panzer!*, pp. 35-38.

105. Lerecouvreux, *L'Armée Giraud*, pp. 254ff, 283ff; d'Ornano, "La 25me DIM," p. 8; *GU françaises* II, pp. 342ff; [General Molinié], *Mai 1940: La 25e Division motorisée (Division d'Auvergne) de Bréda à Lille et à Dunkerque* (Colombes: Imprimerie G. Leroux, 1956 [?]), pp. 8-9.

106. *Overzicht*, p. 132; Lerecouvreux, *L'Armée Giraud*, p. 259; Cras, *Forces maritimes* II, pp. 56ff.

107. France, Commandement en chef des forces aériennes, EMG, 3° Bureau, "Projet de historique de la collaboration aérienne franco-britannique" (unpub-

lished, GQGA, no date), p. 4; Bond, *Chief of Staff*, p. 315; Danel, "La Conquête de la Hollande," pp. 46ff.

108. "Situation des avions disponibles"; d'Astier, *Le Ciel n'était pas vide*, pp. 109ff; Seive, *Aviation d'assaut*, p. 125; Danel, "En Mai Juin . . . ," p. 56.

109. Zeitzler, "Panzer-Gruppe," May article, p. 241; Guderian, *Erinnerungen*, pp. 94ff; Ellis, *War in France and Flanders*, pp. 54ff; Adolf Galland, *The First and the Last: The Rise and Fall of the German Fighter Forces, 1938-1945*, trans. Mervyn Savill (New York: Holt, 1954), pp. 4ff.

110. Minart, *P. C. Vincennes* II, pp. 149ff; Gamelin, *Servir* I, p. 340, III, pp. 400ff; "Extraits du rapport du général Georges," *Titre* V, p. 32; "Communications sécrètes," November 8 issue, p. 4; Roton, *Années cruciales*, pp. 174ff; *GU françaises* III, pp. 400ff.

111. Quote from Charles de Gaulle, *War Memoirs* I, trans. Jonathan Griffin (London: Collins, 1955), p. 37; Cdt. d'Ornano, "La 4e D.C.R. à Montcornet (Mai 1940)," *Revue de défense nationale* (May 1950): 525ff; *GU françaises* III, pp. 508ff.

112. France, Commandement en chef du front nord-est, EM, 3° Bureau: N° 1495-3/Op., "Ordre particulier n° 92" (unpublished, May 14, 1940, at 7:15 a.m.); France, FACNE, EM, Section d'opérations: *numéraux* 901- and 902-0, Messages from Têtu to d'Astier (unpublished, May 15, 1940, at 9:45 and 10:30 a.m.); Prételat, *Destin tragique*, p. 258.

113. Doumenc, *Dunkerque*, pp. 34, 93ff; *GU françaises* II, pp. 48ff, 120ff; Lyet, *La Bataille de France*, pp. 93ff.

114. Winston S. Churchill, *The Second World War* II: *Their Finest Hour* (London: Cassell, 1949), p. 39.

115. "Extraits du rapport du général Georges," *Titre* V, pp. 33ff; Roton, *Années cruciales*, pp. 179ff; Gendry, *La Guerre 1939-1940*, pp. 59ff; Héring's testimony in James de Coquet, *Le Procès de Riom* (Paris: Fayard, 1945), p. 226.

116. Le Goyet, "Contre-attaques manquées," p. 125.

117. Pierre Billotte, *Le Temps des armes*, pp. 39ff; Flavigny's letter in *Événements . . . Témoignages* V, pp. 1255ff; *GU françaises* III, pp. 500ff; Lerecouvreux, *Huit mois d'attente*, pp. 168ff.

118. Guderian, *Erinnerungen*, pp. 95ff; Kielmansegg, *Panzer zwischen Warschau und Atlantik*, pp. 122ff; *GU françaises* II, pp. 190ff, 618ff, III, pp. 384ff, 552ff; Simond, *Décrochages*, pp. 81-89, 183-185.

119. Lyet, "Mitrailleurs malgaches à Monthermé mai 1940," *Revue historique de l'armée* (no. 4 1963); Gabriel Delaunay, *Toute honte bue* (Paris: Nouvelles éditions latines, 1953), pp. 59ff; *GU françaises* II, pp. 706ff, III, pp. 626ff; Reinhardt, "Im Schatten Guderians," pp. 338ff.

120. Bourgin's report in Le Goyet, "Dans la tourmente de mai 1940," pp. 153ff; *GU françaises* I, pp. 448ff.

121. Bourdon, *Le Second drame de Maubeuge*, pp. 72ff, 102ff.

122. Testimony of General Bruneau in *Événements . . . Témoignages* V, pp. 1174ff; testimony of General Martin in de Coquet, *Riom*, p. 255; *The Rommel Papers*, pp. 15ff.

123. Hoth, "Schicksal," pp. 373ff; Bruneau's testimony in *Événements . . . Témoignages* V, pp. 1178ff; Hautecler, "Rommel contre Corap," pp. 102ff; *GU françaises* III, pp. 460ff; de Bellescize, "Carnet," pp. 22ff.

124. Zimmermann, *Griff ins Ungewisse*, pp. 116 passim; Aymes, *Gembloux*, pp. 32ff; *GU françaises* I, pp. 92-93, 116-117, II, pp. 12-13, 206-207, 876-877, 970-971; report of Jean Ragaine in ED, 4DA11, Dr 1, sdr b, pp. 24-25; Cdt. d'Ornano, *La 1re division marocaine dans la bataille de Gembloux* (Bordeaux: Imprimerie Castera, 1951), pp. 34-42; Jungenfeld, *So kämpften Panzer!*, pp. 39-41; Pierre Porthault, *L'Armée du sacrifice (1939-1940)* (Paris: Guy Victor, 1965), passim.

125. Zimmermann, *Griff ins Ungewisse*, pp. 132ff; Aymes, *Gembloux*, pp. 32ff.

126. Bond, *Chief of Staff*, p. 316.

127. "Situation des avions disponibles"; d'Astier, *Le Ciel n'était pas vide*, pp. 127ff; Danel, "En Mai Juin . . . ," p. 57; "Historique succint [*sic*] des opérations aériennes," *Titre* II, Chap. 1, p. 29.

128. Danel, "En Mai Juin . . . ," p. 57; Ellis, *War in France and Flanders*, p. 58; Richards, *Fight at Odds*, pp. 122ff; Sir John Slessor, *The Central Blue: The Autobiography of Sir John Slessor, Marshal of the RAF* (New York: Praeger, 1957), pp. 294ff; *The Diary of a Staff Officer*, pp. 16ff; Robert Wright, *The Man Who Won the Battle of Britain* (New York: Charles Scribner's Sons, 1969), pp. 100ff.

129. Minart, *P. C. Vincennes* II, pp. 151ff, 163; Gamelin's testimony in *Événements . . . Témoignages* II, pp. 403ff and Georges' testimony in III, pp. 670 passim; Georges' report in Reynaud, *La France a sauvé l'Europe* II, pp. 137ff; Gamelin, *Servir* III, pp. 407ff; Daladier's impressions in ED, 3DA8, Dr 1, sdr a.

130. Georges' order in Gendry, *La Guerre 1939-1940*, p. 61; Roton, *Années cruciales*, pp. 179ff; *GU françaises* III, pp. 478ff.

131. Doumenc, *Dunkerque*, pp. 101ff, 122 and Doumenc, *Histoire de la neuvième armée*, pp. 200ff, 222ff; Billotte's directive in Van Overstraeten, *Albert I-Léopold III*, p. 615.

132. France, FACNE, EM, Section d'opérations: 918-0, Message from Têtu to Vuillemin (unpublished, May 16, 1940, at 9:30 a.m.); France, FACNE, EM, Section d'opérations: 917-0, Message from Têtu to Vuillemin (unpublished, May 16, 1940, at 9:00 a.m.); Prételat, *Destin tragique*, p. 258; *La Manoeuvre pour la bataille: Les Transports pendant la guerre 1939-1940* (Paris: Charles-Lavauzelle, 1941), pp. 34ff; "Extraits du rapport du général Georges," *Titre* V, p. 36.

133. France, Commandement en chef du front nord-est, EM, 3° Bureau, "Ordre particulier (Suite à l'ordre général N° 14—N° 1507 3/Op.)" (unpublished, May 16, 1940).

134. Doumenc, *Histoire de la neuvième armée*, pp. 193ff; France, Commandement en chef du front nord-est, EM, 3° Bureau: N° 1537 3/Op., "Ordre particulier n° 93 pour les généraux Giraud et Touchon" (unpublished, May 16, 1940); *GU françaises* III, pp. 358ff; Commandement des Facne, EM, Section opérations [*sic*]: N° 933-0, "Instruction concernant l'application de l'ordre particulier n°93 cijoint" (unpublished, May 16, 1940); Gendry, *La Guerre 1939-1940*, p. 63; "Extraits du rapport du général Georges," *Titre* V, pp. 36ff.

135. Pierre Billotte, *Le Temps des armes*, pp. 39ff; Guderian, *Erinnerungen*, p. 96; Kielmansegg, *Panzer zwischen Warschau und Atlantik*, pp. 126ff.

136. Diary entry of a lieutenant in the unit in France, École spéciale militaire et école militaire interarmes, SHA, *Cours d'histoire militaire: Scènes de la vie militaire: Témoignages de combattants recueillis par le Lt.-Col. Robert Vial du SHA* (St.-Cyr: Librairie militaire, 1962); Pierre Voisin, *Ceux des chars 45 jours 45 nuits* (Lyon

and Paris: Éditions Archat, 1941), pp. 22ff; Le Goyet, "Dans la tourmente de mai 1940," pp. 155ff; Kielmansegg, *Panzer zwischen Warschau und Atlantik*, p. 129.

137. Teske, *Bewegungskrieg*, pp. 31ff; Bourdon, *Le Second drame de Maubeuge*, pp. 121ff.

138. Bruneau's testimony in *Événements . . . Témoignages* V, p. 1180.

139. De Bellescize, "Carnet," p. 24; Doumenc, *Histoire de la neuvième armée*, pp. 200ff, 213; *GU françaises* II, pp. 120ff.

140. *The Rommel Papers*, pp. 17ff; Bourdon, *Le Second drame de Maubeuge*, pp. 129 passim; *GU françaises* III, pp. 462ff.

141. Bertin, "Le 129e R.I.," pp. 99ff; Doumenc, *Dunkerque*, p. 147; *GU françaises* I, pp. 84ff, II, pp. 62ff; Dufieux's report in ED, 3DA9, Dr1, sdr d, p. 72.

142. Doumenc, *Dunkerque*, pp. 113ff; Gort, *Despatches*, p. 5912; Bond, *Chief of Staff*, pp. 316ff; Ellis, *War in France and Flanders*, pp. 59ff.

143. M. Fouillien and J. Bouhon, *Mai 1940: La Bataille de Belgique, Essai d'historique de la campagne, d'après les témoignages et les documents* (Brussels: L'Édition universelle, [1944?]), p. 90; Henri de Man, *Cavalier seul: 45 Années de socialisme européen* (Geneva: Les Editions du cheval ailé, 1948), pp. 223ff; Ehrengardt, "Aéronavale en guerre," pp. 58ff; General Fagalde, "L'Affaire des iles de Zélande: (Walcheren et Sud Beveland). Mai 1940," *Revue militaire suisse* nos. 11 and 12 (November and December 1953): December article, pp. 633 ff; Cras, *Forces maritimes* II, p. 83; Aron, *Léopold III*, pp. 47-48.

144. D'Astier, *Le Ciel n'était pas vide*, pp. 135ff; "Situation des avions disponibles"; Romatet, "Groupement de chasse 23," pp. 82ff; Danel, "En Mai Juin . . . ," pp. 57ff; Danel, "Au service de l'armée de terre," p. 88.

145. Williame, *L'Escadrille des cigognes*, p. 207; Bougerol, *Ceux qu'on n'a jamais vus*, pp. 108ff; Seive, *Aviation d'assaut*, p. 126; Paquier, *Aviation de bombardement*, pp. 59ff.

146. D'Astier, *Le Ciel n'était pas vide*, p. 146; "Projet de historique de la collaboration aérienne franco-britannique," pp. 4ff; Richards, *Fight at Odds*, pp. 124ff; Wright, *The Man Who Won*, pp. 117ff.

147. Quotes from Lord Hastings Ismay, *The Memoirs of General the Lord Ismay K.G., P.C., G.C.B., C.H., D.S.O.* (London: Heinemann, 1960), pp. 127ff and Churchill, *The Second World War* II, p. 44.

148. Jacques Weygand, *Weygand mon père* (Paris: Flammarion, 1970), p. 269; ED, 4DA9, Dr 1, sdr a, "Notes GENEBRIER: 9 mai-6 juin 40" (unpublished), pp. 9-10.

chapter 9

A SECOND MIRACLE OF THE MARNE? (MAY 17-21, 1940)

The eighth day of operations in the west opened on a world in an uproar. France had begun as badly in World War I, only to stave off disaster at the Marne—why not again? Such thoughts were in the mind of Maurice Gamelin, who had stood at Joffre's side in 1914. It was only a question of when, where, and how; but he had to act fast for the situation would soon be out of his hands.

In the morning of May 17 Reynaud rearranged his government, taking charge of the Ministry of National Defense and War at midnight, May 18. He intended to have Weygand replace Gamelin, but Weygand was in the Levant. Weygand called for a fast light bomber to carry him back to France, but decided he could not leave until the next morning, May 18.[1] Gamelin, all unknowing, got a brief reprieve.

May 17: The View from the Top

Vincennes began to shake off the panic of May 16. Papers captured on a German colonel indicated that the enemy target was not Paris, but the Somme River line and Calais, to cut off Allied forces in Belgium. GQG confirmed this before noon: the threat of immediate disaster was past. Gamelin, meanwhile, worked on a long analysis of the causes of the disaster in response to a request of May 16 from Daladier. But if Gamelin took time to prepare a long report, the sense of urgency did not abate elsewhere: talk began at headquarters of the British Air Forces in France of an evacuation of the BEF to England. One British officer noted in his diary that "this seems deplorable"; the British expected the French to rise to an emergency, "but it looks as if this time it was too late. . . ."[2] Gamelin was aware of the mood at the front: egged on by Reynaud he issued a second order of the day—

> The fate of our country, that of our allies, the destinies of the world depend on the battle now taking place.

> English, Belgian, Polish soldiers and foreign volunteers are all fighting at our sides.
>
> The British Air Force is totally committed to battle, as is ours.
>
> Any unit which cannot advance must stand to the death in place rather than abandon the parcel of national soil which has been confided to it.
>
> As always in the dark hours of our history, the order of the day is: Conquer or die. We must conquer.[3]

Georges struggled meanwhile to re-form a front, specifying new lines for the First Army Group at 7:00 a.m. If Billotte could not hold in place, he was to fall back to the Forest of Mormal and to the frontier position farther north, then south from the Mormal along the Sambre and then the Oise rivers to join Touchon's army at La Fère. If that line could not be held, Billotte could hold the Escaut in Belgium and bring his right flank down the French Escaut from Valenciennes to Cambrai, then through Le Catelet to Saint-Quentin and the Crozat Canal to Touchon. Georges withdrew the 25th Motorized from Antwerp and—finally—drew on the reserves of the BEF, ordering elements on the British lines of communication to form a stop line to halt the enemy's drive toward the sea. But by first light, hours before Georges' order went out, Rommel reached Landrecies at the threshold of the second position Georges prescribed; farther south Panzers were already attacking the Oise bridges.[4]

At 10:00 a.m. Georges gave the Second Army, locked in indecisive fighting, to Prételat, freeing himself to concentrate on action farther west. What happened at La Ferté later that morning is not clear, but at 1:00 p.m. Georges issued a new order reflecting despair at re-forming his center. Georges described the situation: "Before the German menace aimed at the right flank of Army Group One, it is important from this moment on to prepare the defense of Paris by barring the valley of the Oise. . . ."[5] Georges ordered the Seventh Army, free from its mission in the Netherlands, to form a front between Touchon's left wing and Péronne—facing *north* into the rear of lines which that morning he had ordered Billotte to defend facing *east* against the Panzers! The Seventh Army was to leave its 16th Corps with the series B 60th and 68th Infantry under Belgian command, while moving its 1st Motorized Corps to its new front. The Second and Third Army Groups would send four infantry divisions to join the 21st Division from the Seventh Army in the area Amiens-Compiègne. Thus Georges seemed to take for granted Billotte's inability to hold the lines specified that morning. He began a new defensive front farther west covering Paris. Georges knew that the enemy's intention was to cut off Army Group One: he seemed to accept that as a fait accompli, leaving Billotte to fend for himself. After 11:30 p.m. Villelume called on Georges to get the latest news for Reynaud. Introduced into Georges' bedchamber,

Villelume learned that reserve divisions were converging by rail on the threatened zone. But the enemy might get there first. In Reynaud's name, Villelume asked if a second maneuver had been prepared in case the present plan failed. That question, said Georges, should be put to Gamelin. Thus hopes for a new Miracle of the Marne rested on Gamelin, and on Billotte.

Billotte was in a serious situation, facing the enemy on May 17 with only fourteen Belgian, eight British, and eighteen French divisions, including three DLMs, parts of the 2nd and remains of the 1st DCR. Against his force the enemy had ten Panzers and thirty other divisions with a further twenty-five in support; seven faced the Belgians, six the British, twenty-two—including nine Panzers—faced the First and Ninth Armies.[6] Belgian and British numerical superiority continued to go to waste for lack of central Allied direction. Given the 7th Panzer's penetration to Landrecies, Billotte decided that afternoon to withdraw his right to the French Sambre, ordering the 4th Infantry and the Cavalry Corps to the west of the Mormal Forest. Shortly after, however, he allowed the First Army to keep the Cavalry Corps, which Blanchard claimed he needed to cover the First Army's retreat.

Meanwhile, Billotte haggled with the British and Belgians over the schedule of the retreat to the Escaut position. Billotte originally wanted to complete the withdrawal in four nights. In the morning of the 17th, Van Overstraeten and Léopold found orders, apparently from the preceding day, prescribing a one-day delay to adhere to Georges' timetable. By the morning of May 17 Georges' order from the morning of May 16 and Billotte's message from the afternoon were out of date; that evening a liaison officer brought in Billotte's order to retreat as originally planned. These mixups raised hackles at British headquarters, where Pownall complained of contradictions between Georges and Billotte, castigated Billotte in his diary as "weak" and his staff as "badly shaken" and added that "Billotte will not coordinate, although nominated."[7]

In the Field

The French center was in a critical state. General Bruché, commander of the scattered 2nd DCR, got hold of his radio units that morning—but they were of no use since his elements had received no common radio wavelength![8] That morning the 2nd DCR had eighty tanks along forty kilometers of the Oise River: a French reconnaissance spotted Panzers driving westward while isolated French tanks picketed intact bridges. To the southeast, however, Colonel de Gaulle launched his "4th DCR"—a battalion of B tanks, a company of D2 mediums, a battalion of infantry support tanks, a few hundred artillerymen fighting on foot, and some elements of the 3rd Light Cavalry—against Montcornet early that morning. De Gaulle pushed his armor forward in two columns against reconnaissance elements, then strongpoints of Guderian's flank. German light tanks and armored cars were no match for the French, who reached Montcornet in the morning but had to withdraw to resupply. Meanwhile, Georges ordered the 4th DCR to establish itself at Montcornet but without risking the bulk of its forces. De Gaulle ordered his tanks into Montcornet where they fought off German mechanized elements. But the infantry of the unit did not appear; tanks alone could not clean out the town. Enemy artillery and air attacks increased; de Gaulle pulled back.

The 4th DCR had taken the 1st Panzer by surprise, stopping its southern wing and killing or wounding staff officers caught in Montcornet. However, other Panzers crossed the Oise and drove off the tanks of the 2nd DCR. To the German command these counterattacks seemed uncoordinated, thus ineffective. Guderian called his 10th Panzer from Stonne to deal with the 4th DCR.[9]

But the German High Command was nervous. Army Group A noted that its Sixteenth Army at Sedan had difficulty holding French counterattacks; Hitler visited the headquarters that afternoon, fearing a French success along the south flank of the German advance.[10] As a result Kleist told Guderian to halt. The fiery Guderian offered his resignation on the spot, but received permission to push "reconnaissances in force" forward. He resumed his course as if the incident had never happened.

To the north Giraud and Billotte tried to form a front on the right wing of Army Group One. Giraud learned by midnight of May 16-17 that Martin was abandoning the frontier; he ordered Martin and Didelet, commanding the 9th Motorized arriving from the north, to line the Sambre facing east and then the Oise facing southeast. At 3:00 a.m. Giraud defined three successive lines to be held: the last was to be reached no earlier than the morning of May 19. The first consisted of positions then held; the second a line from the Forest of Nouvion to Avesnes; the third a line along the Oise and Sambre from Ribemont to Landrecies. The 1st and 2nd DCR were to regroup at Landrecies and Wassigny.[11] Rommel's 7th Panzer reached Landrecies as this order went out, as Giraud soon learned. The French discovered from prisoners that the Rommel raid was separate from the units which had pushed over the Oise against the 9th Motorized's vanguard the day before, but the impression that these were from the same force had an unfortunate effect, particularly on the 9th Motorized which was trying to regroup after its columns were split by the 7th Panzer.

That morning Billotte, unable to contact Giraud and annoyed at the delay, chased him down and spent an hour with him in the front lines within a few hundred meters of a parked group of German tanks. Billotte seemed "energetic and confident" as he talked to Doumenc that afternoon but thought that conferences in the front lines "'aren't worth a damn'" *(ne valent rien).*[12] Billotte ordered Giraud to hold on the Sambre and Oise; he would send the Cavalry Corps to the Sambre to support him. He also gave Giraud the 1st DLM which was on the way. Doumenc, talking to Billotte later, insisted that the First Army Group must do more toward the south: he wanted the whole Cavalry Corps sent to Saint-Quentin. Billotte "understood the necessity for it" but demurred, wanting it to aid the First Army; he did, however, direct the 25th Motorized on to Douai. Billotte's assurance that the 23rd Infantry, coming from Lorraine, was about to arrive at Saint-Quentin and the 1st DLM at Solesmes rekindled Giraud's hope that he could weather the storm.

On May 17 pieces of Martin's 11th Corps, including the 1st North African Infantry, the 4th North African, and remains of the 18th and 22nd Infantry and the 1st Light Cavalry, clung all day to the frontier despite Martin's order to retreat, while cavalry and parts of the 9th Motorized faced south on the Oise at Hirson. German attacks brought quick counterattacks: elements of the 1st Light Cavalry with a few tanks from the 2nd DCR fought their way against the 7th Panzer into Landrecies that night, although they had to give ground later.[13] Farther north portions of the 101st Fortress Infantry panicked following Rommel's raid, but the majority stood firm at Maubeuge and on the Sambre, in line with Billotte's order.

However, the rest of Hoth's force followed Rommel, whose Panzers were heavily engaged to the west in relative isolation, losing contact with their motorcycle elements, who tangled with the remains of the 1st DCR that morning in Avesnes.[14] The last French tanks in Avesnes were destroyed by 4:00 a.m.; Rommel pushed toward Landrecies and the passages over the Sambre. His lead elements made good time but most of his force bogged down in resistance along the route. Rommel drove back to regain contact with his division, while his Panzers to the west faced the counterattack (noted above) of the 1st Light Cavalry and 9th Motorized. The Germans finally secured Landrecies but could go no farther. Faced with this lodgement, Giraud could only reroute the 1st DLM to counterattack the next morning, while Martin fell back to the Mormal Forest with whatever came to hand.

West of the patchy Ninth Army, Georges' orders reached the Territorial divisions of the BEF laboring on the British lines of communication. The two British divisions were to occupy key points west of the Oise between the Somme to the south and the First Army Group to the north. Gort reinforced these units as best he could, but the defense was tenuous.[15] More strength was available farther north: Prioux saw Blanchard that day, insisting on the regrouping of his Cavalry Corps plus the 1st DLM to counterattack on both sides of the Mormal Forest. Getting no satisfaction, he turned directly to Georges, who agreed. But Prioux would have to talk with Billotte first. Prioux saw Billotte at Douai, but the latter expected the Cavalry Corps to stay with the First Army during its retreat.

And that retreat went none too well: Hoepner's Panzers recovered from their drubbing and pressed the French.[16] General René Altmayer's 5th Corps, the right wing of the First Army, had a particularly difficult time with the mass of military and civilian elements on the roads. The 5th Corps was moving back toward the focal point of the attacks of Hoepner's and Hoth's corps; the unit temporarily lost touch with the First Army. The neighboring 4th Corps regained liaison by radio, but the hampered retreat of the 5th broke the rhythm of the First Army's withdrawal.

In Zeeland the expedition to Walcheren ended as the panicky French reservists gave way despite the leadership of General Deslaurens. The French navy improvised an evacuation under cover of the naval air arm; the majority got away. The General and a few troops covered the embarkation; Deslaurens died weapon in hand.[17]

In the Air

May 17 saw a reorganization of the Armée de l'air. D'Astier withdrew the remaining reconnaissance and observation units of the Ninth and First Armies; a new fighter group and two modern bomber groups arrived, but incomplete returns showed only 149 fighters in the Northern Zone that morning (with seventy-two in the Eastern and thirty-four in the Southern Zones), plus twenty-four modern and thirty old bombers.[18] That morning Vuillemin met Barratt and a RAF officer from Britain at Georges' headquarters, pleading for British fighters. Têtu sent a message to Vuillemin: noting the shortage of fighters, he suggested ending daylight bombing so that the fighters could concentrate on air defense. Unable to obtain British reinforcements, Vuillemin agreed; however, should enemy columns break Allied lines, bombers would be engaged without escort.[19]

This order came too late to stop an attack by twenty-four night fighters followed by ten Lioré 451's over the frontier defenses at Trélon in response to a plea from Giraud that came early that morning. Six fighters and four bombers failed to return.[20] Têtu ordered fighters to cover rail lines bringing reinforcements toward the Oise. That evening Groupment 21 was down to fifty-one fighters; Groupment 23 had only seventy-one. The RAF sent twelve Blenheims over the lines following a sweep by Hurricanes, only to lose eleven to resurgent German fighters—the RAF still hesitated to "waste" fighters in direct escort. This disaster led Air Marshal Newall to again halt daylight bombing, but the injunction soon ended before the pleas of the BEF. Thus the Luftwaffe succeeded in limiting the daylight offensive action of Allied airpower. The loss rate played a major part in the British refusal to commit the whole RAF to combat in French skies. But the British refusal guaranteed German numerical superiority, thus helping cause the high loss rate. The ability of Allied air forces to affect events dwindled.

May 18: The View from the Top

In the Levant a seventy-two-year-old French general crawled into a crew seat of a bomber as the sun rose on May 18 for the long flight to France. Maxime Weygand knew why Reynaud was calling him back; during the flight he jotted down his thoughts:

> ". . . the life of France is at stake in this battle as well as the whole of western civilization, the fate of the small powers, the dignity of man. Therefore we must . . . stop the enemy and then beat him.
>
> But . . . it is the offensive spirit which yields victory . . . everyone must have the determination to do as much damage as possible to the enemy, to hold him in constant fear . . . of our reactions. . . . An enemy penetration, even a deep one, offers chances to react, especially when that penetration is based on machines and the enemy's logistics become a matter of unprecedented importance. . . ."[21]

Weygand planned to drain the Maginot Line of field units and pull back in Belgium to the Escaut or even the Yser River to scrape up strength for the center: "'Above all, everyone into battle.'"

Meanwhile, Gamelin dispatched his report to the Defense Minister. He accurately detailed enemy dispositions during the attack. The German offensive might be aimed at Calais or Paris, but Calais was more likely. French forces from the east barred the direction of Paris; the situation with respect to Calais was "difficult." Gamelin complained that the 25 mm antitank gun was too weak and emphasized "moral faults" which led to breakdowns in the field. But he defended his advance into Belgium: the enemy had not been able to penetrate there, nor had he dared attack the Maginot Line. It seemed to him that the main factor was the action of enemy mechanized divisions which paralyzed attempts to seal off the breakthrough: "'. . . the worst of it is that the ideas which inspired the German high command to use its armor in mass are French ideas.'" If French forces had not performed at the level of French conceptions, the fault lay in the decision following World War I to accept only a defensive war, in the lack of arms production, and in weak training under the one-year service. But, "'above all, the German success is the consequence of the physical training and moral exaltation of the [German] popular masses.'" The French soldier was not morally prepared; the "'old national instinct'" proved insufficient. The enemy breakthrough "'was too often the result of a local, then quasi-general panic'" particularly in reserve units; the Allies gave way above all before the numbers of enemy tanks and planes.[22] Having defended himself, Gamelin turned to the battle.

Early on May 18 he drove to La Ferté to meet Georges and Doumenc. Georges' obvious fatigue and the disorder of his headquarters made a bad impression: Gamelin discussed this with Doumenc, who thought Gamelin would have to take charge. Still, it would be best if it could be arranged without bruising anyone's feelings. Gamelin understood—"'Let me know when the time and the occasion appear.'"[23] Gamelin had something in mind: he was more "in form" that morning at Vincennes, ignoring details, examining the general situation. At 8:15 a.m. he sent Vuillemin two questions for air reconnaissance: What forces were behind the enemy motorized columns? How much German infantry was there before Touchon's Sixth Army? Gamelin was thinking of ordering the Sixth forward in liaison with Huntziger's army to threaten the Panzers' communications. That afternoon the intelligence came in: the German rear contained supply and antiaircraft units—little else. Roton accurately detailed the location and directions of the seven Panzers plus motorized infantry operating in the French center, as well as the two Panzers operating in the Gembloux gap and the single Panzer in the Antwerp area; it seemed likely that by the evening of May 18 no more than six enemy infantry divisions could reach the line Hirson-Beaumont behind the German advance. If the Allies could sever the German spearhead from its shaft of conventional infantry, they could achieve another Miracle of the Marne! But it had to be done soon, for the German infantry was moving fast.

That afternoon Reynaud took Daladier and Pétain, called to be Vice Premier, to Vincennes. The possibility of command changes came up, but Gamelin—thinking of Georges—considered that command changes might affect morale. He intended to take charge of operations himself anyway. Following, Pétain took Gamelin by the hand and told him, "'I pity you with all my heart'"; Gamelin replied, "'My thoughts are for the country alone.'"[24] Time was running out.

That morning Georges had decided it might still be possible—despite his order to the Seventh Army of the day before—to reestablish his center. At 10:00 a.m. he ordered counterattacks on the Oise at Origny to throw Guderian's corps back; at 10:30 he ordered the Seventh and Ninth Armies to link up with each other. The new order to the Seventh Army prescribed that while maintaining its initial mission its new commander, General Aubert Frère, was to reach the right wing of the Ninth Army on the Oise, first at La Fère where elements of the 2nd DCR assigned to the Ninth stood, later farther north at Ribemont.[25] At 5:00 p.m. Georges repeated this order to Billotte and Touchon; they were to retreat no farther than a line along the French Escaut at Valenciennes, south to Saint-Quentin, then east to La Fère. These orders were completely out of touch with reality. The Oise was lost the previous evening; by the time Georges' order reached its destination the enemy was west of the last line Georges prescribed. No large

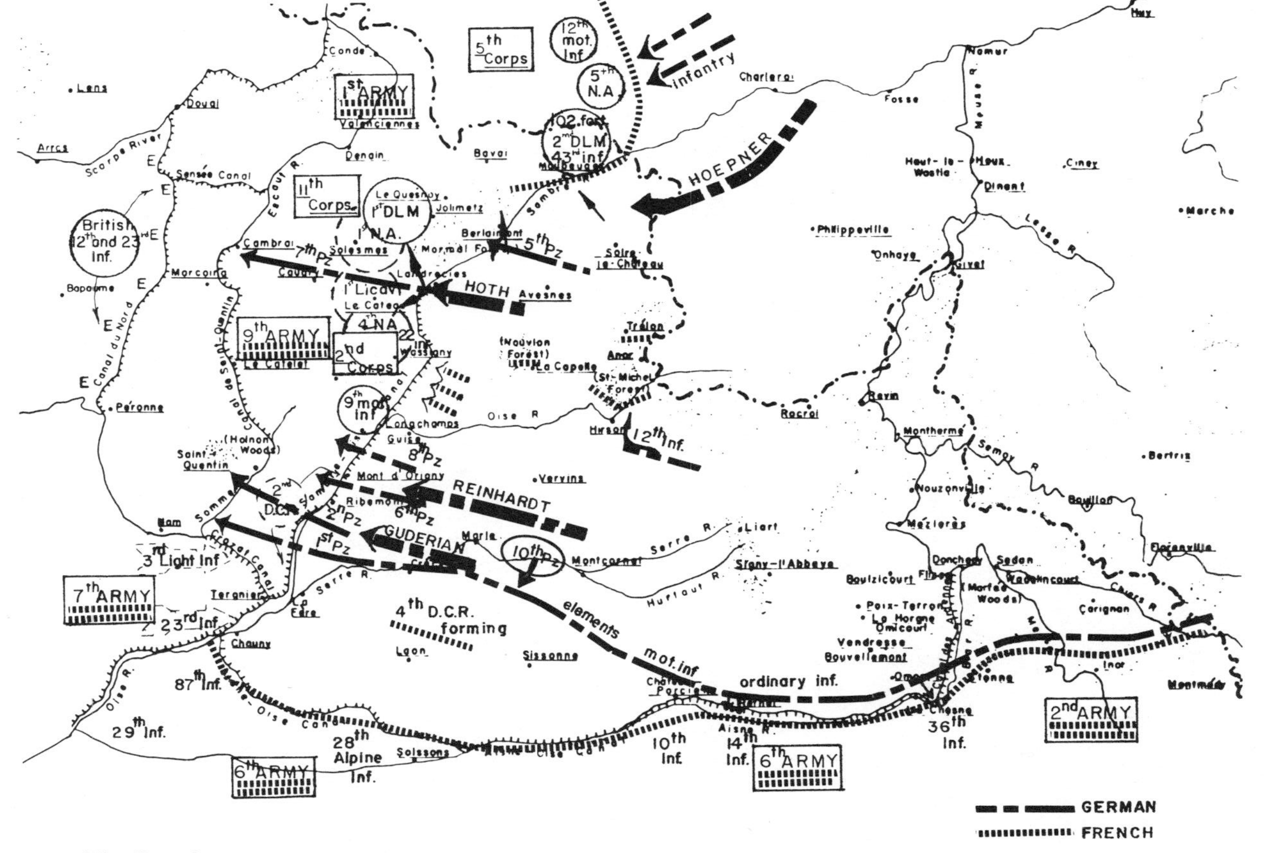

The Situation, May 18, 1940, in the Morning

French force had arrived in the area since the 17th—what made Georges think the enemy would allow this front to knit itself back together?

By 7:25 p.m. information reached Georges that the enemy had breached the fronts he prescribed that morning. He gave up hope of stopping the Panzers, choosing to canalize and slow the enemy while holding the Somme to cover Paris—although he knew Calais was the enemy goal.[26] After a conversation with Billotte he issued another order at 11:00 p.m. Noting that the German advance continued between Maubeuge and Péronne, he ordered a "barrage" along the Somme. But the Seventh Army was to form in depth ready to counterattack: "It is important to profit from the exposed position of the force of Panzerdivisionen engaged on the front from Maubeuge to La Fère,"[27] since these had only a screen of infantry covering their south flank. The 4th DCR was to advance from Laon toward Crécy, under Touchon, while the First Army Group "will do all it can" to intervene from Cambrai toward Saint-Quentin with mechanized cavalry.

Billotte had difficulty following Georges' rapid shifts. In the morning of May 18 no new German advances were reported; French movements continued uninterrupted, creating optimism in various French headquarters.[28] This illusory glow explains Georges' order that morning. At 9:15 a.m. Billotte reported his forces holding on all fronts; the retreat of Belgian and British forces went according to plan and Giraud was "*'content'.*" Billotte dispatched liaison agents to Touchon; the next morning he would move the Cavalry Corps south to reinforce his junction with the main body of the French army. Billotte was convinced that once his units reached their assigned positions the decisive battle would begin. During the day he learned of enemy crossings over the Oise and rerouted the 25th Motorized toward Cambrai; the First Army was to regroup the remains of the 5th Motorized from the Ninth Army and place it, facing south, along the Sensée Canal to cover the First Army's rear. By noon the Army Group could no longer contact the Ninth Army; as night fell, it became clear that the front on the Sambre and Oise had crumbled. Just as his armies reached the Escaut position, Billotte's whole battle plan foundered.

Billotte talked to Georges again that night, telling him "'we are twenty-four hours late'" trying to seal off the enemy advance since the 1st DLM and the 25th Motorized had not yet reached assigned positions. He intended to cling to Condé west of Maubeuge on the frontier but did not know if he could extend his forces sufficiently far south to reach Georges—"'Therefore we must reflect on what line of conduct to adopt in case our forces find themselves separated from each other'."[29] This was a heavy blow to Georges; Billotte for the first time realized his terrible vulnerability. He had to make what arrangements he could to stave off catastrophe.

At 8:25 Billotte ordered the First and Ninth Armies to hold the French Escaut and Maubeuge; the Cavalry Corps would gather north of the Sensée Canal for offensive action toward Le Cateau or Saint-Quentin to clear out the Panzers. Following his conversation with Georges, at 11:30 p.m. Billotte ordered the Cavalry Corps to act the next day toward Saint-Quentin.[30] At midnight Billotte visited the BEF, asking—for the first time—what aid the British could provide. Gort replied that he had no tanks, although his tank brigade had not yet been engaged, but said he was expecting General Evans' Armoured Division soon. Billotte, "quite calm but very tired" as he seemed to Pownall, discussed the measures taken to prop up the Ninth Army, but "clearly had mighty little hope that they would be effective."[31] Thus when Billotte finally asked his Allies for help, Gort and Pownall had lost confidence in the French, and made little effort to provide aid.

In the Field

On May 18 the isolated tanks of the 2nd DCR gave way before Guderian's and Reinhardt's corps, many escaping south of the Crozat Canal where they joined the new Seventh Army.[32] Farther north Giraud issued a general order at 9:45 a.m. He claimed that the Ninth Army was established from the Sambre to the Oise except for enemy tanks at Landrecies and a single crossing of the Oise west of Longchamps; efforts had begun to clear these lodgements. He ordered the 2nd Corps to stand on his right along the Oise with the 23rd Infantry on its right, then the 4th North African and the 1st Light Cavalry. In fact the 23rd ran into the enemy while trying to move north from the Crozat Canal and stood there, joining the new Seventh Army. On his left, Martin's 11th Corps was to hold the Sambre with the 9th Motorized and the 1st North African, while the 1st DLM and 4th Light Cavalry and the remains of the 1st and 2nd DCR were to regroup in reserve.[33]

Actually, Giraud's front was extremely tenuous: German reinforcements poured through the bridgeheads over the Sambre and Oise—Hoth's, Reinhardt's, and Guderian's corps hit the remnants of the Ninth Army. The single new element in Giraud's lineup was the 1st DLM, which finally got its SOMUA tanks via Belgian railroads from the First Army which had held them to cover its retreat. Following Giraud's order of the previous day, the 1st DLM moved in two groups to clear the Mormal Forest and regain the Sambre south of Maubeuge. But it took the division commander most of the day to regroup his unit: Martin had taken some of it to hold the Sambre the day before. The attack of the 1st DLM went in at 6:30 p.m. The French ran into strong enemy armor which had advanced that day through the Mormal Forest and beyond. This was the baptism of fire for the SOMUA tanks of the 1st DLM. The western column drove the enemy back to the Mormal; but the Germans had a heavy preponderance, and as night fell more Panzers swung up from the southwest to flank the French. The 1st DLM stood at Le Quesnoy securing the right rear of the First Army.

The eastern column of the 1st DLM was to advance through the Mormal to Berlaimont on the Sambre. Twenty SOMUA tanks plus motorized cavalry had penetrated the area the previous day, spotting undamaged B tanks abandoned for lack of gasoline. The French could not signal the presence of the tanks because their radios, in this unit always delicate, were not functioning. During the night of May 17-18 the commander, Pierre Dunoyer de Segonzac, pulled back, unwilling to leave his tanks sitting blind on the riverbank. On May 18, joining some North African infantry, they fought for the western exits of the Mormal at Jolimetz. Despite counterattacks by the French armor, the enemy assaulted with some sixty tanks and artillery support and cleared Jolimetz by day's end.[34] The failure to clear the Mormal Forest left elements of the 5th Motorized and 1st North African alone in the area—faced soon by the whole of Hoepner's force which the enemy command ordered down from the north—while the 1st DLM stood west of the Mormal at Le Quesnoy.

On the 18th the remains of the 1st Light Cavalry fell back from Landrecies to the west where they, with the exhausted and in part munitionless remains of other units, were overrun by Reinhardt's and Hoth's corps that night or the next day.[35] The same fate met the staff of the Ninth Army which, fixed in place by order, defended itself until overrun. Generals Thierry d'Argenlieu and Augereau were killed. Giraud was captured the following day. The Ninth Army ceased to exist.

To the north the right wing of the First Army, Altmayer's 5th Corps, was in a critical situation. Retreating toward the frontier at Maubeuge which it was to occupy by May 19, the 5th Corps found the enemy across the Sambre inside the Mormal Forest; the Germans acquired bridgeheads within Maubeuge from the south. Altmayer intended to hold Maubeuge with his 43rd Infantry and the 4th Infantry arriving by rail from the old Seventh Army, but learning of the situation in his right rear, he called on the 2nd DLM, aiding his retreat, to intervene. The tanks of the 2nd DLM were in place that night, but meanwhile the 43rd Infantry and the 101st Fortress Infantry had to hold on alone; only parts of the 4th Infantry arrived. Its commander, General Musse, decided, in view of the confusion, to debark behind the Escaut at Valenciennes. That night the 5th Corps covered the right of the First Army, but it lost touch with Army headquarters during the confusion—and lost the chance to act together with the 1st DLM and the remains of the Ninth Army.[36]

During the night Altmayer received an order from Blanchard, issued that morning, to join in clearing out the Mormal. The situation had changed much since the morning, but Altmayer gave the mission to his 5th North African Infantry for the next day. The 43rd and 12th Motorized would cover its rear.[37] Meanwhile, on May 18 Blanchard ordered the Cavalry Corps regrouped at noon in compliance with Billotte's intention to launch it south; but Blanchard's subordinates were loath to part with tanks, and

Altmayer was out of touch. Billotte sent a strong telegram to pry them loose.

The retreat of Blanchard's 3rd and 4th Corps went fairly easily on the 18th, although the troops were tired. Hoepner did not follow; French intelligence deduced that the Panzers had withdrawn. They appeared in the Mormal Forest soon after.[38] To Blanchard's left the BEF met no serious problem in its retreat. But Billotte's midnight visit left Gort pondering withdrawal toward the Somme or the coast; since the Panzers lay between the BEF and the Somme, he began to consider evacuation. To the British left the Belgian army was vigorously pressed: panic broke out in elements of its 3rd Corps on the Willebroek Canal during the night of May 17. Every step backward was a costly blow to the morale of the Belgian army.

In the Air

In the morning of May 18 incomplete figures showed d'Astier with 191 fighters mostly concentrated under Groupment 23; the Eastern Zone had twenty-three, the Southern, thirty one. The French air force had twenty-four modern and twenty older bombers ready.[39] Part of Groupment 18 of the assault aviation entered the fray flying the unreliable Breguet 691 planes previously used as trainers. The Allies continued to fly fighter cover and reconnaissance missions; the dire situation forced French and British bombers to intervene that afternoon and night over the Ninth Army. Twelve Lioré 451's, unable to find their escort, attacked anyway after 4:00 p.m., followed an hour later by eight Breguet: four were lost. The combined Flak from the corps of Hoth, Reinhardt, and Guderian was devastating.

May 19: The View from the Top

May 19 was a day of decision for the French High Command. Around 5:00 a.m. Doumenc called Gamelin at Vincennes: Doumenc had been at La Ferté since 1:00 a.m.; the time had come for Gamelin to take command. Gamelin asked Doumenc and Vuillemin to meet him at La Ferté at 8:00 a.m. Gamelin had not lost his faith in victory. Defeat would mean the end of Western civilization—"it would be Nazism that would triumph and not just that strange force named Hitler, half evil genius and half folly, but all the unleashed violence of the old Germanism."[40]

Gamelin arrived at La Ferté before 9:00 a.m. and met Georges, Doumenc, and Roton. He knew that the First Army Group intended to hold the Escaut position from Ghent to Condé and Maubeuge, although Billotte felt a threat in the Landrecies-Le Quesnoy area.[41] At last Gamelin had the stable base for which he had been waiting, or so he later said, to start his maneuver. He told Georges that British and Belgian forces must be brought into the maneuver—at last—and added that Billotte's authority needed reinforcement. Then the Commander in Chief drafted his plan of battle.

The gap torn in the French center had narrowed to roughly forty kilometers between the new Seventh Army at Péronne and the First Army Group at Cambrai. Gamelin knew the Panzers had outdistanced their conventional infantry: Allied strength in the north could bear on the rear of the German vanguard and separate it from its support; farther east Huntziger could threaten German communications on the Meuse. Here were prospects for another Miracle of the Marne! Gamelin read the draft to some of the staff; General Louis Koeltz suggested that he make it a formal directive. Gamelin signed the order at 9:45 a.m. The directive, addressed to Vuillemin and Georges, approved the measures taken by Georges and stated, to salve Georges' pride, that Gamelin did not wish to intervene in the conduct of the battle, which came under Georges' authority. Gamelin approved the extension of the Seventh Army front to cover Paris and join up with Army Group One but added that, as far as Billotte's force was concerned, "rather than allow it to be encircled, we must act with extreme audacity: on the one hand by opening its route toward the Somme if necessary; on the other hand by throwing especially mobile forces onto the rear of the German Panzers and motorized infantry divisions."[42] Gamelin added, "It seems that for the moment there is a vacuum behind this first echelon." Georges was to prepare an offensive toward the German communications at Mézières. All Allied air forces were to join the battle. And—"*It is all a question of hours.*"

Giving the directive to Georges and Têtu, Gamelin stayed to talk with Vuillemin. But disconcerting news arrived: Weygand was in France. Gamelin gave Weygand an appointment at the same time he was to meet General Sir John Dill, Vice Chief of the British Imperial General Staff, who came from London to discuss the crisis. Meanwhile, Georges began to work on Gamelin's directive. Perhaps Georges knew of Weygand's arrival—he made no move to implement the directive, which he later insisted was only a set of "suggestions."[43] Georges had already ordered the extension of the Seventh Army and the massing of the Cavalry Corps on Billotte's right, although he left that at Billotte's option. That evening he brought General Besson and his Third Army Group headquarters to oversee the Sixth and Seventh Armies on the Somme.[44] And that was as far as he went. Gamelin's word carried no weight.

Gamelin met Dill, who reaffirmed that the BEF would remain under French orders; he brought an offer from General Ironside to join Gamelin in the north where they could make their authority felt to advantage. Georges joined them, then left to take a call from Billotte. Billotte told him that the Cavalry Corps had not yet regrouped to strike toward Saint-Quentin, although reconnaissances in that direction found no major enemy units.[45] The enemy seemed to be pressing rather weakly to the west and south of the Mormal Forest. Billotte expected to lose Le Quesnoy and perhaps Bavai. The 3rd Corps of the First Army was behind the frontier, but the 5th Corps had been held up in the Maubeuge area, and, with the enemy on its right and perhaps on its rear, would try to break out to the

French Escaut. Then Billotte dropped a bombshell: he had seen Gort in the first hours of the morning; they had reached no decision but he had heard that the British were going to evacuate the Continent. He proposed to ask Gort to join in a common retreat to the northwest. Georges replied that he preferred a retreat toward Arras with a screen of armor to the south; he would ask the British to join this movement. Georges returned to the Gamelin-Dill conference and unloaded the news. But Gamelin repeated Dill's assurance that the British would remain under French command; Georges passed this assurance to Billotte.

In fact, the British command in London faced the same problem with the BEF that Gamelin had with Georges. After Billotte's meeting with Gort, Pownall and apparently Gort too got the impression that most of the French First Army—not just the Ninth Army—was lost or shortly would be. The British commanders scraped together forces, including the 50th Infantry, for a front to their rear. They believed that the BEF would find itself cut off from the French to the southeast "except for such remnants of III French Corps as might adhere to us"; Gort and Pownall thought they might have to retreat to a Channel port for evacuation. That afternoon Pownall called the Director of Military Operations in London and told him "in guarded language . . . the way our minds were running, what might become necessary if circumstances went wrong. He was singularly stupid and unhelpful. . . ." Pownall's suggestion that the BEF might abandon the fight touched off a furor in the British War Cabinet and staff. Later, however,

> The First French Army reappeared from somewhere . . . and the evening ended tranquilly.
>
> But my God what a morning! And my God how awful to be allied to so tempermental a race![46]

The threat of British evacuation was over for the moment. But more serious was Léopold's decision to capitulate, although he took no action for the moment. The alliance was crumbling just as Gamelin, Ironside, and Dill prepared to try one last time to reestablish a coalition front.

That afternoon Georges built up his front on the Somme; at 1:50 p.m. he sent Billotte a telegram approving

> 'your earlier intentions aimed at launching—with the maximum of armored forces regrouped on your right wing—a braking attack *[coup d'arrêt]* toward the south onto the rear of the first echelon of the enemy forces in order to favor [your] withdrawal and reestablishment. . . . if the situation, of which you alone are the judge, allows you to envisage it, you might act with extreme audacity to avoid encirclement by forcing your way south to the Somme. You would have to regulate the British and Belgian retreat to match.'[47]

Billotte requested clarification, and at 4:45 p.m. Georges sent another telegram:

> '*Primo*—Feel it necessary that the three armies [Belgian, British, and French First] remain unified for the retreat which you will choose,
> *Secundo*—the most advantageous solution would be retreat direction south-west, the First Army withdrawing onto the Somme which I am hastening to occupy,
> *Tertio*—You alone remain judge of the choice of direction of the retreat in view of the situation on your right.'[48]

Georges thus reduced Gamelin's maneuver to an operation that Billotte would have to carry out on his own responsibility.

Billotte had a busy morning on the 19th. He decided to fix the new defense line on the Escaut as far south as Cambrai. From there the front would follow the incomplete Canal du Nord to the Seventh Army on the Somme. Billotte intended the Cavalry Corps, reinforced with the 1st DLM, to reach the Somme by moving from Cambrai toward Saint-Quentin. But the Cavalry Corps still lacked its armor; Billotte sent out another order that evening demanding that the armor return to Prioux immediately.[49] Meanwhile, the enemy command reinforced the breakthrough area with Hoepner's Panzers; that evening leading German elements reached the line Le Quesnoy-Solesmes-Cambrai facing north, and Péronne facing south.

Gamelin met Weygand that afternoon at Vincennes. Weygand caught up on the situation, then asked permission to visit Georges. Gamelin gave it, adding that Weygand might help prop Georges up; Weygand turned to go, remarking, "'You know that Paul Reynaud has no love for you?'" to which Gamelin could only reply "'I know'."[50] There could be no doubt in Gamelin's mind—Weygand was to replace him. In fact Gamelin had lost the confidence of the troops and officer corps. Gamelin phoned Georges to ask if the operation was proceeding smoothly—"'But of course'"—but it made little difference now. Minart that evening reported that nothing was being done: Georges must be replaced. "General Gamelin listened silently. His hands separated, then lifted in a gesture which meant: 'What for?' There was nothing left to do but click heels and leave."[51]

Weygand met Reynaud and Pétain that evening; he accepted the supreme command: "Distance had spared me the psychological shock of the first reverses; I felt myself capable of an intense energy. I hoped that I had the force to communicate to all those who might have lost courage for an instant, the faith and will which drove me."[52] Weygand had had only three hours of sleep on the flight to France—he was going to bed. He agreed by phone with Gamelin to take command the next morning: the High Command sat motionless, waiting for its new chief. But the news that Weygand was taking over renewed hopes: perhaps France would still be saved!

In the Field

In the morning of May 19 the 4th DCR, reinforced with a battalion of infantry support tanks and some SOMUA tanks, attacked from Laon toward Crécy in Guderian's left rear. By 9:00 a.m. D2 tanks broke into Crécy, but the town was full of mines, antitank defenses, and PzKpfw IV's. The enemy counterattacked from the west; that night the 4th DCR, having suffered heavy losses, fought to hold Laon.[53] Air cover was arranged with d'Astier, but last minute changes in plan did not reach air headquarters until too late: the 4th DCR suffered from the attentions of the Luftwaffe.

To the west Guderian, beset by logistics problems, was surprised when tanks of the 2nd DCR counterattacked in the Saint-Quentin area toward the Oise and approached his advanced headquarters. But his 10th Panzer forced the French back to the Crozat Canal that evening.[54] To Guderian the counterattacks seemed scattered and planless. That night he had his 1st and 2nd Panzers on a front from Cambrai to Péronne while his 10th secured his left flank: he gave the order to go for the coast the next day.

The 5th Corps of the First Army again lost touch with neighboring units, worrying General Aymes commanding the 4th Corps. Finding his right rear open to the enemy, Aymes swung his whole force about, facing southeast on the French Escaut at Denain near Valenciennes. But the enemy put no pressure on him on the 19th[55]—and with good reason, for they were locked in bitter and confused combat in the Mormal Forest with the 5th Corps, elements of the 1st DLM, and other bits and pieces of the Ninth Army. Altmayer's 5th was in a terrible position: his 12th Motorized was in Belgium retreating toward the frontier; his 43rd Infantry was fighting in Maubeuge against German mechanized troops from the south and east; and that evening his 5th North African sortied to try to clear the Mormal.

Eight battalions of North Africans (two from the 43rd) attacked behind a battalion of infantry support tanks, two squadrons of Hotchkiss and some SOMUA tanks from the 2nd DLM. In confused fighting the eastern column moved down the Sambre almost as far south as Berlaimont by nightfall; the western column pushed a bit south of Bavai before grinding to a halt.[56] Meanwhile, part of the 1st DLM lay encircled near Le Quesnoy, while the rest withdrew to the French Escaut, joining the Cavalry Corps. German attacks across the Sambre north of Maubeuge failed before the 101st Fortress Infantry and the 5th Corps. But Altmayer's position, surrounded on three sides and under heavy pressure from the south and southwest, was critical.

The rest of Blanchard's tired troops reached the frontier while elements of the Ninth Army and the 25th Motorized from the old Seventh Army built a new line at Douai to face south, covering the rear of the First Army Group.[57] The reconnaissance group of the 25th was driven out of Cambrai, while the mass of the division languished in Belgian trains waiting to move south. General Molinié complained of sabotage and a Belgian railroad strike! Whatever the reasons, his division was not in place until May 21. Prioux spent the day trying to regroup his cavalry. He waited vainly for the First Army to release the tank brigades of his 2nd and 3rd DLM, while the 1st DLM fought alone west of the Mormal. He reported this situation to Billotte, who ordered him to place his force between Douai and Arras facing south on the Scarpe River. At the end of the day most of his men were in place, but there was no sign of his tanks or of the 1st DLM.

During the 19th Gort did his best to prolong the front facing south through the rear area of the BEF. He ordered his reconnaissance regiment to Arras and put his 50th Infantry just north of the city.[58] Inside Belgium, the German Army Group B conquered a bridgehead over the Belgian Escaut, although the BEF counterattacked. By day's end the BEF was mostly on the Belgian Escaut; its 50th Division was concentrating north of Arras with the British 5th Division nearby in reserve.

By this time the incomplete 12th and 23rd British Territorial Infantry Divisions were the only Allied elements between Guderian and the sea. The 23rd held sixteen miles of the incomplete Canal du Nord; the 12th had strongpoints in Albert, Doullens, Amiens, and Abbeville. On May 19 the Panzers forced the Canal du Nord and flanked the 23rd through Péronne, pushing its remains toward Arras.[59]

In the Air

Gort and his air commanders agreed that the British Air Component, exposed to the enemy advance, should leave France; three squadrons of fighters did so on May 19. Meanwhile, the 600 first-line and 200 reserve machines of Fighter Command sat idle in England.[60] D'Astier mustered a bare 154 fighters (there were a further 65 in the Eastern and 37 in the Southern Zones) and 11 modern and 30 old bombers. He concentrated his forces to give Groupment 23 130 fighters plus a further group due from the rear. Early that morning Têtu ordered the bombing effort to support de Gaulle; British bombers attacked a German tank formation, but a force of Lioré 451's preparing to hit the same target was put out of action on the ground by the Luftwaffe. Twenty dive-bombers of the French navy attacked enemy mechanized forces east of the Mormal Forest, doing heavy damage; half did not return. That evening Têtu gave first priority for fighter cover for the next day to the First Army, second to the Somme front; bombers were to act on enemy columns in the First Army's rear.[61]

May 20: The View from the Top

At 9:00 a.m. Weygand took over direction of the defense of the West. He spoke with Gamelin, discussing his directive of the previous day, the Levant, even the political situation. The two toured the headquarters, then

Gamelin left, ending fifty years of military service. It seemed to Weygand that Gamelin was glad to be relieved of the responsibility. In any case Weygand still believed in victory.[62] There had been blunders, bad luck; the enemy was better armed and more "maneuverable" than expected; France's Allies had not furnished the support counted on; but "in pulling things back in hand, I thought it possible to hold out until the moment when the elite divisions of the Wehrmacht ran out of breath, when we would find units of lesser quality before us. Then we would have a respite and a chance to reestablish ourselves. . . ."[63] Weygand saw Georges at La Ferté, then talked to General Besson of Army Group Three, arriving to command the Sixth and new Seventh Armies. Besson's force was to attack north as soon as possible from the Somme toward Arras; to lead the attack he was to get the 4th DCR and 3rd Light Cavalry from the Sixth Army and the 2nd DCR, to be rebuilt with three battalions formed at tank-training centers, and six squadrons of tanks from cavalry-training centers forming the de Langle de Cary group. None of these units was immediately ready. That afternoon Weygand talked by telephone with Prételat. He asked if Gamelin's order for the Second Army's counteroffensive had been acted on; Prételat replied that he had never heard of it—Huntziger, however, was conducting an active defense with the 3rd DCR. Weygand withdrew the 7th Corps with two infantry divisions from its position facing Switzerland.[64] He adopted the thrust of Gamelin's directive: he would cut the enemy in two where the gap in the Allied front was smallest, between Arras and Péronne. Besson's attack was the southern jaw of the pincers. The problem was the northern jaw: Billotte had to provide the major effort. His forces were the most threatened, but they were ready while Besson's were still forming. Unfortunately, by this time the Allies had already lost 27 out of 137 major units. The Germans too had suffered, particularly their airborne, mechanized, and motorized troops, but no units other than airborne forces had yet fallen out of their order of battle.

That morning Dill came to see Georges and Weygand with an urgent message. Unless "energetic measures" were taken, the BEF would find its communications cut and might have to retreat to the Channel and evacuate. Dill had an alternative: Billotte should attack southward. Dill promised the cooperation of the BEF in this venture, then put the question to Georges, who replied that Billotte could do no more than fill the gaps in his front. Just then Billotte called; Weygand took the line. The decisive moment had come: Billotte must attack toward Cambrai with all his strength—

> It is by attacking and fighting like dogs that we will finish the Panzers, which must be at the end of their tether *[à bout de souffle]*. We must not limit our operations to installing ourselves on obstacles and remaining on the defensive, that would be to play their game. We will always be outflanked and forestalled. Attack to the south.[65]

This order came just as the commanders in the north reached crucial decisions. Morale at Billotte's headquarters was in a perilous state that morning, as the Belgian liaison officer reported, leading Van Overstraeten to propose that the First Army Group form a huge bridgehead in the Pas de Calais. If that were not done, he feared the BEF might evacuate the Continent. Meanwhile, General Ironside, the Chief of the Imperial General Staff, arrived at BEF headquarters carrying a message from the War Cabinet that the BEF was to fight toward Amiens to the southwest—a move that Pownall thought a "scandalous (i.e. Winstonian) thing to do and in fact quite impossible. . . ."[66] Gort agreed that an attack toward Amiens was impossible; he proposed an operation southward with his 5th and 50th Divisions. With that commitment in hand Ironside hurried off with Pownall to see Billotte and Blanchard.

The British officers found the French at Blanchard's headquarters; as Pownall described in his diary, "They were in a proper dither, even Blanchard who is not *nerveux.* But the two of them and Alombert [Blanchard's chief of staff] were all three *shouting* at one moment—Billotte shouted loudest, trembling, that he had no means to deal with tanks and that if his infantry were put into line they would not withstand attack." Ironside wrote in his diary that he found Billotte and Blanchard ". . . in a state of complete depression. No plan, no thought of a plan. Ready to be slaughtered. Defeated at the head without casualties. *Très fatigués* [worn out] and nothing doing. I lost my temper and shook Billotte by the button of his tunic. The man is completely beaten." Ironside's intervention had a calming effect; Gort telephoned to confirm his attack plan for the next morning, and Billotte agreed to join the operation. Pownall confided to his diary that "Nobody minds going down fighting but the long and many days of defence and recently the entire lack of higher direction and action, have been terribly wearing on the nerves of all of us."[67] But it was the French who bore the weight of the assault, and Billotte who suffered most from the lack of direction by Gamelin and Georges.

Billotte then talked by phone with Weygand, as noted above, and Pownall remarked that Weygand gave him "a good shake up."[68] Ironside told Weygand that Billotte should be removed, but Weygand planned to come north himself the next morning. In Pownall's mind the attack they were planning would be "do or die"—he so informed the French.[69] Ironside, noting that Weygand would be there the next day, returned to London. In retrospect this was a mistake. Ironside's determination to reach an interallied solution and his authority would be sorely missed.

Around noon on May 20 the British mission at Belgian headquarters reported that Gort was concentrating three divisions for a stroke south and asked the Belgians to replace the British 4th Infantry at Audenarde. Léopold agreed, but that night put off the relief until the evening of the 21st.[70] Following his conference with Ironside, Billotte gathered forces for the

French attack. French cavalry discovered the enemy moving south of Cambrai and Arras, but the enemy advance was only lightly covered to the north: the French ran into General Rommel escorted by a couple of armored vehicles, knocked out the armor and held Rommel surrounded for several hours. That afternoon, finding that the First Army had still not given up Prioux's tanks, Billotte demanded they return immediately, threatening to court-martial any who disobeyed the order.

In the Field

On May 20 Panzers reached the sea, severing Allied forces in Belgium from the French army to the south. Along the southern flank of the German breakthrough, the French Second and Sixth Armies fought indecisively with conventional and, farther west, motorized German infantry. Only the 10th Panzer stood behind this screen, but its intervention pinned down the 4th DCR, which withdrew to move west during the day, and the 2nd DCR which, reduced by 64 percent in material and 18 percent in personnel and changing commanders (Perré replaced Bruché), had to muster its tanks just to hold the Crozat Canal.[71] Just north of the Somme Guderian's Panzers trampled the two British Territorial divisions which stood between them and the sea. Amiens and Albert fell by that evening, their defenders in flight. That night the 1st Panzer faced both north toward the rear of Army Group One and south toward the remains of the British Territorials and the new Seventh Army. Guderian's 2nd Panzer drove to Abbeville and pushed elements to the coast that night. Then Guderian waited for Kleist to decide the next move. Only a few of the British in Abbeville got back over the Somme; farther north the British in Doullens were driven out by the 6th Panzer. By the end of May 20 the British 12th and 23rd Infantry were practically out of action. Farther north the 8th Panzer met practically no resistance between Doullens and the southern elements of the First Army Group; on its right Rommel's 7th Panzer found tougher going from Cambrai toward Arras.

At Arras, meanwhile, Gort assembled his 5th and 50th Infantry and his 1st Army Tank Brigade, reduced by breakdowns to fifty-eight weakly armed Mark I and only sixteen powerful Mark II tanks, under General Sir Harold Franklyn. Gort ordered Franklyn to cut the roads south of Arras to prevent the enemy using it as a communications center. Franklyn was also to occupy the Scarpe River east of Arras to reach the French. After Ironside's arrival the idea began to circulate that Franklyn was to begin an offensive to the south, but no new orders went to Franklyn—he was not told that his operation was now part of an Allied counteroffensive.[72] Gort and Pownall, while promising Ironside and the French to participate in the interallied counteroffensive, contemplated only a limited operation to protect their rear.

Prioux regrouped his cavalry on the Scarpe in preparation for a thrust southwest of Arras with the tanks of the 3rd DLM which had finally arrived. Prioux intended to contact the British in Arras, then probe south. The orders were issued when word came in from First Army to hold on the Scarpe. This counterorder disillusioned the cavalry; it resulted from the decision to employ the whole Cavalry Corps as part of the counteroffensive. Then General Franklyn arrived, finding Prioux with Blanchard and Altmayer; Billotte came in later. The French generals discussed possible operations to the south: Franklyn first learned of the projected Allied offensive. The French asked if Franklyn could attack toward Bapaume the next day; he declined to go beyond his orders, but proposed that Prioux reinforce the operation south of Arras, British troops relieving the French cavalry on the Scarpe. Prioux agreed. Later the French generals decided they could not begin their operation toward Cambrai until May 22—again disillusioning BEF headquarters; Franklyn went ahead with his planned operation, receiving no further orders from Gort. That night the British relieved Prioux's 3rd DLM which moved west of Arras; Prioux recovered most of the 1st DLM—forty-five tanks and two battalions of motorized cavalry at 35 percent strength—but the remainder, one battalion of motorized cavalry and ten tanks, stood siege in Le Quesnoy.

While the Allies formed a front around Arras, Altmayer's 5th Corps had to fight through the 3rd, 4th, and 5th Panzers to reach the First Army on the French Escaut. Pockets of troops from the First and Ninth Armies continued to hold the lower Sambre and Maubeuge for some time, but on the evening of May 20 remaining units of the 5th North African in the Mormal Forest fought their way out to the northwest, bringing back ten tanks.[73] The 43rd Infantry got back via Bavai to Valenciennes under cover of the remaining tanks of the 2nd DLM; the 12th Motorized came back through Valenciennes in fairly good shape since enemy pressure from the north was not so strong. The 12th went into reserve for the 4th Corps; the 5th North African and the 43rd Infantry had to be regrouped. Meanwhile, General Aymes relieved his tired 1st Moroccans, who had lost heavily in the Gembloux gap, with the 4th Infantry which finally arrived via the Belgian railroads.

By the end of May 20 the First Army held a stable front on the frontier facing into Belgium at Condé, then southeast along the French Escaut until the Cavalry Corps and Franklyn's force prolonged the front facing south along the Scarpe to Arras. The 25th Motorized from the old Seventh Army would provide the offensive punch of the First Army on May 22;[74] Franklyn's force and the 3rd DLM would attack the next day from Arras. Could these attacks regain the initiative, or would the four tired Panzers, already west of Arras, be able to swing north into the open rear of the First Army Group between Arras and the sea?

In the Air

On the 20th the last of the British Air Component flew back to England. Of the 261 Hurricanes sent to France, 66 returned. However the sixteen Hurricane squadrons of No. 11 Group in England were charged with air cover for the First Army Group, which by now was almost out of effective range of the Armée de l'air.[75] D'Astier mustered 110 fighters in the morning of May 20 (there were 45 in the Eastern and 35 in the Southern Zones), and had 24 modern and 33 old bombers plus some naval dive-bombers. The British Advanced Air Striking Force, based now behind the Sixth Army, was down to 30 fighters and 30 bombers; Bomber Command in Britain had 200 machines in line.

The High Command directed maximum effort to hindering the movements of enemy columns toward the right rear of the First Army Group. Bomber Command in England sent two expeditions of twenty-four planes over Saint-Quentin and Cambrai, but these operated on intelligence several hours old; the RAF took no effective part in the day's fighting.[76] The French sent six Lioré 451's and fourteen assault bombers into the same area. Three Allied bombers were lost. It was at this point that Assault Groupment 19 began to use its Potez 633 trainers in combat. Fourteen French naval dive-bombers hit a crossing point over the Oise; seven were lost. These efforts were insufficient to halt the German exploitation: only ground forces could do that. Weygand's trip to the north and the decisions resulting from it would be decisive.

May 21: The View from the Top

Weygand flew up to the First Army Group in the early morning of May 21. Reynaud and Pétain expressed their unhappiness over his taking such risks; Weygand later claimed that he had to promise to return the same evening (Reynaud later denied this). But Weygand's presence was vital if the Allies were to mount a coherent operation.[77] He drove to Le Bourget and after some confusion found a fast bomber and escort. At his behest the bomber flew over the Somme battlefield and the terrain farther north, then landed at Norrent-Fontes—to find the airfield deserted! Weygand set off himself but returned shortly after, and the group took off again, this time landing near Calais. Weygand ordered the fighters back: they would be needed. The bomber was to wait until 7:00 p.m.: if he had not returned by then, it would return without him.[78] At Calais he met General Champon, head of the French Military Mission to Belgium, and they set out to meet King Léopold at Ypres.

Meanwhile, Georges issued a new general order at 10:20 a.m. The tired German Panzers seemed to have marked time on May 20 on the line Cambrai-Péronne while covering their southern flank with two Panzers in

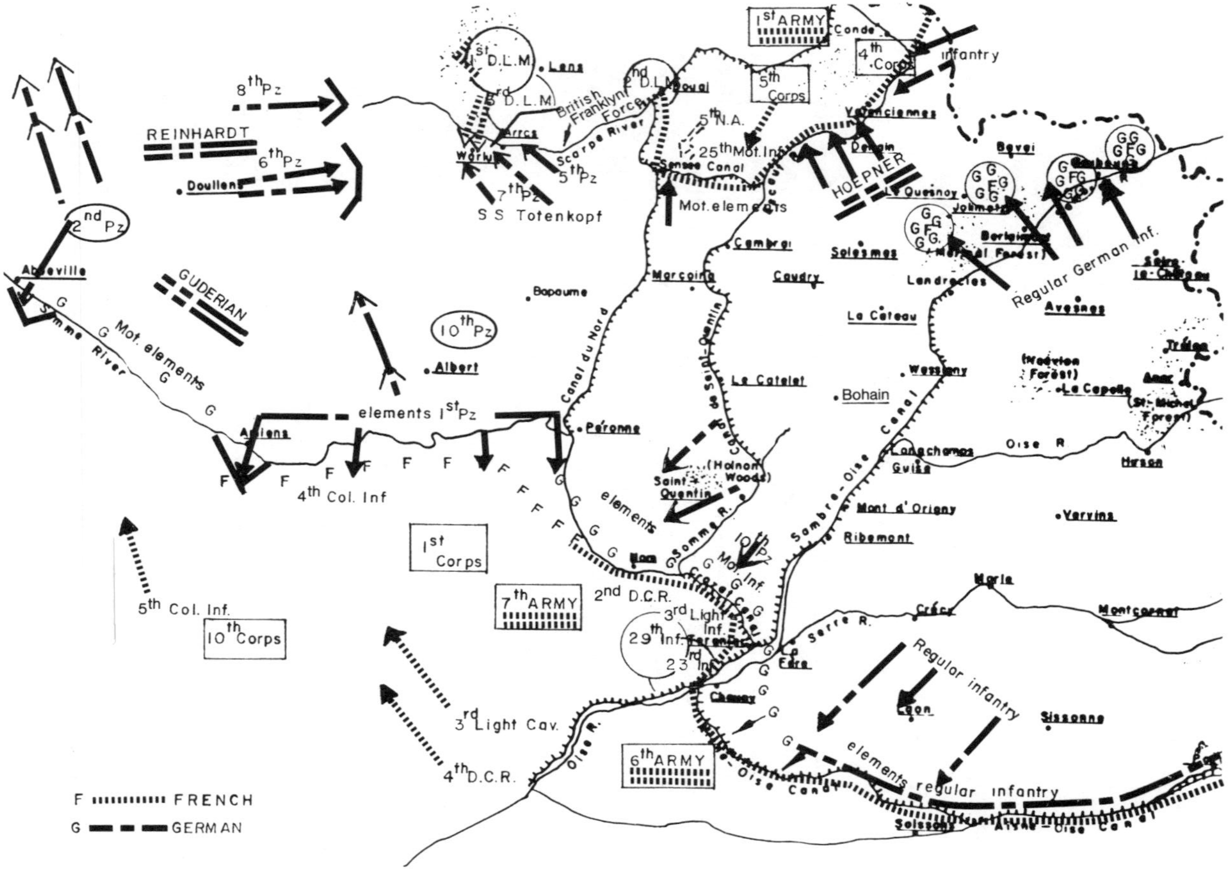

F FRENCH

G GERMAN

The Situation, May 21, 1940

the Ham-Laon area and conventional infantry farther east; the enemy might still pursue his advance to the northwest on May 21. Georges urged his troops to maintain a strong antitank barrage and to conduct an active defense, penetrating the rear areas of the enemy forces facing south. The Seventh Army was to prepare an offensive from Péronne toward Bapaume as soon as possible, the Second Army an offensive toward Sedan.[79] But the Seventh Army was not yet assembled.

Weygand reached Ypres where he was to meet Léopold at 3:00 p.m. Arriving early, he met the chief ministers of the Belgian government. He told them he wanted the Belgian army to retreat west to shorten the Allied front facing north so more troops could attack south. The Belgian ministers agreed. To them Belgium was a member of the coalition and must stand by the Allies, who had marched to their aid on May 10. Léopold, however, felt no great sense of responsibility toward his Allies—it was their defeat that had forced him to abandon most of his country. Besides, Léopold thought the Allied cause hopeless. He and the ministers divided sharply. The ministers eventually retired to sanctuary in France after Léopold excluded them from the meeting. Léopold and Van Overstraeten went into conference with Weygand and Champon. Weygand wanted the Belgian army to fall back onto the Yser River to the southwest. Moving by night the Belgian army—which still had substantial forces—could free most or all of the BEF and the French First Army for the strike south. But time was of the essence: that day two British infantry divisions were to attack from Arras, while the next day three French divisions would attack north from the Somme and the 5th Corps would attack south at Cambrai. Weygand asked that the motorized Belgian Cavalry Corps join these operations, offering the two series B infantry divisions of General Fagalde's 16th Corps, already on the Belgian left, in exchange.[80] Léopold asked Van Overstraeten for his opinion.

Van Overstraeten felt that another retreat would ruin the Belgian army; the left of the army should stand in place while its right swung around to the coast, forming a bridgehead which could be supplied by sea.[81] Weygand insisted that the Belgian army remain linked to Allied forces. Léopold wanted to hear the British view. Van Overstraeten then set out to contact Lord Gort who, it seems, had not received notice of the time and place of the meeting. Van Overstraeten finally reached him and Gort left for Ypres.

As Van Overstraeten returned, Generals Billotte and Fagalde arrived; a second conference started. Weygand had not seen Billotte for a long time: "the fatigue and the anguish of the last two weeks had left a heavy mark on him, but he [Billotte] understood the capital interest of the maneuver to be executed and shared my feeling of its urgency." Billotte reviewed the situation:

> He insisted with conviction on the irresistibility of the attack of the Panzer-divisionen: "Under their assault combined with ground attacks by *Stukas*, whether it be in the open field or on well prepared positions (excepting permanent fortifications), ordinary divisions are broken in an incredibly short time. The Ninth Army suffered the experience three times."[82]

This was an exaggeration: the First Army withstood the Panzers in the Gembloux gap, while the fronts of the Ninth Army were improvised and strung out. Billotte estimated that seven Panzers were on the meridian of Cambrai (most were farther west by this time) with 3,000-3,500 tanks—a gross exaggeration. Several divisions of the First Army had suffered severely; all were exhausted. Billotte thought the BEF possessed offensive potential, but the British attitude was uncertain; the Belgian attitude would also be important. Indeed British and Belgian participation was essential. But although Weygand did not know it, Léopold was thinking mostly of the how's and when's of capitulation; Gort and Pownall had lost faith in their Allies and did not believe that a British attack from the north could be decisive. At this crucial meeting Léopold was less than candid; the British failed to appear at all. Weygand did the best he could under the circumstances, leaving Billotte to fill in the gaps.

Weygand stated that it would be acceptable if the Belgians, instead of moving to the Yser, relieved part of the BEF. Léopold accepted; the French could retrieve Fagalde's corps as well. Weygand agreed, or so Van Overstraeten felt; all that remained was to get British agreement. Weygand also wanted to call the RAF into action. Van Overstraeten went to search for Gort.[83] Gort's failure to appear left Weygand in a dilemma: as Foch's chief of staff in 1918 he had learned how important personal contact between Allied leaders was. He considered staying overnight, counting on his plane to get back to Paris for the government meeting the next day. But Admiral Jean Abrial arrived with news that Calais airfield was being bombed: Weygand ordered his aircraft back, fearing it would be destroyed. He accepted Abrial's offer of a destroyer to return to France and set off that evening for Dunkirk.

Back at Ypres a third conference opened as Gort and Pownall finally arrived. Accounts of this meeting disagree, but the outlines are clear. Gort told Billotte that the offensive at Arras had gone in and would continue the next day—this was not true—and then asked about French participation. Billotte replied that only the 25th Motorized and 2nd North African Infantry were fit for an attack: he asked for more British troops, offering to relieve British units in line. Pownall objected that logistical difficulties made it impossible for the BEF to deliver a major offensive, but the discussion turned to details of the relief.[84] Gort stated that his corps commanders insisted that the BEF in Belgium first fall back to the French frontier defenses; the relief would have to take place in the night of May 22-23. The

Belgian army would relieve one British division in the night of May 22-23, another the next night, but the Belgians refused to send their Cavalry Corps south to Saint-Omer where Billotte's flank lay open between Arras and the sea. Billotte replied that then he would have to keep the 1st DLM in line. Billotte also decided to leave Fagalde's corps with the Belgians. Finally, there was the Belgian retreat: Gort's decision to pull back to the frontier forced the Belgians to fall back in step. According to Gort and Pownall, the Belgian command accepted a retreat to the Yser; Van Overstraeten recorded that they would go no farther than the Lys River. After the conference, however, he claimed that he decided to continue to the Yser.

Be that as it may, vital decisions came out of these conferences. First, Weygand imposed his plan for an offensive from the north. Second, at Billotte's urging it was agreed that the main effort was to come from the BEF which had not yet seen heavy action as a whole. The Belgians and French agreed to relieve British divisions starting the next night to bolster this offensive, despite Pownall's objections. The British and Belgians decided on a retreat to the French frontier and the Lys (eventually perhaps the Yser), delaying the relief of the British units. But Weygand had not met Gort, had not convinced him of the necessity of the British offensive. The interallied support and authority that Ironside had exercised were sorely missed on the 21st. Pownall and Gort agreed to the offensive, but they clearly had reservations, as Van Overstraeten noted:

> The conference closed towards 9:30 p.m. on the affirmation of the French generals that the British attack could still have a decisive influence, but neither Gort nor Pownall seemed convinced of it.
>
> "You must do it, Sir" [in English] Fagalde put in.
>
> But Gort confided to the King in leaving: "It's a bad job!" [in English].[85]

Hope for another Miracle of the Marne hung by a thread.

In the Field

On May 21 Guderian received orders from Kleist to advance north, although his 10th Panzer was taken from him to form a reserve. Guderian ordered his 1st and 2nd Panzers toward Calais and Boulogne, directly threatening Billotte's flank west of Arras. Guderian's forces did not move until the next day; in the meantime, he noted, Kleist's staff "became a bit nervous"[86]—the Allies had counterattacked. In the morning of May 21 Franklyn mustered two columns under General Sir Giffard le Q. Martel, the 1st Army Tank Brigade leading two battalions of infantry—all that Franklyn felt he could spare. Prioux put in the 3rd DLM west of the city, reinforcing it with tanks from the First Army. Prioux's 2nd DLM fought off attacks east of Arras, while he grouped tanks from the 1st DLM west of Arras to protect the open flank of the array. Prioux was unhappy: the Arras attack was stronger than the probing operation he had been forced to cancel on May 20, but it lacked flexibility—a mistake in his view. Early that afternoon the British and then the French attacked. Ground resistance and air attacks were heavy; the British suffered heavy tank losses although the attack made progress. That evening Franklyn decided that the enemy was going to flank his position to the west; he ordered his columns back to Arras. The French held that night while their mechanized units assisted infantry of the British right column; later Prioux pulled his 2nd and 3rd DLM into defensive positions and sent his 1st DLM west to counter the flanking threat.[87] But if the operation seemed no more than a raid from the Allied point of view—and gave rise to no thought of a further advance, despite what Gort said at Ypres—it impressed the SS Totenkopf Division, a green formation, and Rommel's 7th Panzer. Rommel estimated the Allied strength at *five* divisions; when SS troops panicked, Rommel had to personally take charge of artillery and Flak firing at pointblank range.

The German command ordered Reinhardt's corps to swing back east toward Arras to contain the threat. It also put out a call for infantry: "A certain air of panic *[eine leichte Panikstimmung]* dominated the staffs. We remembered well the 'Miracle of the Marne'. . . ."[88] General Franz Halder, Chief of Staff of the German Army, noted in his diary that the Arras battle would be decisive: when German infantry reached Arras behind the mechanized and motorized elements, the battle would be won. In the meantime Rundstedt's Army Group A was to stand on the defensive there while Guderian resumed his advance to the Channel ports. The Allies at Arras had gained the initiative locally, but Panzers farther west remained free to press into Billotte's open flank.

Into that gap Billotte, unable to obtain Belgian cavalry, could only send his own cavalry, although the French 21st Infantry (from the old Seventh Army at Ghent) boarded Belgian trains that night. Many of its elements ended up defending Boulogne.[89] Some French fortress troops and scratch British formations were also there; soon part of the 1st Armoured Division arrived from Britain. The bulk of the 1st Armoured began concentrating west of Paris. That evening the incomplete formation was ordered to the Somme to join the new Seventh Army to strike north. But the British armor did not reach its post for several days.

General Frère's Seventh Army could not attack northward with the 1st and 10th Corps until May 23, despite Besson's urgings. As Besson put it on May 21, "'It is no longer a question of retreating or of defending ourselves. We must attack, attack, attack to regain moral ascendancy and win the battle.'"[90]

Meanwhile, von Bock's Army Group B pressed the British on the Belgian Escaut, gaining a bridgehead and retraining it despite counterattacks.[91]

This threat led Gort's corps commanders to insist that the BEF retreat to the French frontier, delaying the relief of British divisions intended to join the offensive to the south. Altmayer's 5th Corps was still preparing its counterstroke. Two reconnaissance groups and an infantry regiment fought on the 22nd to within a few kilometers of Cambrai before the overextension of their front and heavy German air attacks halted them. Then the First Army ordered them back. Guderian's Panzers were free to push north on May 22; the Allied effort of the day consisted only of Altmayer's sortie.

In the Air

The RAF in England fought on May 21 to cover the armies in Belgium while the Armée de l'air supported the Somme front. That morning d'Astier had 110 fighters plus two groups arriving from the rear at the end of the day, while the Eastern Zone had forty-seven and the Southern eight. The arrival of new assault bombers raised d'Astier's total of modern bombers to thirty-four, plus fifty-three old machines; the British Advanced Air Striking Force in France added thirty-five bombers and thirty fighters.[92] The elements of the Armée de l'air training and reequipping enabled Vuillemin to shore up his frontline units. Georges ordered the effort concentrated on the lower Somme where seven assault bombers operated in two missions.

Georges still met resistance from the RAF which wanted to pursue attacks on the Ruhr. Georges wrote to Barratt, asking that Bomber Command concentrate on the rear of the German advance. The RAF gave in to this plea.[93] Meanwhile, fifty-seven Blenheims in four raids hit German columns between Arras and the coast, but these targets were attacked on the basis of hours-old reconnaissance reports—the only intelligence available to the RAF once the Air Component was back in England. French fighters from Groupment 23 were active covering the debarkation of troops on the Somme; a further mission was executed over the southern flank of the First Army. French fighters flew 320 sorties, losing, principally over the First Army, seven pilots killed and five wounded but claiming nineteen "certain" victories and six "probables."

But only an Allied counteroffensive could hope to change the situation. The chance lay in joint effort following the plans laid out at Ypres. Everything depended on General Gaston Billotte in the north. He had to drive Weygand's plan to execution. That night—May 21—as the last conference at Ypres broke up, word came in that refugee-crowded Béthune had been bombed. Billotte remarked his apprehension at having to pass that way in the dark: that night the Allied Commander in Chief in the north, speeding by car toward his headquarters, was in a terrible crash.[94] Billotte never regained consciousness and died two days later. General Champon tried to fill in Blanchard, who succeeded Billotte as the senior French commander, on the situation; but the thread that held the hope of salvation snapped. There would be no new Miracle of the Marne.

NOTES

1. General [Maxime] Weygand, *Mémoires* III (Paris: Flammarion, 1957), p. 79.

2. Pierre Bourget, "Les 'communications sécrètes du grand quartier général (10 mai-25 juin 1940),'" *L'Aurore* (November 5-6 to December 6, 1949), issue of November 10, p. 4; Jacques Minart, *P. C. Vincennes: Secteur 4* II (Paris: Berger-Levrault, 1945), pp. 164ff; quotes from Anonymous, *The Diary of a Staff Officer: (Air Intelligence Liaison Officer) at Advanced Headquarters North B.A.F.F. 1940* (London: Meuthuen, 1941), p. 21.

3. France, Le Général commandant en chef, Chef d'EM de la défense nationale, Commandant en chef les forces terrestres, "Ordre du jour n° 4" (unpublished, May 17, 1940).

4. "Extraits du rapport du général Georges," *Titre* V, p. 44; General G[aston] Roton, *Années cruciales: La Course aux armements (1933-1939). La Campagne 1939-1940)* (Paris: Charles-Lavauzelle, 1947), pp. 194ff; Georges' order in France, ESG, École d'état-major, [Lt.-Col. P. Gendry], *La Guerre 1939-1940 sur le front occidental* (Paris: Société française de presse, 1947), p. 64.

5. General [Gaston] Prételat, *Le Destin tragique de la ligne Maginot* (Paris: Berger-Levrault, 1950), p. 142; quote from France, Commandement en chef du front nord-est, EM, 3° Bureau: N° 1770 [?] 3/Op., "Ordre particulier n° 96 pour la VIIe Armée" (unpublished, May 17, 1940, at 1:00 p.m.); General Paul de Villelume, *Journal d'une défaite: Août 1939-Juin 1940* ([Paris]: Fayard, 1976), pp. 338ff.

6. Doumenc, *Dunkerque*, pp. 127, 136; Lyet, *La Bataille de France*, p. 65.

7. General [Raoul] Van Overstraeten, *Albert I-Léopold III: Vingt ans de politique militaire belge 1920-1940* ([Bruges]: Desclée de Brouwer, [1946?]) pp. 621ff; quotes from Brian Bond, ed., *Chief of Staff: The Diaries of Lieutenant-General Sir Henry Pownall.* I: *1933-1940* (Hamden, Conn.: Archon Books, 1973), pp. 318ff.

8. Bruché's testimony in France, Parlement, Assemblée nationale, *Les Événements survenus en France de 1933 à 1945: Témoignages et documents recueillis par la commission d'enquête parlementaire* V (Paris: Presses universitaires de France, [1950?]), p. 1230; testimony of Col. Perré in James de Coquet, *Le Procès de Riom* (Paris: Fayard, 1945), p. 287; R. P. Guy Bougerol, *Ceux qu'on n'a jamais vus . . .* (Grenoble and Paris: Arthaud, 1943), p. 113; Cdt. d'Ornano, "La 4e D.C.R. à Montcornet (Mai 1940)," *Revue de défense nationale* (May 1950):532ff; France, Ministère des armées, EMAT, Service historique, *Guerre, 1939-1945: Les Grandes unités françaises: Historiques succincts* III (Paris: Atelier d'impressions de l'armée, 1967), pp. 508ff; Charles de Gaulle, *War Memoirs* I, trans. Jonathan Griffin (London: Collins, 1955), pp. 38ff; Pierre Voisin, *Ceux des chars 45 jours 45 nuits* (Lyon and Paris: Éditions Archat, 1941), pp. 90ff.

9. Graf J[ohann] A. Kielmansegg, *Panzer zwischen Warschau und Atlantik* (Berlin: Verlag "Die Wehrmacht," 1941), pp. 133ff; General Heinz Guderian, *Erinnerungen eines Soldaten* (Heidelberg: Kurt Vowinckel Verlag, 1951), pp. 98ff;

Le Goyet, "Dans la tourmente de mai 1940: L'Engagement de la 2e division cuirassée française," *Revue historique de l'armée* (no. 1 1964): 161.

10. Hans-Adolf Jacobsen, ed., *Dokumente zum Westfeldzug 1940* (Göttingen: Musterschmidt Verlag, 1960), pp. 41ff; Guderian, *Erinnerungen*, pp. 98ff.

11. General A. [Joseph] Doumenc, *Histoire de la neuvième armée* (Grenoble and Paris: Arthaud, 1945), pp. 196ff, 241ff; *GU françaises* II, pp. 122ff.

12. Doumenc, *Histoire de la neuvième armée*, pp. 228ff, 243.

13. Capt. de Bellescize, "Carnet de route du Capitaine de Bellescize du 5e Régiment de dragons portés (10 mai au 18 mai 1940)," *Revue de l'armée française* no. 1 (October 1941): 24ff; Cdt. N[arcisse] Bourdon, *Le Second drame de Maubeuge: Histoire de la 101e Division de forteresse (84e et 87e R.I.F.)* (Fontenay-le-Comte: Imprimerie Lussaud frères, 1947), p. 157; Josef Remold, *Tagebuch eines Bataillons-Kommandeurs: Das III. Gebirgs-jäger-Rgt. 99 im Frankreichfeldzug* (Tettnang: Schild-Verlag, 1967), pp. 21ff; Hermann Teske, *Bewegungskrieg: Führungsprobleme einer Infanterie-Division im Westfeldzug 1940* (Heidelberg: Kurt Vowinckel Verlag, 1955), pp. 34ff.

14. Bourdon, *Le Second drame de Maubeuge*, pp. 171 passim; B[asil] H. Liddell Hart with Lucie-Maria and Manfred Rommel and General Fritz Bayerlein, eds., *The Rommel Papers*, trans. Paul Findlay (New York: Harcourt, Brace and Co., 1953), pp. 20ff.

15. Lord John Gort, *Despatches* (London: H.M.S.O., 1941), p. 5913; Major L. F. Ellis, *The War in France and Flanders 1939-1940* (London: H.M.S.O., 1953), p. 65; General René Prioux, *Souvenirs de guerre: 1939-1943* (Paris: Flammarion, 1947), pp. 85ff.

16. General de la Laurencie, *Les Opérations du IIIe corps d'armée en 1939-1940* (Paris: Charles-Lavauzelle, 1948), p. 63; General Henri Aymes, *Gembloux: Succès français. Le 4e Corps d'armée dans la bataille de la 1re armée en Belgique et en France 10 mai-3 juin 1940* (Paris: Berger-Levrault, 1948), p. 50; *GU françaises* I, pp. 136ff.

17. General Fagalde, "L'Affaire des îles de Zélande: (Walcheren et Sud Beveland). Mai 1940," *Revue militaire suisse* nos. 11 and 12 (November and December 1953): December article, p. 636; France, Marine nationale, EMG: Service historique, Hervé Cras, *Les Forces maritimes du Nord (1939-1940)* II (no place given, 1955), pp. 73ff; [Marcel] Lerecouvreux, *L'Armée Giraud en Hollande: (1939-1940)* (Paris: Nouvelles éditions latines, 1951), pp. 326ff.

18. France, [ZOAN], "Situation des avions disponibles: 10-31 mai 1940" (unpublished, no date); "Historique succint [sic] des opérations aériennes," *Titre* II, Chap. 3, pp. 38ff.

19. France, Message from Têtu to Vuillemin and response (unpublished, May 17, [1940] at 11:45 a.m. and 12:45 p.m.).

20. France, FACNE, EM, Section d'opérations, Message from Giraud at 6:15 a.m. (unpublished, May 17, 1940); "Historique succint [sic] des opérations aériennes," *Titre* II, Chap. 3., p. 41; France, FACNE, EM, Section d'opérations, Message from Têtu to d'Astier (unpublished, May 17, 1940, at 11:30 a.m.); Danel, "En Mai Juin . . .," p. 57.

21. Weygand, *Mémoires* III, pp. 80ff.

22. Gamelin's report in Jacques Weygand, *Weygand mon père* (Paris: Flammarion, 1970), pp. 486ff.

23. Quote from Gamelin, *Servir* III, p. 415; Minart, *P. C. Vincennes* II, pp. 176ff; France, Commandement en chef sur le front du nord-est, EM, 2ème Bureau: N° 1502/2.S., "Instruction pour la recherche du renseignement" (unpublished, May 18, 1940).

24. Quotes from Gamelin, *Servir* III, pp. 417ff; "Communications sécrètes," November 10 issue, p. 4.

25. Georges' order in Gendry, *La Guerre 1939-1940*, p. 66; France, Commandement en chef du front nord-est, EM, 3e Bureau: N° 1975 [?] 3/Op., "Ordre particulier n° 98 pour la VIIe Armée" (unpublished, May 18, 1940).

26. Gendry, *La Guerre 1939-1940*, p. 66; "Extraits du rapport du général Georges," *Titre* V, p. 46.

27. France, Commandement en chef du front nord-est, EM, 3° Bureau: N° 1596 3/Op., "Ordre particulier n° 102" (unpublished, May 18, 1940).

28. *Diary of a Staff Officer*, p. 22; Billotte's report in Roton, *Années cruciales*, p. 199; Doumenc, *Dunkerque*, pp. 148, 163.

29. Billotte's statement in Roton, *Années cruciales*, p. 200.

30. Billotte's orders in Lyet, *La Bataille de France*, pp. 71, 80.

31. Quotes from Bond, *Chief of Staff*, pp. 321ff; Gort, *Despatches*, p. 5915; Doumenc, *Dunkerque*, p. 166; Miles Reid, *Last on the List* (London: Leo Cooper, 1974), pp. 31-39; Brian Bond, *France and Belgium 1939-1940* (London: Davis-Poynter, 1975), pp. 107ff.

32. Le Goyet, "Dans la tourmente de mai 1940," p. 162.

33. *GU françaises* II, pp. 306ff; Giraud's order in Doumenc, *Histoire de la neuvième armée*, pp. 250ff.

34. Pierre Dunoyer de Segonzac, *Pierre Dunoyer de Segonzac le vieux chef: Mémoires et pages choisies* (Paris: Éditions du Seuil, 1971), pp. 69-72; Bourdon, *Le Second drame de Maubeuge*, pp. 205ff, 218; *GU françaises* III, pp. 400ff.

35. De Bellescize, "Carnets," pp. 26ff; testimony of General Véron in *Événements . . . Témoignages* V, pp. 1282, 1303.

36. Doumenc, *Dunkerque*, pp. 138ff; *GU françaises* II, pp. 48ff, 534ff.

37. Doumenc, *Dunkerque*, pp. 149, 168ff.

38. Ibid., p. 138; Ellis, *War in France and Flanders*, pp. 66ff; Van Overstraeten, *Albert I-Léopold III*, p. 626. For a differing account of the mood at British GHQ see Reid, *Last on the List*, pp. 37ff. This account however, written from memory in a German prisoner of war camp in 1942, is dubious.

39. "Situation des avions disponibles"; General [François] d'Astier de la Vigerie, *Le Ciel n'était pas vide: 1940* (Paris: Julliard, 1952), pp. 158ff; Paquier, *Aviation de bombardement*, pp. 68ff; "Historique succint [sic] des opérations aériennes," *Titre* II, Chap. 3., pp. 45ff; Danel, "L'Aviation d'assaut," pp. 25ff.

40. Gamelin, *Servir* III, pp. 427ff.

41. "Communications sécrètes," November 11 issue, p. 4; Maurice Gamelin, parts of a letter of November 14, 1949, *L'Aurore* (November 21, 1949): 4; Gamelin, *Servir* III, p. 430.

42. Minart, *P. C. Vincennes* II, p. 188; quotes from Gamelin, *Servir* I, pp. 3ff.

43. Interview with Georges in *Résistance* (July 17, 1946): 3; "Extraits du rapport du général Georges," *Titre* V, pp. 53ff. For a different interpretation of the events of May 19, see Pierre Le Goyet, *Le Mystère Gamelin* (Paris: Presses de la Cité, 197[6]), pp. 341-346.

44. France, Commandement en chef du front nord-est, EM, 3° Bureau: N° 1621 3/Op., "Ordre de service" (unpublished, May 19, 1940, at 9:00 p.m.).

45. Lyet, *La Bataille de France*, pp. 79ff; Roton, *Années cruciales*, pp. 207ff; Gamelin, *Servir* III, pp. 431ff; Doumenc, *Dunkerque*, pp. 173ff.

46. Quotes from Bond, *Chief of Staff*, pp. 321ff; James R. M. Butler, *Grand Strategy. Volume II: September 1939-June 1941* (London: H.M.S.O., 1957), p. 187; Henri de Man, *Cavalier seul: 45 Années de socialisme européen* (Geneva: Les Éditions du cheval ailé, 1948), pp. 223ff; letter from Admiral Keyes to Gort of June 6, 1940, in Joseph P. Kennedy and James M. Landis, *The Surrender of King Léopold* (New York: Kennedy Memorial Foundation, 1950), pp. 40ff. For a differing but dubious account of British intentions, see Reid, *Last on the List*, pp. 38ff.

47. Georges' telegram in Roton, *Années cruciales*, p. 208.

48. Ibid., pp. 208ff.

49. Doumenc, *Dunkerque*, pp. 168ff; Lyet, *La Bataille de France*, p. 81; Jacobsen, *Dokumente zum Westfeldzug*, pp. 50ff.

50. Quotes from Gamelin, *Servir* III, pp. 432ff; Weygand, *Mémoires* III, pp. 82ff.

51. Alain Darlan, *L'Amiral Darlan parle . . .* [sic] (Paris: Amiot Dumont, 1952), p. 54; Gamelin, *Servir* III, pp. 433ff; quote from Minart, *P. C. Vincennes* II, pp. 196ff.

52. Quote from Weygand, *Mémoires* III, pp. 85ff; Paul Baudouin, *Neuf mois au gouvernement (avril-décembre 1940)* (Paris: Éditions de la table ronde, 1948), p. 61; Gamelin, *Servir* III, p. 434; Edmond Jouhaux, *La Vie est un combat: Souvenirs (1924-1944)* ([Paris]: Fayard, 1974), pp. 170ff.

53. Pierre Voisin, *Ceux des chars 45 jours 45 nuits* (Lyon and Paris: Éditions Archat, 1941), pp. 101ff; *GU françaises* III, pp. 508ff; de Gaulle, *War Memoirs* I, pp. 40ff; Puget, "Historique des opérations," pp. 45ff.

54. Guderian, *Erinnerungen*, pp. 99ff; Le Goyet, "Dans la tourmente de mai 1940," pp. 162ff; *GU françaises* III, pp. 482ff; Kielmansegg, *Panzer zwischen Warschau und Atlantik*, pp. 136ff.

55. Aymes, *Gembloux*, pp. 58ff; *GU françaises* I, pp. 138ff.

56. Doumenc, *Dunkerque*, pp. 153ff; *GU françaises* II, pp. 920ff, III, pp. 402ff; Bourdon, *Le Second drame de Maubeuge*, pp. 216 passim; report of Capt. d'Almont of the 2nd DLM in ED, 4DA7, Dr 4, "Fiche N° 300"; France, SHAT, Baron Ernest Gedult von Jungenfeld, *So kämpften Panzer!* (French translation, no other information given), pp. 47-48.

57. De la Laurencie, *IIIe Corps*, pp. 65ff; Doumenc, *Dunkerque*, pp. 176ff; Prioux, *Souvenirs*, pp. 87ff; [General Molinié], *Mai 1940: La 25e Division motorisée (Division d'Auvergne) de Bréda à Lille et à Dunkerque* (Colombes: Imprimerie G. Leroux, 1956 [?]), p. 11.

58. Gort, *Despatches*, p. 5915; Ellis, *War in France and Flanders*, pp. 69ff.

59. Ellis, *War in France and Flanders*, pp. 76ff.

60. Richards, *Fight at Odds*, , p. 126; Danel, "En Mai Juin . . . ," p. 59; "Situation des avions disponibles"; d'Astier, *Le Ciel n'était pas vide*, p. 165; France, FACNE, EM, Section d'opérations, Message from Têtu to d'Astier (unpublished, May 19, 1940, at 2:30 a.m.).

61. Col. Pierre Paquier, *L'Aviation de bombardement française en 1939-1940* (Paris: Berger-Levrault, 1948), p. 73; Christian-Jacques Ehrengardt, "Bilan et chronologie de l'Aéronavale en guerre," *Icare* no. 61 (Winter-Spring 1972): 58ff; France,

FACNE, EM, Section d'opérations: 973-0, Message from Têtu to d'Astier (unpublished, May 19, 1940, at 7:05 p.m.).

62. Gamelin, *Servir* III, pp. 434ff; Weygand, *Mémoires* III, p. 87.

63. Jacques Weygand, *Weygand mon père*, p. 346.

64. Lyet, *La Bataille de France*, p. 86; Prételat, *Destin tragique*, pp. 150ff; *GU françaises* I, pp. 174ff, III, pp. 500ff; Weygand, *Mémoires* III, p. 93. For Allied losses in major units see Henri Michel, *The Second World War*, trans. Douglas Parmée (New York: Praeger, 1975), p. 114.

65. Dill's report in Ellis, *War in France and Flanders*, pp. 104ff; Weygand, *Mémoires* III, p. 93.

66. Van Overstraeten, *Albert I-Léopold III*, pp. 639ff; Bond, *Chief of Staff*, p. 323; Gort, *Despatches*, p. 5916.

67. Quotes from Bond, *Chief of Staff*, pp. 323ff and Sir Edmund Ironside, *Time Unguarded: The Ironside Diaries 1937-1940* (Edinburgh: Constable, 1962), pp. 321ff.

68. Ironside, *Time Unguarded*, pp. 321ff; quote from Bond, *Chief of Staff*, p. 324; Bond, *France and Belgium*, p. 115.

69. A different but rather dubious view in René de Chambrun, *I Saw France Fall: Will She Rise Again?* (New York: William Morrow, 1940), pp. 136ff.

70. Van Overstraeten, *Albert I-Léopold III*, pp. 642ff; Lyet, *La Bataille de France*, p. 81; Ellis, *War in France and Flanders*, p. 80.

71. Le Goyet, "Dans la tourmente de mai 1940," pp. 164ff; *GU françaises* III, pp. 482ff; Kielmansegg, *Panzer zwischen Warschau und Atlantik*, pp. 138ff; Guderian, *Erinnerungen*, pp. 100ff; Ellis, *War in France and Flanders*, pp. 80ff.

72. Ellis, *War in France and Flanders*, pp. 87ff; Prioux, *Souvenirs*, pp. 93ff.

73. Bourdon, *Le Second drame de Maubeuge*, pp. 215, 229ff; Doumenc, *Dunkerque*, pp. 154ff; Aymes, *Gembloux*, pp. 65ff.

74. *GU françaises* II, pp. 342ff.

75. Danel, "En Mai Juin . . . ," p. 59; "Situation des avions disponibles."

76. Ellis, *War in France and Flanders*, p. 83; "Historique succint [sic] des opérations aériennes," *Titre* II, Chap. 3, pp. 54ff; Ehrengardt, "Aéronavale en guerre," pp. 58ff; Danel, "L'Aviation d'assaut," pp. 25ff.

77. Weygand, *Mémoires* III, p. 95; Reynaud's testimony in *Événements . . . Témoignages* VIII, p. 2391; Paul-Alexandre Bourget, *De Beyrouth à Bordeaux: La Guerre 1939-40 vue du P. C. Weygand* (Paris: Berger-Levrault, 1946), pp. 33ff.

78. Col. Henri Lafitte, "Sur Amiot jusqu'au front . . . [sic]," and Col. Victor Veniel, "20 [sic] Mai 1940: À la recherche de l'armée française avec Weygand," *Icare* no. 55 (Autumn-Winter 1970): 68ff; Bourget, *De Beyrouth à Bordeaux*, pp. 33ff.

79. France, Commandement en chef du front nord-est, EM, 3° Bureau: N° 1636 3/Op., "Ordre général n° 16" (unpublished, May 21, 1940, at 10:20 a.m.).

80. Weygand, *Mémoires* III, pp. 98ff; Van Overstraeten, *Albert I-Léopold III*, p. 649.

81. Van Overstraeten, *Albert I- Léopold III*, pp. 649ff; Weygand, *Mémoires* III, pp. 99ff; Ellis, *War in France and Flanders*, pp. 106ff.

82. Quote from Weygand, *Mémoires* III, p. 101; Billotte's remarks in Van Overstraeten, *Albert I-Léopold III*, pp. 651ff.

83. Van Overstraeten, *Albert I-Léopold III*, pp. 652ff; Weygand, *Mémoires* III, pp. 102ff.

84. Van Overstraeten, *Albert I-Léopold III*, pp. 653ff; Bond, *Chief of Staff*, pp. 328ff; Gort, *Despatches*, p. 5918.

85. Van Overstraeten, *Albert I-Léopold III*, pp. 655ff.

86. Quote from Guderian, *Erinnerungen*, p. 102; Prioux, *Souvenirs*, pp. 96ff; Ellis, *War in France and Flanders*, pp. 88ff.

87. Prioux, *Souvenirs*, pp. 96ff; Ellis, *War in France and Flanders*, pp. 90ff; *The Rommel Papers*, pp. 30ff.

88. Quote from Teske, *Bewegungskrieg*, pp. 44ff; Jacobsen, *Dokumente zum Westfeldzug*, pp. 58ff.

89. Fagalde, "Odyssée d'une division française (La 21e Division française dans les Flandres en mai-juin 1940)," *Revue militaire suisse* nos. 3 and 5 (March and May 1954); Evans, "1st Armoured Division," November article, pp. 65ff.

90. *GU françaises* I, pp. 68ff, 242ff; Besson's order in Maxime Weygand, *Le Général Frère: Un chef. Un héros. Un martyr* (Paris: Flammarion, 1949), pp. 167ff.

91. Ellis, *War in France and Flanders*, pp. 100ff; *GU françaises* I, pp. 138ff; Molinié, *25e Division motorisée*, pp. 12-14.

92. "Situation des avions disponibles"; General Fleury Seive, *L'Aviation d'assaut dans la bataille de 1940* (Paris: Berger-Levrault, 1948), pp. 128ff; Paquier, *Aviation de bombardement*, pp. 80ff.

93. Paquier, *Aviation de bombardement*, pp. 81ff; Ellis, *War in France and Flanders*, pp. 97ff; Lt.-Col. Salesse, *L'Aviation de chasse française en 1939-1940* (Paris: Berger-Levrault, 1948), pp. 112ff.

94. Van Overstraeten, *Albert I-Léopold III*, pp. 654ff; Lyet, *La Bataille de France*, pp. 87ff.

chapter 10

EPILOGUE AND CONCLUSIONS

THE "FALL OF FRANCE"

Billotte's death eliminated the last hope for centralized direction of the Allied effort in the north. General Blanchard formally replaced Billotte on May 25, but Blanchard totally lacked the prestige necessary to influence the British and Belgians. The Allied armies tended even more to follow their own paths with a minimum of cooperation. The French and Belgians relieved part of the BEF, but by that time the enemy had regained the initiative from Valenciennes to the sea, and was making dangerous progress into the junction of the British and Belgian armies. Lord Gort diverted his strength to protect the front between Arras and the sea and to shore up the Belgian junction. Planning for an offensive continued, but the initiative had passed to the enemy for good.

Besson's Third Army Group attacked enemy bridgeheads south of the Somme with some success on May 23 and 24, but German infantry was by then present in force.[1] The chance for a strategic success was gone. The same situation prevailed in the north, where the Allies improvised a continuous front, aided by Rundstedt's and Hitler's desire to rest and refit their mechanized units; thereafter the British tended to plan for an evacuation. By May 26 it was clear there would be no Allied offensive. On May 28 Léopold, his army's morale shattered by German pressure while the remaining area of Belgium filled with refugees, capitulated. This doomed Weygand's last-minute hope of holding a viable bridgehead in the north. From that moment Gort hurried to get out, leaving part of the French First Army to cover the retreat of the British and remaining French forces. Several hundred thousand troops, mostly British, got away from Dunkirk under cover of the Spitfires of the RAF, which finally swung its whole weight into the battle. But the entire British force had to be rearmed and reorganized before it could reenter the fray.

Hitler had no intention of giving the Allies time to make good their losses. His forces had eliminated the Dutch and Belgians, driven the BEF, save one infantry and part of one armored division, from the Continent, and destroyed the best equipped of the French forces. Weygand's remaining force was spread behind the Maginot Line, the Aisne River, and the Somme, where his remaining armor fought unsuccessfully to drive the Germans from their bridgeheads. Weygand hoped to hold out until the forces that escaped from the north could reenter the battle. On June 5 the Wehrmacht dashed that hope by thrusting over the Somme and then the Aisne. The Germans now had better than a two to one superiority. The fighting was savage; for a day or two it seemed the French might hold. But the German preponderance was overwhelming: within a week the French armies broke. From then on the Battle of France was a panorama of endless retreats and rearguard actions. Once through the lines, German mechanized and motorized forces outran the French infantry, encircling and capturing much French strength including Prételat's Second Army Group on the Maginot Line.[2]

No regime could survive such a defeat. On June 16 Paul Reynaud, his cabinet split between those who urged an armistice and those who rejected it, resigned. By then Paris was in enemy hands; the Panzers had reached Cherbourg on the one hand and Switzerland on the other. Pétain succeeded Reynaud and on June 17 asked for an armistice. Charles de Gaulle, whose star had risen high after he left the 4th DCR on June 5 to become Reynaud's Undersecretary of National Defense and War, broadcast his famous appeal of June 18 from London. Thenceforth Frenchmen could choose between the old Marshal and his seemingly legitimate government and the upstart Brigadier—Weygand promoted de Gaulle for his handling of the 4th DCR—who stood for Resistance.

THE CAUSES OF A DEFEAT

The problem of numbers dominated French strategy and played a critical role in the 1940 campaign. It is essential to remember that in 1940 Germany had double the population and perhaps three times the industry of France. Britain also had a larger population and industrial base than France—but it was unprepared for war; its contribution was far too small to redress the balance. With the start of the German offensive an improvised coalition formed, the Netherlands and Belgium joining the Allies. They were small but relatively well prepared and their ground forces—three times the strength of the BEF—swung the balance between the ground forces of the Allies and Germany into rough equilibrium. But the Dutch army was isolated by the enemy, despite Gamelin's Breda maneuver, and overrun on the fifth day of hostilities. The Belgian army played a major role in the battle in the north, following plans sketched out with the Allies prior to hostilities. When the crisis came, the Belgian command accepted Billotte as the "co-ordinator" of operations in the north, but made no further commitment. When Billotte was killed, the armies of the three nations in the north followed their own courses. The Belgian King refused to abandon more Belgian soil and when pressed, capitulated. Lord Gort, despite pronouncements from London and Paris, decided on evacuation. Blanchard struggled to mount an offensive southward; when that proved impossible, he tried to hold in the north as long as possible: every day helped Weygand rebuild. Under these conditions the German command, with unified control over its forces in pursuance of a preconceived plan, had an enormous advantage.

It is not surprising that the nations of the Western coalition of May 10 each sought to maximize its own interests at the expense of solidarity before the fighting began. It is not surprising that Belgians, Dutch, British—and some of the French—regarded Gamelin's attempt to weld the Allies together through the Dyle-Breda Plan with skepticism. The tragedy was that once the fighting began the West failed to form a solid block: as events developed the Allies chose to follow the same individualistic policies they had pursued before the invasion. Thus Winkelman capitulated in isolation in Holland; thus Léopold limited Belgian efforts to the defense of Belgian territory and preferred unilateral capitulation when the defense of that territory became hopeless; thus Britains refused to give priority to the coalition effort on the Continent. Gamelin knew that France alone could not face Hitler: he had to bind the Allies together. He tried to do this by advancing the Allied front as far into northeastern Belgium and the southeastern Netherlands as possible, into an area where all the Allies had common vital interests. This strategy, the Dyle-Breda Plan, failed in part because of military miscalculations, in part because of Allied disunity. Perhaps the biggest failure was that Gamelin, Georges, and Billotte could not hold the Allies together with a common maneuver once Gamelin's initial plan collapsed. Finally, Gamelin and then Ironside and Weygand tried to reunify the Allies; but by then Winkelman had capitulated, Léopold had lost hope, and Gort and Pownall were—at best—wavering. Billotte's death destroyed whatever hope remained for a unified action. After that the numerically superior Germans, having divided their opponents, conquered.

There is a second aspect to the question of numbers. Germany, with double the population of France, fielded a force in 1940 perhaps one and one half times as large as the French. The Germans kept a larger proportion of their adult males in the factories, and set higher standards for those in their field forces. The French, Belgians, and Dutch had to scrape the bottom of the barrel to match German numbers. They opposed German shock troops with series B infantry, or Belgian or Dutch equivalents, because neither France nor Belgium nor the Netherlands had enough first-class troops to defend its whole frontier. The British fielded an army of quality, but it was much too small to reverse the balance.

German industry was perhaps three times as powerful as the French, although the addition of Britain, Belgium, and the Netherlands reversed that situation. But only France was well armed for war on land; in the air, France and Britain nearly matched the German effort. But the RAF withheld most of its strength until it was too late. The French actually had more heavy weapons—tanks and guns—despite France's industrial inferiority. On a unit for unit basis, the French army was more motorized and more mechanized than its German rival. The Allies had much more artillery, more—and more powerful—tanks, and more motorized infantry than the Germans. The Germans, however, had ten Panzerdivisionen to the eight Allied armored divisions—three DLM's, four DCR's, and one British armored division—that participated in the fighting before the outcome of the battle was decided. Officers from six of the French mechanized divisions, reporting after the campaign, generally praised the quality both of their men and of their equipment, save for the old 37 mm tank gun and, sometimes, the radios. But they complained of being thrown into battle piecemeal, without proper support, often by local infantry commanders who chanced upon them—all of this contrary to doctrine. In short, men and material and doctrine were good, but they were misused in battle by commanders facing an unexpected strategic crisis.[3]

To make up for Allied superiority on land, Germany counted on the Luftwaffe. In May 1940 the Luftwaffe had far more bombers and attack planes than the Allies, but was slightly inferior in fighters. Due, however, to the British decision not to commit the bulk of the RAF, the Luftwaffe enjoyed a substantial edge in fighters—an overwhelming lead in bombers—over the Continent, allowing it to intervene decisively at Sedan and to make its weight felt at all times and places.

Finally, in 1940 the Wehrmacht enjoyed more effective radio communications than the Allies. Although all the French units were supposed to have radio, and most actually did, a striking number of French accounts mention the ineffectiveness of their radio equipment: for example, Dunoyer de Segonzac's squadron of SOMUA tanks of the 1st DLM. Communication was an element in the German ability to make more effective use of airpower on the battlefield, although numerical preponderance was the key factor. The difference in radio gear hardly explains the Allied defeat.

By 1940 the French and German armies had a similar conception of warfare. Both planned to use mechanized divisions for quick, deep, disruptive thrusts. Both counted on applying the force of combined arms, including airpower, on decisive points, employing tanks in mass with artillery and air support, neutralizing fortifications by direct fire of high velocity guns. Both French and Germans decided that defense in depth was the solution to mechanized, combined-arms attacks. Both, and the Belgians too, dug into circular strongpoints on the defensive, both developed antitank minefields, both utilized artificial and natural antitank obstacles.

There was, however, a major difference between French and German doctrine. French doctrine advocated methodical operations and constant attention to tactical security (except in exploiting a victory), at the beginning of a campaign in particular. German doctrine sought encounter battles, ordained that strength should be pushed to the front, and ruled that initiative must be given to the lower command so that every opportunity could be seized. The French were aware of German doctrine and of the danger its audacity and flexibility posed. But the French command realized that the German system carried dangers for the Germans too:

> If it [the German system] is examined . . . by cool heads, . . . if our formations are well adapted to the situation and to the terrain, our flank guards vigilant, the depth [of our defense] sufficient, our antiaircraft and antitank weapons well posted at all times; if our officers demonstrate the spirit of quick decision, solid nerves and sure reactions—then it is the German who will be caught in his own trap, for he will have compromised the equilibrium of his forces for a premature action—and we will, from that moment on, have acquired over him a first and serious advantage and an indisputable moral ascendancy.[4]

It was not in the French interest to stake everything on the first throw of the dice: better to hold on until large British forces or others tipped the scales in the Allies' favor, as in 1918. But in 1940, with each side fielding no more than 150 divisions, the situation differed from 1918. Despite extensive lines of fortifications on both sides, neither could "saturate" its front, particularly facing the neutral Low Countries: decisive maneuver was possible. Whether it occurred depended on the strategies adopted and the execution of those strategies.

French strategy was based on the Maginot Line and the defenses of the Rhine River and the Saar. These covered the bulk of French territory. The French command concentrated on the two wings: (1) Switzerland and (2) Luxemburg, Belgium, and the Netherlands. Eager to redress the numerical balance, Gamelin decided to link up with the Belgians, then the Dutch and the Swiss should their countries be invaded. These projected maneuvers absorbed forces, besides which the French command invested in advanced positions, such as Longwy, in front of the Maginot position, and left strong garrisons on the Line.[5] An unusually small force lay in central reserve as operations began, although Georges could recover forces from the Maginot Line and the Breda maneuver once operations began.

The maneuver into Belgium lay at the heart of French plans. By thrusting to the Dyle, the Allies would gather in the Belgian army and shorten their front. But the advance would be dangerous, for the enemy was as close to the projected front as (and in parts closer than) the French: timing would be crucial. Because of this condition the French army employed most of its motorized and mechanized forces in the Belgian and Dutch maneuvers, reducing its ability to react quickly on other parts of the front. As the senior Allied commander on the Continent, Gamelin decided to risk French mobile forces in an attempt to solder the Dutch, Belgian, and British forces together with the French into a coherent front in an advantageous position. The operation, if successful, thus presented a double advantage; but as Georges constantly repeated, the risks were high. Since French motorized and mechanized forces were limited, the initial thrust into Belgium would be limited: the French would not have material preponderance over their Allies in the north. Thus operations beyond the maneuver to the Dyle would depend heavily on Allied cooperation. But this was the weakest element of the Dyle Plan. No interallied command arrangements were made until after the battle started—and then Georges threw Gamelin's plan out of gear by delegating his authority to a subordinate, Billotte. This system would work well enough if Georges kept firm control over operations. But when Billotte was cut off from the main armies, his position as "coordinator" became difficult if not impossible; Ironside's and Weygand's interventions failed to correct this vital problem.

Thus the Dyle Plan offered advantages if it could be implemented, but carried the risk of degenerating into an encounter battle in which the enemy, operating under unified command from nearby bases with air superiority, would have the advantage. Further, it absorbed most of the mechanized and motorized strength of the French army, making it difficult to parry an enemy threat against other parts of the front.[6] When Gamelin added the Breda maneuver, over Georges' objections, he upped the stakes on the first throw of the dice, reaching out for further gains at the cost of further risks.

Gamelin designed the Dyle-Breda Plan, in part, to rise above the divergence of French, British, Belgian, and Dutch interests, to build an Allied front in northeastern Belgium and the southeastern Netherlands—near the Ruhr—in which all the Allies shared a vital interest. Gamelin took serious risks in this endeavor, and in the end it failed in part because of German skill and audacity, in part because of the very interallied difficulties it was designed to correct.

The Breda Plan strained the limits of French doctrine. Gamelin imposed it, but in so doing opened a chasm between himself and Georges. And it was all for nothing: interallied friction, cautious execution, Dutch incredulity, and German audacity laid it in ruins. Its only result was to divert desperately needed French strength from the decisive action.

The German plan took advantage of the weak French center. The French command counted on the Ardennes and the cavalry action there to allow time for reinforcement of the center should the enemy make a strong effort there. Gamelin and Georges also counted heavily on the Meuse River which, fortified in French territory, presented a real obstacle. Initially, the French command worried more about the Gembloux gap—ideal Blitzkrieg terrain—where quick enemy success would have had disastrous consequences.[7] By thrusting seven of ten Panzerdivisionen through the Ardennes backed by the bulk of its reserves, the German command deprived Georges of time to reinforce the Meuse. Crossing the river quickly, the Germans had a headstart into the center of the French array, while Allied mechanized and motorized forces were to the north. But had the Germans failed to break quickly over the Meuse, their Panzers would have been stranded in the Ardennes and threatened with a dire fate—a fate they met there in the Battle of the Bulge in early 1945. But for Hitler it was all or nothing.

Once the offensive began timing became decisive. The coup against Eben Emael and Holland sufficed to distract the French command, but above all it posed a threat to the Gembloux gap that the French had to take seriously. Georges was aware of the German mechanized threat in the Ardennes from the first day of operations, but his first reaction was to reinforce the Gembloux gap. He planned to reinforce the Ninth, Second, and Third Armies from May 11, but he did not do so with urgency, relying on the terrain and the Meuse to hold the Germans until sufficient French strength could be gathered. The Panzers outpaced the French timetable by forty-eight hours or so, forcing a decisive action before the French were prepared on the French Meuse, and bringing on what was almost an encounter battle on the Belgian Meuse where Corap was badly outnumbered. Roton and Doumenc sent two motorized formations, the 3rd Motorized and the 3rd DCR, toward Sedan on May 12 when it became clear that Guderian had selected that point for his attack. But the French command paid little attention to Reinhardt's stroke at Monthermé since the defense there held initially while the front at Sedan and Dinant cracked.

Leaving Billotte to worry about the Belgian Meuse, Georges concentrated on Sedan—although his subordinates' caution ruined his plan for an immediate counterattack. Meanwhile, however, Reinhardt's corps broke through at Monthermé. Since the French High Command had ordered *no* reinforcements there, Reinhardt's Panzers had little trouble pushing into the clear to Montcornet. It was *this* stroke, and not the crossing of the Meuse by Guderian's corps, which tore open the French front.

Georges depended on the defenders at the front to gain time for reserves to come up. Once the 3rd Motorized and the 3rd DCR were committed, he had only the 2nd DCR available as a mobile reserve: other reserve units moved by rail, requiring several days to reach new positions—and the German advance was too quick for that. Grandsard at Sedan waited too long to get his own reserves into position. Nor had Georges foreseen the ease with which the enemy moved cumbersome armored formations over the river despite the Allied air forces.

The French succeeded in getting reserves to the Sedan area although the 3rd Motorized and the 3rd DCR did not move with the urgency Georges seemed to expect. Nonetheless, due to French command inexperience and German audacity, Guderian's corps was able to cross the Meuse against one echelon of French forces on May 13, then destroy Grandsard's reserve in a separate action the next morning, and then push west against a third echelon of French forces in the afternoon of May 14. Had all three echelons met Guderian's Panzers at once, things might have been different. Finally, the late arrival of the 3rd DCR and the 3rd Motorized and Flavigny's caution freed Guderian to continue his maneuver. Similarly, General Berniquet of the 2nd Light Cavalry of the Roucaud group failed to order an advance to support the 71st Infantry which was still in line, enabling the Germans to secure Sedan behind Guderian. Were these hesitations the result of French doctrine with its emphasis on tactical prudence? Perhaps, yet it seems that the principal factor was inexperience. Groping through the fog of war, Flavigny and Berniquet failed to spot the glimmer of opportunity.

On the Belgian Meuse the question of time was even more critical. Corap received no reinforcements other than the 1st DCR, which arrived very late in part because Billotte wanted to mass armor behind Gembloux, in part because the division had difficulty moving over the refugee-choked roads. When the 1st DCR finally arrived, it was given a suicidal mission by Martin; the division then fought, hamstrung by lack of fuel and the failure of its commander to take charge, against Hoth's corps. German Panzer commanders demonstrated the experience they had gained in Poland as well as confidence and technical mastery in defeating the 1st DCR while Rommel's 7th Panzer continued its pursuit. Nonetheless, the commander of the German Fourth Army held up for a day, giving the Ninth Army time to establish itself on the frontier. Gamelin's "suggestion" of the morning of May 15 that Billotte group his mechanized forces at the right of the First Army to counterattack southward might have produced significant results, but Billotte was unwilling to pull armor from behind Gembloux, which Hoepner's Panzers hit that day. From that point on Billotte had to give ground. By the end of May 15 both Hoth and Guderian still faced weak French fronts, but then Reinhardt's corps tore open the center of the Ninth Army.

From that moment, it is clear (in retrospect) that the only Allied hope lay in giving ground to gain time to bring up reinforcements by rail from the east and by road from Belgium.[8] Above all, the Allies had to concentrate sufficient mechanized and motorized strength from the north to regain the initiative on the flank of the German penetration. Only thus could they slow down the enemy advance long enough for conventional French reserves to arrive from the south and east to reestablish the front. But such concentrations had to be planned and imposed by the High Command—this Gamelin and Georges and Billotte failed to do. Georges brought in Touchon to take charge of the breakthrough area, but he issued orders to re-form the front in the immediate area, refusing major withdrawals in his center (although Billotte received permission late on May 15 to go back to the Escaut position in Belgium). Georges' morale sank to rock bottom in the early morning of May 14: to him the situation seemed desperate, although the bulk of his force was still intact. By refusing to yield ground, he made it impossible for Touchon to take effective action; in the resulting grab by local commanders for available reserves, the 2nd DCR met its lamentable fate. Once the mechanized reserves failed, Georges had no choice but to try to stop the enemy with ordinary infantry.

Also in retrospect, it seems clear that after May 16 or 17, the Allies could no longer hope to maintain a continuous front strong enough to stop the German exploitation to the sea. They might have done better to concentrate units instead to seize the initiative on the flanks of the breakthrough, hoping to distract and slow the German advance until reinforcements could arrive. This, however, would have been an act of desperation, for Paris and France's northern industrial zone lay close to the breakthrough area. Given these circumstances, Gamelin bided his time until the enemy turned west away from Paris. Georges merely continued to try to patch together a continuous line.

While Giraud struggled to rebuild the Ninth Army's front, the self-confidence and experience of the German command showed to advantage. Giraud's attempts failed, for his reinforcements from the old Seventh Army arrived over refugee-crowded roads piecemeal, hampered by the reluctance of their commanders to hurl them into uncertain situations—as in the cases of the 9th Motorized and 4th Infantry Divisions. Guderian's, Hoth's, Reinhardt's, and then Hoepner's Panzers were able to meet Giraud's forces in a succession of actions in which they always had local superiority. The raid of Rommel's 7th Panzer to Landrecies provoked disarray in the French command; Guderian met the raids of the 2nd and 4th DCR with relative calm. On the morning of May 18 Giraud thought he could hold the Sambre and the Oise; actually his army was about to disappear under an avalanche of Panzers. Billotte kept the desperately needed Cavalry Corps tied to the First Army, and when he finally recognized, prompted by Georges, that the Ninth had greater need of it, he lost two precious days before the armor was released.

Thus the 1st DLM was thrown against superior forces in the Mormal Forest to save the remains of the Ninth Army, only to be followed a day or so later by parts of the 2nd DLM and the 5th North African Infantry. Had these operations been coordinated they would have been much more effective, although as it was they tied down the Panzers in the area. But

Billotte was under the gun from the start of operations. Bearing responsibility for the battle in the north, he suffered severely from Gamelin's and Georges' failure to provide strong central direction; nor, as the third ranking French commander, had he the prestige to dominate his Allies whose strength in the north was little inferior to his own. He conducted his battle using French reserves only—ignoring the substantial British and Belgian reserves.

On May 19 Gamelin finally intervened with a plan for a full-scale Allied maneuver. Why did he wait so long? It seems likely that he was waiting, as he later claimed, for the First Army Group to anchor its front facing northeast on the Escaut position while the Sixth and the new Seventh Armies covered Paris. Unfortunately, the defense of the Second, Sixth, and new Seventh Armies tied down most of the reinforcements from the east, making it difficult to concentrate forces to regain the initiative on the southern flank of the breakthrough. The 2nd and 4th DCR ran raids, but the French never achieved the concentration necessary to exploit local successes. Here the French command proved as selfishly shortsighted as its Allies. By thinking first of covering Paris, rather than of regaining the initiative to close the gap in the front, the French command helped ensure the loss of the Allied armies—and ultimately the fall of Paris ten days after the enemy had finished off Allied forces in the north. As a result, the major counterattack had to come initially from Billotte's force.

On May 20 Ironside and Weygand pressured Billotte, by that time weakening under the strain, to attack south. But precious time had been lost and every passing hour, as Gamelin emphasized in the morning of May 19, brought the mass of German infantry closer to the decisive area. By that time, with Dutch and some Belgian forces out of the picture and the Ninth Army in bits and pieces, the enemy had numerical superiority on the ground as well as in the air. When Weygand arrived in the north on May 21, time had all but run out. Weygand convinced Billotte to strike southward, but he failed to meet and convince Gort. The counterattack at Arras shook the German command and regained local initiative, but further operations were essential. However, Billotte's accident removed the last hope of unified command in the north, and the coalition dissolved on the battlefield. The same forces of mutual cynicism and narrow national self-interest which had helped make Hitler's rise possible gave him his greatest triumph in the spring of 1940.

It was tempting for many to claim that the French of 1940 did not fight as well as those of 1914. German combatants of 1940 frequently mentioned the bitterness of the fighting, although there were cases in which units of the French—and Allied and German—armies broke under pressure. A number of series B units panicked: at Longwy, Walcheren, and most importantly, Sedan. But French reservists broke under their baptism of fire in 1914 too. The reservists at Sedan faced overhelming superiority in air and ground firepower; it is not surprising that many panicked, although some fought to the end in their casemates. Yet the series B 53rd Infantry fought fairly well in the open field against Guderian's Panzers west of the Meuse. And many of these same troops, for example, those engaged at Walcheren who later played a heroic part at Dunkirk, recouped their reputations.

Hitler took up the question in a letter to Benito Mussolini on May 25. The Dutch had fought harder than expected, he wrote, many fighting very bravely, although in general they lacked training and experience. The average Belgian soldier also fought bravely and showed more experience than the Dutch, holding out "amazingly," particularly early in the campaign. Morale suffered, however (so Hitler wrote) when Belgian troops discovered they were merely covering the British retreat. As for the English, Hitler felt they performed much as in World War I—"very brave and tough in the defense, clumsy in the attack, miserable in leadership." Hitler found French units variable: "In general the difference in value between the active and reserve units is extraordinarily apparent. Many of the [French] active units defended themselves bitterly, while the reserve units in large part were not up to the moral impact of the battle."[9]

Losses provide insight into the bitterness of the fighting. In its communiqué of June 4, 1940, the German High Command listed casualties for May 10 to June 3 as 10,000 killed, 42,500 wounded, and 8,500 missing; the communiqué of July 2 put casualties through June 25 as 27,000 killed, 111,000 wounded, and 18,500 missing.[10] Most of these losses—particularly in the opening phase of the campaign—came from mechanized and motorized units. On May 23 the Kleist group, including Guderian's and Reinhardt's corps, listed armor losses over 50 percent; Hoth's Panzers lost some 50 officers and 1,500 men each and some 30 percent of their armor, with heavy losses in weapons due to frequent encounters with Allied tanks. The German figures reflected tanks lost to breakdowns; in compensation they probably did not count tanks that had been knocked out, then repaired and returned to action.

Casualties on the Allied side were much higher since much of the fighting saw German mechanized units, low in manpower, pitted against Allied infantry. Dutch losses ran to some 3,000.[11] The Belgians lost some 7,500 killed in their force which was roughly double the size of the BEF; casualties for the British army in France through the May-June campaign were about 68,000—the great majority of these taken prisoner. Of the British total some 3,500 were killed; the RAF lost a further 1,500 or so.[12] The French bore the brunt of the fighting losing some 120,000 killed, 250,000 wounded, and 1,500,000 prisoners during the six weeks of the campaign. French losses were higher than those for a comparable period at Verdun in World War I. A great many Frenchmen did fight. Some French reservists panicked in their first action, but that fact—particularly the breakdown at Sedan—had more impact on the morale of the French High Command than on the strategic situation itself.

The Luftwaffe lost 1,469 combat planes including those shot down, lost by accident, or more than 10 percent damaged in May and June 1940. Of these 635 were medium bombers, 147 ground attack planes, and 457 fighters. Despite these very heavy losses reserves made up most of the deficit.[13] During the campaign the RAF lost 931 planes including those that failed to return from operations, those destroyed on the ground, and those irreparably damaged. The Armée de l'air lost, from May 10 to June 10, 306 planes shot down, 229 destroyed on the ground and 222 in accidents: 757 planes. However, French production and American aircraft boosted the strength of the French air force to 575 modern fighters, 300 bombers—250 modern, and 200 modern reconnaissance and observation planes on the day of the armistice.[14] But by then it made no difference.

The essential cause of the defeat of France in 1940 was that a nation of 40 million dared to oppose the will to conquest of a nation of double the population and almost triple the industry. By straining France's resources the French High Command, reinforced at the last moment by Belgian and Dutch forces, managed, with limited British aid, to balance German might, at least on the ground. But a disastrous misjudgment in the disposition of Allied forces combined with a small but fatal error in gauging the speed of the enemy advance gave Hitler's Wehrmacht a golden opportunity. Under the pressure of events the loosely knit Allied military complex began to unravel. When similar events threatened disaster in 1914, the unshakable General Joffre had not only the time to learn the lessons of his initial defeat, but also the resolution to conceive an effective countermaneuver and the moral authority to impose its execution. In 1940 the Allies had precious little time and precious little unity.[15] Georges and Billotte lacked resolution and moral authority; when Gamelin at last intervened he was already on the way out. Weygand had the resolution, had the authority; he lacked the time.

But one must ask why the morale of so many Allied military leaders—Georges, Billotte, Léopold, Gort, Pownall—proved so fragile. Certainly, many members of western Europe's military aristocracy—and Germany's too—had misgivings about the steadiness of their troops, particularly their reservists, in this new and unwanted second world war. In the case of the British generals, misgivings were directed toward the mass armies of their Allies. The collapse of the French 55th and 71st Divisions at Sedan seemed to confirm these doubts; Gamelin himself reflected them in his analysis of the campaign on May 18. Was politically inspired defeatism a major factor in the defeat of 1940? Here the historian comes up against two roadblocks: the lack of conclusive evidence, and his inability to read men's souls. One can only conclude that Georges, Billotte, Léopold, Gort, and Pownall lacked the resolution to recover from the initial blow and seize the small but real opportunity that lay open. Gamelin, his own authority sapped by Reynaud, wavered before recovering his resolution—only to be removed from command. Weygand, however, despite his outspoken criticisms of the Third Republic, still burned with faith in victory. But his and Ironside's interventions came very late.

Above the generals, of course, the government leaders—and above them the organs of public opinion and the electorates of the Allied nations—must bear ultimate responsibility. If Gamelin lacked Reynaud's confidence, why did Reynaud not force the issue? Was the Third Republic so weak that it could not fire its leading general? Hardly! In the spring of 1940 few in the West fully understood how dangerous the German menace was; only when the catastrophe was already on them did Westerners realize their peril. By then it was too late to take those stern measures—resolution of the Reynaud-Gamelin-Georges quarrel, imposition of an all-out military effort and a total commitment to the alliance by Great Britain, decision by Belgians and Dutch and Luxemburgers to join the Western alliance—that would have made the defense of the West so much more effective. And so the West went down to defeat.

Yet one must not to be too severe with Westerners who shied away from a stand against Hitler. Europe had just finished the most terrible war in history. Westerners would fight Hitler only when his actions made their peril immediate and obvious. They were sane enough—politicians and generals and the public too—to foresee the price they would have to pay. But in the end force proved the only means of self-defense. By the time that was clear, unfortunately, it was too late.

THE MEANING OF A DEFEAT

Perhaps never before May 1940 had the forces of rationality and measure stood so alone amid a cowed and cynical community of nations, facing a foe who personified the lust for conquest. The French High Command never doubted that it stood as the vanguard in a struggle between Good and Evil. Therefore, the speed with which its plans collapsed seemed doubly diabolic. The scope and rapidity of the defeat deeply undermined French self-confidence. The Third Republic disappeared, replaced by the Vichy regime which vacillated between conservatism and collaboration with the enemy under old Marshal Pétain. With the rise of Charles de Gaulle, France found a new cause; by the end of World War II Frenchmen could again face the future with some sense of self-respect. But the France of the Third Republic—the triumphant, powerful France of 1918—was gone.

For Germans and for Adolf Hitler, the triumph of 1940 seemed the realization of all their hopes and dreams. Hitler, certain now of the validity of his wildest ideas and impressed by his own genius, held Germany in the palm of his hand and had the rest of—occupied—Europe wondering if the New Order were not the way of the future. From that point on there was no stopping him as he plunged the world into struggle in fulfillment of the mad ideas expressed in *Mein Kampf.* Great Britain withstood German attack and, gathering the governments-in-exile of the West, waited for "the New World to come to the rescue of the Old." Hitler forced this new world—the United States and the Soviet Union—into the war. As Maurice Gamelin predicted before the fighting, a new world order emerged from the trial of strength.

But it was a world he would not have recognized. Western Europe, its colonial empires shattered by loss of prestige and strength and then by Japan, which took advantage of Germany's triumph to launch its expansion, was left helpless. Many of its cities in ruins, populations bloodied and exhausted by six years of total war and divided by the deeply antagonistic political currents that ebbed and flowed as the fortunes of war shifted back and forth, the states of western Europe sank to the level of second-rate powers. Those powers that had held the centerstage of international relations for centuries—the core of Western civilization—gave way to the new world. The defeat of 1940 was one of the most decisive battles of Western history.

NOTES

1. France, Commandement en chef du front nord-est, EM, 3° Bureau: N° 1682 3/Op., "Ordre général n° 17" (unpublished, May 22, 1940, at 1:00 p.m.); Hans-Adolf Jacobsen, ed., *Dokumente zum Westfeldzug 1940* (Göttingen: Musterschmidt Verlag, 1960), pp. 114ff; Major L. F. Ellis, *The War in France and Flanders 1939-1940* (London: H.M.S.O., 1953), pp. 201ff, 333ff; General [Raoul] Van Overstraeten, *Albert I-Léopold III: Vingt ans de politique militaire belge 1920-1940* ([Bruges]: Desclée de Brouwer, [1946?]), pp. 692ff; Cdt Pierre Lyet, *La Bataille de France: (Mai-juin 1940)* (Paris: Payot, 1947), pp. 100ff.

2. Lyet, *La Bataille de France*, pp. 114ff; Jacobsen, *Dokumente zum Westfeldzug*, pp. 152ff; Ellis, *War in France and Flanders*, pp. 271ff.

3. Testimony of officers from six mechanized divisions in ED, 4DA7, Dr 3 and Dr 4.

4. France, École spéciale militaire, *Cours d'emploi des armes: 2ème Année. 3ème Partie* (Saint-Cyr: Imprimerie de l'école spéciale militaire [1939 or 1940?]), p. 512.

5. France, ESG, École d'état-major, [Lt.-Col. P. Gendry], *La Guerre 1939-1940 sur le front occidental* (Paris: Société française de presse, 1947), p. 45.

6. Georges' preface to General G[aston] Roton, *Années cruciales: La Course aux armements (1933-1939). La Campagne (1939-1940)* (Paris: Charles-Lavauzelle, 1947), p. x; France, "Extraits du rapport du général Georges," *Titre* VI (unpublished, January 12, [1940]), pp. 1ff.

7. "Extraits du rapport du général Georges," *Titre* VI, p. 4.

8. Gendry, *La Guerre 1939-1940,* pp. 65ff; "Extraits du rapport du général Georges," *Titre* VI, p. 7.

9. Jacobsen, *Dokumente zum Westfeldzug,* pp. 135ff.

10. Ibid., pp. 151, 287; Ellis, *War in France and Flanders,* p. 151.

11. The Netherlands, Ministerie van Oorlog, Hoofdkwartier van de generale Staf, Krijgsgeschiedkundige Afdeling, Generaal-Majoor Tit. B.D.V.E. Nierstrasz et al., *De Strijd op Nederlands grondgebied tijdens de Wereldoorlog II: Hoofdeel III: Nederlands Verdediging tegen De Duitse Aanval van 10-19 Mei 1940. Deel I: Inleiding en algemeen Overzicht van de Gevechtsdagen van 10-19 Mei 1940* (The Hague: Staatsdrukkerijen Uitgeverijbedrijf, 1957), p. 154.

12. Ellis, *War in France and Flanders,* pp. 325ff; Jean Perré, *Les Mutations de la guerre moderne: De la révolution française à la révolution nucléaire* (Paris: Payot, 1962), p. 237; Lyet, *La Bataille de France,* p. 149; Robert Darcy, *Oraison funèbre pour la vielle armée* (Paris: Boivin et cie., 1947), p. 54.

13. Raymond Danel, "En Mai Juin: *Ils étaient les plus forts,*" *Icare* no. 54 (Summer 1970): 65, Ellis, *War in France and Flanders,* p. 325.

14. France, Inspection générale de l'armée de l'air, 3e Bureau: N° 151 5/0/IGAA, "Un bilan de la bataille aérienne sur le front français du 10 mai au 10 juin 1940" (unpublished, July 29, 1940).

15. See Bond, *France and Belgium,* pp. 43, 96; Robert Aron, *Léopold III ou le choix impossible: Février 1934-juillet 1940* ([Paris]: Plon, 1977).

GLOSSARY

AASF	Advanced Air Striking Force (part of the RAF based in France)
BEF	British Expeditionary Force in France and Belgium
BCR	*bombardement, chasse, reconnaissance*—"multipurpose" aircraft designed to work as fighters, bombers, and reconnaissance planes
CSA	*Conseil supérieur de l'air*—Superior Council of the French Air Force
CSG	*Conseil supérieur de guerre*—Superior Council of the French Army
DA	*Division aérienne*—Air Division of the French air service
DAT	*Défense aérienne du territoire*—Air Defense of the (French) Interior
DCA	*défense contre avions*—French anti-aircraft artillery
DCR	*division cuirassée de réserve*—French heavy armored division
DEM	*détection éléctromagnétique*—Electromagnetic Detection System against air raids
DLM	*division légère mécanique*—French mechanized division
DN	*Défense nationale*—(department of French National defense)
ECPA or E.C.P. *Armées*	*Éstablissement Cinématographique et Photographique des Armées:* the movie and photo service of the French armed forces, at the Fort d'Ivry near Paris
ED	papers of Édouard Daladier at the Fondation Nationale des Sciences Politiques, Paris
EM	*état-major*—French term for any staff
EMA or EMAT or EMG	French Army General Staff
EMAA or EMGAA	French Air Force General Staff
ESG	*École supérieure de guerre*—French Army Staff College
FA	*Forces aériennes*—French air forces
FACNE	*Forces aériennes de coopération du front nord-est*—air headquarters attached to the northeastern front of the French army
FCM	French arms manufacturer
Flak	*Fliegerabwehrkanonen*—German anti-aircraft artillery
FT	*Forces terrestres*—French land forces

FTCA or FTAA	French anti-aircraft artillery forces
GA	*Groupe d'armées*—French army group
GHQ	British General Headquarters
GQG	*Grand quartier général*—French or Belgian General Headquarters
GQGA or GQGAé	*Grand quartier général aérien*—French Air Force General Headquarters
IG	inspector general
IGU	*Instruction sur les grandes unités*—title for major tactical manuals of the French army and air force
MA	*Ministère de l'air*—French Air Ministry
MDN and G	*Ministre de la défense nationale et de la guerre*—French national defense and war ministry
MG	*Ministère de la guerre*—French war ministry
mm	millimeters
Panzer	German armored division; also refers to individual tanks
PzKpfw	*Panzerkampfwagen*—standard abbreviation for German tank types, e.g. PzKpfw I
RAF	British Royal Air Force
SHA or SHAT	*Service historique de l'armée de terre*—French Army Historical Service
SHAA	*Service historique de l'armée de l'air*—French Air Force Historical Service
SOMUA	a subsidiary of the French Schneider arms manufacturing company
Stuka	*Sturzkampfflieger*—German dive-bomber
Supreme Council	chief organ for the direction of the Allied war effort, composed of the French Premier, the British Prime Minister, and such others as they might choose
Théâtre d'opérations du NE or TONE	*Théâtre d'opérations du nord-est*—Georges' northeastern theater of operations facing Germany
ZOA	*Zone d'opérations aériennes*—French air operations zone
ZOAE	Eastern Air Operations Zone
ZOAN	Northern Air Operations Zone
ZOAS	Southern Air Operations Zone

APPENDIX A
ALLIED ORDER OF BATTLE

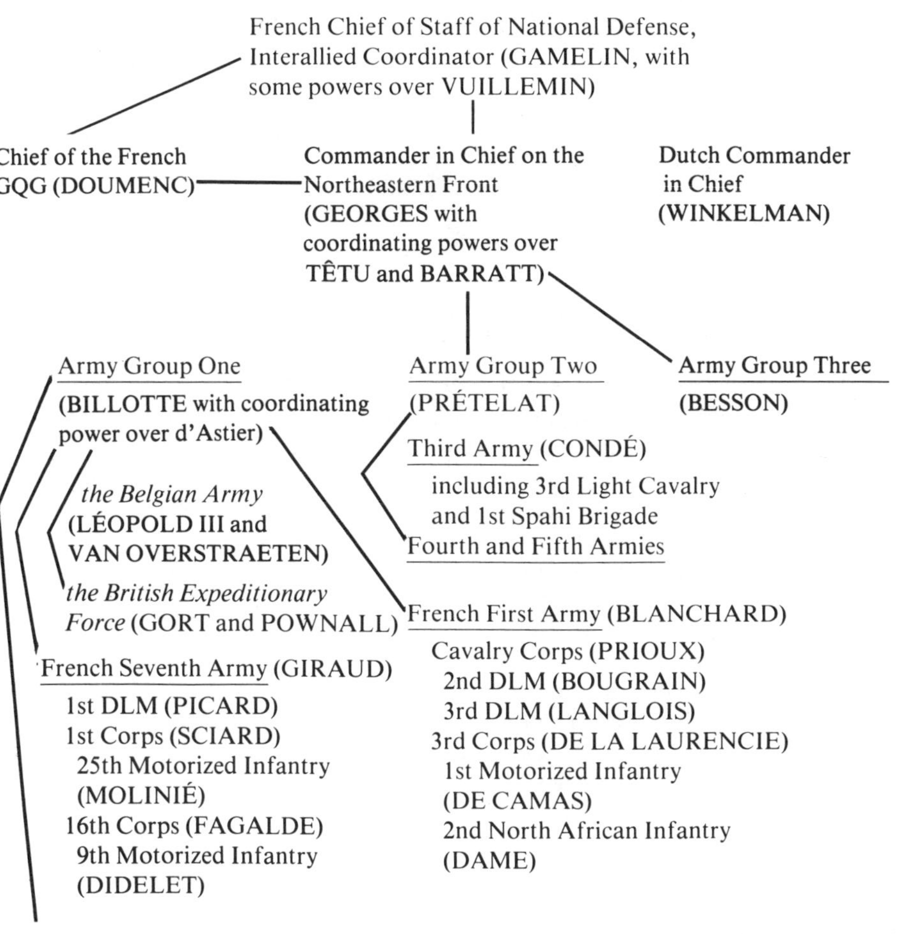

plus in Army reserve —
21st Infantry (LANQUETOT)
60th Infantry (DESLAURENS)
and temporarily delegated to
Admiral Abrial, 68th Infantry
(BEAUFRÈRE)

French Ninth Army (CORAP)
2nd Corps (BOUFFET)
5th Motorized Infantry (BOUCHER)
4th Light Cavalry (BARBE)
11th Corps (MARTIN)
1st Light Cavalry (D'ARRAS)
18th Infantry (DUFFET)
4th North African Infantry
(SANCELME)
22nd Infantry (BEZIERS-LAFOSSE)
41st Fortress Corps (LIBAUD)
3rd Spahi Brigade (MARC)
102nd Fortress Infantry (PORTZERT)
61st Infantry (VAUTHIER)
53rd Infantry (ETCHEBERRIGARAY);
plus soon to begin arriving
in reserve, 14th Infantry
(DE LATTRE DE TASSIGNY)

French Second Army HUNTZIGER)
(in principle, under Billotte's command
until midnight on May 13-14, at which
time it passed directly under Georges'
command)
10th Corps (GRANDSARD)
55th Infantry (LAFONTAINE)
71st Infantry (BAUDET)
3rd North African Infantry
(CHAPOUILLY)
5th Light Cavalry (CHANOINE)
18th Corps (ROCHARD)
plus in Army reserve — 2nd Light Cavalry
(BERNIQUET) and 1st Colonial Infantry
(ROUCAUD) forming the Roucaud
Groupment; 3rd DCR (BROCARD),
1st Cavalry Brigade
plus soon to arrive — 21st Corps
(FLAVIGNY) and 3rd Motorized
Infantry (BERTIN-Boussus)

4th Corps (AYME)
1st Moroccan Infantry
(MELLIER)
15th Motorized Infantry
(JUIN)
5th Corps (RENÉ ALTMAYER)
7th Belgian Corps (at Namur)
5th North African Infantry
(AGLIANY)
12th Motorized Infantry (JANSS
plus in Army reserve — 32nd Infa
(LUCAS),
43rd Infantry (VERNILLAT)
plus in general reserve in the area -
1st DCR (BRUNEAU), 1st North
African Infantry (TARRIT) and
temporarily 2nd DCR (BRUCHÉ

APPENDIX B
GERMAN ORDER OF BATTLE

Hitler

Army Commander in Chief
(BRAUSCHITSCH with HALDER
as Chief of Staff)

my Group B (BOCK)

ghteenth Army (KÜCHLER)
9th Panzer (HUBICKI)

th Army (REICHENAU)
16th Corps (HOEPNER)
3rd Panzer (STUMPFF)
4th Panzer (STEVER)
tal of 3 Panzers and
other divisions

Army Group A (RUNDSTEDT)

Fourth Army (KLUGE)
15th Corps (HOTH) which during the battle controlled 5th Panzer (HARTLIEB) and 7th Panzer (ROMMEL)
Total of 2 Panzers and 12 other divisions

Twelfth Army (LIST)
41st Corps (REINHARDT)—under control of KLEIST
6th Panzer (KEMPF)
8th Panzer (KUNTZEN)
Total of 2 Panzers and 17 other divisions

Sixteenth Army (BUSCH)
Total of 12 divisions

Kleist Group (KLEIST)
19th Corps (GUDERIAN)
1st Panzer (KIRCHNER)
2nd Panzer (VEIEL)
10th Panzer (SCHAAL)
Grossdeutschland Infantry Regiment (SCHWERIN)

Total of 7 Panzers and 38 other divisions

Army Group C (LEEB)

BIBLIOGRAPHIC ESSAY

Because of the bitter controversy resulting from the collapse of 1940 and the scope and complexity of the events, a vast literature sprang up within months after the French armistice of June 22, 1940: contributions continue to this day. This mass of several thousand works is of mixed quality, much of it consisting of partisan works written in at least partial ignorance of the facts and putting forth particular points of view. Such, for example, are Heinz Pol's *Suicide of a Democracy* (New York: Reynal and Hitchcock, 1940), "Pertinax"'s (André Geraud's) better informed *Les Fossoyeurs* (New York: Éditions de la Maison française, 1943), and the impressionistic work of the great medievalist Marc Bloch, *L'Étrange défaite* (Paris: Armand Colin, 1957).

Most of these works found political or ideological reasons for the collapse, paying little attention to the military aspects of the defeat which came so fast as to appear inevitable. This line continued in Jean Dutourd's *Les Taxis de la Marne* (Paris: Gallimard, 1956) and the scholar Herbert Tint's *The Decline of French Patriotism* (London: Weidenfeld and Nicolson, 1964); elements of it appear in the five most recent syntheses: Jacques Benoist-Méchin's dated *Soixante jours qui ébranlèrent l'occident* (Paris: Albin Michel, 1956), Guy Chapman's *Why France Fell* (New York: Holt, Rinehart and Winston, 1968), Alistair Horne's *To Lose a Battle* (London: Macmillan, 1969), William Shirer's *The Collapse of the Third Republic* (New York: Simon and Schuster, 1969), and John Williams' *The Ides of May* (London: Constable, 1968).

However, another interpretation developed, concentrating on the military aspects of the defeat. Such were Colonel Raphaël de Bardies' *La Campagne 39-40* (Paris: Fayard, 1947), and the works of officers who participated at various levels in the fighting such as General Joseph Doumenc, Colonel Georges Ferré, and General Charles Menu; they stressed individual mistakes and the numerical preponderance of German arms. Similarly the officers of the French Army Historical Service, principally Colonel Lyet, and Lieutenant-Colonel Lugand et al., *La Campagne de France (mai-juin*

1940) (Paris: Presses universitaires de France, 1953) concentrated on the military aspects, introducing a debate over the question of French military doctrine.

In 1956 Colonel Adolphe Goutard's *1940: La Guerre des occasions perdues* (Paris: Hachette), taking advantage of newly discovered details of the German effort, asserted that the Allies could have won the battle in 1940. Such thinking appears to some degree in the works of Georges Beau and L. Gaubusseau, *Dix erreurs une défaite* (Paris: Presses de la Cité, 1967); Jean Beaux, *Dunkerque 1940* (Paris: Presses de la Cité, 1967); General Paul Berben and Bernard Iselin, *Les Panzers passent la Meuse* (Paris: Laffont, 1967); and Claude Gounelle, *Sedan: Mai 1940* (Paris: Presses de la Cité, 1965). These all focused on certain aspects of the opening days of the 1940 battle and tended to rehabilitate the French soldier and army of 1940. However, the most popular explanation for the defeat of 1940 undoubtedly remains the political and ideological one.

My contribution is to introduce new documentary material demonstrating that the doctrine of the French military was *not* deficient in 1940. A new synthesis of the 1940 defeat makes clear the vital importance of the Allied nations in what was an *Allied* collapse. In addition, I have added a major section on the development of the French air force and the part it played in 1940—a story that has never been fully told before and about which the most patent falsehoods are commonly accepted. This work tends toward the conclusion that the defeat of the West in 1940 can be largely explained in strategic and military terms with little recourse to ideology. If that is correct, it is possible to see the defeat as the major *cause*, or at least the major precipitating factor, and not the *effect*, of those political and ideological divisions which tore western Europe asunder in the years following.

Post scriptum: After the completion of this manuscript, Professor Robert J. Young published his *In Command of France: French Foreign Policy and Military Planning 1933-1940* (Cambridge, Mass. and London: Harvard University Press, 1978). This is primarily a diplomatic and grand strategic account of French defense policy from 1933 to the outbreak of World War II; as such it complements this work and tends toward the same conclusion —that French policy was both rational and competent given France's relative isolation.

The following bibliography contains citations to the most important published works used in the preparation of this book. It is highly selective: citations to published and unpublished documents of the French armed forces, and to works used only occasionally, appear in the notes.

PRIMARY WORKS

Armengaud, General [Paul]. *Batailles politiques et militaires sur l'Europe: Témoignages (1932-1940).* Paris: Éditions du Myrte, 1948.

d'Astier de la Vigerie, General [François]. *Le Ciel n'était pas vide: 1940.* Paris: Julliard, 1952.

Belgium. Ministère des affaires étrangères. *Documents diplomatiques belges 1920-1940: La Politique de sécurité extérieure.* Brussels: C. de Visscher and F. Vanlangenhove, 1964-1966, 5 vols.

Bond, Brian, ed. *Chief of Staff: The Diaries of Lieutenant-General Sir Henry Pownall.* Vol. I: *1933-1940.* Hamden, Conn.: Archon Books, 1973.

Doumenc, General A. [Joseph]. *Dunkerque et la campagne de Flandre.* Paris: Arthaud, 1947.

______. *Histoire de la neuvième armée.* Grenoble and Paris: Arthaud, 1945.

France. Ministère des affaires étrangères. Commission de publication des documents relatifs aux origines de la guerre 1939-1945. *Documents diplomatiques français 1932-1939.* Paris: Imprimerie nationale, 1963 onward.

France. Ministère des armées. EMAT, Service historique. *Les Grandes unités françaises: Historiques succincts.* No place given: Atelier d'impressions de l'armée, 1967, 1970, 4 vols.

France. Parlement. Assemblée nationale. *Les Événements survenus en France de 1933 à 1945: Rapport de M. Charles Serre, député au nom de la commission d'enquête parlementaire.* Paris: Presses universitaires de France, [1947], 2 vols.

______. *Les Événements survenus en France de 1933 à 1945: Témoignages et documents recueillis par la commission d'enquête parlementaire.* Paris: Presses universitaires de France, 1947-1950, 9 vols.

Gamelin, General Maurice. *Servir.* Paris: Plon, 1946-1947, 3 vols.

Guderian, General Heinz. *Erinnerungen eines Soldaten.* Heidelberg: Kurt Vowinckel, 1951.

Ironside, Sir Edmund. *Time Unguarded: The Ironside Diaries 1937-1940.* Edited by Col. Roderick Macleod and Denis Kelly. Edinburgh: T. and A. Constable [Constable Publishers, London], 1962.

Jacobsen, Hans-Adolf, ed. *Dokumente zur Vorgeschichte des Westfeldzuges 1939-1940.* Göttingen: Musterschmidt Verlag, 1956.

______. *Dokumente zum Westfeldzug 1940* (Göttingen: Musterschmidt Verlag, 1960).

Jacomet, Robert. *L'Armement de la France 1936-1939.* Paris: Les Éditions de Lajeunesse, 1945.

Minart, Jacques. *P. C. Vincennes: Secteur 4.* Paris: Berger-Levrault, 1945, 2 vols.

The Netherlands. Ministerie van Oorlog. Hoofdkwartier van de generale Staf. Krijgsgeschiedkundige Afdeling. Generaal-Majoor Tit. B.D.V.E. Nierstrasz et al. *De Strijd op Nederlands grondgebied tijdens de Wereldoorlog II: Hoofdeel III: Nederlands Verdediging tegen de Duitse Aanval van 10-19 Mei 1940.* The Hague: Staatsdrukkerijen Uitgeverijbedrijf, 1953-1961, 8 vols.

[______. Staten Generaal. Tweede Kamer]. *Enquêtecommissie Regeringsbeleid 1940-1945: Verslag Houdende De Uitkomsten Van Het Onderzoek. Deel I^A en I^B: Algemene Inleiding/Militair Beleid 1939-1940 (Punt A Van Het Enquêtebesluit)* and *Deel I^B/Bijlagen* and *Deel I^C: Algemene Inleiding/Militair Beleid 1939-1940 (Punt A Van Het Enquêtebesluit).* The Hague: Staatsdrukkerijen Uitgeverijbedrijf, 1949.

Roton, General G[aston]. *Années cruciales: La Course aux armements (1933-1939). La Campagne (1939-1940).* Paris: Charles-Lavauzelle, 1947.

Van Overstraeten, [Raoul]. *Albert I-Léopold III: Vingt ans de politique militaire belge 1920-1940.* [Bruges]: Desclée de Brouwer [now of Paris], [1946?].

Weygand, General [Maxime]. *Mémoires.* Paris: Flammarion, 1950-1957, 3 vols.

Numerous articles in *Icare: Revue de l'aviation française.*

SECONDARY WORKS

Duvignac, Colonel André. *Histoire de l'armée motorisée.* Paris: Imprimerie nationale, 1947.

Ellis, Major L. F. *The War in France and Flanders 1939-1940.* London: H.M.S.O., 1960.

France, ESG. École d'état-major. *La Guerre 1939-1940 sur le front occidental (conférences du Lt.-Col. P. Gendry, mai-juin 1946).* Paris: Société française de presse, 1947.

Jacobsen, Hans-Adolf with K. J. Müller. *Fall Gelb: Der Kampf um den deutschen Operationsplan zur Westoffensive 1940.* Wiesbaden: Franz Steiner Verlag, 1957.

Les Relations militaires franco-belges de mars 1936 au 10 mai 1940: Travaux d'un colloque d'historiens belges et français. Paris: Éditions du CNRS, 1968.

Lyet, Commandant Pierre. *La Bataille de France: (Mai-juin 1940).* Paris: Payot, 1947.

Tournoux, General P[aul]-É[mile]. *Haut commandement Gouvernement et Défense des frontières du nord et de l'est 1919-1939.* Paris: Nouvelles éditions latines, 1960.

INDEX

Military units in this index are listed under their respective armed forces in decreasing order of magnitude; within each order of magnitude, they are listed numerically or alphabetically, according to their titles.

ABOUT THE AUTHOR

Jeffery A. Gunsburg is Assistant Professor of History at the Virginia Military Institute in Lexington. He has contributed articles to *Virginia Cavalcade, Armor,* and *The Simon and Schuster Encyclopedia of World War II.*